GEORGE WASHINGTON

and the New Nation

(*1783–1793*)

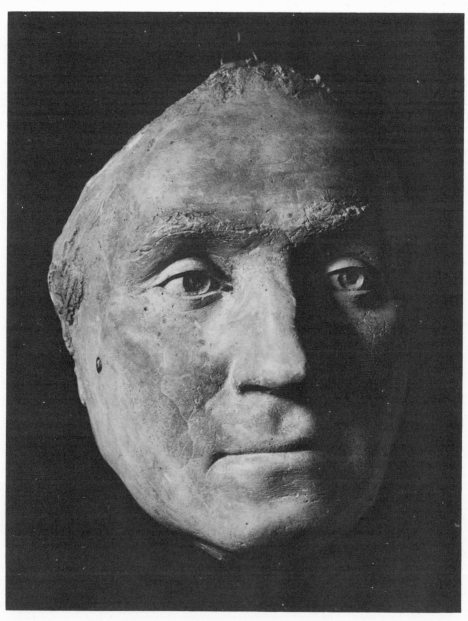

Life mask of Washington taken by Houdon at Mount Vernon in 1785.
Courtesy of the Pierpont Morgan Library

GEORGE WASHINGTON

and the New Nation

(1783–1793)

by JAMES THOMAS FLEXNER

with photographs

LITTLE, BROWN AND COMPANY · BOSTON · TORONTO

LIBRARY OF CONGRESS CATALOG CARD NO. 78–117042

FIRST EDITION

Portions of this book have appeared in slightly different form in
American Heritage and *The American Art Journal*.

*Published simultaneously in Canada
by Little, Brown & Company (Canada) Limited*

PRINTED IN THE UNITED STATES OF AMERICA

To
LLEWELLYN HOWLAND III
A brilliant editor and a good friend

Contents

CONTENTS

List of Illustrations

[xi]

GEORGE
WASHINGTON
and the New Nation
(1783–1793)

Introduction

THIS book tells the story of George Washington's personal experiences and public efforts in the crucial period when it was necessary to follow up the military victory won in the Revolution with a great political and philosophical victory.

That mankind could, in modern times and on a large scale, govern themselves without recourse to kings or dictators was a proposition doubted by most practical thinkers and seemingly disproved by history. The effort of the new United States to demonstrate, once and for all, the possibility of effective republican government was, indeed, a more difficult and a more visionary task than winning the Revolutionary War—and also infinitely more significant for the future of mankind. In the experiment, George Washington played the crucial role. Had he refused to walk this enlarged stage or had he moved differently upon it, there would have been a different ending, quite possibly a tragedy from which the whole future of human freedom would have suffered.

The story begins with the return to his farm of an exhausted soldier who had gleefully renounced any further part in public leadership. His mind had for years been "on the stretch." As exterior pressures relaxed, his character opened out into its natural, wide-ranging idiosyncrasy. This, however, was only a brief respite. Washington found himself with no choice but to preside over the Constitutional Convention. It was then inevitable that the popular hero should become the first President of the United States. He led the new government as it coalesced into a form which, although new to the history of the world, was effective and earned the almost universal acceptance of the people. By the end of Washington's first term, the viability of republican institutions seemed to have been proved for all history to see.

Convinced that the government had been so successfully launched that his services were no longer needed, Washington eagerly foresaw a return to his beloved acres. But the French Revolution whipped up a great international storm which threatened the United States with interior turmoil and foreign war. The two men who have remained as symbols of opposing tendencies in American life—Thomas Jefferson and Alexander Hamilton—both insisted that if in this crisis Washington relinquished the helm, the government might founder. This volume ends as Washington, old now, fearful that his mental as well as his physical powers were failing, agreed to four more years of national servitude.

Although designed to stand on its own feet, this book is the third in a four-part life of George Washington. The effort has not been to define the history of the times by grouping far-spread events around Washington's career. This is intended to be biography in the true sense: an account of the odyssey through time of an individual human being, with, like the rest of us, two eyes, a single heart, and a brain that by no means always churned up what the will commanded. To the best of the author's ability, Washington is shown in all his fallibility and also in all his greatness.

Nowadays, there is as active a popular desire to destroy heroes as there was in the nineteenth century to exalt them. We have exchanged the nauseous treacle which our predecessors poured over Washington for equal amounts of gall. The attempt is here made to ignore both extremes, to eschew furthermore all fashions of interpretation (whether "traditional" or "revisionist"), to re-create the actual man.

I

Philosophic Shades

1

Soldier's Return

GEORGE WASHINGTON remembered that when he awoke in the silent mornings his mind would instantly become a whirlpool of grievous things. Urgency was upon him as it had daily been for his eight years as Commander in Chief: the need to clothe thousands of almost naked men, to fill empty bellies, procure gunpowder, write and persuade Congress: the need to build defenses, place cannon, withstand attack with inadequate forces. He had to march, explore strange countrysides, march, interrogate spies and prisoners, march. How could he find some way to defeat a stronger enemy, some miraculous way to achieve what seemed past the power and will of an emerging and wavering nation: victory that would end this interminable war and establish the independence of the United States?

Then, as his long body thrashed around in an oddly comfortable bed, a strange realization flooded over him. Although he was engulfed in darkness (for this was winter and he always woke early), Washington knew that outside there stretched not a military camp but the peaceful countryside of his childhood memories. The sighing he heard was the wind in his own trees, and out there the Potomac, his ancestral river, pulsed gently under the bluff on which stood his beloved home, Mount Vernon. He was amazed to find that the war was over, that he was home, that "I was no longer a public man, or had anything to do with public transactions.'

At such moments, so Washington remembered, he felt "as I conceive a wearied traveler must do who, after treading many a painful step with a heavy burden on his shoulders, is eased . . . and from his housetop is looking back and tracing with a grateful eye the meanders by which he escaped the quicksands and mires which lay in his way, and into which none but the all-powerful guide and great disposer of human events could have prevented his falling."[1]

After the peace treaty with Britain had been signed, when the British had finally evacuated New York City, Washington rode to Annapolis, where, on December 23, 1783, he had returned his commission as Commander in Chief to the Continental Congress. Then, with his aide David Humphreys beside him, he had galloped for Mount Vernon, hurrying to arrive home, as he successfully did, on Christmas Eve.[2]

Humphreys wrote, "No person who had not the advantage of being present when General Washington received the intelligence of the peace, and who did not accompany him to his domestic retirement, can describe the relief which that joyful event brought to his laboring mind, or the satisfaction with which he withdrew to the shades of private life."[3]

Yet, when Washington rose from his bed into calm; as his days, so recently abrim with excitement, drowsed slowly along; as the plantation which had once been golden with unattainable longing lay around him clogged down with snow, Washington was plagued with restlessness and melancholy. He complained of "the torpid state into which the severity of the season has thrown things." To Jefferson, he wrote, "If you have any news that you are at liberty to impart, it would be charity to communicate a little of it to a body."[4]

Less than a month after he had returned his commission to the Continental Congress, Washington wrote to ask if he could not have the document back. The paper, he explained, "may serve *my grandchildren* some fifty or a hundred years hence for a theme to ruminate upon, *if they should be* contemplatively disposed."[5]

Washington had no grandchildren and no children to create them. He could not have been referring to his wife's grandchildren, descended from her first husband, since he did not consider them his own. He had, he stated on other occasions, "no family . . . nobody to provide for."[6]

Yet the man who had achieved so much could not give up the hope that the children which were so freely accorded others would not in the end be vouchsafed to him. True, he had been married to Martha for twenty-five years, and always without issue. The implications raised by his wife's fecundity during her brief first marriage—she had had in rapid succession four children—could not have been excluded from the ruminations of a man who so steeled himself to look at facts. Yet the magnificent athlete could not accept the conclusion that he was, in fact, sterile.* Surely, his childless state was linked to his marriage with Martha!

"If Mrs. Washington should survive me," he decided, "there is a moral certainty of my dying without issue." However, even a man who loved his wife as George Washington did could not exclude from his meditations another alternative. Its possibility was, indeed, strengthened because Martha was now "scarce ever well . . . Bilious fevers and colics attack her very often and reduce her low." He tried to comfort her by ordering from England "a handsome and fashionable gold watch," the hands to "be set with diamonds," but he could not help speculating what would happen if she did not survive him but he survived her.[7]

Would he marry again? Would his new wife give him a child? He feared that she would not if he selected "a woman of an age suitable to my own." But supposing he married "a girl"? He hoped that, "Whilst I retain the reasoning faculties, I shall never marry a girl," yet he remained haunted by the vision of a child of his own. Not only did he request Congress to return his commission as a souvenir for his grandchildren, but he was careful not to exclude from his promises to his collateral heirs the possibility that a newborn babe would suddenly appear and from the cradle pre-empt all.[8]

A child of his own! Such a newcomer would give permanence to all that Washington had achieved, to the fame for which he had labored so steadfastly, to the landed estate he was amassing according to ancestral patterns aimed at the establishment of a dynasty. And the knowledge that he was leaving his seed behind him would make less menacing the "shades of darkness" into which he felt himself descending.

---

* It is, of course, impossible to be absolutely certain that Washington never sired an illegitimate child. However, no authentic documents point in that direction.

The returned soldier, as he struggled to find his way back to the peace and happiness he had once known, often heard, as a sound almost physical, the inexorable tramping of the years. He imagined that "those trees which my hands have planted . . . by their rapid growth, at once indicate a knowledge of my declination and their disposition to spread their mantles over me before I go hence to return no more. For this, their gratitude, I will nurture them while I stay."9

Washington's closest military friend, the Marquis of Lafayette, lingered in America but had, at last, to return to his French home. Washington accompanied him as far as Annapolis. He soon wrote his vanished companion, "I often asked myself, as our carriages distended, whether that was the last sight I ever should have of you? And though I wished to say no, my fears answered yes. I called to mind the days of my youth and found they had long since fled to return no more; that I was now descending the hill I had been fifty-two years climbing, and that though I was blessed with a good constitution, I was of a short-lived family, and might soon expect to be entombed in the dreary mansions of my fathers. These things darkened the shades and gave a gloom to the picture, consequently to my prospects of seeing you again. But I will not repine: I have had my day."10

Had some prophet whispered to Washington that his day had by no means passed; that his most valuable services to the United States and humanity still lay ahead, he would have been horrified. The returned warrior was desperately tired; he needed above everything else to relax. But for Washington there was no relaxation in inactivity.

After Jefferson had come to know Washington well, he wrote that his friend was haunted by "gloomy apprehensions."11 Washington's mind was, indeed, so prone to darkness that he had been early forced to work out, lest he be overwhelmed, how to keep the shades from closing in across his temperamental skies. His expedient had long been to keep forever busy; his body active, his mind filled with detail. As Commander in Chief, he had kept himself so incessantly occupied that historians accuse him of having concerned himself with many more small matters than efficient leadership allowed.

With the vanishing of the winter snows and the loosening of his own almost murderous exhaustion, Washington exploded into perpetual motion. However, all his activity was for him quiet. As he himself explained it, the multitudinous details of his military life, which affected the lives of men and the destiny of nations (to say nothing of his own reputation) had kept his mind disagreeably "on the stretch." By contrast, the business of his retirement kept his mind "agreeably amused."[12]

And so, pursuing simultaneously the roles of expansive host, family and neighborhood patriarch, farmer, agricultural experimenter, landscape architect, interior decorator, merchandiser, landlord, exploiter of western lands, road and canal builder, Washington at last found the peace which he had dreamed of in military camps and thus described to his most beloved friend, Lafayette:

"At length, my dear Marquis, I am become a private citizen on the banks of the Potomac, and under the shadow of my own vine and my own fig tree. Free from the bustle of a camp and the busy scenes of public life, I am solacing myself with those tranquil enjoyments of which the soldier who is ever in pursuit of fame, the statesman whose watchful days and sleepless nights are spent in devising schemes to promote the welfare of his own, perhaps the ruin of other countries (as if this globe was insufficient for us all); and the courtier who is always watching the countenance of his prince, in hopes of catching a gracious smile, can have very little conception. I am not only retired from all public employments, but I am retiring within myself, and shall be able to view the solitary walk and tread the paths of private life with heartfelt satisfaction. Envious of none, I am determined to be pleased with all, and this, my dear friend, being the order for my march, I will move gently down the stream of life until I sleep with my fathers."[13]

2

Mount Vernon:
A Well-Resorted Tavern

GEORGE WASHINGTON had brought home with him to Mount Vernon a priceless acquisition, the very jewel he had most longed for in his most ambitious dreams. Since he had become familiar as a youth with Stoic philosophy, he had considered that the greatest reward any man could earn was the confidence, affection, and gratitude of his countrymen. It had been to win this boon that, refusing pay and spurning opportunities to grasp further power, he had faithfully served his fellow citizens as military commander year after unbroken year. Now the labor was over: this admiration, this love, this gratitude were his to turn, like a many-faceted crystal, quietly in his hands.

Washington's brightest personal hope had been, as he dreamed by the campfires, to merge his achievement, in memory and in reality, with the even tenor of the peaceful walks he had inherited from his ancestors and had himself happily pursued. All was to be contained within those magic acres which his dear dead half-brother Lawrence, who had willed them to him, had named Mount Vernon.

Here, fashioned from wood on land which his grandfather had purchased in 1674, was tangible continuity, the past moving with beauty into the present. When his prosperity increased, Washington had not torn down his ancestral house and erected (as his neighbor George Mason had done) a new elegant structure according to a plan bought from a professional architect. The center of Mount Vernon rested on seventeenth-century foundations. The room where, on domestic evenings, George sat with Martha while her grandchildren prattled, was the same cramped space he had himself prattled in as a child. Placing furniture was difficult because his grandfather (or was it his father?) had parsimoniously erected the fireplaces in the corners of the rooms so that one outside chimney could serve a pair. Washington had not altered this clumsiness.[1]

Above and on both sides of the tiny old rooms stretched an extensive house, which Washington, his own architect, had improvised in stages as his needs had grown. There were awkward solutions: unsupported beam-ends, false windows where the façade argued with the interior, an extensive waste area between the floor of one room and the ceiling of another, but there was also harmony, dignity, a moving and lyrical sobriety that testified to the temperament of the creator.

"The *mansion house* itself, though much embellished but yet not perfectly satisfactory to the chaste taste of the present possessor, appears venerable and convenient," so wrote Humphreys in 1786. "A superb banqueting room has been finished since he returned from the army. A lofty portico, ninety-six feet in length, supported by eight pillars, has a pleasing effect when viewed from the water."[2]

The whole area was so flat that the "mount" on which the house stood, although it rose only two hundred feet above the Potomac, seemed an imposing height. From the two-story colonnaded porch (which was Washington's architectural invention and was to have many descendants in the south), one could walk a hundred paces on a flat lawn. Then the land dropped to the river "about 400 paces, adorned with a hanging wood with shady walks." From the mount, "the perspective view" was magnificent, the river being some two miles wide and taking a wide curve so that it seemed to embrace Washington's extensive acres. Some foreigners, it is true, found the broad panorama of the Maryland shore deficient in "houses and villages," but the mostly unbroken vegetation pleased the eye of a man who had spent so many still hours in the wilderness. Near both flanks of the house he had, indeed, created artificial wildernesses that mediated between the wild and the planned: woods full of botanical specimens and flowering trees.

On the land side of the mansion, a lawn of about five acres was shaped, by the twin driveways that defined its outer limits, to resemble a copiously rounded bell. From each periphery, "gravel walks planted with weeping willows and umbrageous shrubs" led to large, shield-shaped gardens contained within decorative brick walls. Whether devoted to flowers or kitchen vegetables, the gardens were planned for promenading, being laid out in squares by walks lined with espaliered fruit trees and low box hedges.[3]

An English visitor commented on "the astonishing . . . number of small houses the General has upon his estate." These included the greenhouse, a schoolhouse, extensive stables, quarters for white servants and slaves, shops for brewers, carpenters, blacksmiths, and other artisans, and even "a well-appointed store" serving the neighbors, family, and servants. According to Humphreys, "The *tout ensemble* . . . when seen from the countryside, bears a resemblance to a rural village, especially as the lands in the site are laid out somewhat according to the form of English gardens, in meadows and grass-grounds, ornamented with little copses, circular clumps, and single trees. A small park on the margin of the river, where the English fallow deer and the American wild deer are seen through the thickets alternately with the vessels as they are sailing along, adds a romantic and picturesque appearance to the whole scenery. Such are the philosophic shades to which the late Commander in Chief of the American armies has retired from the tumultuous scenes of a busy world."[4]

Washington had comforted himself in the military camps with the thought that after victory had somehow been achieved, he would return to Mount Vernon and "contemplate" in "philosophic retirement" the excitements and anguishes he had experienced, the rigors he had overcome. It was not only his own restlessness that undermined this vision: his retirement could not conceivably be that of an ordinary man. The triumphant hero, who had returned like the mythical Cincinnatus to the plough, was the most conspicuous symbol of the most portentous political event of the eighteenth century. His character and appearance and way of life were of fascinating interest not only to his fellow Americans but to the entire western world. The dust of his driveway was agitated by the hoofs of horses and the feet of men.

Many visitors came by invitation, for Washington rarely wrote to a companion of the old, hectic days without asking him to Mount Vernon. Others brought letters of introduction, or were men of moment who felt by definition entitled to call on "His Excellency." Some were supplicants for this or that. Some appeared utterly without auspices. Thus Washington noted, "A gentleman calling himself the Count de Cheiza D'Arteignan, officer of the French Guards, came here to dinner, but bringing no letters of introduction nor any authentic testimonials. . . . I was at a loss how to receive or treat him." Washington invited him to stay for dinner and the evening, and continued to extend the invitation until the bogus officer (there is no record of him in the French army lists) had spent two nights at Mount Vernon. Then Washington sent him "with my horses today, at his own request, to Alexandria."[5]

Washington was under pressure to put up all callers—with their servants and horses—who arrived towards evening, since Alexandria, the village that contained the nearest inns, was nine miles away, a journey of several hours. The road was rough and travelers had to stop every few minutes to open and then close gates built across the road to regulate the local cows and pigs. Mount Vernon, so Washington wrote, could be "compared to a well-resorted tavern, as scarcely any strangers who are going from north to south or from south to north do not spend a day or two at it." But, of course, the Virginia gentleman could charge nothing for room and board.[6]

To intimates like Humphreys,* whom he invited for long visits, Washington would write, "The only stipulations I shall contend for are that in all things you shall do as you please—I will do the same—and that no ceremony may be used or any restraint be imposed on anyone." And again, "My manner of living is plain. I do not mean to be put out of it. A glass of wine and a bit of mutton are always ready, and such as will be content to partake of them are welcome. Those who expect more will be disappointed, but no change will be affected by it."[7]

However, Washington's guests never had cause to complain of being treated slackly, of any lack of opulence or elegance. Their host liked to talk of republican simplicity, and he did achieve it in the sense that Mount Vernon was very much less grand than the mansions of Europe: it could have been absorbed twenty times over in a great

---

* Humphreys was Washington's one friend with literary ambitions (he wrote some mediocre poetry which has resulted in his being classified among the "Hartford Wits"). He collected, with Washington's encouragement and assistance, material for a biography of the hero. The manuscript, although often quoted from here, never got beyond an incoherent jumble.

English country house. But for America it was sumptuous, and Washington did his best to improve it in the latest taste.

The current object of Washington's particular architectural attention was what he called the "new room," a banqueting hall which occupied most of the north quarter of the mansion house. The whole building had gone up piecemeal. First there had been the simple story-and-a-half farmhouse where Washington had lived in childhood. This he had raised to two and a half stories when he married Martha. In 1774, he had extended the building to the south with an addition as high and wide as the main block. This supplied private living quarters for the family, but left the house lopsided. A balancing wing to the north had been begun when Washington rode off to the Revolution. It was roofed over in 1776, and then waited unfinished for the General's return.

Washington's intention was to make the interior of the banqueting hall more up to date than the rest of the house, and, within reason, more elegant. When a marble mantelpiece given him by an English admirer arrived in ten packing boxes, he expressed apprehension that it would prove "too elegant and costly by far," for his "republican style of living," but the three panels which celebrated in high relief the agricultural way of life, proved to be just what he wanted for the "new room." All other rooms at Mount Vernon were small; here there was to be space. The banqueting hall occupied the entire width of the house. Washington had planned to raise it two full stories, but, on trial, his eye told him that this would make the room disproportionately high. He dropped the ceiling some three feet, committing the sin (to professional architects) of leaving a considerable slice of waste space, but achieving triumphantly the visual effect he desired.

Washington hoped to carry out or at least approximate wall decorations in the Adam style then so fashionable in England. However, he was far from sure how to go about it. He sent a Philadelphia merchant a query about a possible shortcut: "I have seen rooms with gilded borders made, I believe, of papier mâché, fastened with brads or cement round the doors and window casings, surbase, etc., and which gives a plain blue or green paper a rich and handsome look. Is there any to be had in Philadelphia?" But off to an English gentleman went a request for information concerning the real thing: the use of stucco for finishing interiors. He wanted to know whether the "rooms with which it is encrusted are painted generally, or are they left of the

Pair of paintings of Mount Vernon made by an unidentified artist about 1792. *Above:* East front overlooking the Potomac. *Below:* West front with circular driveway in foreground. Courtesy of the Mount Vernon Ladies' Association

The north lane at Mount Vernon, the driveway and the low fenced lawn in the middle distance being part of the circular courtyard in front of the mansion house. On the right a salthouse or storehouse, next a house used by the gardener or the shoemaker, and, beyond the circle, a storehouse. On the left, the servants' hall, and, beyond the circle a corner of the family kitchen.

Courtesy of the Mount Vernon Ladies' Association

Washington's architectural conceptions at their most elegant: the banqueting
hall at Mount Vernon. Courtesy of the Mount Vernon Ladies' Association

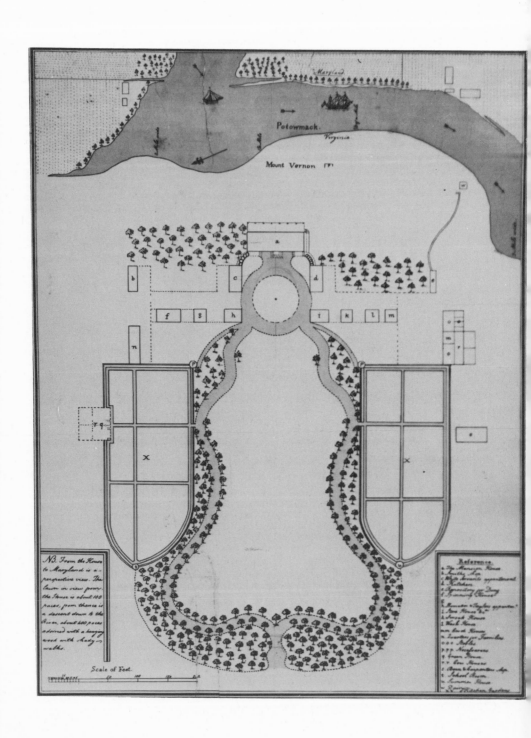

Maryland

Potowmack.

Virginia

Mount Vernon [F]

N.B. From the House to Maryland is a perspective view. The lawn in view from the House is about 100 paces, from thence is a descent down to the River about 400 paces adorned with a hanging wood with shady walks.

Scale of Feet

Reference.

The mansion house grounds at Mount Vernon, engraved by Von Glomer after a plan drawn in 1785 by Samuel Vaughan and corrected by Washington. The inscriptions read:

"N.B. From the house to Maryland is a perspective view. The lawn in view from the house is about 100 paces, from thence is a descent down to the river, about 400 paces adorned with a hanging wood with shady walks.

References

"a   The Mansion House
b   Smith's Shop
c   White Servants' appartment
d   Kitchen
e   Repository for Dung
f   Spinning House
g
h   Shoemakers and Tailors appartment
i   Storehouse, etc.
k   Smokehouse
l   Work House
mm   Coach House
n   Quarters for Families
ooo   Stables
ppp   Necessaries
q   Green House
rr   Cow Houses
s   Barn and Carpenters Ap.
t   School House
u   Summer House
w   Dairy
xx   Kitchen Gardens"

natural color which is given by the cement made according to Mr. Higgins's mode of preparing it? And also whether the rooms thus finished are stuccoed below the surbase (chair high) or from thence upwards only."[8]

In the end, Washington decided that "stucco and plaster of Paris" it had to be—but where in America was he to find a craftsman capable of executing the work? A Mr. Turner, who had surfaced in Philadelphia, proved, on investigation, unavailable or incompetent. Then he signed an agreement with Richard Boulton, a house joiner and contractor from Baltimore. Boulton appeared at Mount Vernon but disappeared again, probably dismissed by the General. Next to be considered was John Rawlins, also of Baltimore. His abilities seemed promising but his price was exorbitant. Washington hesitated but, having been frustrated for so long, finally agreed.

Work had hardly begun in April 1786, when Rawlins announced that he would delegate the finishing of the job to one Richard Tharpe, who had just arrived from England. Although Washington had received from a friend overseas a recommendation for Tharpe, he complained, insisting that Rawlins had promised to complete the job. Rawlins turned a deaf ear and departed.

Time passed; there were the usual misunderstandings and absences and shortages of materials, and then in April 1787 the decorations were completed. Although he complained to Rawlins that the finishing was imperfect in some particulars, Washington considered the entire effect "very pretty."

The banqueting hall, which has been reconditioned to stand as Washington designed it, is not one of America's great architectural monuments, but the room breathes that charm, intimately linked with Washington's own personality, that characterizes so much of Mount Vernon. By wandering through the buildings and over the grounds of the home he so cherished, one can, perhaps, get the best sense of the side of the hero which made so many of his acquaintances describe him—particularly before he became awe-inspiringly famous—with the adjective "amiable." No note of grandiloquence is struck anywhere at Mount Vernon, and the striving for grandeur, which receives its fullest expression in the "new room," has about it a touching simplicity. There is more eagerness than pretension, a feeling of Washington's own pleasure in the realization of a personal vision. In the banqueting hall, he had achieved exactly what he had described when he wrote, "That which is most light and airy I would prefer."[9]

One morning, as Washington was preparing to set out for his daily circuit of his farms, he saw coming up his driveway a young stranger on a scruffy horse. As the youth, Elisha Ayers, later described it, he rode up to Washington and announced "that I was from Connecticut and going west to teach school."

Washington politely "inquired my name and what part of Connecticut I was from."

The youth gave his name and added that he came from near Preston Village, seven miles east of Norwich.

"I know where Norwich is," said Washington.

At this, Ayers said that the General, on his way to take command of the army, had passed not only through Norwich but through Preston. "At Preston Village you were joined by Colonel Samuel Mott," a fact, so Ayers continued sententiously, Washington should not have forgotten since Mott had contributed so greatly to the conquest of Canada. What's more, Washington had also been joined by Captain Nathan Peters and Captain Jeremiah Halsey. "These three—or part of them—went with you several miles on your journey to Boston."

Washington said, "I remember something about it."

Ayers then told him that he "went in sight of my father's house two miles north of Preston Village."

"Very likely," said Washington.

Ayers now confessed that "I had a curiosity to call to see his park of deer, some curious fowls, jacks, mules, etc."

Having ascertained that the youth had not breakfasted, Washington told "his black man Peter" to feed Ayers and show him around. Then Washington proceeded on his own circuit of his farms.[10]

When Washington returned in the early afternoons, he found that departures and arrivals had altered the crowd of guests he had said good night to on the previous evening. Often completely strange faces stared at him with a curiosity embarrassingly undisguised.

The man the newcomers studied, although he moved with a springy lightness, was for those days a very big man, somewhere (accounts differ) between six feet and six foot three in height.[11] His shoulders were narrow and sloping but his limbs—forearms and thighs, hands and feet—startlingly large. His head was massive. The forehead, under a plentiful thatch of graying hair, was broad and high, yet seemed small compared to the rest of his face. Set widely apart, his gray-blue eyes were deep in huge sockets, surrounded with heavy lids. The unusually wide bridge of his nose had on it a ridge of flesh. The nose protruded powerfully; it would have seemed longer and more strongly hooked had it not been for the width of his nostrils. His mouth varied in shape from year to year, depending on his current set of false teeth, but was always full with strong lips. High cheekbones gave the lower part of his head the appearance of greater width than it actually possessed, but it was far from narrow. The depth and jut of his chin, which would have dominated any other face, seemed no more than correctly proportioned in Washington's.

Such a head could inspire fear. But every strength in Washington's appearance, as in his character, incorporated within it its own restraint. He gave an impression of reserve tempered with affability. Unless quickened by recognition of an old friend, his eyes, as they politely looked from face to face, lurked in their deep sockets without animation. Some visitors considered him austere; others were amazed to conclude that the great man was shy. An Englishman noted, "He speaks with great diffidence, and sometimes hesitates for a word, but it is always to find one particularly well adapted to his meaning. His language is manly and expressive."[12]

Having ceremoniously greeted each visitor, Washington would sit for a few minutes, and then go upstairs to change out of his farming costume. In half an hour or so, he would reappear, wearing on one occasion (as a guest noted) his hair neatly powdered, a clean shirt, a new plain drab coat, and white stockings.

Dinner was served at two or three. "Whether there be company or not," Humphreys remembered, "the table is always prepared by its elegance and exuberance for their reception." Another visitor tells us that Washington served not only the produce of "his large estate" but "the luxuries of every clime." And Washington himself boasted in 1786 of a Christmas pie "on which all the company, although pretty numerous, were hardly able to make an impression."[13]

For his own part, Washington did not stuff. He ate commonly a single dish and drank from half a pint to a pint of Madeira wine. If the company permitted of relaxation, he remained "an hour after dinner in familiar conversation and convivial hilarity. He is more cheerful," so Humphreys continued, "than he was in the army. Notwithstanding his temper is rather of a serious cast and his countenance commonly carries the impression of thoughtfulness, he perfectly relishes a pleasant story, an unaffected sally of wit, or a burlesque description which surprises by its suddenness and incongruity with the ordinary appearance of the same object."* [14]

When he finally rose from the dinner table, Washington disappeared into his library or outdoors into his gardens. Towards evening, he drank "one small glass of punch, a draught of beer, and two dishes of tea." Commonly, although a "very elegant" supper was served to his guests, he did not appear, but went to bed at nine. If, however, intimate friends or individuals who brought interesting news arrived towards evening, Washington would come to the supper table. Then he would drink several glasses of champagne and get "quite merry," and "laugh and talk . . . a great deal."[15]

That Washington by no means always showed to visitors his merry side was revealed by the memories of Gijsbert Karel van Hogendorp, a twenty-two-year-old Dutchman who had been heralded at Mount Vernon in a letter from Jefferson saying that he was "the best informed man of his age I have ever seen." Hogendorp wrote home that, on being announced, he was taken into a room occupied by Martha Washington with several ladies and gentlemen. "They greeted my arrival with dismal silence, regarding me with the careless manner I have met so often in America. After a brief conversation, carried on almost entirely by me, I heard the door behind me open, and saw Washington himself enter the room." Hogendorp thought he recognized "integrity" in Washington's face. However, "his mien and conversation seemed to me so commonplace that I was bewildered by what I observed."

As the young Dutchman held forth with "the vivacity and enthusiasm" which he himself considered so fascinating a part of his own character, Washington acted "embarrassed," presumably because, being "slow of perception, he expresses himself slowly." When the youth gave the Commander an opportunity to talk of his campaigns, Wash-

---

* This statement is an excellent definition of Washington's particular sense of humor, which was concerned not with exaggeration or fantasy, but the comic side of actual living.

ington refrained, "fearing," Hogendorp assumed, "to speak." Then Hogendorp tried him on subjects of general importance. Washington responded by "giving his opinions vaguely or repeating his annoying, 'In truth, I know nothing about it.' . . . Transition from one subject to another," Hogendorp deduced, "is difficult for him. . . . I could never be on familiar terms with . . . a man so cold, so cautious." And Washington, instead of kicking the puppy out, tried so hard to be courteous that the Dutchman considered him "obsequious."

Hogendorp decided that Martha was smarter than her husband and told her. The good lady, who lived perpetually in the shadow of the great man she had married, could not help smiling with pleasure. At which, Hogendorp concluded that she, with "eyes more perceptive than her husband," agreed that Washington was not very bright.[16]

Another visitor, Steuben's young aide William North, was bored. He resented the lack of sexual contact between the Mansion House and the slave quarters: "Will you believe it, I have not humped a single mulatto since I am here." He summarized, "Here we are, three meals a day and a quadrille at night, the great man retiring to his study after breakfast and we to our room. . . . The Woman has a certain goodness of heart, but then she is such a figure, and squeaks so damnably that there is no hearing her."[17]

Very different was the testimony of Elkanah Watson, who shared with Washington a passion for canal building. The General, Watson wrote, "soon put me at ease by unbending in a free and affable conversation. The cautious reserve, which wisdom and policy dictated whilst engaged in rearing the glorious fabric of our independence, was evidently the result of consummate prudence and not characteristic of his nature. . . . I observed a peculiarity in his smile which seemed to illuminate his eye: his whole countenance beamed with intelligence, while it commanded confidence and respect. . . . I found him kind and benignant in the domestic circle, revered and beloved by all around him, agreeably sociable, without ostentation, delighting in anecdote and adventures without assumption, his domestic arrangements harmonious and systematic." The servants (particularly his valet Will) kept an eye on Washington to anticipate his every want.

Watson had a bad cough. Washington (who himself avoided taking medicines) tried vainly to press some nostrum on his visitor. During the night, Watson's cough increased and then he heard a noise. "On drawing my bed curtains, to my utter astonishment, I beheld Washington himself standing at my bedside, with a bowl of hot tea in his hand. I was mortified and distressed beyond expression."[18]

Among the more complimentary (and plaguing) of Washington's visitors were artists who wished to spread his likeness through an eager world. From the time when he was first painted as an uncelebrated Virginia planter, Washington had found it embarrassing to sit still and be stared at. During 1785: he responded to a letter introducing the English artist Robert Edge Pine: "In for a penny, in for a pound is an old adage. I am so hackneyed to the touches of the painters' pencil that I am now altogether at their beck and sit like patience on a monument whilst they are delineating the lines of my face. It is a proof among many others of what habit and custom can effect. At first, I was as impatient at the request and as restive under the operation as a colt is of the saddle. The next time, I submitted very reluctantly, but with less flouncing. Now no dray moves more readily to the thill than I do to the painters' chair."[19]

Sculptors came, first the obscure Joseph Wright, operating on a private speculation, and then the celebrated French artist Jean-Antoine Houdon, who had been employed in Paris by Jefferson and Franklin to create a heroic statue which had been commissioned by the Commonwealth of Virginia. Both sculptors started out by making life masks. Concerning Wright's effort, Washington stated, "I consented with some reluctance. He oiled my features over, and, placing me flat upon my back upon a cot, proceeded to daub my face with the plaster. Whilst in this ludicrous attitude, Mrs. Washington entered the room, and seeing my face thus overspread with the plaster, involuntarily exclaimed. Her cry excited in me a disposition to smile, which gave my mouth a slight twist or compression of the lips that is now observable in the busts which Wright afterwards made."[20]

Houdon appeared from across the ocean with three assistants. Jefferson, who seems to have feared that Washington would hesitate to receive an artist, had written that the sculptor moved in the best French circles. Jefferson need not have worried: Washington was used to entertaining men of all ranks. He was interested enough in the plaster that was to be laid on his face with a brush to note minutely in his diary how it was prepared. After he had entertained the sculptor and his assistants for more than two weeks, he sent them up the Potomac in his "barge." They carried with them measurements and the life mask, which were combined in Paris into the statue.[21]

Eventually, Washington wrote Jefferson, objecting diffidently—"not having sufficient knowledge in the art of sculpture to oppose my judgment to the taste of connoisseurs"—against being shown dressed as Cincinnatus in an ancient toga. He urged at least "some little deviation in favor of the modern costume," adding that he would not have dared make this suggestion had he not been told that Benjamin West, the leading American painter resident in London, had pressed such modernity on Houdon, and that "this taste, which has been introduced in painting by West, I understand is received with applause and prevails extensively."[22]

In May 1785 there rolled up the driveway one of England's most notorious women, Catherine Sawbridge Macaulay Graham, who had struck out for liberty and excoriated the Tories in her eight-volume *History of England from the Accession of James I to that of the Brunswick Line.* She surely wore more rouge than any other lady ever entertained at Mount Vernon—John Wilkes described her as "painted to the eyes" and "looking as rotten as an old Catherine peach"—and she had in tow a lower-class youth in his twenties whom, at the age of almost fifty, she had married, to the publicly expressed despair of her elderly lover and the titters of British society. The bridegroom's elder brother was a notorious quack who operated at fashionable Bath a Temple of Health (the future Lady Hamilton was said to have acted as Goddess) which featured the electrified Royal Pantogonian bed that was supposed to enhance sexual pleasures and was reputed to be the inspiration of the marriage of the elderly "historian in petticoats" to her juvenile surgeon's mate.[23]

As she made expansive gestures, Mrs. Macaulay Graham talked at the top of her lungs almost without stop, laying down the law on political matters that the eighteenth century considered the exclusive concern of men. Washington was deeply impressed with this friend "of liberty and of mankind" who was clearly as brilliant as she was eccentric. He wrote General Knox, "A visit from a lady so celebrated in the literary world could not but be very flattering to me." In sending out invitations to dine with her and her boyish husband, he explained to the neighbors: "I wish to show them all the respect I can." He placed his military records in her hands "for her perusal and amusement." When the Grahams departed after a stay of ten days, Washington accompanied them some distance on the road. The General and the bluestocking continued to correspond during the many years until she died, her letters being crammed with political advice, and his written with that special care he employed in addressing those whom he considered more educated than he himself.[24]

Washington had "a most delightful bowling green" in front of his house. He kept "an amazing number of horses,"* and frequented the Annapolis Races (to which his slaves were allowed to go). But his favorite sport was foxhunting.[25]

Lafayette had sent him seven foxhounds from France. A few days after their arrival, Washington "took my French hounds with me" on his farming rounds, "for the purpose of airing them and giving them a knowledge of the grounds round about this place." When he tried them in an actual hunt, he borrowed from George Mason two local dogs to show them the ways. The hounds "found a fox which was run tolerably well by two French bitches and one of Mason's dogs." To Washington's disgust, the other French dogs and Mason's unpatriotic second beast wandered around aimlessly, until they came on another fox "which was followed slow and indifferently by some and not at all by the rest, until the scent became so cold it could not be followed at all."

A few days later, he had the French dogs out before sunrise. He exercised them by dragging a bag full of scent over the ground and making them follow. Then he introduced a live fox. Most of the canine messieurs and mesdames sat down to droop with homesickness or boredom. However, Washington had fought off the British with militia: he kept trying, and eventually made the immigrants "understand more fully the kind of game they are intended to run."[26]

In 1789, Washington's kennels were among the most international residences in America. The inhabitants were Vulcan and Venus from France, Ragman and two other dogs from England, Dutchess and Doxey from Philadelphia, and Jupiter and Countess, American-born descendants from the French. Washington visited the kennels every

---

* Two of his horses were elderly pensioners from his military days: Old Nelson, best in battle, and Blueskin, who had stood up less well under fire.[27]

morning and evening (as he also did his stables) and labored to keep the dogs so well matched in point of speed and wind that, as they coursed, the whole pack could be covered with a coat.[28]

Vulcan was so large that Washington's step-grandson could in infancy ride him, and so determined that he stole a ham, intended for a large company, from the kitchen, and then stood off with his fangs all efforts on the part of the kitchen staff to retrieve the prize. No one dared tell Martha until, as the guests were eating, she noticed the "loss of a dish which formed the pride of her table." The sad news communicated, she excoriated Vulcan and went on to express her opinion of dogs in general, while her husband rocked with laughter.[29]

Washington often took his hounds along as he rode between his farms, gleefully abandoning business if they started a fox. "The regular hunts," he wrote Humphreys, "are once a week or oftener." On those mornings, Will laid out for the General a blue coat, scarlet waistcoat, buckskin breeches, top boots, velvet cap, and a whip with a long thong. The driveway in front of Mount Vernon soon pulsed with male voices, since all the neighborhood was regularly invited.

No ladies rode after the hounds, but roads were cut through the woods that enabled them gently to follow the hunt in carriages. Once the fox and the hounds were off, Washington was all passion, his cries resounding across the fields, his long body leaning forward over his mount's head as he galloped among the first of the riders. Knowing the terrain and considered the finest horseman of his time, "he was always in at the death and yielded to no man the honor of the brush."

After the hunt, there was a party at Mount Vernon, featuring a well-spread board and clusters of decanters of imported wine. Like every other aspect of Washington's life, this was very expensive.[30]

Even as Washington, the living symbol of republican revolution, was much more than a country squire, Mount Vernon played a vastly larger social role than that of a gentleman's country residence. Since what national government existed did not rank in importance with the governments of the thirteen individual states, there was no national capital. Having no Chief Executive,* the United States could have no President's house. Mount Vernon was the most prominent building in

---

* The President of Congress was the chairman of the central council of a regional alliance.

America, and the scene of the most impressive entertaining done for the United States. Despite his admission that his own predilections were opposed to doing anything in "too . . . niggardly a manner," Washington had some justice on his side when he asserted that he was "as it were, involuntarily compelled" to keep up a grand and expensive establishment.[31]

He had hardly returned from his military service when the Supreme Executive Council of Pennsylvania instructed its delegates to call his situation to the attention of the Continental Congress. Their resolution stated that although Washington considered himself "amply *rewarded* for all his labors and cares by the love and prosperity of his fellow citizens," yet "they ought not to suffer those merits to be burdensome to him."[32]

Washington had no intention of allowing even one facet of the jewel of reputation he had carried with him to retirement to be clouded by any suspicion that his services had not been altogether disinterested. He had during the war refused all pay. Now he replied that, although he welcomed this further "mark of the approbation of my fellow citizens," his "sentiments" on the subject of remuneration had "been long and well known to the public." His refusal of assistance was a self-sacrificing and impressive stand—but he was living dangerously beyond his income.[33]

3

Family Matters

THE man who rode away from Mount Vernon to lead a revolution that pointed to the future of the western world, had come back eager to gather soothingly around him his personal past. Much re-emerged easily, but there remained an aching gap.

Every time Washington came out of his front door after nightfall and looked over his left shoulder, he felt a sadness (as he wrote) to see dark where the lights of Belvoir should be gleaming.[1] He knew the mansion had caught fire during the war. To find out how much of it still stood would have been the first step towards what he greatly desired—to persuade some of the old inhabitants to come back and rebuild. Yet for more than a year Washington could not summon the fortitude to ride the short, familiar distance and face the ruins.

When, in his young manhood, Washington had stared at the now vanished lights, he had visualized moving behind them people who epitomized grace and grandeur and, indeed, love. There had been Lord Fairfax, whose royal grant included much of Virginia and who had befriended a provincial lad amazingly skillful at riding to hounds. There had been his Lordship's cousin, William Fairfax, who had tried to teach Washington how to wheedle the great and who had succeeded in interesting him in Stoic philosophy. William's son, George William Fairfax, had been a gentle weakling who, although seven years the elder, had become Washington's disciple. And, above all, there had been George William's wife, the incomparable Sally, a slightly older coquette with whom the stripling conducted year after year the hopeless yet hopeful love affair which, whether or not it was (as history fails to communicate) ever consummated, was surely the most passionate experience George Washington ever had with a woman.[2]

Lord Fairfax and William Fairfax were dead, but George William and the delightful Sally still lived in England. In a letter to George William, Washington described how, in February 1785, he finally directed his horse along the road, now knee-high in underbrush, which he had so often traversed when it was rutted by the wheels of fine carriages. The ruins, he discovered, were "ruins indeed." Although some walls and chimneys still stood, "the whole are, or very soon will be, a heap of ruins."

"When I viewed them," Washington continued, "when I considered that the happiest moments of my life had been spent there; when I could not trace a room in the house (now all rubbish) that did not bring to my mind the recollection of pleasing scenes, I was obliged to fly from them." Surely with tears in his eyes—for the General was not ashamed to weep—Washington rode home "with painful sensations and sorrowing for the contrast."[3]

The strength of Washington's emotions raises questions which only a clairvoyant could answer. Was he mourning only vanished friends and the memory of a disturbing, exhilarating love? Or did he suffer also from the nostalgia of the successful hunter for the beauty of his quarry that will course the fields or fly the skies no more? Within Washington's experience, Belvoir stood as the happiest symbol of the British aristocratic way of life, of those institutions which he had done so much to expel from American shores. He did not want this way of life or those institutions to return to the nation—he would have fought again to repel them. Yet he did long to have the Fairfaxes come back. They should rebuild Belvoir and re-create those old times when, after he had married Martha and the heat of his passion for Sally had abated, the two families had been intimate neighbors. He begged "that you would consider Mount Vernon as your home until you could build with convenience, in which request Mrs. Washington joins very sincerely."[4]

If Washington's old love for Sally had created strains at the start of his life with Martha, that was far in the past. His long-range satisfaction in his marriage shone out from a thousand words and deeds, but nowhere more eloquently than in letters to French fellow veterans of the Revolution congratulating them on entering what Washington seemed to consider the purely American institution of marriage. He was "pleased if not surprised" to find the Marquis de Rouerie thinking "quite like an American on the subject of matrimony and domestic felicity. For in my estimation, more permanent and genuine happiness is to be found in the sequestered walks of connubial life than in the giddy rounds of promiscuous pleasure, or the more tumultuous and imposing scenes of successful ambition. This sentiment will account, in a degree, for my not making a visit to Europe." To the Marquis of Chastellux, he commented, that marriage "is quite good enough for you. Now you are well served for coming to fight in favor of the American Rebels, all the way across the Atlantic Ocean, by catching that terrible contagion, domestic felicity, which time, like the smallpox or the plague, a man can have only once in his life, because it commonly lasts him (at least with us in America; I don't know how you manage these matters in France) for his whole lifetime."[5]

Martha—in what seems to have been an act of possessiveness after having been forced to share her husband so relentlessly with the world—burnt their correspondence when her husband was dead. This has raised whispers that there were rifts in the marriage to hide.[6] However, there is no indication in the floods of documents that have survived of any serious rift. Martha (except for her failure to give him a child) filled satisfactorily the role she played in Washington's life. Characterized by the Massachusetts bluestocking Mercy Warren with the words affability, candor, and gentleness, Martha was a bringer of relaxation, a creator of comfort. That her mind was far from brilliant may well have been an advantage in her marriage, because it excluded her from active participation in the stormy aspects of her husband's life. Her function was not to advise or even to amuse but to support.[7]

A postwar visitor to Mount Vernon noted, "It is astonishing with what raptures Mrs. Washington spoke about the discipline of the army." She said that towards the close of the war, there had been no superior troops on earth. Even the British acknowledged it. "What a pleasure she took," Martha continued, "in the sound of the fife and drums, preferring it to any music that was ever heard." To see the army march, a few weeks before it was disbanded, when the men were all well clothed, had been "a heavenly sight." Almost all the soldiers had shed tears at being parted from the General—"a melancholy sight." So Martha rattled loyally on, to the affectionate pleasure of her listeners.[8]

At about five feet, Martha was a full foot shorter than her husband. When he was abstracted and she wanted to tell him something, she would pull on one of his buttons till he smiled down on her. To Charles Thomson, the Secretary of Congress, Washington commented, "Mrs. Washington, if she knew I was writing to you in the style of invitation, would, I am certain, adduce arguments to prove that I ought to include Mrs. Thomson, but before she should have half spun the thread of her discourse, it is more than probable I should have nonplussed her by yielding readily to the force of her reasoning."[9]

If Martha lacked the variety and edge to keep her transcendently able husband continually interested, her greatest gift made this unnecessary. Her greatest gift was social, the ability to get on with all kinds of people. She contributed to keeping Mount Vernon so full of humanity that, as Washington noted in 1797, he had not dined alone with his wife for twenty years.[10]

Martha was now caught up in a passionate concern that ordinarily removed her husband from the center of her attention. She was absorbed in her own grandchildren, a fixation which must have heightened Washington's consciousness that he had no descendants truly his own.

All of Martha's children by her first marriage were dead, and only one, John Parke Custis, had left heirs. Elizabeth had been, when Washington returned from the war, seven years old; Martha, six; Eleanor, known as "Nellie," four; and George Washington Parke Custis, almost three. Their mother had remarried, to Dr. David Stuart. Stuart was distantly related to Bonnie Prince Charlie, whose defeat had caused his father to flee to America; he had been well educated, having studied medicine in Edinburgh; and Washington was, after returning to public life, to place much confidence in him as an intimate correspondent. However, Stuart made little use of his medical training and, as a planter, he was financially incompetent; his family's fortunes declined. Finding their stepfather "morose," the older Custis children, as they grew up in his household, envied their younger brother and sister, Nellie and Washington, who were raised at Mount Vernon (and later the President's mansions) as unofficially "adopted" children under Martha's wing.

Nellie—whom Washington referred to in his correspondence as "Miss Custis"—must have showed signs of growing up into the charming beauty she became. Yet the boy, known as "Tub" or "Little Washington," was, as big Washington put it, "the pet of the family." Nellie complained "Grandmama always spoiled Washington." As for the step-grandfather, he wrote affectionately of Tub being "as fat and saucy as ever."[11]

To a former house guest who sent Tub a pony, the General exulted, "It is not in my power to describe his delight. . . . He finds beauty in every part, and, though shy at first, he begins now to ride with a degree of boldness which will soon do honor to his horsemanship."[12]

Having stood helplessly by the deathbeds not only of her first husband but of all four of the children she had by him, Martha was, as she admitted, made miserable if a child "complains, let the cause be ever so trifling."[13] She feared that "the Almighty" might not "spare him to me." Her anxieties were perpetual. Years before, Washington had succeeded, over her protests, in sending Tub's father away to school, but now the diminutive lady was adamant; little Washington must remain with her at Mount Vernon until ready for college.* Washington later asserted that he had discovered in his step-grandson "from his infancy . . . an almost unconquerable disposition to indolence in everything that did not tend to his amusements." However, since the grandmother ruffled her feathers so much when her husband tried to intervene, the major responsibility had to be left to Martha, while the boy's soft and ingratiating disposition made him abandon bad behavior before punishment was really necessary. And Washington, in any case, believed that "the first rudiments of education" should be "mere amusement, because it is not my desire that the children should be confined closely." What tutoring was done was a minor task of Washington's secretaries.[14]

This did not mean that Washington took education lightly. Throughout his life assailed by an uneasy consciousness of his own lack of formal schooling, he made the prevention of this inadequacy in others his favorite charity. He offered the Academy in nearby Alexandria a thousand pounds as endowment for the education of poor scholars. Finding that he could not raise the sum, he gave the Acad-

---

* Since girls were correctly educated at home, there was no such problem in relation to Nellie.

emy what would be the interest—fifty pounds annually—and left them the principal in his will.[15]

Washington financed the education of the sons of several of his friends. When Samuel Washington died bankrupt ("In God's name," Washington asked, "how did my brother Samuel contrive to get himself so enormously in debt?") George sent his nephews, George Steptoe and Lawrence Augustine Washington,* to the Academy at Georgetown. He asked that they be taught French and such parts of mathematics as would contribute to that "practical surveying" which he considered "useful to every man who has landed property."[16]

When the Georgetown Academy insisted on giving the nephews the conventional education of English gentlemen, Washington angrily threatened that he would withdraw them: "To find boys who have been six or seven years at the classics *entirely* unacquainted with those parts of literature which are to fit them for the *ordinary* purposes of life, incapable of writing legibly, and *altogether* ignorant in accounts, does not in the smallest degree comport with my ideas of useful and essential education."[17]

Another nephew, Colonel George Augustine Washington, was in a plight harrowing to his uncle's recollections. The most tragic aspect of Washington's young manhood had been his vain efforts to help his beloved half-brother Lawrence recover from tuberculosis. He had accompanied Lawrence to the Indies: now George Augustine was "buffeting the seas from clime to clime in pursuit of health." Washington's memories would not let him believe reports that the sufferer was improving. He wrote encouragingly to the "poor fellow" but confided to Lafayette that he feared all was "in vain."[18]

To Washington's surprise, George Augustine appeared at Mount Vernon, claiming to be almost cured. He was soon perpetually in company with another invalid, Martha's niece Fanny Bassett, who had been sent there from nearer the ocean in the hope that "the change of air and exercise will soon give her health." The two decided to get married. Washington wrote Lafayette with grim humor that George Augustine had gone to "the Sweet Springs" (which had done Lawrence no good) in search of health "sufficient to fit him for a matrimonial voyage in the frigate F. Bassett, on board which he means to

---

* Samuel's daughter Harriot joined the family circle at Mount Vernon. The mess in which she kept her room and her carelessness about hanging up her clothes became one of Washington's concerns when President.[19]

embark at his return in October. How far his case is desperate, I leave you to judge. If it is so, the remedy, however pleasing at first, will certainly be violent."[20]

However, as "I have always considered marriage as the most interesting event of one's life, the foundation of happiness or misery . . . to prevent a union which is prompted by mutual esteem and affection is what I never could reconcile to my feelings." He noted in his diary under October 10, 1785: "After the candles were lighted, George Augustine Washington and Frances Bassett were married by Mr. Grayson."[21]

Washington promised that, saving the most unlikely possibility that he himself should father a child, he would leave George Augustine a specified part of the Mount Vernon estate. He wished George Augustine to build and settle there, on Washington's assurance that he would be reimbursed for all improvements should some change in Washington's matrimonial status make the now unforeseeable child appear. The nephew would help Washington in the management of Mount Vernon and would with his wife, Martha's beloved niece, live in the mansion house until his own buildings were ready. To all this, George Augustine agreed. For the time being, his health held up, and the arrangement was a happy one.[22]

The explosion in Washington's personal relations took place in the oldest connection of all and the psychologically most intimate. His mother was in her late seventies but, as he wrote, in "good health" and in "the full enjoyment of her mental faculties." As soon as the weather had abated after his first return to Mount Vernon, Washington had journeyed to Fredericksburg to pay her a duty call in the small but elegant house he had erected for her there. When the "Mayor and Commonalty" of the town had presented him with a congratulatory address, he thanked them for "the honorable mention which is made of my revered mother, by whose maternal hand (early deprived of a father) I was led from childhood."[23]

It was, however, normal for him to avoid, as far as possible, lengthy sessions in his mother's presence. If, now that her son stood before her as one of the world's acclaimed heroes, she added a word to the general praise or did not try to make him feel inadequate, it would have been a prodigy. She had been, during the Revolution, so uncomplimentary about Washington's activities that she generally had been considered a Tory. To those who had lauded her son in her presence, she had replied that he was off doing things that were none of his business and allowing her to starve. Washington had heard "from very good authority that she is upon all occasions and in all companies complaining of the hardness of the times, of her wants and distresses; and, if not in direct terms at least by strong innuendoes, inviting favors." This, Washington continued from one of his military camps, was "too much." However, Washington quickly added that he would prefer not to remonstrate with his mother himself. He urged his favorite brother, John Augustine Washington, to do so.[24]

The irritations extended back to Washington's childhood. His father had died when the boy was eleven, leaving the best part of a modest estate to two sons of a previous marriage, and, on an impoverished farm, a second family of which George was the eldest. His mother preferred George to her other children, but demanded of him total service. He struggled to escape. How great was her power over him, even after he had set up his own bachelor household at Mount Vernon, was revealed when he allowed her unexpected appearance there to keep him from what he then considered the most important appointment of his life.

The French and Indian War was in full swing, and he was just setting out to meet with the British regular general, Edward Braddock, with whom he hoped to secure the conspicuous and educational post of aide-de-camp. His mother had come to importune him to honor what she considered his duties to her rather than go off and risk his life on battlefields. Hour after hour, he argued with her, allowing himself to slight the British general in a way that might well have ended all his chances for glory and military preferment. However, when his relationship with Braddock proved not to have been ruined, he accepted the appointment as aide despite his mother's disapproval.[25] Her resentment had been as great then as it was to be during her son's absence when leading the Continental Army.

Down the years, mediation by John Augustine Washington had kept the relations between George and his mother from open fireworks, but in January 1787, the mediator died.[26] A month later, Washington's control broke.

His mother had again asked for money. He sent her fifteen guineas, which he stated was all the cash he had, and then pointed out angrily what a drain her activities had been on his estate. She had requisitioned all the supplies from a plantation he conducted near Fredericksburg, and, in addition, he had during the war advanced her between three and four hundred pounds from his own pocket. Despite this, she had talked in such a way that he was "viewed as a delinquent and considered perhaps by the world an unjust and undutiful son."

She should rent her farms, which would supply her with ample support, should break up housekeeping, hire out all her servants except a man and a maid, keep only a phaeton and two horses, and live with one of her children. "This would relieve you entirely from the cares of this world and leave your mind at ease to reflect undisturbedly on that which ought to come." Since her expenses would use up only a quarter of her income, she could "make ample amends to the child you live with." She might then be "perfectly happy," that is "if you are so disposed . . . for happiness depends more upon the internal frame of a person's own mind than on the externals in the world."

Washington hastened to add that he was not suggesting that she come to Mount Vernon: "Candor requires me to say it will never answer your purposes in any shape whatsoever." Since the house was always crowded with strangers she would be forced to do one of three things: be always dressed for company, appear in dishabille, or be a prisoner in her own chamber. The first she would not like as being too fatiguing for one in her time of life. The second he would not like, as his guests were often "people of the first distinction." Nor would it do for her to stay in her own room, "for what with the sitting up of company, the noise and bustle of servants, and many other things, you would not be able to enjoy that calmness and serenity of mind which, in my opinion, you ought now to prefer to every other consideration in life."[27]

Mary Washington no more relished her son's desire to make her into a conventional fireside figure than he had relished her wish to make him into the epitome of dutiful and obedient sons. She did not rent out her land or break up her personal housekeeping. But, on the other hand, she did not permit George's interference and scolding to displace the one family antagonist who was worthy of her own mettle from his position as the favorite of her children. When she finally died in 1789, she left the lion's share of her estate to the descendant who least needed the bequest, George Washington.[28]

4

Farmer Washington

D URING 1786, speaking strangely in the past tense, Washington expressed his attitude towards slavery: "The unfortunate condition of the persons whose labors in part I employed has been the only unavoidable subject of regret. To make the adults among them as easy and comfortable as their actual state of ignorance and improvidence would admit; and to lay a foundation to prepare the rising generation for a destiny different from that in which they were born, afforded some satisfaction to my mind, and could not, I hoped, be displeasing to the justice of the Creator."[1]

These sentences defined a temporary halting place in Washington's continuing mental march from the ideas of his fathers to his own eventual conclusions and acts on the subject of slavery. He inherited the institution, and had been raised in an environment where slavery was the accepted—and necessary—foundation of the economic system according to which almost everyone lived. However, even before his Revolutionary command detached him violently from his Virginia environment, his conscience increasingly bothered him. He concluded that in addition to being humane in his treatment of his slaves, he would not relocate or sell a slave unless he could secure (as was rarely the case) that individual's consent.[2] This, as the birth rate in his slave quarters soared, left him with an economically damaging surplus of labor.

During his military service, Washington made close friends—Lafayette, John Laurens, and others—who denounced the entire institution of slavery as iniquitous. Furthermore, he was then surrounded with an economy that was not fundamentally geared to what—so it became more evident to him every day as he led a war for "freedom"—was unjustifiable tyranny. He sometimes wondered whether he could not shift from one economic system to the other, could not cease to be a slaveholder and make his peacetime living the way men like Robert Morris did, as an urban businessman.[3] However, he utterly lacked skill in the management of capital. He disliked cities and, as the strain of his military duties went on and on, his one tangible dream of peace and relaxation was to return to his old way of life at Mount Vernon.

In 1794, Washington was to write a Virginia neighbor, "With respect to the other species of property concerning which you ask my opinion, I shall frankly declare to you that I do not like to even think, much less talk, of it."[4] Yet he could not keep from thinking about it, and in the end, as the final radical act of his life, Washington freed all his slaves.*

On his return from nine years of war and political experiment, Washington needed above all else to cease pioneering, to mend his spirit by total immersion in the traditional and familiar. Attending to his farms became the major expedient of a mind that needed to be forever filled with detail, of a body that sickened without exercise.

Mount Vernon was no longer the modest plantation Washington had inherited. Using to get himself going the money which had come to him from his marriage to Martha Dandridge Custis (who had been a rich widow), expanding into surrounding property whenever a piece could somehow be brought on the market or even rented for a long term, Washington had amassed a huge estate. It stretched for some ten miles along the river shore and penetrated inland at its widest point for about four. In December 1793, he had 3265 acres under cultivation. However, his farms covered less than half his land. Birds looking down on the Mount Vernon plantation saw wide areas of scrub woods alternating with patches of cultivation, the whole cut by two broad tributaries of the Potomac.[5]

In addition to the settlement around the mansion house, there were five semi-independent farms. Each contained a simple house for the overseer, slave cabins, barns, tool sheds, stables, pastures. Washington

---

* The evolution of Washington's reactions to the subject of slavery is discussed in more detail in Volume IV.

operated a ferry across the Potomac,[6] a commercial mill that ground for his neighbors as well as his own farms, and a variety of home industries aimed at reducing, to the lowest possible minimum, what he had to buy from the outside with that commodity always rare for farmers however large their operations: cash. Humphreys tells us that he manufactured linen or woolen cloth almost sufficient for his "numerous household."[7]

How numerous was that household is indicated by a list he drew up in 1786 of the slaves who constituted his principal work force. At the Mansion House Farm were Washington's valet Will, two waiters, two male cooks, three drivers and stablers, three women past service, three seamstresses, two housemaids, two washers, four spinners, a stock keeper, an "odd-jobber," seven laborers, one wagoner, one carter, one gardener, four carpenters, two smiths, one knitter, and twenty-six children thirteen years of age or younger. Four men operated the mill. At River Plantation there were a slave overseer and his wife, ten laboring men, seventeen laboring women, and twenty-three children. At Dogue Run Plantation there were twenty-one adults, including another black overseer, one man described as ruptured and another as old. Also seventeen children. Ferry Plantation was inhabited by five laboring men, ten laboring women, and fifteen children. At Muddy Hole Plantation there was a third slave overseer, fourteen workers, and eleven children. In all there were one hundred twenty-four black adults and ninety-two children for a total of two hundred sixteen.[8]

This was by no means the total of Washington's work force. Although he was trying (for their own sake as well as his own) to train up likely Negro boys as artisans, he still needed white workmen to carry out the more skilled crafts. Hardly any such were available in Virginia for wages, and thus Washington (although he could by no means always find the opportunity or afford the price) bought the time of indentured servants who had contracted to work out the cost of their passage from Europe after they had arrived in America. In 1786, he paid twenty-four pounds for three years' service of two Irishmen: a shoemaker and a tailor.[9]

A Virginia estate, manned mostly by a work force without personal incentive and often commanded on the lower level by unenlightened overseers who too easily became brutalized, could (as Washington

[41]

pointed out) only operate successfully if supervised perpetually and in detail by the proprietor.[10]

As he had in wartime, Washington arose early, with the dawn in summer, by candlelight during the rest of the year. He was instantly attended by his "valet de chambre," Will (also known as Billy Lee), an aging mulatto slave who had been at his side during both his wars. Will was a privileged servant with duties hardly extending beyond serving a master who needed little personal service, and with a gift for procuring, in the byways of the intricate household, liquor that would get him drunk by evening.* In the mornings (presumably) Will was sober, if a little bleary-eyed. He had already laid out the costume in which Washington would attend to his farms: on a recorded occasion a plain blue coat, white cashmere waistcoat, black breeches, and black boots.[11]

Washington shaved himself. Then Will brushed his master's long hair, pulled it back tightly in what was considered "a military manner" (as it left no curls at the side), and tied the queue firmly with a ribbon.

It had been Washington's habit, when on military travels, to ride for several hours before finding breakfast. Now he read or did accounts until seven o'clock, when his meal was invariably the same: "three small Indian hoecakes (buttered) with as many dishes of tea (without cream)."

Almost every day except Sundays, Washington stepped out the door to where a groom waited with one of his horses. He leapt into the saddle and cantered rapidly down the driveway (he enjoyed moving fast) in anticipation of hours of refreshing exercise and relaxing attention to a flood of continuing practical details. Often he made the circuit of all five farms, a ride of about twenty miles, before he returned in time to dress for a three o'clock dinner.[12]

Most of Washington's farmhands were kept, of course, at routine tasks of producing food. They grew primarily corn and wheat. (Washington did not return to Virginia's traditional tobacco economy, which he had abandoned before the Revolution as uneconomic.) When fish ran in the Potomac, they manned the seines: some of the catch was

---

* Inviting Humphreys for an extended visit in 1786, Washington wrote, "Your old acquaintance Will, who is scarcely fit for anything else, can whiten your head, and many idlers about the house can blacken your shoes." In 1793, Washington added that Will had been "ruined by idleness."

dried for year-round food, some sold, bringing fifteen shillings a hundred for shad and four shillings a thousand for herring in 1785. They tended the stock, which Washington listed in that same year as one hundred and thirty horses (twenty-three unbroken): three hundred and thirty-six cattle including six bulls and twenty-six draught oxen; two hundred and eighty-three sheep. The hogs, he noted, could not be counted since they ran wild in the woods, but there were enough to send eight tons of pork to the smokehouses.[13]

The economic aspects of farming were obviously essential, yet they lay to one side of Washington's true pleasure. How agreeable it was for a released warrior not to destroy but create! "To see plants rise from the earth and flourish by the superior skill and bounty of the laborer fills a contemplative mind," Washington wrote, "with ideas which are more easy to be conceived, than expressed." How pleasing "to see the work of one's own hands, fostered by care and attention, rising to maturity in a beautiful display of those advantages and ornaments which, by the combination of nature and taste of the projector in the disposal of them, is always regaling to the eye, at the same time [that], in their seasons, they are . . . grateful to the palate."[14]

Beauty was always in Washington's mind as he directed his laborers or stripped off his coat to work beside them in the fields. Carefully planned drainage was not only necessary to preserve what thin topsoil remained, but the gullies the rains scooped out were unsightly scars on his fields. Neat hedges that served as what he called "live fences" did more than conserve lumber and keep the hogs from the corn: they soothed Washington's soul as he galloped from field to field. And then there were the extensive grounds at the Mansion House where ornament was not the handmaiden but the overlord of utility. As he rode, he kept his eyes out for trees that could be transplanted with aesthetic effect in "my walks, groves, and wildernesses." He designed ha-has (ditches that contained sunken fences) so that his cattle would seem to be grazing freely but were kept at a suitable distance from the house.[15]

A visitor commented that Washington had a great turn for "mechanics." He made minor inventions and supervised the erection of the farm buildings, "condescending even to measure things himself, that all may be perfectly uniform."[16] The whole estate, as it stretched mile after mile, was his own creation, always to some extent satisfying, always capable of improvement.

Improvement in agriculture, Humphreys wrote, was Washington's passion. Every day, he engaged in experimentation. Seeking to find new or more abundant crops that would grow in Virginia soil (and also new decorative plants) he established "botanical gardens" at Mount Vernon and then, as he needed more land, at others of his plantations. His eminence brought him seeds and cuttings from all over the world. (He reciprocated, sending, for instance, seed from Kentucky to Louis XVI for the gardens at Versailles.[17]) The exotics he planted in different ways at different spots with different kinds of fertilizer. Typically, they did badly, the "seeds from China," for instance, coming up sparsely the first year and not at all the second. Also typically, he was cautious about his conclusions, asking himself whether the Chinese seeds were unfit for the climate or whether he had planted them wrongly. However, he did decide that, as a general rule, better results came from domesticating indigenous wild plants than importing outsiders. Thus, believing that French grapes ripened too soon in Virginia's hot climate, he collected two thousand cuttings from all the "spontaneous" vines he could locate, hoping that a happy chance would enable him to establish an American wine. "Wine," he observed, "would be a valuable produce," but his efforts as a vintner came to little.[18]

The great need, Washington realized, was somehow to improve Virginia's basic agricultural patterns. "I never ride to my plantations," he wrote, "without seeing something which makes me regret having continued so long in the ruinous mode of farming which we are in." Indeed, everywhere in tidewater Virginia, the land was "gullied and exhausted." Since the common farmer could not be expected to "hazard" a departure "from the *old* road till the *new* one is made so plain and easy that he is sure it cannot be mistaken," Washington felt that it was up to large holders like himself to apply part of their resources and leisure to what alone could solve the problems: "a *course* of experiments." Although he studied English agricultural books and corresponded copiously with Arthur Young, who was considered the greatest English writer on agriculture, he was convinced that ideas from abroad had to be carefully re-examined under American conditions: "What is good and profitable husbandry in one country may not be so in another." Towards determining which crops "are useful on our farms or salable in our markets," and would also improve rather than further exhaust the land, "every experiment is a treasure."[19]

Typically, Washington divided a field at Muddy Hole Plantation into three parts with crosswise furrows and then subdivided so that the same corn could be identifiably planted in six different ways.[20] The suspense was fascinating as findings came in according to nature's slow rhythm—and always, in the end, Washington was left with another riddle. His results might have turned on such an irritating circumstance as inadequate hoeing by his slaves; or perhaps all had been set topsy-turvy by freaks of that untamable giant, the weather.

In June 1785, Washington decided to find out what "a thoroughbred *practical* English farmer" could achieve on a Virginia plantation. He wrote his old friend George William Fairfax (the Fairfaxes had not responded to his urgings that they return to America) to find him a man "who understands the best course [system of rotation] of crops, how to plough, to sow, to mow, to hedge, to ditch, and above all, Midas-like, one who can convert everything he touches into manure [fertilizer] as the first transmutation towards gold."[21]

A year later, James Bloxham of Gloucestershire arrived at Mount Vernon. He looked around him in horror. "The old man" had expected, so Washington wrote, "well-organized farms." Washington bravely defended Virginia's reputation by blaming the state of agriculture on "the ravages of a nine years' war" and pointed out humbly that if the farms at Mount Vernon were as "perfect" as English farms, "there would have been no occasion for his services." But when Bloxham, after hesitating to send for his wife and family, finally did so, Washington instantly began putting English perfection to practical tests. As Bloxham planted wheat in the English manner, Washington was right beside him planting other furrows in the American manner.* [22]

For every working day, Washington noted in his diaries (which were primarily agricultural records) what had been done on every farm. On Saturdays, his overseers presented him with reports that

---

* Bloxham remained Washington's farmer until 1790. He was, Washington summarized, "perfectly acquainted with every part of a farmer's business and peculiarly so . . . in the management and use of oxen for the cart or plough. . . . Yet, finding it a little troublesome to instruct the Negroes and to compel them to the practice of *his* modes, he slided into theirs."[23]

were entered in ledgers. The amount of detail was tremendous and recording it occupied innumerable hours. Jefferson was to hint that these "agricultural notations" served to occupy Washington's leisure hours as reading would fill those of a more bookish man.[24] Certain it is that Washington very rarely attempted (as he had done so often during his military career) to boil the complicated facts down into a written synthesis.

From his letters, we gather that the major agricultural reforms he was trying to work out for his neighbors were the growing of grass specifically for grazing: the establishment, with a superior line of sheep, of economic wool production; the development of fertilizers indigenous to Virginia; the invention of a method for rotating crops that would replenish the fertility of the fields; and the breeding of a line of super-mules.*

Although Washington loved to discuss his agricultural practices and wrote about them in letters, he felt that to publish his ideas or findings "might be imputed to me as a piece of ostentation." When an old man, he concluded, "I have made very little proficiency in acquiring knowledge either in the principles or practice of husbandry. My employments through life have been so diversified, my absences from home have been so frequent and so long at a time as to have prevented me from bestowing the attention and from making the experiments which are necessary to establish facts in the science of agriculture." Yet

---

* Virginia needed to be instructed in the merits of pasturage. Cows, for instance, browsed on twigs and weeds, which meant they could not be caught to be milked every day, and their manure was uncollectible to be used as fertilizer.

That there could be an "intimate connection . . . between agriculture and chemistry" came to Washington in 1796 as a "curious and interesting" idea. He tried to use effectively as fertilizer all farm waste and the waste from his fisheries. He also hopefully spread over his fields year after year mud dug up from the bottom of the Potomac.[25]

There was a British law against exporting blooded sheep. Having boasted that he never, by purchasing a smuggled animal, encouraged a captain to break the law, Washington added that he had no objection to buying the offspring of such illegal arrivals. In 1788, he raised two hundred lambs and a year later was getting five and a quarter pounds of wool per head. However, while he was too busy as President to attend to his flock, the yield fell to two and a half pounds.[26]

According to Freeman, Washington's most useful agricultural discovery was his method of crop rotation, which expanded the usual Virginia routine—corn, wheat, then hay—from three years to six: 1. Corn, with Irish potatoes or carrots between the rows. 2. Buckwheat as fertilizer—ploughed in, allowed to grow again, again ploughed. In the fall, wheat. 3. Wheat harvested. 4. Peas. 5. Spring barley and oats, with red clover. 6. Clover. 7. Top of cycle: corn again.[27]

Washington's adventures with mules will be described in a moment.

[46]

"agricultural pursuits and rural amusements" had always been "the most pleasing occupation of my life and most congenial with my temper."[28]

It was natural for Washington to lump together "agricultural pursuits" and "rural amusements." It would, indeed, have been impossible for him to decide where at Mount Vernon work stopped and play began. Take, for instance, the matter of the jackasses.

Whether Washington knew this or not, it all started as an aspect of international intrigue. Spain, the possessor of the mouth of the Mississippi, wished acceptance of her policy that citizens of the United States might not trade through into the ocean. Washington wished to improve Virginia's mules by putting to American mares some of Spain's sensational jackasses. Spain had a law against the export of such jackasses. Washington was heard to wonder how he could secure a jack who had not been doctored by the wily Spaniards. Those that could be bought, he had been warned, "very frequently have their generative parts so injured by squeezing as to render them as unfit for the purpose of begetting colts, as castration would, when, from a superficial view, no imperfection appears." The Spanish foreign office got wind of Washington's quandary, and the King himself dispatched across the ocean, as a present to the most influential man in the United States, two jackasses from his own royal stables.[29]

Hearing that the jacks, each accompanied by a personal attendant, were expected to disembark in Boston, Washington hurried off one of his overseers to meet them and escort them overland to Mount Vernon. He tried to prepare this overseer for all foreseeable eventualities with instructions as elaborate as those he had given General Wayne before the attack on Stony Point. The jacks would surely pine if separated from their grooms. Since the grooms would equally surely speak no English, the overseer should seek out an interpreter in Boston and settle all issues that might arise on the road including "the kind and quantity of liquor" with which the Spaniards were to be supplied daily. Should any controversy arise in this discussion, the Lieutenant Governor of Massachusetts should be asked to mediate. Washington hoped that once the cavalcade was en route, there would be no mutterings, screamings, or fist-wavings; but if there were, the overseer should, on their arrival in New York, dash for assistance to the Spanish ministry.[30]

One jack proved to have died on shipboard. When the other (after what bilingual explosions we know not) arrived with his attendant safely at Mount Vernon, Washington was delighted with the physique of the animal, whom he named Royal Gift. The majestic jackass was not only "about fifteen hands high" but "his body and limbs [were] very large in proportion to his height." For the eagerly expected newcomer, Washington had, by depriving his Arabian stallion Magnolio, prepared a bounteous harem: thirty-three eager fillies awaited the Spaniard's ministrations.[31]

Surely Washington was leaning over the fence when the first of the mares was introduced into the paddock where the now well-rested jackass preened his impressive anatomy. Royal Gift sniffed at the mare and then turned away in disgust.

As the Spaniard repudiated bride after bride, Washington had flashes of rage in which he suspected that His Most Catholic Majesty had played a trick on him by sending him a damaged beast,* but more often his reaction was mirth at the ridiculous denouement to all his efforts and hopes. He wondered to Lafayette whether the jackass was not being the perfect courtier by imitating the behavior of the elderly Spanish king: "His late royal master, though past his grand climacteric cannot be less moved by female allurements than he is, or, when prompted, can proceed with more deliberation and majestic solemnity to the act of procreation."

At other times, Washington speculated that, as an aristocrat, Royal Gift was superior to "republican enjoyments." He seemed "too full of royalty to have anything to do with a plebeian race. Perhaps his stomach may come to him. If not, I shall wish he had never come from His Most Catholic Majesty's stables."[32]

Magnolio had been reinstated as the sultan of Mount Vernon's equine harem and most of the nubile mares had been rerouted to him when Washington tried an experiment that again changed the situation. He introduced Royal Gift not, as always formerly, to a mare but to a female ass borrowed from a neighbor. This time, as he wrote the owner of the "jenny," the view over the fence was different: "Though in appearance quite unequal to the match, yet, like a true female, she

---

* Washington wrote officially of "my gratitude for so condescending a mark of esteem from one of the first crowned heads in Europe," but stated privately that if the jack had been tampered with, "I shall have no disinclination to present His Catholic Majesty with as valuable a present as I received from him."[33]

was not terrified at the disproportionate size of her paramour, and, having renewed the conflict twice or thrice, it is to be hoped the issue will be favorable."[34]

Washington then discovered that if a she-ass were employed to rouse Royal Gift from his "slothful humors," and a mare quickly substituted, the jack would, although "slow in covering" be "sure." Washington now regretted having sent most of the harem to Magnolio.[35]

Lafayette, who had been working abroad on the mule enterprise, procured from Malta what Washington called "the most valuable things you could have sent me": another jack and two jennies. When these proved lighter and more graceful than the ponderous Royal Gift, Washington resolved to set in motion two races of mules which would, since mules require less fodder, make horses obsolete in Virginia. Royal Gift's descendants would take care of "heavy, slow draught," while the Knight of Malta's would be good for the saddle and light carriages. "In a few years, I intend to drive no other in my carriage."[36]

There is no record that Washington ever set out in his ornamental coach drawn by six mules. He offered Magnolio and his jackasses, and as time went on, their descendants, at stud for a fee. However, as he wrote, such pursuits always contributed "more to the amusement than profit of the raiser."* [37] The same thing could be said of the whole Mount Vernon operation. In 1785, Washington had to buy corn, as he had not succeeded in growing enough to feed the many mouths on his plantations. In 1786, he did manage to feed everyone from his crops, but had no surplus with which to raise cash. In 1787, he wrote, "My estate for the last eleven years has not been able to make both ends meet."[38]

The basic cause of the economic limpness of the Mount Vernon operation was that the topsoil there had been so completely exhausted that Washington's best efforts to renew its fertility could accomplish little. The soil, furthermore, was only a thin layer over clay or marl, which, by preventing rain from sinking down, kept the fields unmanageably wet for long periods of time, and also encouraged washouts which further reduced the amount of topsoil. The general sterility was

* They also contributed to the amusement of the slaves. Washington wrote that Peter "will do nothing but peddle [trifle] about the stables and conceives it to be a kind of degradation to bestow his attention on horses of plebeian birth."[39]

attested to by the trees on the areas between the farms which were so stunted that Washington had difficulty finding timber even large enough for fencing.[40]

A further problem was the inefficiency and wastefulness of slave labor. Add the fact that Washington kept his gangs working so much of the time at what pleased his eye or interested his mind but did not serve immediate utility. And then there was the produce which disappeared unprofitably into his expansive entertaining at the Mansion House.

A man who followed middle-class business ideas would have been discouraged to the point of despair by watching a concern to which he devoted his principal energies lose money season after season. Washington was full of cheer. His bodily health was never better, and now, when he awoke in the mornings, his brain revolved not grievous matters but only little problems that merged with anticipations of pleasure.[41]

Still, in the long run he would have somehow to meet his expenses. When chivied by bill collectors he felt not only resentful but incompetent since, so he complained, he had never learned how to "parry a dun."[42] To disentangle himself was made more difficult by his principles. His position, he had concluded, required more of him than just refusing governmental rewards: He should not now place his prestige behind any speculations that were larger than the transactions of every day. It followed that he would have to extract the funds he needed from the old speculations he had set in motion before the Revolution, before he had become a marked and famous man.

5

Business Worries

W ASHINGTON had foreseen that the business papers he
had left behind at Mount Vernon when he rode unexpectedly to war would, on his return, be in some confusion.
However, the extent of the "disorder" proved horrifying. The files had
been thoroughly scrambled (and some completely lost) during "frequent hasty removals of them" when there had been danger that
Mount Vernon might be set on fire by British raiders. Furthermore,
Washington's wartime manager, his cousin Lund Washington, had
abhorred keeping books. Thus, when the General wished to collect
an old debt or was asked to pay one, he had little to go on except
imperfect memory. His overall financial situation was completely
hidden from view. And to make everything more confused, mixed
up with his own papers were documents dealing with the estates of
deceased friends which before the war he had agreed to handle. Concerning these, embarrassing queries came in.[1]

Washington perpetually expressed his resolution to straighten out
the mare's nest. He had, since he was a boy, found it soothing to keep
day-by-day accounts, but only because the balancing of figures was a
finite act "in a clouded state of existence, where so many things appear
precarious to . . . bewildered research." Stirring around in a huge
mass of incoherent financial data he found repellent. If the sun shone,
he would flee from his desk to his gardens. During succeeding winters,
his conscience welcomed the inclement weather with the hope that
"the dreariness of the season" would give him "leisure" to organize
those nagging papers. But when he was immured in his library, he had

his farming diary to scribble in, or he could copy passages out of agricultural books. He could read. And then there was always a huge pile of letters waiting to be answered.[2]

Washington complained that he was bothered with "letters (often of an unmeaning nature) from foreigners; inquiries after Dick, Tom, and Harry who *may have been* in some part or at *some time* in the Continental service; . . . introductions; applications for copies of papers; references of a thousand old matters with which I *ought* not to be troubled more than the Great Mogul." When Humphreys pointed out that he encouraged this "truly distressing and almost incredible" flow by answering the letters, Washington replied firmly that each "must receive an answer of some kind." Indeed, because it involved human contact and presented possibilities for kindness, Washington found struggling with his mail more congenial than straightening out his financial records.[3]

After having growled that a correspondent was imposing on him, Washington would carefully and exquisitely word his reply to keep from giving offense. "I am," he wrote on one such occasion, "sorry it has been your lot to be brought before a court, much more so for the issue, and if I could with propriety place you in full enjoyment of everything you wish, I should have pleasure in doing it, but it is not in my power."[4]

Sometimes Washington's correspondence enabled him to enjoy the pleasures of literary expression. Such was the case when he received from his friend, the politician and amateur composer Francis Hopkinson, *Seven Songs for the Harpsichord.* In the dedication to Washington, Hopkinson claimed to be "the first native of the United States who has produced a musical composition"* and requested Washington's musical patronage.

Washington replied, "We are told of the amazing powers of music in ancient times . . . The poets of old (whatever they may do in these days) were strangely addicted to the marvelous; and if I before *doubted* the truth of their relations with respect to the power of music, I am now fully convinced of their falsity, because I would not, for the honor of my country, allow that we are left by ancients at an im-

---

* No man who had fought in the Revolution and seen men march to William Billings's "Chester" could doubt that the New England singing master had anticipated Hopkinson. Hopkinson, Washington probably realized, based his claim on being the first Europeanized gentleman composer.

measurable distance in everything; and if they could soothe the ferocity of wild beasts, could draw the trees and the stones after them, and could even charm the powers of Hell by their music, I am sure that your productions would have had at least virtue enough in them (without the aid of voice or instrument) to melt the ice of the Delaware and Potomac, and in that case you should have had an earlier acknowledgment of your favor of the first of December."

Hopkinson, Washington continued, had not used judgment in choosing him as "a coadjutor"; should he have "any doubts about the reception which your work would meet with . . . For, should the tide of prejudice not flow in favor of it (and so various are the tastes, opinions, and whims of men that even the sanction of divinity does not ensure universal concurrence), what alas! can I do to support it? I can neither sing one of the songs nor raise a single note on any instrument to convince the unbelieving. But I have, however, one argument which will prevail with persons of true taste (at least in America): I can tell them that it is the production of Mr. Hopkinson."⁵

Washington's business records would probably never have been straightened out had not the President of Harvard intervened as a *deus ex machina* by recommending a long-nosed, lantern-jawed young Yankee named Tobias Lear to be Washington's private secretary and tutor to Martha's grandchildren. That his arrival was a gift of Providence was at first not altogether clear. As was so often the case with those entering the service of the man reputed to be so great, Lear came in defensively, determined (as he put it) to "conduct myself in such a manner as to preserve my independence at all times." Watching his employer closely, he felt towards himself a "reserve and coldness" which made his "pride take alarm" as he wondered whether the General did not desire "servility." Lear was meditating on resigning, when Washington "began to relax and gradually drew me towards him by every tender and endearing tie." He then concluded that Washington's "caution and circumspection, striking traits in his character," had induced his previous behavior.

Lear was now, as he boasted, "treated in every respect as a child of it [the family]." He had, indeed, to hide his need for new shirts to keep Martha from postponing, so he could be served, some work the seamstresses were doing for her husband. This the young man could not think of permitting; his original fear of Washington had turned to idolatry. He wrote an old New England friend, "General Washington is, I believe, almost the only man of an exalted character who does not lose some part of his respectability [right to respect] by an intimate acquaintance. I have lived with him near two years, have received as many marks of his affection and esteem as perhaps any young man ever did, and have occasions to be with him in every situation in which a man is placed in his family—have ate and drank with him constantly, and almost every evening played at cards with him, and I declare that I have never found a single thing that could lessen my respect for him. A complete knowledge of his honesty, uprightness, and candor in all his private transactions have sometimes led one to think him more than a man."[6]

Loyal, controlled, humorless, tense, very competent, Lear remained Washington's right-hand man for most of the rest of the hero's career— and the paragon started by making sense out of the recalcitrant papers. The General was enabled to conclude that he had sustained a loss of at least ten thousand pounds sterling during his Revolutionary service, mostly as the result of wartime inflation. His debtors—"ungenerous, not to say dishonest"—had taken advantage of the paper money to pay off what they owed him at "a shilling or sixpence in the pound." His creditors, on the other hand, had taken advantage of the national leader's unwillingness to make personal profit from the inflation. They had let "their claims rest till the annihilation of paper money, and are now receiving (as, indeed, every person ought to do) specie or an equivalent to the full amount."[7]

Freeman asserts that, despite Lear's accountings, Washington did not realize how bad his financial situation actually was. The debts still owed him were largely uncollectible, partly because a large proportion were held by his or Martha's relations, partly because he could not bring himself to distress men who had been so honest as not to pay him off during the inflation; and partly because many whom he did try to press would not pay unless sued, and, in Washington's opinion, "to sue is to do nothing." The debts he himself owed he found it difficult, if not impossible, to meet. Virginia was, indeed, suffering from the opposite of the old inflation: a shortage of money that made cash almost impossible to come by.[8]

To Washington, with his innate passion for land, the most painful of all his postwar renunciations must have been his share (which his position as Commander in Chief would have made tremendous) in the grants of land being made to veterans. The tracts he had previously claimed, many as a result of his service in the previous war, remained his most promising unexploited assets.

Washington had been home less than two months when he wrote sarcastically to Gilbert Simpson, who managed a mill he had built on a tributary (now called Washington's Run) of the Youghiogheny River, not far from Pittsburgh: "How profitable our partnership has been, *you best can tell.*" Washington was sure "I ought to have a good deal of wealth in your hands," as he was told "that it is the best mill and has had more custom than any other on the west side [of] the Allegheny Mountains." He expected, so he wrote, immediately to receive complete accounts and payments that would "give the lie to these reports" that Simpson was cheating him. Back from the miller came seventy-nine pieces of Virginia paper money of various denominations but all so worthless that Washington tossed the packet into a drawer, where it remained until, long after Washington's death, the bills became valuable as antiques.[9]

Washington's next effort was to advertise for rent his favorite and most extensive western possession, "30,000 acres of land on the Ohio and Great Kanawha," which he had personally explored in 1770, when this tract of virgin wilderness was deep in the Indian country. It was still far beyond the boundaries of ordinary settlement. Lyrically, Washington described how ten thousand of his acres lay "upon the Ohio between the mouths of the two Kanawhas, having a front upon the river of fifteen miles and beautifully bordered by it."* The other twenty thousand acres stretched up the Great Kanawha "from the mouth or near it" for more than forty miles, being all "river low-grounds of the first quality. . . . A great deal of it may be converted into the finest mowing ground imaginable, with little or no labor, nature and the water-stops which have been made by the beaver having done *more* to effect this than years of hard labor in most other rich soils."

Washington specified that the first three years would be rent-free, on condition that for every hundred acres, five be cleared and a "comfortable" house erected. During specified terms, the house would be changed to one of "brick or stone or framed work with a stone or brick

---

* Today, this land lies between Point Pleasant and Parkersburg, West Virginia.

chimney"; other improvements would be made; and the rent would rise slowly to three shillings an acre, where it would remain for the remainder of a lease running 999 years.

In reply to a query from the Rev. John Witherspoon, President of the College of New Jersey (later renamed Princeton), Washington stated that he hoped to lure from Europe "societies or religious sectaries with their pastors." The isolation of his so distant acres, he added cannily, "would be a means of connecting friends in a small circle, and making life in a new and rising empire (to the inhabitants of which and their habits newcomers would be strangers) pass much more agreeably."

Washington confessed to Witherspoon that he had been puzzled as to terms. Short leases would be most advantageous to him, but he assumed that the prospective settlers would not want the improvements they made to revert to the landlord. Yet how, "in an infant country where lands rise progressively," to set the rent without making it frighteningly high at first and yet without allowing its inadequacy in the long run to "injure the landlord"? Whether the terms he had hit on were low enough to be "inviting" and whether arrived "strangers" might not feel they had been cheated "upon seeing a wide, a wild and an extensive country before them," where other land (though not so "valuable and pleasant") might be got cheaper, "is not with me to decide. Experiment alone can determine it. But it is for me to declare that I cannot think of separating forever from lands which are beautifully situated upon navigable rivers, rich in quality, and abundantly blessed with many natural advantages, upon less beneficial terms to myself." Outright sale, the method of western settlement approved of by democrats, was not according to traditional Virginia patterns, and not Washington's choice for his favorite tract.

The General added to Witherspoon that it was his intention "to be perfectly candid, for my feelings would be as much hurt, if I should deceive others. . . . as theirs would be who might suffer by the deception." However, his candor was limited. "The title to these lands is indisputable," he wrote, although less than two weeks later he asked the legal help of Edmund Randolph because "my ignorance of the existing laws of this state, since the change of its constitution" made him unsure how his claims stood. In his advertisement, he commented that since the land lay on the southeast side of the Ohio, their occupancy "can give no jealousy to the Indians; the proprietors of it, therefore, may cultivate their farms in peace, and fish, fowl, and hunt without fear of molestation." Yet when he planned to visit his Kanawha lands later that same year, he asked the commandant at Fort Pitt to lend him, in addition to a boat, an escort of "three or four trusty soldiers."* And, in the end, Indian troubles on the frontier made it too dangerous for him to visit the land.[10]

The properties Washington claimed west of the Blue Ridge and again west of the Alleghenies were in various states of disarray: some occupied by tenants who did not pay, some unoccupied, some even being advertised for sale by rival claimants. A personal tour of investigation and amendment being called for, Washington set out in September 1784.

Although he was careful to include in his party no one "who would soon get tired and embarrass my movements," he did not stint himself when it came to baggage. From his military storage, he took an officer's marquee for the gentlemen and a horseman's tent for the servants. In the "equipage trunk" and one linen and two leather valises he carried clothes, bed linen, and silver cups and spoons; and also containers that seconded separate canteens and "two kegs of spirits" in making sure that there would be no shortage of oil, vinegar, madeira, port wine, and cherry bounce. Washington did not forget extra horseshoes, "spices of all sorts," and "my fishing lines."[11]

His route could hardly have been more rich in exciting memories. It carried him by Fort Cumberland, which had during his first war been his headquarters, and along Braddock's Road through a region where he had fought the French and Indians year after year. No military reminiscences found their way into his journal. At the Great Meadows, where he had built Fort Necessity and suffered his first defeat, he wrote, "The whole of the ground called the Meadows may be reclaimed at an easy comparative expense, and is a very good stand for a tavern." The land, indeed, belonged to him, since an agent had bought it for him in 1770 for thirty pistoles which (due to an obvious quirk in his mind) he wrote down as "pistols."[12]

His partnership with Simpson having ended in what he regarded as fraud, Washington had advertised that he would auction off the mill property. He considered it very valuable. As he cantered onto the site,

---

* Washington added to the commandant that he saw "no impropriety in my request respecting the boat and soldiers. If I had thought there was, I pledge myself to you I should not have made it."

he found the mill drooping and ragged, while, under a broken dam, the race was almost empty of water. "Little rent or good," he sadly concluded, "is to be expected from the present aspect of her."[13]

Washington had noted in 1770, when he had last seen the property, that veins of coal rose to the top of the ground and appeared to be "of the very best kind, burning freely." However, native coal was rarely used in America because it was hard to transport and the fumes were believed to cause epidemic diseases. During this visit, Washington did not mention the black outcroppings (which were eventually to make the land extremely valuable) except insofar as they contributed to the discouraging infertility of the farm around the mill.[14]

On the day of the sale, a satisfactory crowd gathered, but they had come to stare at General Washington. Little money was realized, although a cow sold for £2.10. No one wanted to take over the mill, despite Washington's offer of fifteen months' rent free. Although he believed that his cooperation with Simpson had already lost him more than a thousand pounds in hard money, he was forced to let the miscreant stay on the farm for a rent to be paid in wheat. As for the mill, being unable to "rent or sell her," Washington was willing to "let her return to dust."[15]

At Simpson's there appeared representatives of the Scotch-Irish families who had for more than ten years lived on a tract of 2813 acres, beside a tributary of the Ohio called Miller's Run, which Washington claimed as his own property. The delegation, so Washington noted, attempted "to discover all the flaws they could in my deed . . . and to establish a fair and upright intention in themselves." However, all their expostulating could not budge Washington from his insistence that, even if it had been they who had changed the wilderness into farms, the land was legally his. They would have to pay him rent.

To stand up against America's greatest hero (after whom Pennsylvania had named the county in which they had squatted) required great fortitude. The deputation, having conferred long among themselves, finally announced that they would have to return home and consult further with their fellow settlers. They would give Washington "their definite determination when I should come to the land."[16]

Washington arrived near the settlement on the next Sunday. He decided that, since "the people living on my land" were "*apparently* very religious," he would not visit them until the next day. Then he hired a neighbor for six shillings to be his "pilot," and visited one by one the thirteen farms, making a note of the situation of each. Thus Samuel McBride had "five acres of meadow and thirty of arable land under good fencing—a logged dwelling house with a puncheon roof and stable or small barn of the same kind—the land rather hilly but good, chiefly white oak."

The settlers gave Washington dinner in David Reed's "good logged dwelling house with a bad roof." They asked on what terms he would sell his claim. They were convinced they could not be dispossessed, "yet to avoid contention, they would buy if my terms were moderate."

"I told them I had no inclination to sell."

The settlers then talked "a great deal of their hardships, their religious principles (which had brought them together as a society of seceders), and unwillingness to separate or remove."

Washington finally agreed that he might sell. This started arguments about price, which Washington brought to an end by stating that his "last offer" was twenty-five shillings an acre, to be paid in three annual installments with interest. Otherwise, he would give them 999-year leases at an annual rent of ten pounds "per ct."

The farmers withdrew to another room. Finally, they filed back. The spokesman asked Washington if he would take the purchase price "at a longer credit" and without interest.

Washington replied that he would not.

Under the circumstances, said the spokesman, they were "determined to stand suit."

It having been "suggested that there were among them some who were disposed to relinquish their claim," Washington called out the names individually: "James Scott, William Stewart, etc., etc." One by one the squatters rose and answered "that they meant to stand suit and abide the issue of the law."[17]

Washington was angry.* Since the squatters had ignored warnings he had sent them when he was away on military service, he felt that "a very ungenerous advantage has been taken of a situation in which I could not attend to my private concerns." For once, he put a dispute in the hands of lawyers. He was soon writing that since the local

---

* A tradition remains in the neighborhood that he used profane language and was fined on the spot by one of the squatters, who happened to be a justice of the peace.[18]

community sided with the squatters, he did not expect a fair trial, yet the issues were so clear that there could be no doubt of a favorable verdict from an impartial jury.[19]

As a matter of fact, Washington could attribute correctly to his military service only delays which had prevented him from trying to enforce his claims before the squatters became so well established. As the letters he now wrote to his lawyer reveal, the basic weaknesses of his position dated from before the Revolution. They were, indeed, not untypical of the ever-vexed original titles to western land.

During 1771, William Crawford, a surveyor Washington often employed, found the tract "at my request" and made a survey. Some settlers (not the present group) appearing, Crawford bought them out, built a cabin, "and placed a man therein to keep possession of the land." Then, in October 1773, the present squatters arrived, drove away the man, and built a cabin of their own which so blocked the door of Washington's cabin that it became uninhabitable.

Washington still had none of the warrants he would have to present in order to change his private survey into a deed of possession. The warrants he finally bought were dated November 15, 1773. They had belonged to John Posey, who had secured them as a French and Indian War veteran under the King's Proclamation of 1763. This added confusion, since Crawford's legal authorization as a surveyor did not extend to patents made under this proclamation. And when, at the request of his lawyers, Washington now tried to locate the survey, it was not to be found in the official records where it should have been. However, Washington argued that even if the survey was not exactly regular, it was the only one ever made of the land; and, even if it could not now be found, it must have existed since otherwise he would not have been granted his legal patent. The patent was dated October 30, 1774, almost a year after the settlers had moved in.

The squatters had never sought a patent. They argued that Washington's had been secured illegally, and that therefore they possessed the land by right of occupancy. Washington's answer was that should occupancy prove the criterion, most of the tract was still his because the first building on it had been the cabin Crawford had erected at his orders.[20]

As the suit dragged on, Washington's anger smoldered. A rumor that the settlers had decided to give up and move made him write that, since they had withheld his land for ten or twelve years and, "after all the admonition I could give and the favorable offers which have been made them," had put him to the expense of a suit, he wished that, whether they left the land voluntarily or were finally evicted, "you will sue them respectively for trespasses, rents, or otherwise . . . to obtain justice for me." However, he soon thought better of this, deciding that perhaps, after all, they were not "willful and obstinate sinners."[21]

In November 1786, Washington learned that he had won the case. "Although the present occupants have little right to look to me for indulgences, . . . yet, as they are now in my power, it is neither my wish nor intention to distress them further. . . . They may therefore become tenants upon terms equitable between man and man, or purchasers, it being my intention to dispose of the land."* He had resolved to sell all his land in western Pennsylvania because of the impossibility of getting good managers: honest men were too busy to pay much attention, and those who had time to work for him, cheated him.[22]

Washington had even steeled himself to abandoning his dream-acres on the Ohio and the Kanawhas if he could find suitable purchasers in Europe. He had, he explained to a French correspondent, "no family" and he "wished to live easy and to spend the remainder of my days with as little trouble as possible." He would accept thirty thousand English guineas for what he now put down as 32,373 acres.[23]

But it was one thing to offer western lands for sale and another to get anyone to buy them. Most remained on his hands, to be rented out if possible. He entrusted to Battaile Muse, probably the son of one of his old French and Indian War companions, the management of those tracts which were occupied or, unlike the too-distant Kanawha lands, truly available for settlement. He admonished Muse to do for deserving tenants not only those things that were "legal and just but those that are honorable." More than that: Muse was not to deny families who had "no other claim but upon my generosity." However, Muse was to have no pity for those tenants who had "taken advantage of me" during the war by paying their debts in depreciated paper. Even these, if they appealed personally to Washington, found him in the end kind.[24]

Muse surprised Washington by making the lands he managed

---

* Some of the squatters stayed on as tenants, others moved nearby. Washington finally succeeded during 1796 in selling the entire tract to a land agent for $12,000.[25]

profitable.[26] However, Washington remained in the sum of his activities land-poor. He was forced, like any mean frontier farmer, to become the prey of speculators. He took from his strongbox some certificates Congress had given him, in lieu of cash, to pay back money he had expended as Commander in Chief. He sold them for a twentieth of their face value.[27]

6

The Cincinnati Quandary

O N his return from the Revolution, Washington resigned from the vestry of his local Episcopal parish. This reflected no opposition to organized religion—he did not, in principle, disapprove of taxing for the support of churches*—but rather a desire to have nothing more to do with government. In Virginia, the vestries had certain temporal powers.[1]

The organizations with which Washington kept contact were fraternal. He remained a Mason[2] and continued as President-General of the Society of the Cincinnati.

As the association of the officers who had fought at his side, the Cincinnati was dear to Washington's heart, all the more because the order had brought back good fellowship during that unhappy time when Washington had been forced to thwart his officers' rightful expectations by persuading them to go home unpaid rather than aim their weapons at the civil governments. The society, furthermore, had filled in for governmental neglect by establishing a charitable fund to benefit impoverished officers. Washington's first letter from his Mount

---

* When legislation was proposed for "establishing" all Christian religions by having each Virginian taxed for the expenses of his own church, Washington wrote that, although no man was more opposed than he "to *any kind* of restraint upon religious principles," he was not alarmed at the idea of making people "pay towards the support of that which they profess . . . or declare themselves Jews, Mohammedans, or otherwise and thereby obtain proper relief." However, since the bill caused disquiet, even if only to "a respectable minority," Washington hoped it "could die an easy death" lest it "rankle and perhaps convulse the state."[3] The bill died, and eventually Jefferson secured the abolition in Virginia of all religious taxes.

Vernon retirement was a circular letter to the state societies calling a general meeting in Philadelphia during May 1784.[4]

One of the most unpleasant moments in Washington's life was surely the appearance at Mount Vernon of an ill-printed little pamphlet entitled *Considerations on the Society or Order of the Cincinnati . . . Proving That It Creates a Race of Hereditary Patricians or Nobility, Interspersed with Remarks on Its Consequences to the Freedom and Happiness of the Republic.* The work was signed "Cassius," but tentatively attributed to Aedanus Burke, a Chief Justice of South Carolina. The title page quoted from the Bible: "Blow ye the trumpet in Zion."

The trumpet vociferated that what Washington regarded as the main objects of the society, the perpetuation of friendships and the charitable fund, were only cloaks for a sinister plot hidden in two provisions of the charter. Did not the charter provide that membership should be hereditary, in the aristocratic manner, according to primogeniture, and that individuals not officers or officers' descendants could be invited to join? "It is in reality and will turn out to be *an hereditary peerage*," that would rivet on the American people "an order of nobility."

The only hope for the preservation of American republicanism, Cassius believed, was "extirpating the Cincinnati altogether." However, he expressed doubt that this could be achieved. He saw demagogues whipping up every species of unrest until "the sovereign people" marched like lambs to the abattoir of an aristocracy on the European model.[5]

Washington was aghast. Always fearful of faction, he could not fail to wonder whether Cassius's charge that "the order is planted in a fiery hot ambition and thirst for power" might not be true in relation to some—how many?—leaders of the far-flung society. And even if it were completely false, the charge would, were it widely believed, stir up those tensions between the conservatives and the radicals, the richer and the poorer, which it had been Washington's effort throughout the Revolution to keep tamped down. Although Cassius had in his attacks spared Washington, aiming his principal invective against the foreigner General Steuben, who was president of the New York branch, Washington was in fact the national president. His personal position as a national leader was inevitably involved.

From visitors to Mount Vernon, he discovered that the pamphlet was alarming many citizens, particularly New Englanders. He wrote to

A tureen, decorated with the eagle of the Cincinnati, from a 302-piece set of Oriental export porcelain bought by Washington in 1786. Courtesy of the Mount Vernon Ladies' Association

Washington's own sketch for the crest on the Presidential carriage. Courtesy of the Library of Congress

Jefferson, who was in New York representing Virginia at the Continental Congress, asking him to express, "with frankness and the fullest latitude of a friend," his own opinion of the Cincinnati and repeat "what you suppose to be the sentiments of Congress respecting it."[6]

Jefferson replied that the Cincinnati was considered contrary to the American principle of "the natural equality of man . . . particularly the denial of a pre-eminence by birth."[*] Furthermore, the provision for honorary memberships "might draw into the order all men of talents, of office and wealth." Among the congressmen he had interrogated, "I have found but one who is not opposed to the institution, and that with an anguish of mind . . . which I have not seen produced by any circumstance before."

Opponents of the Cincinnati, Jefferson continued, saw no cause for worry as long as Washington led the society, but pointed out that Washington was "not immortal; and his successor or some one of his successors . . . may adopt a more mistaken road to glory." For his own part, Jefferson had long wished to see Washington "stand on a ground separated" from the Cincinnati "so that the character which will be handed to future ages at the head of our Revolution may in no instance be compromitted by subordinate altercations."

Jefferson believed that the only solution was to disband the society. But Washington, still moved by those concepts of fellowship and aid to needy officers which had moved him when the society was founded, went to Philadelphia for the general meeting determined to remake the fraternity without destroying it.[7]

One reason that the Cincinnati was so feared was that the order perpetuated, into this time of decentralization, the federal thinking and organization which had grown up in the Continental Army. Alone among private groups, the Cincinnati had branches in all the states and provisions for national meetings. Those who saw arising an anti-republican rival to the only other national body, the elected Continental Congress, were not reassured by the attendance at the Philadelphia convention of the Cincinnati. Full delegations came from all thirteen

---

[*] Among the many denunciations of the hereditary aspects of the Cincinnati which the mail brought to Mount Vernon was one from Washington's most aristocratically born friend, the Marquis of Lafayette, who added that most of the Americans in Paris, including John Adams and John Jay, "warmly blame the army."[8]

states, such complete representation as the Congress could, in those lax postwar years, very rarely achieve.

Swinging into strong action, Washington urged the convention to "strike out every word, sentence, and clause which has a political tendency. Discontinue the hereditary part in all its connections *absolutely. . . .* Admit no more honorary members." So that there could be no possibility of foreign subversion, accept funds only from American citizens and place what money was collected in the hands of some public body. Allay the fears of a continental combination by holding no more national conventions. "No alterations short of what is here enumerated will, in my opinion, reconcile the society to the community. Whether these will do it, is questionable."[9]

Washington soon wrote General Schuyler, "We have been most amazingly embarrassed in the business that brought us here."[10] Although some delegates admitted the existence of serious opposition within their states, and Washington "confidentially" revealed that Congress was considering legislation against hereditary orders that was aimed at the Cincinnati, the convention balked with angry stubbornness. The veterans felt that they had already made too many concessions to men who had talked and legislated while they had fought, who had allowed them to starve, and finally bilked them of their pay.

Washington, who preferred in deliberative bodies to move behind the scenes, found himself arguing with more "warmth," with more "agitation," with greater "plain language" than he had, in all probability, been forced to display in the give-and-take of a debate since he had been, before the Revolution, a member of the Virginia legislature. The officers with whom he wrangled may have been again resentful, as they had been when he had sent them home with empty pockets, at his placing broader interests so firmly above theirs. Yet, when he threatened to resign as President-General, they seemed to capitulate. They voted all the reforms Washington had suggested except the abolition of general meetings.* However, it was provided that the changes would not take effect until ratified by the state societies. If Washington suspected that this was a subterfuge, he preferred not to

---

* This was certainly the concession to public opinion with which Washington had the least sympathy, since he favored not less but more activity on the federal level.

[67]

act on the suspicion. He did not turn his back on the club of his beloved comrades in arms. He accepted re-election as President-General.[11]

Not in any overt manner but passively, largely by dragging their feet, the state societies blocked the changes. To this day, the Cincinnati is hereditary, and the country has not been subverted. Although various changes were circulated during the debates over the Constitution and over Hamilton's fiscal policies, the Cincinnati seems never to have exerted any overpowering political influence, nor did it remain for long a dangerously divisive force within the minds of most Americans. Does this mean that Washington gave way to hysteria or was being overly cautious of his own reputation?

Certain it is that almost the entire spectrum of major political leaders (with the marked exception of Alexander Hamilton) shared Washington's concern when the issue boiled over in 1784. Perhaps what was feared might have actually developed (at least to a bothersome extent) had not Washington halted the momentum of the Cincinnati, driven it to excuses and inaction, and, in the process, soothed the fears of the opposition. In any case, it should not be forgotten that George Washington—and on an occasion when his own loyalties to his fellow veterans were involved—opposed faction on the conservative side as determinedly as he was later to oppose the Democratic Societies, which he considered faction in the opposite interest.

7

The Arts of Peace

I T is a strange aberration of historical legend that George Washington has been commonly regarded as one of the most Europeanized of American leaders. Many Englishmen and even some Americans believe that he was actually born in England. Writers on both sides of the ocean have liked to characterize him as a not untypical English Whig country gentleman. Again and again, Washington is depicted as a holdover from colonialism whose imported ideas had to be overthrown by Thomas Jefferson's electoral revolution. The fact is that Jefferson—even if his ideas tended to be French rather than English—was much more Europeanized than Washington. No other President of the United States before Andrew Jackson was so largely a product of the west and the frontier as the first President. Washington had served in the wilderness as a surveyor, a messenger traversing unknown trails, an explorer, and an Indian fighter.

When a very young man, it is true, Washington had admired English leadership and dreamed of visiting England. However, that admiration and that dream had been eroded by his tribulations during the French and Indian War with royal governors and officers of the British regular army, by his peacetime experience with London factors who supplied him with inferior goods in exchange for tobacco they undervalued. Well before the Revolution, Washington had reorganized his patterns of planting and distribution so that he no longer had to sell and—by extension—buy in England.

At the beginning of his career, when he would have liked to have sailed to what the Colonials called "home," Washington was too poor to do so, but he had been plenty rich enough during the many years between the French and Indian War and the Revolution. Once, when he was seriously ill, he had been afraid that he would be driven to England for medical attention, but he procrastinated and in the process got well. Then came the Revolution, during which he fought and hated the British.

Although the passage of time and what he came to consider the necessities of national policy blunted and masked that hatred, Washington never again expressed a warm surge of affection for the land he had once called home. Quite the contrary. Visiting Connecticut as President in 1789, he commented in his diary on the still visible "destructive evidences of British cruelty," which "are yet visible both in Norwalk and Fairfield, as there are chimneys of many burnt houses standing in them yet."[1]

After the Revolution, Washington would not have been *persona grata* in England, but France was another matter. There he ranked as a hero. Two of his most beloved wartime friends, Lafayette and Chastellux, importuned him to come to France; so did Benjamin Franklin. Washington did insist that his youthful dependents be taught French, which had become "in a manner the universal language," but he turned aside all suggestions that he himself visit France. Such a voyage, he would explain, was precluded by his "domestic habits," and his need to straighten out his financial affairs.[2]

When in the years that followed the Revolution, he set out on a trip from Mount Vernon, almost always he turned his horses' heads west. And on the rare occasions that he did ride east—let us say to Virginia's capital at Richmond—it was surely on business involving territory west of his starting place. His outlook was revealed by the pattern of his landholdings. With only one important exception,* all his acres not contiguous to Mount Vernon, or his other childhood home at Fredericksburg, were to the west of them. And Mount Vernon, although in the tidewater, was at the very western edge of that long-settled region. It would take many days of riding to go from his front door to where the ocean lapped the Virginia coast, but he could pass quickly beyond the Falls of the Potomac into the Piedmont. He possessed some holdings in the Piedmont, more across the Blue Ridge in the Shenan-

---

* Although the exception was near the seashore, it was more of a howling wilderness than his farthest western lands: a part of the Dismal Swamp which he hoped could be drained by cutting through it a commercially valuable canal.[3]

doah Valley (where he had made his first money and bought his first land) and even more over the Alleghenies (where he had fought Frenchmen and Indians).

In 1893, Frederick Jackson Turner propounded his famous theory that the continuing frontier was a dominating creator of American democracy. George Washington anticipated Turner by a full century. Washington felt that influences coming in from Europe were debilitating, but, so he wrote in 1788, the American people did not need to fear contamination: "Extent of territory and gradual settlement will enable them to maintain something like a war of posts against the invasion of luxury, dissipation, and corruption. For, after the large cities and old establishments on the borders of the Atlantic shall, in the progress of time, have fallen a prey to those invaders, the western states will probably long retain their primeval simplicity of manners and incorruptible love of liberty. May we not reasonably expect that, by those manners and this patriotism, uncommon prosperity will be entailed on the civil institutions of the American world?"[4]

Among the favorite schemes of Washington's later years was the establishment of a National University, and he played, although in a most gingerly manner, with the idea of inviting the ablest professors from Europe. This was in the same spirit as he imported foreign seeds or an English farmer in the uncertain hope that they might prove useful under American conditions. Although he was much impressed with European intellectuals like Chastellux and Mrs. Macaulay Graham, he opposed sending American youths "to foreign countries for the purpose of education . . . where, besides contracting habits of dissipation and extravagance, principles unfriendly to republican government and to the rights of man may be imbibed."[5]

Washington was, indeed, much less concerned with what Europe could contribute to America than with what America could contribute to Europe. One of his greatest desires was that the example of the United States should lead the rest of the world into freedom from bondage to the kings who were, so Washington was convinced, the creators of tyranny, and also of war.

When he meditated on the "thousands of gallant spirits" who had fallen to satisfy the ambition of kings, Washington wondered "for what wise purposes does Providence permit this? Is it as a scourge for mankind, or is it to prevent them from becoming too populous? If the

[71]

latter, would not the fertile plains of the western world receive the redundancy of the old?"

"While you are quarreling among yourselves in Europe," he assured Lafayette, "while one king is running mad and others acting as if they were already so by cutting the throats of the subjects of their neighbors, I think you need not doubt, my dear Marquis, we shall continue in tranquillity here." And, until American political institutions pacified Europe, the United States could serve as a haven to which Europeans could flee.

"I wish to see the sons and daughters of the world in peace and busily employed in the more agreeable amusement [than war] of fulfilling the first and great commandment: *increase and multiply,* as an encouragement to which we have opened the fertile plains of the Ohio to the poor, the needy, and the oppressed of the earth. Anyone therefore who is heavy laden, or who wants land to cultivate, may repair thither and abound, as in the land of promise, with milk and honey."[6]

In the eighteenth century, immigration often passed beyond the settled areas into the frontiers. Thus idealism was for large holders of western land who, like Washington, needed tenants seconded by profit motive.* However, a danger was created: since immigrant inhabitants of the west "will have no particular predilection towards us," they could "become a distinct people from us, have different views, different interests." They might declare their independence or join up with the British possessions to the north of them, the Spanish to the south.[7]

Washington's major public activity during his "retirement" was an effort to forge chains that would tie the central valley to the older settlements. Traversing mountains, these chains were to be made partly of earth but primarily of water.

Today, when the United States has for so long existed as a single nation and the only catastrophic split in our history was between north and south, it is hard to credit what Washington concluded in 1784, during his trip over the mountains: "The western settlers (I speak now

---

* As he tried to recruit immigrants in Europe to settle his Kanawha lands, Washington urged that his personal role in the activity be kept quiet "lest in a malicious world it might be represented that I was officiously using the arts of seduction to depopulate other countries for the sake of peopling our own."[8]

from my own observation) stand as it were upon a pivot. The touch of a feather would turn them [politically] any way."⁹

The Ohio region was endlessly fertile, but the settlers could not get their surplus goods to market. When water transportation supplied the only economical means for transporting bulky goods, no practical way existed to carry produce across the mountain barriers to the eastern seaboard. The central valley had, of course, a central passageway of rivers, but—how Washington blessed what he considered the stupidity of the two European powers!—the ends were being held shut by England and Spain.

England had refused to honor that part of her peace treaty with the United States which dictated surrendering the forts which controlled access to the Great Lakes water system, and she was using what she illegally held to block trade in that direction. Spain was holding closed the mouth of the Mississippi. The crisis, Washington believed, would be grave if either European nation, "instead of throwing stumbling blocks in their [the western settlers'] way as they now do, should hold out lures for their trade and alliance." Then the new west, far from strengthening the American Utopia, might become a very dangerous neighbor.¹⁰

Fortunately, time was being allowed for the United States to conquer the west with "the arts of peace." Washington defined the arts of peace as "clearing rivers, building bridges, and establishing conveniences for traveling, etc." Commercial ties, he believed, should be firmly established between the Ohio Valley and the eastern seaboard before the United States made with Spain "any stir about the navigation of the Mississippi."¹¹

Washington was thus in sympathy with the treaty negotiated by John Jay, the Secretary of Foreign Affairs, in which it was agreed that Spain, in return for other concessions to the United States, might hold the Mississippi closed for twenty-five years. When the settlers reacted to Jay's concession with rage and threats of secession, Washington, it is true, changed his ground. Yet he may not have been too sorry when Spain did not respond to official American urging by opening the navigation.¹²

Washington's prime solution to the problem of the west fitted like a template over what had been, before the Revolution, his favorite public project. Then he had viewed the scheme as helping his own neighborhood and lining his own pocket; now he regarded it as help-ing his own neighborhood and strengthening the internal bonds of the nation.

From his young manhood onward, in peace and in war, Washington had wandered up the Potomac through the Blue Ridge to the sources of the river high in the Alleghenies; he had observed and wrestled with the further rivers which flowed down the western slopes of the moun-tains to carry their waters into the Ohio; and he had concluded that an intelligent linking of waterways could carry the trade of the whole central valley along the very river which flowed by his own door. He had himself, when a teenaged surveyor, laid out the street plan for the village of Alexandria. Now, since Alexandria was at the top of tide-water, at the spot where goods going up or down the Potomac would have to be transshipped between river and oceangoing craft, he visu-alized his boyhood creation as becoming (as New York City was actually to be made, by the Erie Canal) the major metropolis of the United States.

Of course, only a canoe could now traverse what Washington foresaw as a watery highway for cargo vessels, and that canoe would often have to be carried through riverless wildernesses or around falls, yet he was sure that engineering could improve the waterways into canals, while roads (a military road he had himself built had carried the first wheels into the Ohio Valley) could cross the watershed, linking the not too widely separated heads of navigation.

It was a stupendous vision. Statistics could easily reveal that a Potomac Canal would be a much more direct route from the Ohio to the ocean than a trip down the Mississippi (which had the additional problem that you could not get boats up again); or around through the Great Lakes and the Saint Lawrence; or even the almost level route (the future site of the Erie Canal) which New York State hoped to open from Lake Ontario through the Mohawk and Hudson Rivers to New York City.

In the early 1770's, Washington had been the principal mover in the effort to create a private company that would at its own expense open the Potomac from the tidewater 150 miles westward, its earnings to come from the collection of tolls. To get an enabling bill through the Virginia legislature, Washington had been forced to add to the scheme a similar company that would open, farther southward, the James. The next necessary step on the Potomac scheme had been to get another enabling act from Maryland, since that colony controlled the river's northern shore. However, the Baltimore merchants, whose trading center would be bypassed, opposed. The Maryland bill failed. "In this situation things were when I took command of the army."[13]

Washington had been home from the army for only a few months when Jefferson wrote him that unless Virginia got moving at once, New York would engross the western trade by building a canal along the Mohawk-Hudson route.* If Washington would regard placing his prestige behind a Potomac Canal as "only a dignified amusement to you, what a monument of your retirement it would be!"[14]

It took no further argument to convince Washington that leading the canal effort might be made to "comport with those ideas and that line of conduct with which I meant to glide gently down the stream of life." He was off like a lighted rocket.[15]

A conference held at the Virginia capital decided to tackle the Maryland legislature first. Washington was not pleased when his former military rival, General Horatio Gates, "contrived to edge himself into the commission," but he was soon complaining that Gates, by falling ill, had left all the lobbying at Annapolis to him: "It is now near twelve at night, and I am writing with an aching head." After four days of agitation, Washington's prestige bowled over the opposition from Baltimore. Maryland empowered a stock company to improve the Potomac and collect tolls. Public funds were to pay for connecting roads with westerly-flowing rivers.[16]

Virginia quickly passed a twin bill. It added authorization for a James River Canal Company. Determining to override Washington's objection to receiving any reward for his multiple services to the nation, the Assembly decided that (in James Madison's words) "the mode least injurious to his delicacy as well as the least dangerous in precedent" was to give Washington a quantity of stock in both enterprises.[17]

Washington wrote that he was more "embarrassed" by this offer than by any circumstance that has "happened to me since I left the walks of public life." In his perturbation, he could not get the offer—one hundred shares in the James River Company and fifty in the

---

* New York's effort waited on British compliance with the peace treaty, the route being now blocked by England's unwillingness to evacuate Fort Oswego, which controlled the Great Lakes end of the future Erie Canal.

Potomac—straight. Sometimes he stated that he had been offered one hundred fifty, sometimes fifty, in each.

Part of Washington's mental stress could have stemmed from his being tempted. To make a fortune from canals had been one of his favorite pre-Revolutionary dreams. He may well have wished that his principles did not now intervene. If he were to accept the shares, so he confided to George William Fairfax, he would consider them "the *greatest* and most *certain*" foundation for income that could be imagined.

On the public level, Washington was worried lest a refusal be construed as "disrespect" for the "good opinion and affection" of his countrymen. He might even be accused of "an ostentatious display of disinterestedness or public virtue." Yet, "it is really my wish to have my mind, and my actions, which are the result of contemplation, as free and independent as the air, that I may be more at liberty (in things which my opportunities and experience have brought me to the knowledge of) to express my sentiments" without raising the slightest suspicion of "sinister motives." He could not forget that his first public stand, made in 1752 when he was twenty—his warning that French aggression was on its way down the Ohio—had been discounted because his family was concerned with land speculation over the mountains.

He now wrote concerning the canal project: "I would wish that every individual who may hear that it was a favorite plan of mine, may know also that I had no other motive for promoting it, than the advantage I conceive it would be productive of to the Union, and to this state in particular." He asked Jefferson—"I have accustomed myself to communicate matters of difficulty to you"—for advice on what he should do.[18] Jefferson replied that the world would be pleased to see Washington rewarded and that his reputation would suffer "no derogation." However, declining would "add to that reputation."[19] In the end, Washington secured the permission of the legislature to devote the fund "to objects of a public nature." He applied the stock to the education of poor children, particularly descendants of soldiers killed in the war.[20]

With his own capital, Washington bought in the Potomac Company, of which he became president, five shares, and softened his refusal to preside also over the James River Company by buying five shares in that, also. He cast yearning glances at the village of Alexandria, which he intended to make so soon into a metropolis. Having urged his friend, the Philadelphia financier Robert Morris, to establish a major wholesale house there, he added, "Had I inclination and talents to enter into the commercial line, I have no idea of a better opening . . . to make a fortune." But commerce "I never shall engage in."[21]

Washington made no significant new real estate investments connected with his canal hopes. If the ditches would, in fact, greatly increase the values of landholdings he already had,* he shared this situation with landowners along a wide spread of navigable waters.[22]

How wide a spread? Washington's heart was in the Potomac Canal. He bored visitors to Mount Vernon by quoting mileage tables to show that the Potomac route was designed by nature as the commercial outlet for the entire west, including the furs that come from even more distant regions to distant Detroit.[23] Yet he could not resist visualizing canal improvement on a national scale that would stir up for his pet project, many competitors.

Drawing a division between state and federal responsibility, Washington considered it the prerogative of the states to authorize canals through their own territory. However, it was the duty of the Continental Congress to plan an overall system of water transportation. Congress should "have the western waters well explored, the navigation of them fully ascertained, accurately laid down, and a complete and perfect map made of the country." To Madison he exclaimed, "The mind can scarcely take in at one view all the benefits which will result therefrom. . . . This business wants only a beginning." As the advantages of water transportation became manifest, one river after another would be opened, bringing "navigation to almost every man's door."[24]

Washington was much more worried about selling (in a nation where there was so little fluid capital) the necessary shares of Potomac Company stock than he was about opening (in a country where there were no sophisticated engineers) the roaring, mountain river to navigation. He assured Robert Morris that improving the Potomac the two hundred miles from the Great Falls to Fort Cumberland, and even

---

* Not only the Potomac scheme could contribute to Washington's prosperity. The western link of the James was thought of as the Great Kanawha, which might place a city on or near Washington's land at the confluence of the Great Kanawha and the Ohio.

forty miles farther if advisable, presented "no more difficulty or uncertainty in the execution, comparatively speaking, than there is in bringing water to a mill by a common race." But he sent to Jefferson, who was now representing the United States in Paris, for information on how capital could be raised for the enterprise in France, Holland, or England.

However, no need developed for foreign capital. As soon as the subscription was opened, Americans bought, in the company sponsored by Washington, almost twice the minimum necessity of 250 shares. Then Washington's optimism soared to a point where he became concerned lest the tolls authorized by the legislatures had been set too high "considering the harvest which the public is preparing for the adventur[er]s [stockholders]."[25]

When he had gone west in September 1784, to deal with his vexed landholdings, Washington had also sought to discover the best route by which the Potomac Canal system could climb over the mountains. This involved the happiest meshing of three geographic questions: what upper Potomac branch or tributary could most easily be opened to what height; where building a road across the peaks would present the least difficulty; and to what landing on what tributary of the Ohio (which might also have to be opened to navigation) such a road should lead. Washington cross-questioned every traveler he met, and then, leaving most of his baggage behind at Simpson's dilapidated mill, set out with two companions on horseback to explore the divide that had given him so many and often bloody difficulties when he had commanded the Virginia Regiment, had marched with Braddock, had marched with Forbes. His results could at best be tentative,* but he returned more than ever convinced that his Potomac Canal could be linked, with "diffuse navigation," which required no man-made improvements and was "more extensive perhaps than is to be met with in any country upon earth."[26]

---

* The enabling legislation took the solution of geographic problems off Washington's hands, making them the joint responsibility of the governments of Maryland and Virginia, who were also to build the roads. Washington's tentative conclusions had been that a good road, not exceeding thirty miles, could be built from Fort Cumberland to the Youghiogheny, a river impeded by only one falls in its seventy-five-mile flow to Pittsburgh. Or, should the North Branch of the Potomac be cleared for forty miles above Fort Cumberland, a portage to the Cheat would be only twenty miles. If the Cheat could not be opened, a road along its banks would, in another twenty-five miles, carry to the Monongahela.[27]

Earlier on this same western trip Washington had an adventure which seemed to imply that destiny itself was fighting on the side of the Potomac Canal. The scene was the Warm Springs to which he had accompanied his dying brother and his dying stepdaughter, and where he had gone himself when he feared he was dying. What he had known as a wilderness clearing, where sufferers' lives had ebbed away in tents or covered wagons, was now an elegant little community, renamed Bath after the fashionable English watering resort which it was doing its best to emulate. Washington found himself well housed in "a very commodious boardinghouse . . . at the sign of the Liberty Pole and Flag."

The landlord, whose name was James Rumsey, dangled elegant lace cuffs over hands hardened with labor. Blushing and stuttering and yet with an impressive self-confidence, the handsome youth asked if he might speak to the General in private. He looked perpetually over his shoulders to make sure that they were not being followed when he led Washington into the woods to where a stream had been doctored to flow rapidly through a smooth-bottomed channel. Rumsey disappeared into the underbrush, and then returned with a peculiar-looking contraption which he gently placed in the rushing water. He raised his hand and the object, as if propelled by magic, moved up the rapid stream. This was surely one of the moments—like the time when he heard that de Grasse's French fleet had actually arrived off York-town—that Washington jumped up and down with excitement.

The contraption proved to consist of two model boats joined side by side with a paddlewheel between. The current turned the wheel, the wheel activated poles that hung over the sides; the poles walked along the bottom, pushing the boat upstream.*

In the history of invention, it has been common for men to see but not to believe. This was particularly true in the eighteenth century, at the dawn of the Industrial Revolution, when mankind had not got used to the idea that machines could remake the world. The skepticism of eyewitnesses, for instance, delayed the invention of the steamboat, perhaps for a generation. But Washington was instantly convinced (as it turned out, over-convinced) by Rumsey's mechanical pole-boat. He

---

* Since poles pressed against the bottom have more purchase than oars, their use, in the hands of strong men, to push boats along was then a common method of fighting strong currents. In its famous crossing of the Delaware, Washington's army had been propelled by poles.

decided that this wonderful invention solved the worst problem faced by the Potomac venture: how to navigate up a stream too narrow and with too strong a current for oars. Rumsey had made "the present epoch favorable above all others" for opening the Potomac navigation.[28]

Washington geared his canal plans to Rumsey's pole-boat. "Through all the falls and rapids *above the Great Falls*," he wrote in September 1785, "we mean to attempt nothing more than to open a straight passage to avoid, as much as possible, currents, giving sufficient depth and as much smoothness as may be to the surface; and, if Rumsey's project fails (of which he has not the smallest apprehension) to pull the boats up by chains attached to buoys." This would be infinitely less expensive than the usual procedure of cutting beside the river semi-independent waterways where the flow could be controlled, building locks, making paths on which horses or mules could walk as they towed the boats. Furthermore, when once "the passage is opened in a straight direction in the natural bed of the river, it is done as it were forever," whereas special canals and locks "are never safe when there are such sudden inundations and violent torrents as the rivers in this country are subject to."[29]

Even at the Little Falls, where "the river descends in curling waves thirty-six feet in a quarter of a mile," Washington intended to do no more than cut an open, smooth-bottomed channel. But even his optimism could not carry him into believing that this would do at the Great Falls, which created the break between tidewater and piedmont. The Great Falls were described by Washington's visitor Elkanah Watson as "a stupendous exhibition of hydraulic power. The whole river rushing down amid rocks and impediments, wave pressing upon wave like the surging of the ocean in a tempest, producing a roaring which we distinctly heard at the distance of a mile." The entire fall was seventy feet, including a vertical drop of twenty-three "which adds infinitely to the imposing scene."[30]

Washington insisted, that, since it would only take nine miles of road to get around the Great Falls, opening that part of the river to navigation was not absolutely essential. However, he added that only the skeptical "have any doubt of the practicability" of getting boats past the falls into the tidewater. To do so would involve locks and all the other devices of conventional canal-building. Washington admitted that he knew nothing about locks. He wrote Lafayette to send him from France what in his suspicion of theoretical experts he described as "a skillful engineer or rather a person of practical knowledge."[31]

The Potomac Company advertised in American newspapers for an engineer to direct clearing channels through the other two hundred to two hundred forty miles of river. When not a single individual had the temerity to apply, Washington offered the job to Rumsey. The former commander who had (while he was training himself) trained so many other civilians to become effective generals, commented that when it was impossible to find a man with "experimental knowledge" of a "particular kind of work" you should seek a man who "may be possessed of a genius which may soon fit him for it."[32]

The Potomac project was now Washington's passion. Visitors to Mount Vernon were disappointed to find that the hero, shunning military discussions, would talk only about canals. A guest complained of "hearing little else for two days." Washington's countenance glowed when he said that the Baltimore merchants, who had laughed at what they called "a ridiculous plan," were now looking serious and fearing for their trade. As he sent the bottle around "pretty freely" after dinner, the General would toast again and again, "Success to the navigation of the Potomac!"[33]

Washington gave "a turtle feast" at Mount Vernon for the directors of the Potomac Company, and often rode out to meetings held elsewhere. He was perpetually inspecting one part or another of the works, sometimes dashing in a canoe down rapids in order to judge how and where the current should eventually be directed.[34] Yet the works could only be described as going swimmingly in the sense that the workmen were perpetually being washed downstream along with their works. And before there was any chance of trying his mechanical pole-boat out in any reach of the Potomac, Rumsey abandoned the invention (it was, indeed, impractical on a large scale) in favor of still inconclusive experiments with steam.* He proved so unsuccessful at canal-building that he was, in July 1786, discharged.[35] But, there

---

* Rumsey became an important actor in the drama of steamboat invention, both for his own achievements and because of his acrimonious controversies with an even abler inventor, John Fitch. In the controversy between the two men Washington played so minor (if charming) a part that it must be omitted here. Curious readers are referred to another of this writer's books, *Steamboats Come True*.[36]

being no engineer on his way from France, the directors could find no one to replace Rumsey except his equally ineffectual assistant.

The fact was that the engineering know-how then available in America was unequal to either of the tasks the Potomac Company had set itself: it could neither open navigable and permanent channels where locks were not considered necessary, nor build locks where they were. But Washington, who had at very long last bested a professional British army with ragged amateurs, refused to admit the existence or even the possibility of defeat. In May 1787 (when as President of the Constitutional Convention, he was already being drawn to other tasks), Washington wrote Jefferson that "the progress already made in this great national work" justifies "the most sanguine expectations which have been formed of its success."[37]

However, the Potomac Company was to pay no dividends during Washington's lifetime, and only one thereafter. It was moribund when taken over in 1827 by the Chesapeake and Ohio Canal Company, which did eventually open a canal from Fort Cumberland to the Great Falls. As for the metropolis Washington wished to foster on the banks of the Potomac, that he was to achieve in an altogether different way, which he could not yet foresee.[38]

Observing how Washington galloped away from his Mount Vernon retirement on every canal call, Madison commented to Jefferson, "The earnestness with which he espouses the undertaking is hardly to be described, and shows that a mind like his, capable of great views and which has long been occupied with them, cannot bear a vacancy." Washington complained to Benjamin Franklin, with no introspective hint that his own temperament was to blame, "Retirement from the public walks of life has not been so productive of leisure and ease as might have been expected."[39]

II

Thirteen Nations or One

8

The Political Scene Darkens

WASHINGTON had, during 1775, attended the Second Continental Congress as a delegate from what he then regarded as "my country": Virginia. Virginia was considering a military alliance with the other twelve Colonial countries. To achieve this was no easy matter. During their long histories, the Colonies had been jealous of each other, with practically no political connection short of what was now weakening: their common allegiance to the Crown.

In the end, the Congress achieved its alliance not by any direct vote but by electing George Washington to command the forces of all. Although chosen as the visible embodiment of continental cooperation, Washington, when he assumed the leadership of what was still an overwhelmingly New England army, reacted, upon occasion, like any foreign commander of alien troops. The New Englanders, he wrote, were "an exceeding dirty and nasty people."[1]

But soon, as regiments came in from other parts of the alliance and he maneuvered them against a common foe, Washington's allegiance to Virginia gave way to the truly continental point of view, which he had brought home with him from the war. He did continue to feel a special loyalty to his own neighborhood around Mount Vernon, but when he lifted his eyes from that dear region, his vision transcended the confines of Virginia, embracing the Union as a whole.

Although other men, including many of the soldiers who had shared Washington's wartime experiences, also became convinced, during the conflict, of the importance of close continental cooperation, the question of whether the United States was one nation or an alliance of thirteen was never resolved. The Continental Congress remained an assembly of different sovereignties. It proved extremely difficult to draw up any paper that defined their relationship, and the one that was finally achieved after years of negotiation, the Articles of Confederation, provided little more than a firm league of common friendship. Depending on how the provisions were interpreted, this league could either be moderately intimate or conspicuously distant.[2]

In the early stages of the war, political cooperation had been close, but as the conflict dragged on, and particularly after victory seemed assured, the divisive forces became increasingly powerful. The states not only failed to meet the expenses incurred by the central body that was directing the war, but refused the unanimous agreement necessary to allow the Continental Congress taxing powers of its own. The army could not be paid its back or present pay; businessmen who had lent money to the central government could not even secure interest; and the combined dissatisfactions began to coalesce in a manner extremely dangerous to republican institutions. In 1783, Washington was offered the leadership of a movement which could have developed into what we today call fascism.

With the greatest difficulty and in much anguish of mind, by putting his command and his personal prestige in the balance, Washington prevented the army from joining with the businessmen in terrorizing the governments. Promising to do everything he could "consistently with the great duty I owe my country," to procure eventual justice for the soldiers, Washington persuaded them, when they were no longer needed against the enemy, to go home with cruelly empty pockets. The civil creditors (although about these Washington cared less) were also left in the lurch.[3]

Washington had labored to save the American republican form of government. From this he believed the soldiers would profit more greatly, since they were returning to civilian life, than they would have from the pay of which they were being bilked. He had also turned his own back on the possibility of achieving unlimited personal power. As Jefferson acknowledged, "The moderation and virtue of a single character probably prevented this revolution from being closed, as most others have been, by a subversion of that liberty it was intended to establish."[4]

How much responsibility for making the government function effectively did Washington assume when he persuaded the army and forced the other creditors to accept present injustice while placing their reliance on republican forms? His experience had persuaded him that the rightful debts could not be paid, that the glorious possibilities of republicanism could not be achieved, unless Americans pushed sectionalism aside and learned to function as one nation, not thirteen. While still living out his stint in the army, he had, indeed, yearned to achieve major reforms through such a constitutional convention as was not to convene for years.* During July 1783, he wrote privately that he wished "a convention of the people" would establish "a federal constitution" that would leave the determination of local matters to the states, but provide that, "when superior considerations preponderate in favor of the whole, their [the states'] voices should be heard no more."5

However, Washington recognized that this conception was still far beyond the present reach of national opinion. In a circular letter to the states, he publicly urged not the substitution of a new, stronger instrument for the Articles of Confederation, but rather interpretation and amendment of the Articles to give the federal government the strength necessary to meet its obligations and to establish, where reason indicated, necessary central authority.

Eager to give his advice the greatest weight possible, and also anxious to defend himself from any suspicions that political ambitions had made him step outside his authorized military sphere, Washington announced that this, his only major political document to date, was also his last. Once he was released from his military duties, he would never again "take any share in public business."6

As came naturally to him, Washington had struck a dramatic note. His advice came to be known as "Washington's Legacy," and had for a time much of the importance later assumed by his Farewell Address. However, supporters of a stronger central government were dismayed by Washington's insistence that he would return to Mount Vernon and take no further part in government.

To those who, as disunion became more rife, accused him of deserting a sinking cause, Washington replied that the nation would "work

---

* The need for a constitutional convention had for some time been discussed at headquarters. Hamilton, then Washington's aide, had advocated the measure in a letter dated as far back as September 1780.7

its own cure, as there is virtue at the bottom."[8] Thus he demonstrated acceptance of the Romantic doctrine that man was not (as aristocrats said) basically evil and in need of restraint, but rather basically good and to be trusted. However, as was typical of his thinking, he gave the doctrine a twist towards its opposite. Repudiating the Romantic conclusion that, since man was naturally virtuous, the best government was that which imposed the fewest restraints, he believed that their virtue would make the American people impose upon themselves, through republican means, the governmental restraints which he considered necessary to a strong nation, a just and prosperous society.

Furthermore, Washington did not expect the people to find the right answers merely through inspiration supplied by their natural goodness. "I am *sure*," he explained, "the mass of citizens in these United States *mean well,* and I firmly believe they will always *act well* whenever they can obtain a right understanding of matters."[9] His "Legacy" had been an effort to supply such an understanding. However, he did not expect it or any other document to be instantaneously efficacious.

Again applying his particular mental twist, he combined into a single progression "a knowledge of books" and what he called "other knowledge." In this context more a Romantic than a Classicist, he considered traditional knowledge learned from reading as second to "other knowledge" which came from intuition worked on by experience.[10]

But experience, Washington knew from his own memories, is a slow teacher, and insight needs jogging before it will desert habitual ways. "The people must *feel* before they will *see;* consequently, are brought slowly into measures of public utility." And again: "[It] is on *great* occasions *only,* and after time has been given for cool and deliberate reflection, that the *real* voice of the people can be known."[11]

Sure that the people of America would act for the best but not quickly, Washington could, after his return to Mount Vernon, comfortably watch the states go galloping off in as many directions as thirteen half-broken colts, while the Continental Congress often lacked enough representation to transact any business at all. Despite the apprehensiveness of his temperament—that propensity to use his powerful imagination in projecting the worst—Washington was consistently sanguine during the first two and a half years of his retirement. He felt, as did many another optimistic survivor of the triumphant Revolution, that it was only a matter of waiting for "the good sense of the people" to get the better of their prejudices.[12]

Although unwilling to act, Washington kept in touch. He interrogated visitors. If newspapers were stolen before they reached Mount Vernon, he complained, and, when they did arrive, he denounced them for being "too sterile, vague and contradictory on which to form any opinion." He secured from Congressman Jefferson full reports on what was going on in New York. Knox reported as Secretary of War, and, during his vacations, sent news of Massachusetts. In congratulating Humphreys on joining a commission to negotiate trade agreements in Europe, Washington added, "You will have it in your power to contribute much to my amusement and information."[13] He secured other foreign intelligence in correspondence with important Frenchmen whom he had got to know during the war: Luzerne, Rochambeau, Chastellux, Lafayette.

To his well-informed foreign correspondents, Washington penned elaborate speculations on what policies the various European courts would pursue. These closely reasoned essays read like the works of a student being presented for the approval or correction of his professors. For whatever reason, the former general, whose activities had been almost completely limited to American soil, was trying to teach himself foreign affairs.

Washington often boasted or complained of being isolated. Yet so much news came into Mount Vernon and was pulsed out again in Washington's conversations or his letters that Humphreys considered the planter *the focus of political intelligence* for the new world."[14]

However, it was not news coming in from the outside that reentangled Washington in the issue of one nation or thirteen. It was the unavoidable fact that so large a man could not stretch himself without overlapping state lines.

Before he could get his Potomac Canal scheme even started, Washington had been forced to secure cooperation between the two states which bordered the river: Maryland and Virginia. Under Washington's leadership, Virginia then applied to a third state, Pennsylvania, for a road to the Youghiogheny and also for an agreement not to collect tolls on the vast network of Pennsylvanian connecting waters, which would require no expensive opening to navigation. The Virginia legislature also decided to consult with a fourth state, North Carolina, about a possible link between the Elizabeth River and the Roanoke.

The next necessary step in the Virginia-Maryland relationship was a conference to discuss navigation of the Potomac in the tidewater, below where the canal would end. Both states appointed commissioners who met at Alexandria during March 1785. Although Washington was not a commissioner, his presence hovered over the conference, which soon moved to Mount Vernon. The Virginia delegates had not been empowered to discuss navigation in the Chesapeake, but Maryland refused to proceed unless Virginia agreed not to charge tolls at the mouth of that inland sea, and the Virginians finally exceeded their instructions by giving assent. During eight days, agreement was reached on the complicated matters, such as the apportioning of fishing rights, involved in the common use of waters. However, Madison considered that the most important outcome of what has gone down in history as the "Mount Vernon Conference" was the decision that delegates from Maryland and Virginia should meet annually "for keeping up harmony in the commercial relations between the two states."[15]

While ratifying the commissioners' report, the Maryland legislature decided to invite to the annual conferences Delaware and Pennsylvania. Virginia thereupon proposed a conference of all the states "to consider how far a uniform system in their commercial regulations may be necessary to their common interest and their permanent harmony." This call led to the Annapolis Convention, which, in turn, sent out the call that led to the Constitutional Convention. Thus, the historical sequence which dredged up the eventual solution to the question of one or thirteen seemed (in Madison's words) "naturally to grow out" of the Mount Vernon Conference.[16]

Concerning Washington's canal schemes, Madison wrote Jefferson, "He could surely not have chosen an occupation more worthy of succeeding."[17] In that half alliance, half nation the United States, the needs for trade were great and they argued eloquently for unity. That the Potomac Canal, which was sponsored by the continent's most revered man, demanded close interstate cooperation, was an object lesson hard for any intelligent individual to ignore or explain away. Thus, in passionately pursuing a project that began with the view from his own portico, Washington, although still officially retired, was promoting continental union.

In July 1786 Washington wrote Rochambeau that "mankind are becoming more enlightened and humanized. . . . To indulge this idea affords a soothing consolation to a philanthropic mind, insomuch that although it should be founded in illusion, one would hardly wish to be divested of an error so grateful in itself and so innocent in its consequences."[18]

In fact, Washington's confidence was shredding away. Experience, instead of teaching the people effectively to govern themselves, seemed to be presenting its lessons—most unpleasant ones—to optimists like Washington. Far from raising a ground swell for national unity, the years were bringing more division, and also actions by the states that seemed to him destructive of all orderly society. On August 1, he meditated, "We have probably had too good an opinion of human nature in forming our confederation. Experience has taught us that men will not adopt and carry into execution measures the best calculated for their own good, without the intervention of a coercive power. I do not conceive we can exist long as a nation without having lodged somewhere a power which will pervade the whole Union."[19]

Washington was upset that Congress continued to be denied by the states the taxing power that would enable it to have funds of its own with which to operate and pay its debts; his soldiers were still being disappointed.* Washington was upset when the state of New York undermined Congress's exclusive right to make treaties by holding her own land-buying conference at Fort Stanwix with the Six Nations. He was upset because Congress, afraid to take advantage of one of the few powers it actually had, bowed pusillanimously, in regulating the settlement of western lands, to the states. He was upset that attendance at the central legislature was, if anything, even more sparse and impotent than before.[20]

Having so long fought the British, Washington (although he was in some ways glad that the posts were held) could not fail to see "hostile intent" in the refusal of the former enemy to evacuate the western forts which the peace treaty had ceded to the United States. The British justification was that various states had contravened America's obligations under the same treaty through the enactment of laws aimed at preventing Englishmen from collecting prewar debts. Unhappy that no

---

* The total income of the government in 1786 was less than one-third of the annual interest on the national debt.[21]

power existed to make the states act as the united government had agreed, Washington denounced the local violations of the treaty as "impolitic and unfortunate. . . . It is good policy at all times to place one's adversary in the wrong."*22

When the British, in what Washington called their "chagrin and jealousy," passed laws aimed at restricting American trade, his indignation was tempered by his conviction that this effort of the old enemy to weaken the United States would have an opposite effect. Surely the need to substitute, for the rival tariff acts of the various states, uniform retaliation against British discrimination "will facilitate the enlargement of Congressional powers in commercial matters, more than half a century would [otherwise] have effected."23 But Washington's guess proved wrong. Anxious to grind their own little axes, the states would not combine to sharpen an internationally powerful weapon. New York, for instance, did not wish to endanger the customs system she had established to milk Connecticut and New Jersey. And the south, which made so much use of English shipping, was afraid that federal retaliation against British restrictions would put them at the mercy of New England shippers.

Some regional divergence of interest, Washington admonished a southern doubter, would "apply to every matter of general utility." Whatever such a majority as required by the Articles of Confederation (nine or eleven of the thirteen state delegations, depending on the bill) decided was "for the benefit of the whole, should, in my humble opinion, be submitted to by the minority. Let the southern states always be represented; let them act more in union; let them declare freely and boldly what is for the interest of, and what is prejudicial to their constituents; and there will, there *must* be an accommodating spirit." In any case, the British, who were counting on an inability in America to unite, would probably back down as soon as general retaliatory measures threatened. And, if it should become necessary to restrict British trade, the southern states would not necessarily become dependent on New England shipping: they could develop their own.25

The most serious problems under the Confederation were economic. Having no mints or stocks of rare metals of her own, America had

---

* Washington notified his own prewar British factor, Wakelin Welch, that he would not take advantage of any laws to avoid paying the principal he owed. However, only if legally forced would he pay interest for the period of the war, when he had been prevented by British aggression from extinguishing the debt.24

always been dependent for "hard money"—specie on European coins. At the end of the war there had been, as a result of the spending in America by the English and French armies, more specie available than at any other time in the history of the continent. However, there also existed a long-frustrated hunger for European goods. Specie flowed back across the ocean for luxuries; when money began to run out, American merchants bought on credit. The market became glutted, and bust followed boom. What specie did cross the ocean to America was instantly drawn abroad again to pay foreign debts. Practically no currency remained to serve the transaction of local business.

A shortage of money now called the fiscal tunes. It was particularly hard on debtors. Farmers in newly opened areas, who had borrowed to buy land and tools, and indeed all poor men who had for any reason borrowed, often found it impossible, however hard they worked, to raise cash to meet their obligations. Taxes also became extremely difficult to pay. Honest as well as dishonest men lost their farms or were jailed for debt. The natural reaction was political protest which often swung the pendulum too far the other way, wreaking as much injustice on creditors as the debtors had previously suffered.

The various state governments were usually dominated by directly elected legislatures: the governors were (like the President of Congress) no more than legislative tools, and the courts had no jurisdiction beyond the enforcing of whatever laws the legislatures passed. Such laws often declared certain types of debts uncollectible, and brought back into existence what had been the curse of Washington's experiences as military commander: paper money. By 1786, seven of the thirteen states had adopted, as agrarian relief, some kind of paper currency.[26]

We may assume, from the steadfastness with which he later supported Hamilton's fiscal reforms, that Washington sensed the need of new radical cures for the economic illnesses of the thirteen half-united states. But in the choices then presented: between legal obligations enforced or, as relief for the poor, expropriated; between governments supported by effective taxation or bankrupt; between hard or soft money, he had no doubt where he stood. With the question of inflation in particular his emotions were deeply involved.

Although as a young planter Washington had been disturbed when the British government vetoed a Virginia paper money act, his strongest conviction in the realm of finance was now a horror of paper money born of his Revolutionary experiences. During the war, inflation had made it impossible to supply the army, had bankrupted the officers, and had brought great wealth to speculators. Furthermore, Washington's own estate had grievously suffered, since many had paid off their debts to him with worthless paper, while he had felt it dishonest and beneath his station to take a similar advantage of his own creditors.

Washington was, it was true, chronically short of cash and suffered in his land deals from the general lack of currency. Yet he and his immediate neighbors could proceed on their established farms not too uncomfortably by supplementing considerable self-sufficiency with barter. Washington was personally lenient to those of his western tenants who were honestly strapped. He believed that the hardship caused by an adherence to hard money "is represented as greater than it really is." In any case, the alternative would be even worse: "The wisdom of man, in my humble opinion, cannot at this time devise a plan, by which the credit of paper money would be long supported." Since "depreciation keeps pace with the quantity of the emission," the farmer, the planter, the artisan would achieve only temporary benefit in return for long-range loss. The debtor would, admittedly, be better off, but "in proportion to his gain," the creditor would suffer, while the body politic would languish as its tax revenues were received in worthless stuff. "An evil equally great is the door it [paper money] immediately opens for speculation, by which the least designing, and perhaps most valuable, part of the community are preyed upon by the more knowing and crafty speculators."

As for the laws some of the states passed to rescue debtors by impairing the validity of contracts, Washington believed, they would "ruin commerce, oppress the honest, and open a door to every species of fraud and injustice."[27]

"My *opinion* is," Washington wrote during April 1786, "that there is more wickedness than ignorance in the conduct of the states. . . . Until the curtain is withdrawn and the private views and selfish principles upon which these men act are exposed to public notice, I have little hope of amendment without another convulsion."[28]

The basic problem, so Washington and almost all his correspondents believed, was the irresponsibility of the state legislatures. They swayed like saplings to any breeze, and the prevailing wind seemed to be towards what the eighteenth century called "leveling": taking away from the established and giving to the poor what was expropriated. The propertied citizens who were being trampled on could not be expected to submit tamely. Thus the potential political fissure which Washington had spent so much of his energies during the war trying to hold closed, once more threatened to open wide. He had from the military camps feared a split between the conservatives and the radicals, the haves and the have-nots, more than he had feared the British army. He had, as the war closed, stamped out a possible military insurrection to the right. Was the nation now endangered by a possible political insurrection to the left?

The best preventative, Washington and his friends believed, was a stronger federal government that would clip the wings of local demagogues, bring unity where there was chaos, establish a solid economic base on which the government would not teeter in any uncontrolled direction. The expedient nearest at hand was the convention at Annapolis to which all the states had been invited for a discussion of the improvement of commerce.

No effort was made to persuade Washington to represent Virginia at the Annapolis Convention. He was too powerful a trump card to risk on so doubtful a venture.

From the quiet of Mount Vernon, Washington expressed regret that "more objects were not embraced by the meeting" than merely trade. Back from one of the promoters, Secretary of Foreign Affairs John Jay, came a suggestion that Washington must have found disturbing. It comported with conceptions he had long since held, but threatened to carry him back into that public arena he had so passionately renounced.[29]

Might it not be a good idea, Jay asked, to have the Annapolis meeting initiate a call for "a general convention for revising the Articles of Confederation"? Jay was "fervent in my wishes" that, should such a general convention meet, Washington would, for that "important and *single* occasion," return to public life as a delegate.[30]

Washington was upset to learn that Benjamin Franklin, although old enough to be Washington's father, had "again embarked on a troubled ocean." Franklin had accepted the presidency of Pennsylvania in a high-minded effort to reconcile warring political factions. At his relaxed dinner table, Washington commented uneasily on the "slippery ground" Franklin had agreed to tread. Whether the aged leader, who alone among Americans rivaled Washington's prestige, succeeded or failed was, Washington wrote Lafayette, "a question of some magnitude, and of real importance to himself, at least to his quiet."[31]

To Jay, Washington wrote emotionally, "I think often of our situation and view it with concern. From the high ground we stood upon, from the plain path which invited our footsteps, to be so fallen! so lost!" However, he thought the time was not yet ripe for calling a convention to remake the government. "We are certainly in a delicate situation, but my fear is that the people are not yet sufficiently *misled* to retract from error." He made no comment on Jay's suggestion that he himself get in harness again.[32]

Jay continued to pound at Washington, arguing that some terrible crisis, "some revolution" was to be expected, although he was not sure what. The trouble was that "the mass of men are, neither wise or good, and the virtue, like the other resources of a country, can only be drawn to a point by strong circumstances, ably managed, or strong government, ably administered." Jay most feared that "the better kind of people" would be led by the insecurity of their property and their lack of faith in the existing governments "to consider the charms of liberty as imaginary and delusive."[33]

Washington, who would certainly be offered the crown if anyone was,* exclaimed in reply, "What astonishing changes a few years are capable of producing. I am told that even respectable characters speak of a monarchical form of government without horror. From thinking proceeds speaking, thence to acting is often but a single step. But how irrevocable and tremendous! What a triumph for our enemies to verify their predictions! What a triumph for the advocates of despotism to find that we are incapable of governing ourselves, and that systems founded on the basis of equal liberty are merely ideal and fallacious!"[34]

Arriving at almost the same metaphor he had used in relation to Franklin, Washington went on: "Retired as I am from the world, I frankly acknowledge I cannot feel myself an unconcerned spectator.

---

* With the approval of an anonymous political leader (who may have been Nathaniel Gorham, then the President of Congress), the German Revolutionary veteran General Steuben wrote Prince Henry of Prussia asking whether he could consider becoming constitutional monarch of the United States.[35] Yet it is hard to believe that, under any circumstances, Americans would reach into the pool of available and trained European princelings. Among the native-born, only Washington could conceivably receive adequate support. His greatest regal flaw —that he had no heir—could be considered an advantage, as it would have enabled the whole matter to be reconsidered after his death.

Yet, having happily assisted in bringing the ship into port, and having been fairly discharged; it is not my business to embark again on a sea of troubles." Furthermore, the people had not listened to the advice he had "given as a last legacy in the most solemn manner. I had then perhaps some claims to public attention. I consider myself as having none at present. Mrs. Washington joins me in compliments, etc."[36]

Washington awaited word from the Annapolis Convention. The first news was bad: only five of the thirteen states had bothered to send delegations. Then word came that the few delegates had boldly called for a general convention to meet in Philadelphia and "render the constitution of the federal government adequate to the exigencies of the Union."[37]

Washington hardly had time to wonder whether this effort should not have waited, as he had advised, until some more grievous crisis had developed, when there floated in across the autumn landscape reports of a crisis so grievous that it seemed as if all efforts to bring strength to the government might prove too late.

9

Duty's Clamorous Voice

WASHINGTON'S first inkling probably reached Mount Vernon with the *Pennsylvania Packet* for September 23, 1786: a mob of some four hundred men, who were described as ragged, disreputable, and drunken, had threatened a court in western Massachusetts. One insurgent had cried, "I am going to give the court four hours to agree to our terms, and, if they do not, I and my party will force them to it." The court had adjourned hastily "to prevent any coercive measures."[1]

Soon the mail brought a letter Humphreys had written from Hartford: "Everything is in a state of confusion in Massachusetts." There were also "tumults" in New Hampshire, while "Rhode Island continues in a state of frenzy and division on account of their paper currency."[2]

Washington replied, "For God's sake tell me what is the cause of all these commotions: do they proceed from licentiousness, British influence disseminated by the Tories, or real grievances which admit of redress? If the latter, why were they delayed till the public mind had become so much agitated? If the former, why are not the powers of government tried at once?"[3]

The news of what came to be called (after its leader, Captain Daniel Shays) Shays's Rebellion grew increasingly disturbing, all the more because the insurgents menaced, as they milled through western Massachusetts, the Continental arsenal at Springfield, where there were "ten to fifteen thousand stand of arms in excellent order," plenty to supply a shattering rebellion. Congress was considering raising troops but feared this would boomerang, since the central government lacked money to pay any army, and, if unpaid, the troops might join the insurgents. "In great hurry and real distress," Henry Lee wrote Washington from Congress that there was talk of asking him to abandon his retirement and gallop northward, in the hope that, because of his "unbounded influence . . . your appearance among the seditious might bring them back to peace and reconciliation."[4]

Secretary of War Knox, who had been sent into western Massachusetts by Congress to investigate, wrote Washington a hair-raising report. Although the insurgents complained of unpayable taxes, this could not be the true cause since they had "never paid any or but very little taxes. But they see the weakness of the government; they feel at once their own poverty compared with the opulent and their own force; and they are determined to make use of the latter in order to remedy the former." They wished "to annihilate all debts public and private" in a flood of unfunded paper money. Their creed was "that the property of the United States, has been protected from confiscation of Britain by the joint exertions of *all,* and therefore ought to be the *common property* of all. And he that attempts opposition to this creed is an enemy to equity and justice, and ought to be swept from off the face of the earth."

The insurgents, Knox continued, numbered about one-fifth of several populous counties. By combining with people of similar sentiments in Rhode Island, Connecticut, and New Hampshire, they could "constitute a body of twelve or fifteen thousand desperate and unprincipled men" well adapted by youth and activity for fighting. This was a larger number than the Continental Army had possessed during most of the Revolution.[5]

Washington was in extreme agony as winter closed in over his quiet fields. The news that had previously reached him at his listening post had in no way foreshadowed such a calamity. "After what I have heard," he wrote, "I shall be surprised at nothing." Had someone told him, when he retired from the army, "that at this day, I should see such a formidable rebellion against the laws and constitutions of our own making. . . . I should have thought him a bedlamite, a fit subject for a madhouse." Not doubting that what his friends who were nearer the centers wrote him was accurate, he found himself menaced with a conclusion as terrible as it was "unaccountable, that mankind when left to themselves are unfit for their own government." The insurgents exhibited "a melancholy proof of what our transatlantic foe has predicted. . . . I am mortified beyond expression when I view the clouds that have spread over the brightest morn that ever dawned upon any country. In a word, I am lost in amazement when I behold what intrigue [and] the interested views of desperate characters" could achieve. Yet he still believed that the majority, even if they "will not act," could not be "so shortsighted, or enveloped in darkness, as not to see rays of a distant sun through all this mist of intoxication and folly."[6]

Washington's health, which had been startlingly good in his retirement, suddenly collapsed. He suffered from "a violent attack of the fever and ague succeeded by rheumatic pains (to which, till of late, I have been an entire stranger)."[7]

It has become common for historians to view Shays's Rebellion in a sympathetic light. Depression and the shortage of specie were combining to make it impossible for backcountry farmers to pay their taxes and their debts; appeals for relief had been turned down by the wealthier men from longer-settled regions who controlled the Massachusetts government; and finally, rather than have their farms expropriated and be perhaps themselves imprisoned, the western farmers were blocking the sessions of courts that might take such action. The insurgents hoped that the protest and the delay would result in their being accorded legal relief.[8]

This, however, was not the story that penetrated by newspaper and letter to Virginia. After Washington had sent Madison his correspondent Knox's inflammatory report, Madison wrote back that Knox's intelligence was not so black as what Madison had heard "from another channel." In summarizing for his father the situation as it was viewed at the Virginia capital, Madison expressed a fear of what skeptics had prophesied would be the eventual outcome of the American democratic experiment: the violent seizure of property by the poorer classes.* [9]

That Washington, as he rode his own neighborhood, could see nothing menacing, that in Virginia "a perfect calm prevails," did not keep him from believing there were "combustibles in every state." Were the Tories and Britons who had foreseen dreadful events, Washington asked, "wiser than others, or did they judge us from the

---

* Almost every important American leader except Jefferson, who was in France and thus out of touch, viewed Shays's Rebellion with extreme alarm.[10]

corruption and depravity of their own hearts?" And he went on, "When I reflect on the present posture of our affairs, it seems to me to be like the vision of a dream. My mind does not know how to realize it, as a thing in actual existence, so strange, so wonderful does it appear to me! . . . When this spirit first dawned, probably it might easily have been checked, but it is scarcely within the reach of human ken, at this moment, to say when, where, and how it will end."[11]

A major danger of political life is that extremism (real or fancied) at one end of the spectrum stirs up extremism at the other end: many of Washington's former officers saw the counterforce to Shays in the Society of the Cincinnati. And the time for the next "triennial general meeting" of the society was coming round. As he was required to do, Washington summoned the meeting for the first Monday in May of 1787 at Philadelphia. But he then announced that he would not himself attend or accept re-election as President-General. In a circular letter to the state societies, he blamed this on a pressure of affairs that would keep him at Mount Vernon, and on failing health. However, he confided to Madison that he was disassociating himself because the state societies had refused to ratify the changes which he had pushed through at the last general meeting in an effort to remove from the society's charter those clauses which had made a potential anti-republican political force out of what he wished to be no more than a benevolent association of former fellow officers. However great the danger seemed at the moment to be from the radical side, Washington was not going to countenance any faction of conservatives.[12]

Washington had sent to Madison at Richmond extracts from Knox's alarming letter in order to prod the Virginia legislature into electing delegates to the convention which the Annapolis Convention had called to revise the federal government. "What stronger evidence can be given of the want of energy in our governments than these disorders?" Washington asked. "If there exists not a power to check them, what security has a man for life, liberty, or property? . . . Thirteen sovereignties pulling against each other and all tugging at the federal head will soon bring ruin on the whole, whereas a liberal and energetic constitution, well guarded and closely watched to prevent encroachments, might restore us to that degree of respectability and consequence to which we had a fair claim and the brightest prospect of attaining."[13]

Even as Washington thus prodded, he must have foreseen a personally frightening result. Having responded with the news that Virginia would probably be the first state to appoint a delegation, Madison continued, "It has been thought advisable to give this subject a very solemn dress and all the weight that could be derived from a single state." The legislature had therefore placed Washington's name at the head of their delegation. Whether Washington ought in the end to accept the post, Madison added soothingly, did not require immediate decision.[14]

To the suggestions he had been receiving that he toss himself into the current crisis by personally going to Massachusetts and stilling, with his influence, the rebellion, Washington had an answer that was not only grateful to him personally but sound politically: "Influence," he wrote, "is no government." If the insurgents had legitimate grievances, either redress them at once, or if that were impossible, acknowledge (as he himself had so often so successfully done with the army) the justice of the complaints and explain why no remedy was immediately at hand. If the insurgents did not have legitimate grievances, "employ the force of government against them at once." Should the force prove inadequate, "*all* will be convinced that the superstructure is bad or wants support."[15]

The request that he commit his prestige and abilities to the proposed convention menaced more severely his deep-laid plans "to view the solitary walk and tread the paths of private life . . . until I sleep with my fathers." Washington was (or had been until Shays's Rebellion exploded) happier than in any previous period of his life. And he had no faith in the assurances he was given that he could, after attending the convention, return uncommitted to Mount Vernon. Should he go, he would become again, as he had been during the Revolution, the standard-bearer of a vexed cause, to fall with its failure or be exalted with its success. If the convention failed, that would tarnish the shining image which was reflected back to him from the eyes of neighbors and strangers, and which was the great reward he had won with his previous labors. If the convention succeeded, that would mean— how could he doubt it?—demands for further service to help strengthen the government he had helped to create. It was easier, he believed, to avoid taking a step on the wrong path than to return to the right one, and for him the right path—so his heart told him—avoided the political arena.[16]

Washington's immediate reply was that he could not attend the federal convention "with any degree of consistency" because the general meeting of the Cincinnati, which he had announced he would not attend, would be convened in Philadelphia at almost the same time. He could not appear at one and not the other "without giving offense to a very worthy and respectable part of the American community, the late officers of the American army." However, he did not slam the door. As he put it to the Governor of Virginia, Edmund Randolph, "It would be disingenuous not to express a wish that some other character, on whom greater reliance can be had, may be substituted in my place, the probability of my non-attendance being too great to continue my appointment."[17]

Washington's perturbation about his own future course heightened his perturbation about Shays's Rebellion. "What, gracious God, is man!" he asked, "that there should be such inconsistency and perfidiousness in his conduct?" He wondered whether General Nathanael Greene was not lucky to be dead rather than live to see such times. He examined with anxiety the newspapers that came to Mount Vernon, commenting that they "please one hour only to make the moments of the next more bitter." If the news was that the mobs in New England remained disorderly, that darkly foretold anarchy, but if the mobs were said to be orderly, that implied "there are surely men of consequence and abilities behind the curtain who move the puppets, the designs of whom may be deep and dangerous." Perhaps the old enemy, the British, were stirring up disunion so that they might march in and take over after all![18]

Massachusetts called out the militia under the command of Benjamin Lincoln, a general Washington had trained. There being no money in the treasury, rich citizens subscribed the cost. Lincoln marched, the Shaysites fled, and, with almost no fighting at all, the insurrection was (as far as violence went) ended.*

Although Washington was puzzled as to how a revolt which had been made to sound so ominous could have been extinguished "with so little bloodshed," his anxiety was not eased.† As long as the weakness

---

* Future developments were that the protest moved to the ballot box; the conservative power, which had been so indifferent to the plight of the poor farmers was overthrown; many of the reforms the Shaysites had desired were enacted into law; and all the rebels were amnestied.[19]

† In this, Washington was not untypical. Madison, for instance, wrote his father that discontent was still spreading towards "some awful crisis."[20]

of the government remained unremedied, the country lay vulnerable to another insurrection. Might it not, indeed, have been a misfortune that this premonitory disturbance had been stilled before the need for major reforms had been made clear to all? "I believe," Washington wrote, "that the political machine will yet be much tumbled and tossed, and possibly be wrecked altogether," before the people would agree to such a strong central power as the partisans of the coming convention wished to establish. He had times when he wondered whether wisdom did not urge postponing the convention until there was more hope that it could succeed. Or perhaps the idea should be completely abandoned.[21]

In order to understand Washington's tribulations, it is necessary to forget everything that is now known about the success and importance of what came to be called the Constitutional Convention. The name itself could not have been coined as Washington worried, since it was impossible to foresee that the meeting, if held, would even try to write a new constitution. As far as anyone could judge, the gathering might prove no more than another in the long series of efforts to strengthen federal unity which stretched back into Washington's period of military service, and all of which had ended in frustration.

Underlying Washington's confusion was such a nightmarish feeling as he had suffered during the Revolution when he needed to act, but was blind because his intelligence network had failed. That Shays's Rebellion had come to him as such an utter surprise underlined his conviction that, "scarcely ever going off my own farms," he was dangerously "little acquainted with the sentiments of the great world." He begged for facts from those of his friends who had "the wheels of the political machine much more in view than I have." To make up his mind in the manner that was characteristic of him, he needed to weigh the facts on both sides of a question in a mental balance, following in the end the direction which tipped the beam. Unable to do this, his mind spun as in a void, throwing up a chaos of possibilities and alternatives.[22]

On the matter of whether it was wise to hold the convention at all, his thoughts covered a wide gamut. If a meeting collapsed into complete failure, might that not be "the end of federal government"? Or, if the public proved not "matured" for important changes, the convention might patch up the Articles of Confederation in a way that would enable that feeble instrument to stagger along until the situation was past remedy. On the other hand, this might be the final moment when a "peaceable" amendment of the government would be practicable. The convention might be the last opportunity mankind would have to demonstrate that the human animal was capable of ruling himself.[23]

Washington's correspondents wrote him that there was serious talk of grouping the states into two or three separate nations, each unified in interests.* There was also talk of abandoning political experimentation by reverting to that well-tried form, monarchy. Much as he disapproved of both these possibilities, Washington did not exclude them from his ratiocinations. He admitted that, should efforts to strengthen the federal government seem, on "full and dispassionate" examination, "impractical or unwise," wisdom might dictate accepting a different form "to avoid, if possible, civil discord and other ills." Having led one bloody revolution, Washington had no desire to experience another.[24]

To Madison, who wondered in melancholy (as did Jay) whether a king might not prove after all necessary, Washington admitted that perhaps the New Englanders, having gone to the extreme of "the leveling principles" and been disillusioned, were bouncing the other way. However, southerners would not countenance royalty. "Even admitting the utility, nay the necessity of the form, yet . . . the period is not arrived for adopting the change without shaking the peace of this country to its foundation."[25]

As Commander in Chief, Washington had often, in moments of discouragement, written Congress that the war was as good as lost, yet for him depression was never despair. Now he wrote, "I must candidly confess, as we could not remain quiet more than three or four years in time of peace under the [state] constitutions of our own choosing . . . I see little prospect either of our agreeing upon any other, or that we should remain long satisfied under it if we could. Yet I would wish anything and everything essayed to prevent the effusion of blood and to avert the humiliating and contemptible figure we are about to make in the annals of mankind."[26]

His final conclusion was that the convention should be essayed, not

---

* The United States as it then existed—"from the Atlantic to the Mississippi, from the Great Lakes to just short of the Gulf of Mexico"—was already as large as France, Italy, Spain, Britain, and Ireland combined. European politicians were sure that this huge area could not be governed from any center but would become, like Germany or Italy, a grouping of petty sovereignties.[27]

because he thought it could solve the problems but because, if the discussions were fruitful, it could point the way. It should "adopt no temporizing expedient, but probe the defects of the constitution to the bottom and provide radical cures, whether they are agreed to [by the states] or not. A conduct like this will stamp wisdom and dignity on the proceedings, and be looked to as a luminary, which sooner or later will shed its influence."[28]

There remained the question whether, if the convention did meet, Washington should himself attend. "To see this country happy whilst I am gliding down the stream of life in tranquil retirement is so much the wish of my soul," he wrote, "that nothing on this side Elysium can be placed in competition with it." But the two halves of the picture would no longer fit together. He could not be tranquil while his country was not happy. Yet what should he do?[29]

He did not wish to accept his election as a delegate unless there was a good possibility that something useful could be achieved. Surely opposition was to be expected from "the darling sovereignty of the states individually; the governors elected and elect; the legislators, with a long train of etcetera whose political consequence will be lessened, if not annihilated" by any strengthening of the federal power. Perhaps this would mean that there would be no better representation at the new convention than there had been at Annapolis. Why did only five states send delegations to Annapolis? Would there be a fuller representation this time? And even if all the states did send, would not the delegates be so shackled by instructions that all discussion would be useless?[30] "I should not like to be a sharer in this business," Washington stated, unless "the delegates come with such powers as will enable the convention to probe the defects of the constitution to the bottom." If no effective agreement could be reached, the delegates would have to return home "chagrined at their ill-success and disappointment. This would be a disagreeable circumstance for any one of them to be in, but more peculiarly so for a person in my situation."[31]

Washington's often voiced objections to serving unless there was a good chance of success, and the belief which he several times expressed that failure would be more painful for him than the other delegates, have elicited the criticism of later writers. His usually enthusiastic biographer Freeman has ruled that he was "too much the self-conscious national hero and too little the daring patriot. . . . He never could have won the war in the spirit he displayed in this effort to secure the peace."[32]

This judgment would have amazed Washington's contemporaries. The advice he received from his intimates tended to be against his going. Jay, the lawyer, was worried that the convention had been called independently of the amending provisions in the Articles of Confederation: Washington should not countenance what was illegal. Humphreys wished him to stay away because he thought the attendance would be small and the meeting a failure. Knox wrote that if it were known that Washington was going to attend, the eastern states would be induced to send delegates, but "the principles of purest and most respectful friendship" made him add, "I do not wish you to be concerned in any political operations of which there are such various opinions." And Madison, who had been urging Washington to serve, had second thoughts when notified that the General's vacillations were subsiding in that direction. Might it not be best, he asked, if Washington should not appear at once, so that if the opening sessions portended failure, he need not appear at all? "It ought not to be wished by any of his friends that he should participate in any abortive undertaking."[33]

Everyone knew that if Washington did go to the convention, he would be, with Franklin, one of the two most celebrated members, and, being much the younger of the pair, he would probably be called on to play the most conspicuous role. This would give him the furthest to fall. The desire to spare Washington was, in addition to being affectionate, both aesthetic and pragmatic, Washington was the living, spotless standard of the successful Revolution; it would be disgusting to have him splattered with mire. And there was also the fact that, in contrast to Franklin, he was not already enbattled in the political arena. The impact of his emergence from retirement should not be squandered. Even those most passionately desirous of the convention did not envision it (however melodramatically they sometimes expressed themselves) as the final ledge before the abyss of anarchy. Knox, for instance, expressed himself in favor of having the General held in reserve. There might, Knox explained in a letter to Washington, "arise some solemn occasion in which you may conceive it to be your duty again to exert your utmost talents to promote the happiness of your country. But this occasion must be of an unequivocal nature, in which the enlightened and virtuous citizens should generally concur."[34]

Despite the negative advice he received, Washington's thoughts continued to spin. He had promised in his "Legacy" that he would never again accept public office. If he accepted election as a delegate would he not be accused, and rightly so, of having broken his word? And during early March a new fear formed in his mind: should he fail to attend, would his refusal be attributed to "a dereliction to republicanism" which made him want the government to collapse into a tyranny, perhaps one he could himself lead.[35]

With Washington's thoughts, the pains in his body fluctuated. Although he continued trying to calm his nerves with his old panacea of riding restlessly by the hour around his plantations, his rheumatism was sometimes so afflicting that he could not lift his arm to his head or, at night, turn himself in bed. It was at this time of strain that he wrote the angry letter to his mother quoted in Chapter Three.[36]

As Washington looked out of Mount Vernon's windows at the vistas he had so carefully planned and created, as he rode through the fields where he had started so many amusing projects it would take a lifetime to end, his beloved home seemed to dim before his eyes, receding again into the unattainable dream which it had seemed during his eight years of military exile. And the thought of a new exile was driving his wife almost frantic. She could not, Martha admitted sadly, "blame" Washington if, by acting "according to his ideals," he again shattered their domesticity. But she added with great passion that she had little thought that, once the war was ended, "any circumstances could possibly have happened" which would call him "into public life again. I had anticipated that from this moment we should have been left to grow old in solitude and tranquillity together."[37]

The news that now came in from across the countryside was good from the point of view of the nation and republicanism, bad for Washington's hopes of staying home. Indications were multiplying that his faith in the people had not been so misplaced as it had on the surface seemed. A realization of the need for self-discipline, for effective government, had been slowly augmenting like water swelling subterranean streams. It had only been necessary to drill a hole to have the water rise, and that is what Shays's Rebellion had done. The nation had overreacted (as Washington himself did) to that small insurrection because tens of thousands of people had previously felt, even if only unconsciously, that they were vulnerable to chaos. And now support for the coming convention emerged amazingly. Congress gave the meeting a semblance of legality by endorsing it. And in state after state indications pointed to the election of full and influential delegations. Knox changed his advice, writing on April 9, "It is the general wish that you should attend."[38]

Washington had already (on March 28) written Governor Randolph that if his health permitted—a matter concerning which he was far from sure—he would accept election to the Virginia delegation. This would force him, he added, to reach Philadelphia a week before the convention opened on May 14, so that he could "account personally for my conduct to the General Meeting of the Cincinnati."

The Cincinnati situation added to Washington's unhappiness. If he were there in person, he would have personally to disassociate himself from the decisions of his fellow officers for whom "I shall ever retain the liveliest and most affectionate regard."[39]

Washington soon wrote Randolph a second letter in which he repeated his fear that the delegates would arrive so "fettered" by provisos that "the grand object" would be unattainable. He added that he had given his consent "contrary to my judgment." He was now carrying his arm in a sling.[40]

It is usually impossible to foresee where true trouble lies. As Washington worried over what effect the coming convention would have on his reputation, the greatest of all menaces to his place in the national memory appeared at Mount Vernon disguised in trivial routine. Washington's diary states, "The Rev. Mr. Weems and young Dr. Craik, who came here yesterday in the afternoon, left this about noon for Port Tobacco."[41] How could Washington know that Weems, the voluble twenty-eight-year-old clergyman whom he probably hardly noticed, would kidnap his ghost and substitute, in the minds of generations of Americans, a repellent, goody-goody, Sunday-school-inspired prig?

Washington fixed Monday, April 30, as his date of departure. But between four and five o'clock on the afternoon of the 26th, in rushed a messenger "who assures me not a moment is to be lost to see a mother and *only* sister (who are supposed to be in the agonies of death) expire." Washington hurriedly wrote Knox, as Secretary General of the

Cincinnati, that the family summons would preclude his reaching the meeting of the society. In fact, "this journey of mine . . . one hundred miles in the disordered frame of my body, will, I am persuaded, unfit me" to go to Philadelphia at all.[42]

Setting out before sunrise, he galloped into Fredericksburg at about two in the afternoon. He found his mother and sister "better than I expected." The sister had overstrained herself by "watchful attention to my mother," but was out of danger. Although Washington doubted that his seventy-nine-year-old mother could "long survive the disorder which has reduced her to a skeleton," she was "somewhat amended."[43]

Having spent three nights at Fredericksburg, where he saw much company, Washington rode in a leisurely manner back to Mount Vernon, arriving "in a small shower." Since he had made his excuses, he had no intention of hurrying to the Cincinnati. He would immerse himself for a few more days in the happy routine of his retirement before abandoning it (as he feared) forever. "Notwithstanding my fatigue" and with his rheumatism bothering him less than was now usual, he rode to all his farms on the morning of his return. He spent the evening cozily in his study, making agricultural notes in his diary.[44]

The day Washington had now established for his departure, May 8, 1787, moved inexorably around. However, "the weather being squally with showers, I deferred setting off till the morning." When on the morrow he stepped into his coach by candlelight, Martha unhappily watched from Mount Vernon's doorway. "Mrs. Washington," he wrote down not without irritation, "is become too domestic and too attentive to two little grandchildren to leave home."[45]

Washington rode beyond Baltimore to spend the night at Montpelier (the home of this writer's great-great-grandmother) near Elk Ridge Landing, Maryland. He had traversed this region before when vainly seeking shipping that would carry his army and his French allies down the Chesapeake to attack Cornwallis. Old strains, old memories crowded in upon him, jostling away the quiet fields of Mount Vernon. "Feeling very severely a violent headache and sick stomach, I went to bed early."

Four days later, after being buffeted by much bad weather and being delayed for a night because the Susquehanna was too storm-agitated to cross, Washington reached Philadelphia. "On my arrival," he noted, "the bells were chimed."[46]

That Washington had been so reluctant to take part in an event which was to be among the most important in American history was among the reasons that the event became so important. Again, in a way that was past the imagining of less instinctive leaders like John Adams, Washington had, by following his own personal feelings, behaved in the most politically effective manner. Had he leapt to the constitutional call, like a war-horse at the sound of the bugle, suspicion would have been raised that the Virginia landholder was serving his interests and those of his class. His long and painful hesitation not only absolved him of selfish motives (as his refusal of a salary had done at the start of the Revolution) but, when he felt he could no longer refuse, dramatized the significance of the meeting. His obvious self-sacrifice inspired others also to rise above their personal concerns.

In a letter involving three future Presidents of the United States, James Madison wrote Thomas Jefferson about George Washington, "To forsake the honorable retreat to which he had retired and risk the reputation he had so deservedly acquired, manifested a zeal for the public interest that could, after so many and illustrious services, scarcely have been expected of him." And Knox wrote Lafayette, "Secure as he was in his fame, he has again committed it to the mercy of events. Nothing but the critical situation of his country would have induced him to so hazardous a conduct."[47]

10

Widening Political Horizons

O NCE Washington had arrived in Philadelphia to attend the Constitutional Convention, the conditions of his mind and body altered with startling rapidity and completeness. He had often demonstrated during his military command that however long and painful had been his hesitation, when he finally reached the conclusion which he carried into action, doubts no longer modified to the slightest degree his determination. Now the physical ailments that had been plaguing him for months vanished, and he was all energy.

On his entry into the city crowds had gathered, cheering wildly. The warmth of this reception was reassuring to the man who had wondered whether he would be forgiven for returning to public life after he had publicly renounced it, and also to watching Federalists, who wished to judge how much public influence was still possessed by the ace card they wished to play for a new constitution. Madison hurried off to Jefferson in France a happy report on "the acclamations of the people."[1]

Washington had refused a written invitation that he stay with Robert Morris, by reputation the nation's richest man. Now Morris pressed him again, and he abandoned the boardinghouse where he had taken lodgings, moving up High Street to the three-story brick mansion that was considered the grandest in Philadelphia.* The re-

---

* The house had been selected by Washington's opponent, the British commander in chief, Sir William Howe, as his headquarters during the occupation of Philadelphia. Since then Morris had enlarged and improved the house.

strained elegance with which he was surrounded made even Mount Vernon seem shabby. Not only the tables but the doors were of "superb mahogany," polished until Washington could see within them his own vague image. The brass locks and hinges seemed to visitors "curiously bright." Every piece of furniture was a masterpiece of the cabinetmaker's art, many inlaid with sandalwood or embellished with silver. The profusion of decoration brought to eighteenth-century eyes no sense of clutter: comments ran on how neat everything was and how exactly in its place. As Washington was happy to discover, the food, rushed down the long passageway from a separate kitchen, arrived always at the perfect temperature. For the Morrises, the purpose of luxury was not to strike awe but to establish comfort, which exactly suited Washington.[2]

The Convention was supposed to open on the morning after Washington's arrival, May 14, 1787. Exactly on time he walked into the room at the State House (now known as Independence Hall) where he had sat as a member of the Continental Congress and had been elected Commander in Chief. Sunlight poured through the long windows into an almost empty chamber. There was a bustle as a sedan chair—probably the first Washington had ever seen—came in carried by two "trusty convicts" and containing the aged Benjamin Franklin, still President of Pennsylvania. Yet only two delegations made their appearance: Virginia and Pennsylvania. A quorum being seven states, there was nothing to do but shake hands, gossip for a few minutes, and agree to return the next day.[3]

Day after day, Washington returned to find sometimes a few newly arrived delegates, but no quorum. Madison stated bravely that the trouble was not apathy, but bad roads and poor weather. Washington wrote, "These delays greatly impede public measures and serve to sour the temper of the punctual members who do not like to idle away their time."[4]

The Cincinnati convention was still on (although poorly attended). Washington did not go to any sessions. He did, however, dine with the delegates. He allowed himself to be persuaded to accept re-election as President-General on the condition that the Vice-President, Mifflin, should do all the work. As Washington explained to Jefferson, he could not decline "without placing myself in an extremely difficult situation" with his fellow veterans, "that brave and faithful class of men whose persevering friendship I had experienced on so many trying occa-

George Washington, painted at the time of the Constitutional Convention by
Charles Willson Peale. Courtesy of the Pennsylvania Academy
of the Fine Arts

Mrs. Robert Morris: George Washington's hostess and Martha Washington's intimate friend. By Charles Willson Peale, about 1782. Courtesy of the Independence National Historical Park Collection

sions." He added optimistically that the public clamors against the Cincinnati had ceased.* 5

While waiting for his own convention to get under way, Washington attended at daily conferences during which the Virginia delegation hammered out a plan for presentation to the Convention.† The basic conceptions had been prepared by Madison and gone over by Washington before he left Mount Vernon. As refined by the entire delegation, the suggestions were revolutionary and, indeed, illegal, since Congress had specifically limited the power of the Convention to revising the existing Articles of Confederation. What came to be known as the "Virginia Plan" scrapped the Articles and recommended a different government.6

While this bombshell was being secretly prepared, Washington tried to determine, in his conversations with the arriving delegates, how far they would go. He discovered that "much is expected of it [the Convention] by some, but little by others, and nothing by a few." It was hopeful that all agreed "something is necessary," because the existing government "is shaken to its foundation and liable to be overset by every blast. In a word, it is at an end, and unless a remedy is soon applied, anarchy and confusion will inevitably ensue."7

Over convivial tables, Washington did what he could to prepare minds for strong actions. The Pennsylvania delegate Gouverneur Morris quotes him as having said, in reply to arguments that the people would not go along with any radical changes, "It is too probable that no plan we propose will be adopted. Perhaps another dreadful conflict is to be sustained. If, to please the people, we offer what we ourselves

---

* This was one of Washington's convenient evasions. In the Constitutional Convention, a possible takeover by the Cincinnati was a bugaboo raised by opponents of a strong government. The French chargé d'affaires, Louis Guillaume Otto, reported home that the Cincinnati wished to extinguish state divisions and give Washington "all the powers and prerogatives of a crowned head." If the Convention failed to carry out their program, they threatened to achieve it by force of arms. Otto added that the Cincinnati was too weak and unpopular to lead an insurrection.8

† Some writers have doubted that Washington attended these meetings, as they are not mentioned in his diary. However, the diary notations are extremely brief, describing primarily where he dined and supped, while the wording of the principal source about the meetings (a letter from George Mason to his son) seems clearly to include Washington: "The Virginia deputies (who are all here) meet and confer two or three hours a day, in order to form a proper correspondence of sentiments."

disapprove, how can we afterwards defend our work? Let us raise a standard to which the wise and the honest can repair. The event is in the hand of God."* ⁹

On Friday, May 25, after Washington had waited in Philadelphia for thirteen days, the presence of seven states made it at last possible to call the meeting to order. The intention had been that Franklin, the only other possibility for the office, would nominate Washington as president of the Convention. But rain poured and the aged philosopher did not feel well enough even for his sedan chair. The task was handed on to Washington's host, Robert Morris.

Morris could hardly have kept from Washington what was planned. When the Virginian had foreseen that he would be elected Commander in Chief, he had stayed away from the very room where the Convention was now meeting. On this occasion, he decided that such an act would be too coy. He was sitting in his place when Morris, "on behalf of the deputation of Pennsylvania," nominated Washington. "Mr. Jno. Rutledge," so continues Madison's unofficial log, which remains the basic source concerning the Convention, "seconded the motion, expressing his confidence that the choice would be unanimous, and observing that the presence of General Washington forbade any observations on the occasion which might otherwise be proper.

General Washington was accordingly unanimously elected by ballot, and conducted to the chair by Mr. R. Morris and Mr. Rutledge, from which, in a very emphatic manner, he thanked the Convention for the honor they had conferred on him, reminded them of the novelty of the scene of business in which he was to act, lamented his want of better qualifications, and claimed the indulgence of the House towards the involuntary errors which his inexperience might occasion."¹⁰

General Washington was now occupying the seat, on a low dais, which had been, during the Revolution, occupied by his titular civilian commander, the President of Congress. That he looked down on a scant twenty individuals did not bother him: he was used to fighting major battles with very few men.

---

* This famous quotation was not published by Morris until 1799. Although Washington often expressed similar sentiments in his letters, the exact wording of the quotation was probably Morris's, for the metaphor is military, a kind of figure which the peace-loving former general almost never used.

Of the two most important rules of procedure the Convention now adopted, one was foreordained if certainly not what Washington would have preferred: as in Congress, each state, whether large or small, had a single, equal vote. With the other major decision—that the proceedings of the Convention be secret—Washington enthusiastically agreed. He was, indeed, to give way to one of his now rare flashes of temper when a copy of some resolutions was found lying carelessly where a member of the public could pick it up. Having controlled himself until the meeting was ready to adjourn, he then pulled the offending paper from his pocket and stated, "I must entreat gentlemen to be more careful, lest our transactions get into the newspapers and disturb the public repose by premature speculations." Raising the document high in his hand, Washington continued, "I know not whose paper it is, but there it is!" He threw it down on the table. "Let him who owns it take it!" Then (so continued the narrative of the Georgia representative William Pierce) Washington "bowed, picked up his hat, and quitted the room with a dignity so severe that every person seemed alarmed. . . . It is something remarkable that no person ever owned [to] the paper."[11]

Secrecy was of such primary importance because the Constitutional Convention was, in its most creative aspects, less a forum of debate than experimental laboratory in which a group of men educated each other to work out together such a government as existed nowhere in the past or present of the world. No man brought to the Convention a complete vision of the outcome. Groups began, indeed, from widely divergent starting points. Unimpeded mental mobility was therefore indispensable. Any publicity that committed anyone to anything or raised public objections to any aspect of the plan before the total structure was perfected could bring to a halt the essential educational process.

It certainly was a blessing that the political parties which were to become inherent in the American governmental system had not yet evolved. Two or more teams pulling against each other for political advantage would have wrecked the Constitutional Convention.*

---

* In explaining the failure of the 1967 New York State Constitutional Convention, the *New York Times* editorialized, "The most important single cause . . . was the intense rivalry of the two political parties."[12]

Washington's greatest fear had been that the delegates would come with commitments that would prevent persuasion.

Almost a year before, his nephew, Bushrod Washington, had written to ask his opinion of a "Patriotic Society" which was being planned in the lower Virginia counties "to inquire into the conduct of those who represent us and give them our sentiments." Although Bushrod's intention was also Washington's—to further federal power—his uncle replied, "To me, it appears much wiser and more politic to choose able and honest representatives and leave them in all national questions to determine from the evidence of reason and the facts which shall be adduced, when internal and external information is given them in a collective state." Local groups could not be counted on to understand what was to their true interest on a national scale. Furthermore, "may not a few members of this society, more sagacious and designing than the rest, direct the measures of it to private views of their own? . . . What figure then must a delegate make . . . with his hands tied and his judgment forestalled!" Such delegates would be blinded to "all the lights which they may receive."[13]

This correspondence, which supplies further evidence that Washington opposed pressure groups even when he agreed with their objectives, is given particular interest because of the resounding charges made by the historian Charles E. Beard that the Constitutional Convention was a cabal of the propertied to place fetters on the poor. Beard believed that Washington, the presiding officer, was "probably the richest man in the United States in his time," happily possessed of "a large amount of fluid capital." This is, of course, pure balderdash. Although Washington did live high, he complained shortly before the Convention that he owed "more than 500 £, three hundred forty odd of which is due for the tax of 1786, and I know not where or when I shall receive one shilling with which to pay it."[14]

Beard erred certainly in trying to apply to a yet half-grown economic society distinctions that were not to achieve validity for many years. To place Washington (and many of the other delegates) into a consistent economic cubbyhole is impossible. Although a tidewater landowner, Washington could not be indifferent to the interests of the west, since he owned extensive property there which could only assume value with expansion and settlement. He was a creditor but also a debtor. He was a farmer, but much concerned with export, since

Virginia produced more than it could consume, and he wished to build canals that would bring the produce of the central valley to ocean vessels. He had reasons for encouraging local manufactures, since his military experience had proved their importance to national defense, and, as a civilian, he had found purchasing from abroad most unsatisfactory, since he had been so often swindled. Although he owned some government obligations, they were not of major importance to his prosperity, and he was inept in handling them: like lesser farmers, he was swindled by the city slickers. Not himself a city man, he nonetheless hoped that his Potomac Canal would create in his own district the greatest metropolis in the United States. Thus, it is impossible to pin Washington down to narrow economic motivation unless one interprets as such the desire, shared by everyone with any type of property to lose, not to have it expropriated by government action.

This desire was, of course, unsatisfactory to debtors without assets, but the poor did not look far beyond their fields, nor did they sit in the Convention any more than they do in today's Senate. A desire for the stability of property characterized the whole spectrum of effective national leadership. Washington's convictions were shared, for instance, by two younger men who were to become Presidents of the United States as opponents of conservatism. Madison and Monroe both wrote Jefferson that the American danger was the reverse of what Jefferson was seeing in France. Monroe argued that, although the struggle in Europe had always been for the people to extricate themselves from the oppression of rulers, in America the struggle was "to establish the dominion of law over licentiousness." Madison added that wherever power lies, there lies the danger of oppression. In America, the danger was that the masses would tyrannize over the propertied minority. "Invasion of private rights is chiefly to be apprehended."[15]

A method to protect all people from governmental tyranny existed in well-known theory. The trouble with so many of the state governments, it was generally believed, lay in their being controlled by legislatures, often unicameral. What a majority voted instantly became, without any defense for the minority, law. Blackstone and Montesquieu had established in writing the principle that government could be made safe for all legitimate interests by the establishment of different branches, chosen in different manners and for different terms, which had all to agree before a proposition became law. As John

Adams had put it way back in 1776, "A legislative, an executive, and a judicial power comprehend the whole of what is meant and understood by government. It is by balancing each of these powers against the other two that the efforts of human nature towards tyranny can alone be checked." Washington, although he had never made a deep study of political theory, had come to a similar conclusion before the Convention met. Since most of the other delegates had also been similarly convinced, the problem of the Convention was never the wisdom of establishing a balance of powers, but rather what weight to assign on the balance to various interests and forces. The way was thus wide open for dickering, persuasion, and compromise.[16]

The Convention moved with surprising exactitude according to the natural tenor of Washington's mind. It used only as starting points the lessons of history and theories derived from books. As a guide throughout, there was what Washington called "that great line of duty which, though hid under a cloud for some time from a peculiarity of circumstances, may nevertheless bear scrutiny." And the process for reaching new formulations was that in which Washington most believed (and which was becoming the technique of science): seeking new experience through intelligent contact with specific problems.[17]

However, the result, far from being truly scientific, had to bring into conjunction those often irrational entities, human brains. On top of truth, it was necessary to build compromise. The compromises were achieved by the method which Washington had established for himself years before: "In all matters of great national moment, the only true line of conduct in my opinion is dispassionately to compare the advantages and disadvantages of the measure proposed, and decide from the balance. The lesser evil, where there is a choice of them, should yield to the greater."[18]

That the Convention could not, like an ordinary legislative body, establish any final conclusion by a majority or even a three-fourths vote came to Washington as no surprise, for this had been exactly the situation of the Continental Congress during the war. In those embattled years, virtual unanimity was always necessary, since an angry minority would weaken the cause by inaction or by giving actual comfort to the enemy. Now, if a new government were set up in such a way that one or more states would not in the end come along, the continental union which was the great objective would be shattered.

Washington's often-repeated advice that the delegates should advance boldly was not an urging that anyone should be shouted or voted down, but rather that each man should use his own best judgment without fear of what his constituents back home might think. The Convention, Washington realized, was only the first step in the necessary educational process. It would determine how the various interests could be balanced in a manner acceptable to the delegates from the various areas. The assumption had to be that what the delegates would accept could be made (when the constitutional university was expanded to include the entire area of the United States) also acceptable, on explanation, to their constituents. As Washington put it, the Convention should "form such a government as will bear the scrutinizing eye of criticism, and trust it to the good sense and patriotism of the people to carry it into effect."

To bring into unity such "a diversity of sentiments," it was necessary, Washington wrote, to "inform the judgment" by hearing all the arguments that could be advanced, giving at every step "due consideration to circumstances, habits, etc., etc."[19]

But before one can consider circumstances and habits one has to understand them: the first basic need was for the delegates to mingle together. At the start, the men from different areas seemed to each other—as the Massachusetts officers had seemed to Washington in 1775—not only strange but wrongheaded and even (to use Washington's old word) "nasty." (Madison admitted that he knew no more about Georgia than Kamchatka.)[20] Frequent meetings, however, revealed many grounds for agreement. No one (to take a basic example) really wished the nation to break apart. Washington saw repeated, as weeks passed, the process which had successfully unified the army: Americans, after spitting at each other, discovered they were the same breed of cats, different from the European breed, and mutually shaped by the same great, historic adventure. It was the gradual merging during a long summer of strangers into a coherent cultural group which made possible the eventual compromise that was to be the Constitution.

In the educational process, the debates and parliamentary maneuvers at the Convention sessions were symptoms and visible results of what was moving below. They were like the spray and currents on the top of a deep-rolling sea.

Washington took practically no part in the debates, making only one speech and that at the very end of the Convention. This was by no means because he was always the presiding officer. The Convention hammered out drafts for its own final consideration under the parliamentary device of sitting as a "committee of the whole."* On such occasions, Washington handed the gavel to Nathaniel Gorham of Massachusetts, who served as chairman of the committee, and then stepped down to sit with the Virginia delegation. He was now free to vote (which he did) and to speak (which he refrained from doing). He explained that silence was still enjoined by his role, even if temporarily inoperative, as president of the Convention.[21]

When presiding over the Convention's formal sessions, Washington sat hour after hour on the low dais in full view of the other delegates. They were a small group (rarely more than thirty); almost all desired Washington's good opinion; and their remarks were always titularly addressed to him. Much of the time, it is true, he listened torpidly. As his wartime aide John Laurens wrote of him, "When the muscles are in a state of repose, his eye certainly wants animation." But, so Laurens continued, "his countenance, when affected either by joy or anger, is full of expression." There were many stories afloat of how Washington's facial expressions—"anxious solicitude" at acrimony changing to delight at fruitful compromise—affected the debates, and it is hard to see how this could have failed to be the case.[22]

As the months passed, Washington set an example for the delegates by never missing a single session or arriving late. Yet, in all probability, his greatest influence was exerted off the Convention floor. Although many of the delegates had been strangers to him at the start of the Convention, many were his friends or former associates. A half-dozen had voted for him as Commander in Chief; a dozen or so had served with him in the Continental Army; a dozen had met him during the war as congressmen or had visited him at Mount Vernon. And it was a rare delegate who failed to have considerable personal contact with him now.[23]

Concerning most days Washington noted in his diary that he dined in one place, drank tea at another. He received and returned visits. He

---

* This enabled the Convention to take votes which were automatically reexamined when the committeemen submitted the report to themselves now meeting in their formal capacity.

attended clubs of delegates in various taverns. Delegates who went to the theater could often converse with him during intermissions. He was, indeed, so active that he was unable (something that rarely happened even during the Revolution) to find time to read his manager's reports from Mount Vernon. On at least two occasions, he was forced to cut short his letters home because "it is now eleven o'clock at night and I am tired." Almost all general business had to wait for his attention until the Convention was over.[24]

When the real need is for men to get to know and trust each other, to rub off sharp edges by continual contact, the tavern table can be a more effective instrument for achieving decisions than the debating floor. History will never be able accurately to assess the influence Washington exerted during the social occasions he endlessly attended. Yet when we remember how great was his prestige and the almost hypnotic charm he exerted on his fellowmen, we can safely assume that the effects were powerful.

Concerning the grand design of the new government Washington's convictions were strong: it should be republican, grounded on the will of the people, and it should, to the greatest feasible extent, silence the voices of the states in national concerns. These two principles taken together led to a third: the citizens of all states should be given an equal power in the national government, which meant that the citizens of the large states should not be prevented from outvoting the citizens of the small.

As Commander in Chief, Washington had been more hampered by exclusive local loyalties than by any other political phenomenon. "Persuaded I am," he wrote, "that the primary cause of all our disorders lies in the different state governments and in the tenacity of that power. . . . Whilst the local views of each state . . . will not yield to a more enlarged scale of politics," government had to be "weak, inefficient, disgraceful."[25]

Delaware had (according to the first census in 1790) fewer than 60,000 inhabitants, while Virginia (not counting the future Kentucky which by itself was more populous than Delaware) had 750,000. The three giants—Massachusetts, Pennsylvania, and Virginia—boasted almost half the total population of the United States. However, the small states had always possessed their separate entities under the British Crown, and, they had been, since the Declaration of Independence, sovereign within their own boundaries. Naturally their people (or was it only the politicians?) did not wish their prerogatives to be buried under the mass of their larger neighbors. Whether or not in part because he was himself from a large state, Washington had little sympathy with this point of view. He classed "men who are unwilling to lose any of the state consequence" among the principal enemies to political reform, along with "demagogues," and "men who for personal motives" were opposed to "any general government."[26]

Having served unhappily on many military occasions without the powers requisite to achieve his duties, Washington had no doubt that the general government should be entrusted with all the strengths its functions would require. The perennial argument that this would open the road to such a tyranny (or even a worse one!) as the Americans had fought against during the Revolution, he vehemently denied. Tyranny, he argued, could spring from either extreme: not only from unbridled power but also from weakness which left a governmental vacuum for demagogues to fill. There was no remedy for weakness but more strength. And there was no reason why strength had to be unbridled. There was the protective principle of checks and balances.[27]

Concerning the actual machinery which the Constitution should establish, which wheels should mesh with which and where the brakes should be placed, Washington had no strong preconceptions. Having never given deep thought to political organization, he needed an expert political mechanic to guide him—one whom he could trust.

With the rise of constitutional issues as the major concerns of the nation, James Madison became Washington's primary adviser. As a boy, at about the age when Washington had copied down *101 Rules of Civility and Polite Behavior*, Madison had penned what he called *James Madison His Book of Logic*. He undertook at the College of New Jersey (Princeton) a deep study of constitutional law, and then returned to his father's plantation in the Virginia piedmont. Suffering from a hysterical form of epilepsy, he pulled down the blinds against all the outdoor activities on which Washington spent so much energy. He read and thought and thought and read.

Madison was, when the Convention met, thirty-seven years old and (it seemed) a confirmed bachelor. Short and slight, with a large head but thin legs, he seemed to carry the maximum of intellect on the mimimum of body. His eyes were "bluish but not bright blue." Over features that displayed a warm intellectual symmetry, his dark hair

[125]

had withdrawn up his forehead. He had a sallow, indoors complexion. He usually dressed in black. Although his ribald wit could, when the gentlemen were sequestered over their wine, bring the table to a roar, Madison was usually grave.[28]

Washington could hardly have considered the hypochondriacal theorist the most amusing of companions. Yet he found in Madison qualities infinitely more valuable. As long as Madison greatly admired another man—and he now greatly admired Washington—he placed almost selflessly his wisdom at his idol's disposal. And that wisdom comprised what the United States now most needed: a widely examined and deeply meditated knowledge of the machinery of government.

The first business to go before the Convention, after its organization had been completed, was the plan which had been drawn up by the Virginia delegation under Madison's leadership and with Washington's participation. Since Madison's voice was weak and his manner pedestrian, the actual presentation was entrusted to the young Governor of Virginia, Edmund Randolph, who possessed not only "a most harmonious voice" but "a fine person and striking manners."[29]

What has gone down in history as the Virginia Plan, having in effect scrapped the Articles of Confederation, favored a system in which a bicameral legislature, an executive, and judiciary checked and balanced each other. Furthermore, the plan aimed a shattering blow at the smaller states by proposing that all representation should be based on a numeral count of population or on the extent of financial contributions to the government.

The people were to elect the lower legislative house, which would in turn elect the upper house from persons nominated by the state legislatures. The resulting congress would choose the members of the executive and judicial departments. The executive might consist of one or more persons who would be ineligible for re-election. The judiciary would consist of several courts. "A convenient number" of judges would sit with the executive in a Council of Revision that could veto the acts of the legislature. The veto could be overridden by an unspecified number of votes. To establish federal supremacy, the legislature could negate any laws passed by the states contrary to "the articles of union" and could use force against recalcitrant states. Since the state legislatures could not be expected to approve a plan so diminutive of their own powers, the Constitution would, "after the approbation of Congress," be passed on by conventions chosen in each state, for that specific purpose, directly by the people.[30]

This was very strong medicine, but the group of youngish men in the room—their average age was forty-four—listened without visible shock. They then organized themselves into a committee of the whole which discussed the Virginia Plan section by section. Since nearly all the delegates were anxious to establish agreements and postpone difficult issues, Washington was able to write on June 3, "the sentiments of the different members seem to accord more than I expected they would, as far as we have yet gone." On May 30, with eight states present, a giant step had been achieved by a vote of six ayes, one no, and one divided: the Articles of Confederation and purely legislative power were to be scrapped. "A national government," it was decided, "ought to be established consisting of a *supreme* legislative, executive, and judiciary."[31]

However, Washington was not oversanguine. He placed his carriage in a shop to be mended—a labor that would take several months—and wrote his nephew and estate manager, George Augustine Washington, "Send me my blue coat with the crimson collar and one of those made of the cloth sent me by the Spanish minister, to wit that without lapels and lined with white silk, as I see no end to my staying here."[32]

11

Building a New Government[1]

ALTHOUGH tiny Rhode Island, the ever-intransigent, continued what Washington considered its "scandalous conduct"[2] by refusing to appoint delegates, and the representatives from distant New Hampshire were long on the road, eleven states were soon present, if not represented at every session. They continued step by step to refine the Virginia Plan.

Real trouble was presaged during May on the issue of large states versus small. The small states proposed that, although the lower house of the legislature should be apportioned according to population, in the upper house all states should have equal representation. Virginia and Pennsylvania led a juggernaut which rode this proposition down. The smaller states warned that they would not confederate on the basis thus presented, and bided their time.

The committee of the whole eventually reported out thirteen resolutions that were basically refinements of the Virginia Plan. Presiding again as president of the formal Convention, Washington recognized William Paterson, a short, mild-appearing representative from the small state of New Jersey.

The revolt that now exploded reflected in part the outrage of the smaller states and in part the flow-back natural in human beings when men have been washed by an emotional tide far beyond their previous prejudices and behavior patterns. Four smaller states—Delaware, Maryland, New Jersey, Connecticut—were joined in opposition by a scattering of delegates from various sections, and also by New York, which was the fifth largest state and growing, while it recovered from the long British occupation during the war, faster than any other.

As Paterson pointed out, the New Jersey Plan, which he now presented, obeyed (as the Virginia Plan did not) the instructions of the Continental Congress by strengthening rather than jettisoning the Articles of Confederation. It contained many provisions designed to guard the powers of the states. After three days of sharp debate, the juggernaut moved again, and the New Jersey Plan was voted down.

The Virginia Plan was now rediscussed by the formal Convention, with the dissenting states contesting every step. As hot June moved into stifling July—the windows had to be kept closed for fear of eavesdroppers—Washington presided with mounting uneasiness and unhappiness over debates that became more and more angry.

Now that the mood had changed from agreement to controversy, difference of interest writhed over the Convention floor. Should not only population but property values be considered in the apportioning of votes? And what about slavery: would the north ram abolition down the throats of the south; should the southerners be allowed to protect themselves, as a minority, by including their unfranchised slaves in the population count that would determine their representation? And, like sheeted ghosts, the old economic divisions walked again, particularly the southern fear that any federal trade regulations would make them helpless serfs to New England shippers.*

Raw spot after raw spot was uncovered, and it was far from clear that the eventual result would be healing rather than exacerbation. At a dark moment, Washington wrote Hamilton (who had appeared as a delegate, made an indiscreet speech favoring a government on the British pattern, and returned to New York), "I *almost* despair . . . and do therefore repent having had any agency in the business."[3]

The most menacing explosion came at the very end of June when the small states tried again for that equal representation in an upper legislative house which they felt was essential to their continued existence. As, under Madison's leadership, the larger states showed no signs of relenting, the opposition oratory rose to an ever higher tone until Gunning Bedford from Delaware, a man as choleric as he was fat, shouted, "*I do not, gentlemen, trust you!* . . . The small states never can agree

---

* During a meeting of the Committee of the Whole, so Madison recorded, Washington went against the narrow Virginia interest in voting that Congress be empowered to tax exports.[4]

to the Virginia Plan; and why then is it still urged?" Did the large states feel they could confederate on their own terms and then crush the small ones. "Sooner than be ruined," Bedford continued, "there are *foreign powers who will take us by the hand*."[5] On this desperate note, the meeting adjourned until the following Monday, July 2.

That evening Washington went to "ladies' day" at a Philadelphia club and on Sunday he stayed for the most part "home" at Robert Morris's. A delegate who had been temporarily absent from the Convention dropped in to find Washington and his host "much dejected" at what they regarded as "the deplorable state of things. . . . Some of the members were threatening to go home, and, at this alarming crisis, a dissolution of the Convention was hourly to be apprehended."[6]

On Monday the situation darkened. The smaller states and the delegates favoring states' rights placed their all behind a renewed motion that representation in the upper house should be apportioned evenly among the states. When Washington put the question, the count was a tie that settled nothing and pleased nobody. The whole body sat there confusedly. That gnarled former shoemaker from Connecticut, Roger Sherman, rose to say that they appeared to be "at a full stop." But he supposed that no one intended to break up the Convention without attempting something. It was finally decided to appoint a committee, made up of one member from each state, to "devise and report some compromise." The Convention then adjourned till Thursday, July fifth.[7]

Washington went on to a dinner given at the Indian Queen by the delegates staying there. The "many spacious halls" of the tavern were furnished elegantly in the manner of a gentleman's home. The black servants who waited on well-appointed tables wore blue coats, with sleeves and capes of red, buff waistcoats and breeches, their shirt bosoms ruffled and their hair powdered.[8] However, at the delegates' long table there could have been little gaiety.

When the Convention reconvened, the committee reported a compromise that had been suggested by Franklin. Although each state should be allowed equal representation in the upper house, all the important money bills which supplied the fuel of government should originate in the lower—the truly representative—branch. As leader of the large states, Madison was in no way placated. Principle, he croaked in his weak voice, should never be sacrificed to expediency!

The opposition of the smaller states, he continued, could be ignored, since they would dare neither to seek foreign support nor to go it alone. Many historians believe that Madison almost wrecked the Convention.

Washington was, of course, opposed to states' rights. On the other hand, he was no zealot like the scholarly theorist Madison.* When Madison wanted the Virginia delegation to come out strongly for giving the national legislature such a veto over state legislation as the British government had once possessed, he carefully avoided, as he admitted, consulting Washington. There is good evidence that Washington believed that Franklin's compromise would have to be accepted. For some undisclosed reason he was opposed to the sop being thrown the larger states: he did not believe that money bills should originate solely in the lower house. However, he told Madison that "he gave up his judgment . . . because it was not of very material weight with him and was made an essential point with others who, if disappointed, might be less cordial on other points of real weight."⁹

In the end, such moderation as Washington supported triumphed. After more anguished and tearing debate, a group of unidentified delegates, including the leaders of the large states—was Washington among them?—met privately before the Convention reopened and agreed to Franklin's suggestion. A vote in the Convention backed this agreement, which has therefore gone down in history as "the Great Compromise."

The result was like pulling a stick out from between the spokes of a wheel. The Convention, with Washington now usually in the chair, rolled rapidly along, considering and coming to some kind of agreement on every section of the Virginia Plan as it had been reported out by the committee of the whole. However, the result of so much deliberation, so many motions passed, remained chaotic. The Convention resolved to adjourn for two weeks so that, as Washington put it, a committee "might have time to arrange and draw into method and form the several matters which had been agreed to."¹⁰

Washington, who had in Philadelphia accepted so much hospitality and been able to give so little, was distressed that his carriage was still

---

* This difference was signaled as far back as 1774. Madison was all for war. He denounced Washington's temperate reactions to British provocations as characteristic of a lukewarm patriot.¹¹

laid up at the repairers'. Irresistibly impelled to escape from the city during the recess, he had to ride in someone else's coach, although he could offer his own horses. They drew him and Gouverneur Morris in that gentleman's carriage "to the vicinity of Valley Forge to get trout."[12]

While Morris waded and cast in the streams, Washington, as he noted laconically, rode in solitude "over the whole old cantonment of the American army of the winter [of] 1777 and 8. Visited all the works, which were in ruins." The pursuits of peace had obliterated most of the old streets and leveled the shallow indentations that had been made in building hundreds of cellarless huts. Crops grew where men had suffered. Washington could only find remains of "the encampments in [the] woods where the grounds had not been cultivated."[13]

Three days later, he accompanied a large party to fish near Trenton. He wrote down no comment on riding again through streets where he had seen bloody snow, preferring to record that he had "fished, not very successfully."[14]

It was only when—this was after the Convention had reconvened—he visited "my old encampment" at Whitemarsh, that Washington jotted down what he thought on revisiting an old military site. At Whitemarsh, he "contemplated on the dangers which threatened the American army at that place."[15] Then, Philadelphia had just been captured by the enemy, his army was naked and unfed, and his own position as Commander was being endangered by the Conway Cabal. Now, in a peaceful Philadelphia, the voices debating a strong government were becoming ever more amicable.

The report of the Committee on Detail first established in the American vocabulary the words President, Senate, House of Representatives, and Supreme Court. The extensive proceedings had been honed down into twenty-three articles, seven of which were further subdivided into forty-one sections. This text now became the business of the Convention. Every clause, every word had to be discussed and approved. With Washington in the chair, the debate moved slowly, hour after hour, day after day, from section to section in stifling heat (as before, the windows were kept shut lest a word reach an unofficial ear). There were spurts of anger, of course—shouting voices—but the compromises which had previously been found continued to act as sedatives, and the advance was steady, even surprising. Who, for instance, could three months before have guessed that delegates from the north, the middle, and the south, from small states and large, would agree that the federal government could bypass all state bodies and collect taxes directly from individuals in the local streets and fields? It was, indeed, the principle of direct contact between citizen and nation not only in taxes but in judicial proceedings and voting rights that was the Convention's major invention for establishing unity.

Although the delegates, all possessors of property, agreed to forbid the states to print money or pass laws that would impair the validity of contracts, the basic political rights of the poor were not violated. In what was a stunningly radical departure, no property qualifications were established for voting or even for holding office. Leaving this crucial matter to the will of the individual states may have been in part dictated by the need to get the Constitution ratified by the people, but there was more to it than that. As Clinton Rossiter wrote in a masterly passage: "We cannot begin to understand the mind of a man like Washington unless we recognize his consuming belief in the existence of a common, enduring interest of the whole community that encompassed and yet rose above all private interests, that held out the hand of peace, order, and welfare to all men of all classes, and that provided the grand context of liberty, stability, and progress within which each man could pursue his own version of happiness."[16]

Down the months that the Convention met, the issue that cut closest to Washington's personal emotions was the establishment of the executive. If, as was strongly urged, this turned out to be a committee of three men (one from each major section of the country), Washington could surely stay home at Mount Vernon while others served. But if there were a single and powerful President, no one doubted who would be called first.

Whatever were his private desires, Washington's belief in a powerful government urged a strong executive. He voted with the Virginia delegation for a single President; opposed having the executive elected by the legislature rather than directly by the people; and wished to set the legislative vote necessary to override a Presidential veto at three-quarters rather than two-thirds. He showed his very special concern with the Presidency by making his only handwritten corrections on the official account of the Convention in an effort to clarify the highly complicated method of Presidential election—through an electoral college—which was one of the more cumbersome compromises between those who desired and those who feared popular sovereignty.[17]

The delegates, who had suffered under George III and been frightened by the long history of kings, gave the President an amazing amount of power. Although laws were to be established by the legislature rather than executive fiat, the Constitution allowed the Presidency to be held by a single man unencumbered with any board of officially created advisers, occupying a four-year term almost independently of the other governmental branches, indefinitely re-electable (for a lifetime, it could be), and removable from office only for treason or criminal behavior. He was even made, as any tyrant would wish to be, commander in chief of the military forces, not excluding the militia once they were called into the federal service. These decisions were thus explained by Pierce Butler, a delegate from Maryland: "Many of the members cast their eyes towards General Washington as President, and shaped their ideas of the powers to be given to a President by their opinions of his virtue."[18] Historians agree that Washington's personal prestige went far towards inspiring the Constitutional provisions for a strong Presidency. Because of his very existence, Washington had done much to shape the office even before he occupied it.

Paraphrasing closely a statement that had been made to the Convention by Franklin, Washington wrote Lafayette that he could not foresee "the least danger that the President will by any practicable intrigue ever be able to continue himself one moment in office, much less perpetuate himself in it but in the last stage of corrupted morals and political depravity; and even then there is as much danger that any other species of domination would prevail. Though, when a people shall become incapable of governing themselves and fit for a master, it is of little consequence from what quarter he comes."[19]

According to the Articles of Confederation, any alteration in the government set up by that document would require a unanimous vote of the states. But at the Constitutional Convention one state had not even been represented. In providing for specially elected state conventions to ratify the Constitution, the delegates also provided that the government would become operative within the territories that agreed after only a proportion of the states had ratified. In this more radical than most of the delegates, Washington wished that proportion to be a simple majority: seven. The Convention decided on nine.

By September 8, the Convention came to the salubrious conclusion that they could now appoint a "Committee of Style" to put into final form what had been agreed to. Four days later, the committee made its report. Printed copies were given all the members. All followed the text with their eyes as the report was read, but glanced up at every pause to read each other's faces. Looking down from his dais, Washington was delighted to conclude that the delegates were on the whole better pleased than they had expected to be.[20]

The Convention now saw a hope of adjournment. Although the clauses were again considered one by one, discussions of proposed changes were short and the votes quick. Almost no important alterations were made, and on September 15, after Washington had served for four months and one day, the Convention was prepared to take a single, final vote on the entire document. But first they had to hear three dissenters: George Mason and Peyton Randolph of Virginia, and Elbridge Gerry of Massachusetts.

The dissenters expatiated on various matters concerning which they had already been voted down. Mason's overall conclusion that the projected government would end either in "a monarchy or a corrupt, tyrannical aristocracy" could only bring to Washington's face a worried and angry frown as a preview of what seemed to him the irrational opposition the Constitution would have to face.

Mason's defection, indeed, created for Washington a problem of personal loyalty. The stooped, studious Virginian, his close neighbor ever since Washington had inhabited Mount Vernon, had been, in those difficult years when the Revolution was brooding but had not truly broken, his political mentor. The reaction of the two longtime associates to their disagreement over the Constitution was so strong that their friendship was permanently shattered.*

Mason's suggestion, in his speech of opposition, that the Constitution be prefaced, to protect the people from governmental encroachments, with a "bill" listing their rights, was given short shrift by the hurrying delegates, who considered such a bill unnecessary on the ground that, since all rights naturally belonged to the people, everything not specifically granted was automatically reserved to them. A

---

* As Mason later fought ratification by Virginia, Washington first blamed his old friend's actions on the malign influence of Richard Henry Lee (who had during the Revolution tried to unseat Washington as Commander in Chief) and then on Mason's "pride" and "want of manly candor" which kept him from retracting.[21]

bill might, indeed, have the opposite effect from that intended by being interpreted to limit the people's rights to those listed.

Randolph moved, with Mason as seconder, that the state conventions which would consider the Constitution be requested to prepare amendments which would then be submitted to another national Constitutional Convention. The existing document, Mason argued, was "formed without the knowledge or idea of the people. A second convention will know more of the sense of the people. . . . It was improper to say to the people, take this or nothing."[22]

In Washington's view, a second convention could create only chaos, since the amendments to which the various delegates would be tied by their state conventions would be mutually contradictory. The people would, in truth, have to take the existing document or nothing. This fact, Washington believed, would be emotionally the strongest argument for ratification. He hoped that there would be wide agreement with the sentiment Charles Pinckney announced from the floor. Although the document was not perfect, Pinckney stated, "apprehending the danger of a general confusion and an ultimate decision by the sword, he should give the plan his support."[23]

In their eagerness to finish, the delegates remained in their seats for seven hours, without food or drink. It was six in the evening, so Madison noted, before the two crucial votes were taken. On the scheme for proposing a second convention, "all the states answered, 'No.' On the question to agree to the Constitution as amended, all the states, 'Aye.' The Constitution was then ordered to be engrossed, and the House adjourned."[24]

The engrossed document still had to be finally approved, and signed by all the agreeing delegates. On Monday, August 17, the Convention held what was hoped would be its final session. Franklin had written a speech pointing out that no man was infallible and appealing for unanimous support despite any continuing individual reservations. This was read for the aging statesman, and then Franklin, rising shakily to his feet, moved that the Constitution be signed.

Before the vote was taken, Washington finally broke his months-old official silence. His view of the nation did not permit him to care much about state divisions because when his mind left the very big it swung to the very small. The neighborhood was the political unit with which he was most familiar and he felt very strongly its importance. He seems to have foreseen that many people would fear that their interests would be lost in a government too big and too far away. He said (so Madison noted), "Although his situation had hitherto restrained him from offering his sentiments on questions depending in the house, and it might be thought ought now to impose silence on him, yet he could not forbear expressing" his belief that forty thousand was too large a number of citizens to be represented by a single man in the House of Representatives. If the number were reduced to thirty thousand, that would increase "security for the rights and interests of the people. . . . Late as the present moment was for admitting amendments, he thought this of so much consequence that it would give much satisfaction to see it adopted."[25]

Although the smaller number had previously been voted down, it was now unanimously accepted.

The question then came up of what should be done with the records of the Convention. If they became public, it was pointed out, "a bad use would be made of them by those who would wish to prevent the adoption of the Constitution." There was no official repository where they could be locked up. Washington had, in his own person, supplied many needs of the young nation that had not yet created public institutions. He was now to supply another. The Convention voted to put their records in his care. He asked for guidance on what he should do with them. The vote was that he should hold them "subject to the order of Congress," if such a body should be "formed under the Constitution."[26]

Then, as Washington wrote in his diary, "the Constitution received the unanimous assent of eleven states and Colonel Hamilton's from New York (the only delegate from thence in Convention) and was subscribed to by every member present except Governor Randolph and Colonel Mason from Virginia, and Mr. Gerry from Massachusetts.

"The business being thus closed, the members adjourned to the City Tavern, dined together and took a cordial leave of each other; after which I returned to my lodgings, did some business with and received the papers from the Secretary of the Convention, and retired to meditate on the momentous work which had been executed after not less than five, for a large part of the time six, and sometimes seven hours sitting every day, except Sundays and the ten days adjournment . . . for more than four months."[27]

To Lafayette, he wrote wearily that the Constitution "is now a child of fortune, to be fostered by some and buffeted by others. What will be the general opinion on, or the reception of it, is not for me to decide, nor shall I say anything for or against it. If it be good, I suppose it will work its way good. If bad, it will recoil on the framers."[28]

Washington's carriage being at last mended, he set out for Mount Vernon, but, as the early autumn landscape jolted by his windows, he could not relax. He worried about some hounds a Captain Morris had given him. He had been sent a list of names but no hints as to which dog bore which appellation. He had appealed vainly from Philadelphia for identifying marks. Now from his lodgings at the Head of Elk (where General Howe's British army had once landed), he urgently begged that the information be sent him "by the first post after this letter shall have reached you." Otherwise, "I shall find myself at a loss. . . . Though I had eight names, I might not apply one right."[29]

The next morning he found that the Elk River was too high to be forded. However, he could not bear to wait. He sent his carriage inching across "an old, rotten, and long-disused bridge." Suddenly, "one of my horses fell fifteen feet at least, the other very near following, which, had it happened, would have taken the carriage with baggage along with him and destroyed the whole effectually. However, by prompt assistance of some people at a mill just by, and great exertion, the first horse was disengaged from his harness, the second prevented from going quite through and drawn off and the carriage rescued from hurt."[30] General Washington could proceed on his passionate journey to regain that peace which he suspected was now forever lost.

12

The New Constellation
of This Hemisphere

T O secure adoption of the Constitution in the nine states required to make it operative—and the thirteen states necessary
for unity and peace on the continent—was a more formidable
if less creative task than the activity at the Constitutional Convention
itself. Monroe, in writing Jefferson, assessed Washington's role: "Be
assured, his influence carried this government."[1] With Monroe's
judgment, it would be hard to find disagreements either among the
supporters and opponents of the Constitution at that time or among
historians ever since. Yet Washington's influence was exerted in a
way as far from modern publicity techniques as is conceivably possible.

At "the first moment after my return" from Philadelphia to Mount
Vernon, Washington sent copies of the proposed Constitution to three
key Virginia leaders: Patrick Henry, Benjamin Harrison, and Thomas
Nelson. His identical covering letters stated that he would add "no
observations; your own judgment will at once discover the good and
the exceptionable parts of it, and your experience of the difficulties
which have ever arisen when attempts have been made to reconcile
such variety of interests and local prejudices as pervade the several
states will render explanation unnecessary. I wish the Constitution
which is offered had been made more perfect, but I sincerely believe it
is the best that could be obtained at this time; and, as a constitutional
door is opened for amendment hereafter, the adoption of it under the
present circumstances of the Union is, in my opinion, desirable."

In the second and final paragraph of these letters, Washington heated up, but only a little. "From a variety of concurring accounts it appears to me that the political concerns of this country are, in a manner, suspended by a thread," he wrote, and then switched rapidly from advocate to reporter: "The Convention has been looked up to by the reflecting part of the community with a solicitude which is hardly to be conceived, and [it is believed] that, if nothing had been agreed on by that body, anarchy would soon have ensued, the seeds being richly sown in every soil. I am, etc."[2]

When Henry and Harrison wrote back that they could not bring themselves to support the Constitution, Washington responded with no further argument. After the controversy had finally been decided, he explained to Harrison that his silence had not been due to any lessening of friendship because of their disagreement: the differences in men's minds as in their faces "both being the work of nature are equally unavoidable." The explanation was that "I did not incline to appear as a partisan. . . . For it was my sincere wish that the Constitution . . . might, after a fair and dispassionate investigation, stand or fall according to its merits or demerits."[3]

"I defy any anti-Federalist," Washington stated on another occasion, "to say with truth that I ever wrote to or exchanged a word with him on the subject of the new Constitution," unless the subject was "forced on me in a manner not to be avoided." Unwilling to "obtrude my opinions with a view to influence the judgment of anyone," Washington expressed his convictions only to those of his usual correspondents who could be considered—even if their flagging convictions needed bolstering—already on the federal side. Thus, when Madison urged him to throw his weight into the dubious battle in Massachusetts, he answered, "I have no regular correspondent in Massachusetts; otherwise, as the occasional subject of a letter, I should have had no objection to the communication of my sentiments." Then it occurred to him "that General Lincoln and myself frequently interchanged letters." He was soon writing Lincoln: "No one *can* rejoice more than I do at every step the people of this great country take to preserve the Union."[4]

If men to whom it was natural for him to write chose to show their friends the political passages in his letters, that, Washington considered, was their responsibility. To Lafayette, he stated that he would express his sentiments "without reserve, although by passing through the post offices they should become known to all the world." However, when he forwarded to Stuart, the family representative in the Virginia legislature, copies of the propaganda publication later known as *The Federalist*, he cautioned, "I would [not] have it known that they are sent by *me* to *you* for promulgation."[5]

Since the problem was public education, Washington felt that "good pens" were an urgent need on the federal side. However, he himself had "no inclination and still less abilities for scribbling." He was outraged when Colonel Charles Carter, to whom he had written a letter primarily about "wolf dogs, wolves, sheep, experiments in farming, etc., etc., etc.," extracted from the text its one political paragraph, which he sent to a Baltimore newspaper. In the manner of those days, the paragraph was picked up by other gazettes until it had run through almost all the papers on the continent. Washington's annoyance at being put in the position of proselytizing was seconded by literary embarrassment: had he written for publication, he would "have taken some pains to dress the sentiments . . . in less exceptionable language" and would have assigned reasons for what was baldly stated. "You have," he wrote angrily to Carter, "provided food for strictures and criticisms." However, he made no effort to remedy the situation with a better-composed public statement.[6]

To the indications which streamed into Mount Vernon that the people expected Washington to be the first President and that this confidence was a major force for the acceptance of the Constitution, Washington turned as deaf an ear as he could; for months, there is no mention of the matter in his letters. He remained, as perhaps never before in his energetic and gregarious life, altogether in his own neighborhood. "I have not been ten miles from home since my return to it from Philadelphia," he wrote in February 1788, and he repeated this information in letter after letter as if it were a magic spell that would enable him to continue to fend off the world. Most days, he made the circuit as usual of the five home farms, his fishery, his ferry, his mill. He took an inventory of his animals. He scratched away at his agricultural journal. However, he could not keep his attention fixed. The Constitution, he wrote, seemed to have absorbed all lesser matters. There was "nothing interesting or entertaining in this quarter to communicate, our faces being turned to the eastward for news."[7]

The first steps were easily taken. The Continental Congress forwarded the call for ratifying conventions to the states, and by the end of the year all the states, except of course Rhode Island, had set times and places for the election and subsequent convening of delegates. However, Washington was informed that these acts represented little more than passing the buck: it was at the state conventions, where binding decisions would be reached, that the opposition would unmask its batteries.[8]

The Constitution has become so deified that moderns find it difficult to realize how it was viewed at the time of its composition, even by its framers. Each one of these had been forced to give in on various matters against his interest or his judgment; every Founding Father had strong objections to parts of the compromise. These objections, it was expected, would reappear in the various regional conventions.

No claim was made that the document was perfect. Indeed, the letter of transmittal to Congress which the Convention had prepared and Washington, as President, had signed claimed merely that the Constitution was needed and was the best that could be worked out under the circumstances. When combined with the policy Franklin had urged—no delegate should specify his objections lest he give ammunition to the opposition—this approach supplied supporters with an effectively flexible stance.[9] Washington may well have seen a parallel to the first year of the Revolution, when the immediate objective was clear—to oppose British tyranny—but many long-range aspects of the effort were cloaked in a conciliatory vagueness that enabled people of different opinions to stand side by side. In any case, Washington was scrupulous never to add to his admissions that the document had flaws any hint as to where he considered those flaws lay.

It is clear that, from the moment he came home, Washington was convinced that ratification of the text as it stood offered the best alternative to chaos. Yet there rises from his correspondence during the months directly after the Convention an aura of unhappiness with the result. This is, of course, partly to be explained by the unavoidable conclusion that the office of President was a menace to his personal peace. But he seems also to have wondered whether the recommended government could successfully steer its way between the flanking precipices of tyranny and anarchy.

As he interrogated visitors to Mount Vernon and read the flood of polemic literature that the controversy over the Constitution incited, Washington was motivated not only by an anxiety to follow events, but also by his own desire to be further educated and persuaded. "As far as the frailty of nature would permit," he wrote, he had studied with complete "candor," the arguments put forward "to shake the proposed government." Almost all seemed to him addressed not to reason but "the passions of the people."[10]

His "long and laborious investigation . . . resulted in a fixed belief that this Constitution is really in its formation a government of the people; that is to say, a government in which all power is derived from, and, at stated periods, reverts to them; and that, in its operation, it is purely a government of laws, made and executed by the fair substitutes of the people alone. . . .

"Hence I have been induced to conclude that this government must be less obnoxious to well-founded objections than most which have existed in the world. And in that opinion, I am confirmed on three accounts: *first*, because every government ought to be possessed of power adequate to the purposes for which it was instituted; secondly, because no other or greater powers appear to me to be delegated to this government than are essential to accomplish the objects for which it was instituted, to wit, the safety and happiness of the governed; and thirdly, because it is clear to my conception that no government before introduced among mankind ever contained so many checks and such efficacious restraints to prevent it from degenerating into any species of oppression."[11]

When the controversy was at its height, Washington wrote an old friend, "Upon the whole, I doubt whether the opposition to the Constitution will not ultimately be productive of more good than evil. It has called forth, in its defense, abilities which . . . have thrown new light upon the science of government. They have given the rights of man a full and fair discussion, and explained them in so clear and forcible a manner as cannot fail to make a lasting impression upon those who read the best publications on the subject, and particularly the pieces under the signature of Publius."[12] The pieces signed "Publius" are today known as *The Federalist*. As usual, Washington instantly recognized quality.

It is a fascinating addition to our knowledge of the importance of *The Federalist* that the papers had a powerful influence not only on waverers throughout the nation but also on the great man who was to lead and do so much to shape the new government. Another major effect on the future can be read between the lines. Washington had recently written Hamilton a captious letter, criticizing him for getting into a personal squabble with Governor Clinton of New York when unity was so much to be desired. But information that Hamilton had been allied in preparing *The Federalist* with Washington's two friends and advisers Madison and Jay inspired in Washington a renewed warmth towards the old aide from whom he had long been partially estranged. He now wrote Hamilton that the Publius papers would certainly claim "a most distinguished place in my library." He had read every publication he could find on both sides of the Constitutional question "and, without an unmeaning compliment, I will say that I have seen no other so well calculated (in my judgment) to produce conviction. . . . When the transient circumstances and fugitive performances which attended this crisis shall have disappeared, that work will merit the notice of posterity because in it are candidly and ably discussed the principles of freedom and the topics of government, which will always be interesting to mankind so long as they shall be connected in civil society."[13]

As the debate on the Constitution swung into full clamor in all the thirteen states, Washington tried to find personal repose through the conclusion which had enabled him to feel, during the first years of his retirement, no need to interfere in the political confusions under the Confederation: the people would decide correctly. Apart from all complicated considerations, he saw a simplistic argument, convincing and suitable to all minds, which he phrased in four questions: 1. Is the Constitution "preferable to the government (if it can be called one) under which we now live?" 2. Is it probable that a new convention could reach a better agreement? 3. What would be the consequences of non-ratification or long delay? 4. "Is there not a constitutional door open for alterations" when experience showed them necessary?[14]

But would the people be allowed to see this clear picture? Opponents, he felt, were obscuring the issues by alarming "the apprehensions of the ignorant or unthinking" lest their regions or their persons become subject to oppression. He blamed the misrepresentations not only on those who were in fact misguided by local prejudices, but also on men with "sinister views." The latter group he never accurately defined. It seems to have included dishonest debtors who feared laws that would enforce contracts; local politicians afraid that on a national scale their importance would shrink; and demagogues who wished troubled waters to fish in.[15]

Ten days into the new year of 1788, Washington wrote Lafayette a curious blend of overall optimism with specific, practical worry. He began by announcing happily that the only conventions which had so far met—New Jersey, Delaware, and Pennsylvania—had ratified with no hampering objections. Having stated that New England (with the exception, of course, of Rhode Island) "it is believed will cheerfully and fully accept it, and there is little doubt but that the southern states will do the same," Washington added. "In Virginia and New York, its fate is somewhat more questionable." Again pushing all doubts aside, he came to a happy peroration: "Upon this summary view you will perceive, my dear Marquis, the highest probability exists that the proposed Constitution will be adopted by more than nine states at some period early in the coming summer."[16]

Washington enjoyed the thought that "the establishment of an energetic general government will disappoint the hopes and expectations" of Europeans "who are unfriendly to this country." In commenting to Jefferson on what he called the "Assemblée of Notables" that was trying to curb Louis XVI, he wrote proudly, "The rights of mankind, the privileges of the people, and the true principles of liberty seem to have been more generally discussed and better understood throughout Europe since the American Revolution."[17]

Letters from Washington's correspondents in France—Jefferson, Lafayette, Rochambeau, and others—warned of a possible war that would embroil as opponents the nation's co-combatants in the Revolution, England and France. This news, so Washington believed, gave a new urgency to the ratification of the Constitution, since there existed many forces that would tend to draw the United States into such a war. Only a strong central government could "restrain our people within proper bounds."

Washington now saw American policy exactly as he was to see it during his second term as President when the conflicts attendant on the French Revolution finally exploded: "Separated as we are by a world of water from other nations, if we are wise, we shall surely avoid being drawn into the labyrinth of their politics and involved in their destructive wars."[18]

During January, Georgia and Connecticut ratified, bringing the total to five. Massachusetts was next on the tapis—and a state so important that failure there would destroy all. Washington received discouraging prognostications before the Massachusetts convention opened, and as the debate there rolled on, Madison wrote him that the situation was becoming indeed "ominous." Daily, even several times a day, Washington sent horses galloping over the icy roads from Mount Vernon to Alexandria, for letters, for gazettes. "Suspense, of all situations, is the most disagreeable," he complained. But when gazettes arrived, he was horrified to read the speeches of the opposition which, it seemed to him, "would rouse the passions of the most moderate man on earth."* [19]

However, in Massachusetts, as had happened elsewhere, the educational process worked. Delegates who on their arrival were opposed to the Constitution were eventually won over. In the end, the state ratified.

Warnings that the situation was ticklish in Virginia, made Washington urge Madison to come home from his Congressional seat in New York and run for election to the state convention. But in other letters Washington continued to sound notes of aloofness and optimism. Thus to General Lincoln: "There is not perhaps a man in Virginia less qualified than I am to say from his own knowledge and observation what will be the fate of the Constitution here, for I very seldom ride beyond the limits of my own farms and am wholly indebted to those gentlemen who visit me for any information. . . . But from all I can collect, I have not the smallest doubt of its being accepted."[20]

Washington counted heavily on both New Hampshire and Maryland, and maybe also South Carolina, coming in before Virginia decided, which would strengthen the Constitutional cause by eight agreements or perhaps even the ninth needed formally to establish the government in the states that had ratified. His eagerness for information that would confirm or dash these hopes was frustrated by what he described in irritation as the worst winter weather he had ever experienced. When melting ice and snow finally reopened the roads, the news that came in was bad. The sweep for ratification, heretofore

---

* It casts a revealing light on the receptiveness of Washington's mind that he was several times fascinated to the point of fright by arguments in support of causes he considered evil. Concerning the appeal circulated at Newburgh to induce the army to terrorize the civilian authorities, he wrote, "In point of composition, in elegance and force of expression, [it] has rarely been equaled in the English language."[21]

uniformly successful, had received a check. New Hampshire had "baffled all calculation" by postponing her convention. For the first time, Washington expressed real worry about Virginia's decision. It would be argued that New Hampshire was waiting on Virginia, and that thus Virginia, far from being caught in a tide which if opposed might isolate her, was in a position to block the Constitution altogether. Gleeful orators were telling the people that the new government was not "so generally approved of in other states as they had been taught to believe."[22]

More news: despite the favorable action at the state convention which had met in Philadelphia with great haste (partly for the purpose of keeping them away) the Pennsylvanians who lived west of the Susquehanna were alive with "rancor and activity" against the Constitution, which they feared would enslave them to moneylenders and the opponents of free navigation of the Mississippi. Washington knew that similar sentiment was at least latent in western Virginia, which (since it included what subsequently became Kentucky) was populous enough to swing the balance in the state convention. He could only hope that the insurgent Pennsylvanians were "generally speaking, persons of too little importance to endanger the general welfare of the Union by extending their influence to other states, or even any further in their own than to a few counties, or over persons whose characters, dispositions, and situations are conformable to theirs."[23]

His worry over this situation brought with it another worry: the Virginia opponents of the Constitution were a frighteningly formidable group. His secretary Lear wrote nervously of "the persuasive rhetoric of a Mason, a Lee, a Henry, or a Randolph." It was to be hoped that their eloquence would mean less to Virginians than "the favorable decisions of other states."[24]

But then a movement developed in Maryland to have the convention of that state adjourn until Virginia had decided. In his anguish, Washington passed beyond his scruples, writing a hortatory letter to a state official. Thomas Johnson was, it is true, an old friend and Washington assumed that he did not need persuading to be in favor of the Constitution, but the fact remained that he was Governor of Maryland. In his letter to Johnson, Washington admitted that he might have exceeded "the proper limit." If so, "my motive must excuse me. It is that in *peace* and *retirement* I may see this country rescued from the danger which is pending and rise into respectability maugre the intrigues of its public and private enemies."

His message to Johnson was that the proposed postponement in Maryland was a scheme worked out by the opponents of the Constitution not only in that state but also in Virginia. The delay, following after the action in New Hampshire, would "have the worst tendency imaginable." It might bury the Constitution in Virginia, which meant also in South Carolina and for the whole nation.[25]

More than a month before the Virginia convention was to meet, Washington learned that Maryland had ratified by an overwhelming vote. In reporting to General Lincoln, he summed up his attitude in amusingly self-contradictory sentences: "I never have, for my own part, once doubted of its adoption here, and, if I have at any time been wavering in my opinion, the present appearances and concurrent information would have completely fixed it."[26]

South Carolina came in, which put Virginia in position to make the determining ninth ratification. As he waited for the crucial meeting in his home state to convene, Washington was so overcome with restlessness that he undertook his first extensive trip away from Mount Vernon since he had returned from Philadelphia nine months before. He rode as far as the Susquehanna on inspection of the still-struggling Potomac works, and then set out with Martha in their carriage to visit his mother and sister at Fredericksburg. His mother still had the energy to borrow four guineas, but was otherwise so frail that he did not expect ever "to see her more."[27]

The gentlemen of the neighborhood vied to entertain the General, and his presence on Sunday so overloaded the local church that (as he noted laconically) "the congregation being alarmed without cause, and supposing the gallery at the north end was about to fall, were thrown into the utmost confusion, and in the precipitate retreat to the doors, many got hurt."[28]

Washington was home again by the time the Virginia convention met on June 12. The reports he received from Madison were pessimistic but, as he wrote, "more pleasing than suspense." Soon, however, the picture lightened. As had been the case again and again, discussion and elucidation favored the Constitution. On June 25, Virginia ratified, eighty-nine to seventy-nine, thus making the government operative.

As Washington stood on the porch at Mount Vernon savoring his delight at the news, he heard cannon booming up and down the river, and then the water was suddenly alive with small boats. Jubilant neighbors appeared, to invite him to a festivity the next day at Alexandria, where (as Washington wrote) the citizens were "federal to a man." That night there came a further pounding on the door: New Hampshire had also ratified. The Constitution had been accepted by one more than the number of states needed to establish what Washington hailed as "The New Constellation of This Hemisphere."[29]

When Maryland had been on the point of postponing and it seemed that all might be lost, Washington had confided to his former military aide, the Marylander James McHenry, that he had "meddled . . . in this political dispute less perhaps than a man so thoroughly persuaded as I am of the evils and confusions which will result from the rejection of the proposed Constitution ought to have done."

Washington, so he wrote, was "carefully" preserving "as a last anchor of worldly happiness in old age . . . the 'hope'" that he could disentangle himself from government, live out his life at Mount Vernon. Memories of old tribulations appeared like wounds in his mind. Although usually so courteous to all supplicants he now burst out to a former Revolutionary officer who wished him to reconsider the verdict of an old court-martial: "While riveted to the toils and perplexities inseparable from the commission of Commander in Chief, I sought not to avoid trouble. I shunned not to enter into the minutest investigation of innumerable disagreeable subjects, for unfortunately in our army they were but too numerous and too troublesome to my repose. But to rip open again the disagreeable subjects that seemed to be forever closed with the war and my retirement, I could not think of doing it, unless I would first consent to give up all the prospects of tranquillity which, I flattered myself, awaited the last years of a life that had been devoted almost invariably to the services of others. The sacrifice would be too great and the expectation unreasonable."[30]

In expressing pleasure that Madison was coming home from Congress to run for the Virginia convention, Washington had written, "The consciousness of having discharged that duty which we owe to our country is superior to all other considerations." Yet, although the *Pennsylvania Gazette* repeated a rumor that he would himself run, Washington did not do so. Nor did his fellow Federalists—even when the

Virginia convention seemed aimed at failure—ask him to put in an appearance or take any active part.³¹

The truth was that not only at the Virginia convention but at all the state gatherings, Washington was always present, a force more powerful for being insubstantial as a ghost. There was nothing to strike out at, no one present to argue with, but just the brooding fact that Washington had presided over the Constitutional Convention and been the first to sign. How the opposition had to tack around his invisible presence was revealed by Luther Martin at the Maryland convention: "The name of Washington is far above my praise! I would to Heaven that on this occasion one more wreath had been added to the number of those which are twined around his amiable brow—that those with which it is already surrounded may flourish with immortal verdure, nor wither or fade till time shall be no more, is my fervent prayer." But—³²

The weight that Washington had already thrown on the wheel had set up such tremendous momentum that it continued its major role in keeping the wheel aspin. Had Washington acted further, he might well have confused and impeded the drive by getting caught in little squabbles. That he would furthermore have stirred up resentment because of the very extent of the force he wielded is shown by a rumor that reached him at Mount Vernon concerning the one time he had been goaded into "meddling." Washington heard that Governor Johnson had been so greatly "displeased" with his "officiousness" in pleading with Maryland not to postpone that the Governor had, in pique, urged the state to recommend amendments to the Constitution. Johnson's denial did not obviate the fact that the rumor had started and gained currency.³³

In his original letter to Johnson, Washington had been careful to state that his one motive was to be able to live "*in peace and retirement*" in a happy land. He was, indeed, continually afraid that any public action on his part would make it look as if he were campaigning for the Presidency. As set up by the Constitution, the Presidency had tremendous power. No equivalent office had ever existed on American soil; to many citizens, it seemed unpleasantly reminiscent of George III. Jefferson warned Adams that it was "a bad edition of a Polish king."³⁴ Fears of tyranny, indeed, most clustered around the Presidency, and to these fears the expectation that Washington would be the first incumbent was the best antidote. But supposing Washington, instead of staying quietly on his plantation, had campaigned for the Constitution that would give him so powerful a personal weapon?

In many ways it was brought home to Washington that, despite the passive part he had played, the ratification of the Constitution was regarded across the nation as his personal triumph. This was most startlingly symbolized by a weird object he saw moving on the Potomac very early one morning. It appeared as if either a schooner had been shrunk by witchcraft or a giant was coming up the river in an ordinary-sized ship. Certain it was that the head of the single sailor in a beautifully appointed schooner rose high between the masts. The vessel which eventually drew up at the wharf in front of Mount Vernon proved to be a model, fifteen feet long, of a full-rigged ship. It had been, when pulled along on wheels by four horses, the main feature of a parade celebrating in Baltimore the ratification of the Constitution. Finally, the vessel had been launched on the Chesapeake. Captain Joshua Barry, one of the naval heroes of the Revolution, had sailed it down the bay and up the Potomac as a congratulatory present to Washington from the merchants of Baltimore. The gesture was all the more indicative since Washington's Potomac Canal was in direct opposition to Baltimore's commercial interests.[35]

It was Washington's habit, as he often noted, to retire into himself after great events had taken place and meditate in tranquillity on what he had seen. He hailed the Constitution as "a new phenomenon in the political and moral world, and an astonishing victory gained by enlightened reason over brute force."[36] Yet he also viewed the projected new government in such a larger context as "revisionist" historians express today in arguing that the importance of the change from the Confederation has been overemphasized:

"When the people shall find themselves secure under an energetic government," Washington wrote Lafayette; "when foreign nations shall be disposed to give us equal advantages in commerce from dread of retaliation; when the burdens of war shall be in a manner done away by the sale of western lands; when the seeds of happiness which are sown here shall begin to expand themselves; and when everyone (under his own vine and fig tree) shall begin to taste the fruits of freedom; then all these blessings (for all these blessings will come), will be referred to the fostering influence of the new government. Whereas many causes will have conspired to produce them.

"You see I am not less enthusiastic than ever I have been, if a belief that peculiar scenes of felicity are reserved for this country is to be denominated enthusiasm. Indeed, I do not believe that Providence has done so much for nothing. It has always been my creed that we should not be left as an awful monument to prove 'that mankind, under the most favorable circumstances for civil liberty and happiness, are unequal to the task of governing themselves and therefore made for a master.' "[37]

13

On the Brink

W ASHINGTON considered it his duty "to do whatever might be in my power in favor of those whose misfortunes have been unavoidably brought upon them by no fault of their own." He found himself acutely embarrassed when unable to help such petitioners, and in justifying his inability, he sometimes wrote to comparative strangers letters more revealing than those to his close friends. Indeed, his earliest (June 1788) written reference to the popular expectation that he would be the first President was addressed to one Samuel Hanson, with whom his two nephews, George Steptoe Washington and Lawrence Washington, were staying while they attended the academy at Georgetown. Hanson was not proving very satisfactory—he allowed (as Washington had complained) one of the boys' shirts to be ruined in laundering, and fed them on scraps when he had company to dinner. However, in asking that, as President, Washington appoint him to some office, Hanson had complained of misfortunes.

In his reply, Washington stated that it was *"much more* than possible" that he would not be concerned with any new administration. The subject was "peculiarly distressing and perplexing to me." He felt "the impropriety of my anticipating events [the necessary nine states had not yet ratified] or hazarding opinions . . . however slightly." He hoped Hanson would not regard this letter as "actuated by any prejudice against your pretensions."[1]

Seven months and many job applications later, in January 1789, Washington answered firmly to further prodding from Hanson, that, if circumstances should force him to leave his beloved retirement for "the walks of public life, it is my fixed determination to enter there not only unfettered by promises, but even unchargeable with exacting or feeding the expectation of *any man living* for my assistance to office."[2]

The nine months between the acceptance of the Constitution by the minimum number of states and the actual establishment of the new government were for Washington a period of uneasy drift. He refrained from active participation in national affairs, although they absorbed his mind.

When the New York convention met in July 1788, the news that came in to Mount Vernon indicated that the state would not ratify, which would punch a great hole in the new federation. Although he "did not . . . see the means by which it was to be avoided," Washington could not believe that the state would act so irrationally, and the event proved that he was still assaying correctly the deep flow often hidden under surface rippling. New York did come in. This made for the moment negligible the decision—which Washington considered "unaccountable"—of North Carolina to postpone, and also the expected intransigence of what Washington called "the paper-money junto" of the Rhode Island "anarchy."[3]

However, New York's ratification carried a sting in its tail, by reviving the old bugaboo of a second Constitutional Convention. New York stated that she had only agreed in the fullest confidence of an early amending convention to which the various legislatures would be invited to send recommendations. Washington feared that this would rally the unconvinced opposition that lurked in every state. He still believed that a second convention could only create conflict, since various states would make diametrically opposite recommendations.[4]

The need was to carry the educative process which had started at the Constitutional Convention and been continued at the state conventions more forcibly to the people at large. Towards this end, Washington emerged temporarily from behind his veil of noninterference. He protested violently a new post office regulation which impeded the movement of newspapers at the very moment when "the momentous question of a general government" was under consideration. "The friends of the Constitution," he pointed out, wanted "the public to be possessed of everything that might be printed on both sides of the question." Furthermore, any "suppression of intelligence" could be construed by the enemies of the Constitution as "a wicked trick of policy contrived by an aristocratic junto." He asked angrily whether the postmaster general should not be removed from office.[5]

The old Continental Congress, which had been entrusted with settling the details of establishing the new government, was hung up by a debate over what city should be selected as the provisional capital, to serve until the new government could make its own decision. New York and Philadelphia were the principal contenders. Washington, who wished neither of these to become the permanent capital, favored New York as being less central than Philadelphia; it was less likely to be able to hold on to the government. Washington favored a truly central spot. Had not Madison suggested that the government's final resting place might be on the Potomac near Mount Vernon?[6]

However, his main concern was to get matters settled. Congress, he complained, was hanging "the expectations and patience of the Union on tenterhooks." Finally, Congress did fix on New York. It established the first Wednesday in January for electing Presidential electors. They were to meet on the first Wednesday in February, and the Government was to start rolling the first Wednesday in March.[7]

Not only the electors, but all the senators and representatives had to be chosen. Washington feared that the enemies of the Constitution would attempt to "set everything afloat again" by elevating supporters of the second convention that had been urged by New York. He warned of "persons who, upon finding they could not carry their point by an open attack against the Constitution, have some sinister designs to be silently effected, if possible. But I trust in that Providence which has saved us in six troubles, yea in seven, to rescue us again from any imminent, though unseen, dangers. Nothing, however, on our part ought to be left undone. I conceive it to be of unspeakable importance that whatever there be of wisdom and prudence and patriotism on the continent should be concentered in the public councils at the first outset." He wrote this to General Lincoln, the personal correspondent he had established in Massachusetts, adding, "Heaven is my witness that an inextinguishable desire" for "the felicity of my country . . . is my only motive in making these observations."[8]

Some historians claim that the conflicts Washington was now witnessing represented legitimate differences of interest and presaged the eventual birth of useful political parties. Washington failed to see it that way. He saw a government essential to national peace and prosperity, a government that presented its own machinery for orderly change, being sniped at before it could get started. That the opposing factions—local, ill-informed, or evil—should somehow unite on a national basis was among his nightmares. He was, indeed, outraged when opponents of the Constitution pooled their support behind a single candidate, thus violating the old tradition that a local election was a popularity contest between individuals each running on his personal worth and reputation. The supporters of the Constitution would, he warned grimly, in self-defense have also to combine their votes.[9]

Washington was depressed to hear that his favorite adviser, Madison, had been defeated for the Senate by a vote in the Virginia Assembly. Two candidates considered lukewarm to the Constitution had been preferred. However, Madison was successfully elected to the House, and Washington soon received assurance that Virginia's two new senators had agreed not to push for amendments until defects became actually clear in practice. Other fears dissipated, and, towards the end of January, Washington was able to notify Lafayette "that the elections have been hitherto vastly more favorable than we could have expected, that federal sentiments seem to be growing with uncommon rapidity. . . . I cannot help flattering myself the new Congress, on account of the self-created respectability and various talents of its members, will not be inferior to any assembly in the world."[10]

On his return home from the Constitutional Convention, Washington had "found Mrs. Washington and the family tolerably well, but the fruits of the earth almost entirely destroyed by one of the severest droughts," which had affected particularly a small area around Mount Vernon. He needed *"absolutely"* to buy, for the many mouths he had to feed, six hundred barrels of corn, and feared that he would have to agree to exorbitant prices since he lacked the cash to pay on receipt.[11]

The following summer, so he complained, "rains prevailed beyond what has been known in the memory of man." This produced abundant crops "in most parts of the United States," but not at Mount Vernon, where much of "the soil is mixed with clay and so stiff as to be liable to retain the moisture."[12]

Taxes are always a problem for farmers, since they have to be paid not in goods but in money. Washington was worrying how he would raise cash to meet his taxes on the Mount Vernon plantation when his extensive wilderness lands on the Kanawha, which had been lying quiet like a jewel in a strongbox, suddenly emerged as a frightening liability. A member of the Virginia Assembly from over the mountains notified Washington that the sheriff of Greenbrier County "has a considerable demand upon me for the taxes of my land on the Great Kanawha," and made threats of "proceeding to extremities." Complaining that this was "first intimation directly or indirectly I have had of these taxes," Washington tried desperately to find out what the situation actually was. No county lines had existed when he had explored the then distant acres; he did not know what part of his land was in Greenbrier. Some might be in Botetourt or Montgomery, or indeed in a county whose name he did not know. He sent out desperate queries to find out what taxes he owed where, and whether, indeed, some of his land might not already have been sold by the authorities.[13]

Obviously, he would have to raise at least enough income from his Kanawha lands to pay the taxes on them. But how could this be achieved? He wrote around for the name of a nearby resident he could employ as an agent. Thomas Lewis was recommended. He wrote Lewis, asking him to find tenants whose short-term leases would not permanently encumber eventual sales. Lewis did not reply. He wrote again and finally heard that Lewis had land of his own which he wished to settle. Rather than have no agent close enough to effect something, Washington asked Lewis to represent him on the understanding that the agent would take care of his own land first. Lewis replied that he would be deceiving Washington, since he had been unable to get anyone to live on his own land because of Indian depredations.*

So as not to lose what he was sure would someday be really valuable, Washington managed in April 1788 to send west, in various types of certificates, £107.11.9 to meet the taxes in Greenbrier for 1785 and 1786. He hoped this would keep the sheriff quiet until he could raise more money.[14]

Washington wrote his old friend and neighbor Dr. James Craik, "I never felt the want of money so sensibly since I was a boy of fifteen years old."[15] Then he had been living on a rundown farm with his widowed mother, unable to get away to dances because his horse was

---

* More than a year later, some squatters finally appeared in the region, to the pleasure of legal owners, who felt that their presence added to the value of all the surrounding land.

immobilized by lack of feed. Now, of course, he lived in great luxury. He asked a friend who was traveling to Paris to buy him a fine watch, and advanced £25 in specie. He was building, according to plans sent him by the English agricultural reformer Arthur Young, a brick barn which he boasted would be "the largest and most convenient one in this country." He offered a nephew the free use of a house he owned in Alexandria, and rather than "distress" the heirs of his brother-in-law, Bartholomew Dandridge, took for a debt that estate owed him payment in "land which I do not want in lieu of money which I really do want."[16]

As his financial situation continued to go from bad to worse, Washington recognized that, unless some radical change occurred, he would be forced to practice "frugality and economy," virtues which, he added piously, were "undoubtedly commendable."[17] But a way out was becoming ever more likely.

That peculiar institution, the Electoral College, which on its first spin-around worked more or less as the Founders intended it to do, removed from Washington the necessity of stating whether or not he was a candidate for President. Gentlemen were elected to the College by their own names and supposedly in their own right, to vote when the Electors gathered as their judgments then dictated. If a man did promise in advance that he would support Washington, that was not Washington's responsibility.

Again and again, Washington explained that he would not anticipate matters by making up his mind on the Presidency until the College had acted. Perhaps he would not be selected; he did not wish to place himself in the situation of the fox who was reduced to saying that the grapes he had vainly tried to reach were sour. If the College did offer the post to him, he would decide how to act on the basis of the situation as it then appeared.[18]

But Washington must have realized that, since it was universally assumed that he would serve as President, his silence was, in effect, consent. Indeed, the difference between his behavior in this situation and his behavior when he had been worried as to whether he should attend the Constitutional Convention was as between darkness and light. On the earlier occasion he had asked the advice of all his friends, and had suffered from anguishes of indecision and ill-health. It was then that the decisive plunge had been taken. He had, it is true, returned to his acres and his avocations, but his emotions and also his position in history had remained irrevocably entangled with the government in the establishment of which he had already played so important a role.

As his Constitutional Convention beckoned, Washington had sunk into ever deeper depression. Now his spirits were on the rise. The Convention had been a chip thrown down on a gambling table. It might have been carried off—and his own reputation with it—by an unfortunate turn of the wheel. Since then, the idea of a federal government had prospered in a way that seemed truly miraculous. It was as if the Constitution, surrounded by the arguments that brought it into focus, was a beam of light which, wherever it was turned on the darkness of local prejudice, dispelled the shadows. If many shadows remained in corners that the light had not yet touched, it seemed only necessary to enlarge the torch.

Washington was being lured by the pleasure of taking part in an undertaking he considered glorious. "You will permit me to say," he wrote the Irish patriot Sir Edward Newenham, "that a greater drama is now acting on this theater than has heretofore been brought on the American stage, or any other in the world. We exhibit at present the novel and astonishing spectacle of a whole people deliberating calmly on what form of government will be most conducive to their happiness." The Americans were approaching "nearer to perfection than any government hitherto instituted among men."[19] But he knew that only the bare foundations of the government had been established. He could not fail to be excited by the opportunity to lead in raising a daring and just structure for the emulation of all mankind.

Washington did still write, it is true, of the great sacrifice he would make in renouncing his hope of living out "an unclouded evening after the stormy day of life." He could still shudder dramatically, "in a kind of gloom of mind," at the prospect of "entering upon an unexplored field enveloped on every side with clouds and darkness." But he was at least equally worried that he would be "chargeable with levity and inconsistency" in accepting the Presidency after his ancient renunciation of all public office. He wondered whether the world would give him credit for the "unfeigned reluctance," the "real diffidence" with which he viewed the Presidency. Might he not be accused of "rashness and ambition"? Sometimes he feared that he should so accuse himself. He appealed to "the Great Searcher of Human Hearts" as "witness that

I have no wish which aspires beyond the humble and happy lot of living and dying a private citizen on my own farm." Surely he was consenting to his duty rather than giving way to "egotism."[20]

Washington frankly admitted that there existed a financial lure. He intended, it is true, to continue his refusal to receive any public salary. Yet his expenses as President would be paid. This would handle the lion's share of his own support and that of his family. His entertaining would clearly be official entertaining. Since "my means are not adequate to the expense at which I have lived since my retirement to what is called private life," only what he disingenuously called (even in this context) "the event that I dread" would rescue him from "the necessity" of applying those distasteful virtues, "frugality and economy."[21]

Closer to his own flesh was a haunting sense that "I am passing rapidly into the *vale of years,* where the genial warmth of youth that fires its votary with a generous enthusiasm becomes extinct and where the cheerlessness of the prospect often infects the animal spirits." Seeing America prosperous, he continued lugubriously, would be "a consolation amidst the increasing infirmities of nature and the growing love of retirement."[22] But why seek consolations in retirement? He was only fifty-six and comfortably rode twenty miles almost every morning. Why not wash away the specter of old age in floods of purposeful activity?

Discussion by the Federalists* of whom they should support for Vice President pointed at John Adams. Adams was from Massachusetts, and the conception, as old as the Revolutionary cause, of always balancing a man from Virginia with a man from the leading New England state, was still good politics. Furthermore, Adams, unlike his chief Massachusetts rival for the office, John Hancock, was a strong supporter of the Constitution. He had shown great ability as a political leader. But what would Washington's reaction be?

In a letter to Jefferson, Madison confided that some of his col-

---

* At this time, the terms Federalist and anti-Federalist connoted supporters or opponents of the Constitution. With the general acceptance of the new government, the distinction faded to give way to a new use of the same terms. The Federalists became the more conservative political party, opposed by the Jeffersonian Republicans (who were also sometimes called Democrats). Madison, to take a not untypical example, was a Federalist according to the first meaning of the term, but opposed to Federalism according to the second.

leagues, recalling Adams's "cabal during the war against General Washington" and considering the "extravagant self-importance" of the Massachusetts leader, concluded that Washington's attitude towards having Adams as his "second" would hardly be "cordial."[23]

General Lincoln undertook to mediate with his former Commander in Chief. The true intention of those who opposed Adams, Lincoln wrote Washington, was to get an anti-Federalist into the Vice Presidency. The strategy of the opposition was to insinuate that, if Adams became Vice President, "Your Excellency must bid adieu to all future happiness in public life." Lincoln went on to insist that Adams knew and acknowledged every "virtue in your character which the most intimate of your friends have discovered."[24]

It was, of course, impossible for Washington to forget how much trouble had been made him during the Revolution by Adams's determination to keep the army organization temporary and weak, lest a standing army dominate the government, lest Washington make himself king. Now, in replying to Lincoln, Washington did not mention Adams by name. He wrote that, in his desire not to be accused of "electioneering," he had not, to the best of his recollection, discussed the Vice Presidency with anyone. He assumed the official would come from Massachusetts. He assumed the Electors would choose "a true Federalist." Should he himself become President, whoever the states chose would not be disagreeable to him in (he added) his official capacity: "If I had any predilection, I flatter myself I possess patriotism enough to sacrifice it at the shrine of my country."

Lincoln responded by sending Washington some letters by Adams about the Revolution which had been published. Washington replied that Adams had overestimated the strength of the Continental Army (this had been one of his standing irritations during the war) but that the total performance was more "a subject for admiration" than otherwise.

Over two months later, on January 31, Washington notified Lincoln that he had confided to some Electors that the selection of Adams "would be entirely agreeable to me and that I considered it to be the only certain way to prevent the election of an anti-Federalist."[25]

Although the Electoral College had not yet met, Washington was by the start of 1789 in full preparation for the Presidency. He drew up elaborate instructions for the management of his farms in his absence, and engaged in active planning of his future policies.

It is an amazing fact that Washington, the so often diffident, gave no signs of being plagued by the self-doubts that had made his acceptance of the military leadership so painful. He wrote, indeed, to Lafayette, "I think I see a *path* as clear and as direct as a ray of light which leads to the attainment" of "permanent felicity to the Commonwealth."[26]

Washington did not feel that he was undertaking the leadership of an invalid nation which needed to be sustained with elaborate nostrums. He envisioned the United States as a young and growing giant, stupidly entangled in a hampering net. The major necessity was merely to cut away the confining strands. As he put it to Newenham, "We are surrounded by the blessings of nature. . . . In short, it seems as if we should want little besides common sense and common honesty to make us a great and a happy people." For Lafayette, he defined "the four great and essential pillars of public felicity" as "harmony, honesty, industry, and frugality."[27]

With the assistance of Humphreys, Washington prepared a seventy-three-page document which, although it was never delivered, was intended as his inaugural address. The text has been the victim of the most horrendous historical vandalism.

Jared Sparks, in editing the first compendium of Washington's papers, concluded that not only the document, itself, which was all in Washington's hand, but the very fact of its existence should be suppressed. On May 22, 1827, he asked the elderly Madison's approval. Relying on his memory of what he had seen thirty-eight years before, Madison replied, "I concur without hesitation in your remarks on the speech of seventy-three pages and the expediency of not including it among the papers selected for the press. Nothing but extreme delicacy towards the author of the draft, who was no doubt Colonel Humphreys, can account for the respect shown so strange a production." Sparks was thus encouraged not only to omit the draft from his edition but to mutilate it: he cut it up, giving fragments sometimes as small as three lines to autograph collectors. Despite assiduous efforts to reassemble it, between a half and two thirds of the manuscript is still lost.[28]

Even if it had been originally drafted by Humphreys, the fact that the speech existed in Washington's autograph reveals that the General made it his own.*

Washington wrote Madison in February 1787 that, "if it should be your *own* desire," he might discuss the speech with Humphreys. This Madison seems to have done while staying at Mount Vernon later that month. It may well have been Madison who persuaded Washington to abandon the address. Certainly, he helped Washington prepare the shorter speech that was actually delivered.[29]

Why did Sparks and Madison, when they conferred in the 1820's, decide to suppress the speech? It might have been because the text seemed to indicate a greater desire than Washington was to show when President to effect the balance of power by executive leadership of the legislative. Or the objection could have centered on the lengthy defense, cast in an unusually personal vein,† against possible charges that ambition had made Washington break his word that he would retire from public life, a defense not altogether dignified, which might encourage the very suspicions it was aimed at undermining. There remains, of course, the possibility that the mystery will be eternal; that in cutting up the manuscript, Sparks burned the pages he found most unsuited to his vision of Washington.‡

Even in its mutilated form, the discarded inaugural is an extremely important document. If the sections that remain are combined with passages from various of Washington's letters, a good idea may be achieved of the ideas he carried with him to the Presidency.

---

* Since Washington was himself capable of striking poetic metaphors, it is hard to identify Humphreys's contribution. However, the professed poet may have composed: "If the blessings of Heaven showered thick around us should be spilled on the ground or converted to curses through the fault of those for whom they are intended, it would not be the first instance of folly or perverseness in shortsighted mortals."[30]

† Here is an unusually interesting personal passage: "In the next place, it will be recollected that the Divine Providence hath not seen fit that my blood should be transmitted or my name perpetuated by the endearing, though sometimes seducing, channel of immediate offspring. I have no child for whom I could wish to make a provision—no family to build in greatness upon my country's ruins."[31]

‡ Although the copies of letters and other documents which Washington kept among his own papers usually had their doubles that went out into the world, culling of the papers by Sparks presents the most frightening possibility that censorship might have forever altered the record. A common anecdote, that J. P. Morgan bought and burnt a packet of Washington's letters which he considered damaging to the reputation of the hero, is considered wildly unlikely by those most familiar with the financier's behavior; as an avid collector and no prude, he would have been more likely especially to cherish such documents.[32]

The most immediate need, Washington believed, was to assuage the worries of lukewarm citizens and also win the active anti-Federalists over to the government. The Constitution, he pointed out, was self-cleansing because it contained a provision for amendment.³³ To Jefferson, Washington wrote that he did not have "*much* objection" to any of the amendments proposed by the various states except those that would deprive the government of necessary revenue by forbidding direct taxation. In his undelivered speech, Washington urged against starting the government in a mood of tinkering. It would be more intelligent to view "this complicated machine . . . fully in movement" before rearranging the existing checks and powers. However, rapid action should be taken to add to the Constitution what was being widely agitated for: such a Bill of Rights as would give "extreme satisfaction."³⁴

There should be no squabbles within the legislature or other branches of the government that would encourage latent squabbles outside: as in the Constitutional Convention, the spirit should be "accommodation," the result, as far as possible "unanimity." "Rectitude" in the behavior of all officials would elevate minds and disarm criticism. Sectional feeling could be washed away: "A perseverance in temperate measures and good dispositions will produce such a system of national policy as shall be mutually advantageous to all parts of the American Republic."³⁵

Washington felt that the first contribution he could himself make lay in achieving wise and conciliatory appointments to federal offices. This, he realized, would not be easy. His habitual desire to serve the needs and hopes of everyone who applied to him would have to be sternly, even painfully, curbed. That his selections should reflect a fair geographic distribution endlessly complicated matters. In a domain which extended for fifteen hundred miles, his information concerning "the characters of persons" must often be "so imperfect as to make me liable to make mistakes." He ruminated, "So necessary is it, at this crisis, to conciliate the good will of the people, and so impossible is it, in my judgment, to build the edifice of public happiness but upon their affections," that "a single disgust excited in a particular state . . . might, perhaps, raise a flame of opposition that could not easily, if ever, be extinguished."³⁶

Having himself been nipped by inflation on one hand and squeezed, on the other, by the shortage of any adequate circulating medium,

Washington recognized that a primary practical necessity was "to extricate my country from the embarrassments in which it is entangled through want of credit."[37] The scarcity of cash was, indeed, "one of the numerous evils which arise from the want of a general regulating power. For in a country like this, where equal liberty is enjoyed, where every man may reap his own harvest, which by proper attention will afford him much more than is necessary for his own consumption, and where there is so ample a field for every mercantile and mechanical exertion, if there cannot be money found to answer the common purposes of education, not to mention the necessary commercial circulation, it is evident that there is something amiss in the ruling political power, which requires a steady, regulating, and energetic hand to correct and control."

This passage, in which he expressed his belief that it was the government's responsibility to foster a healthy economy, was written in April 1788, well before Washington renewed close contact with his onetime aide, Hamilton. Washington went on to reveal that at this time he visualized the government's role as little more than that of a referee: If "property was well secured, faith and justice well preserved, a stable government well administered, and confidence restored, the tide of wealth and population would flow to us from every part of the globe, and, with a due sense of the blessings, make us the happiest people on earth." As he put it succinctly on another occasion, prosperity would come as "the natural harvest of good government."* [38]

Americans, Washington was convinced, would long remain an agricultural people—this was demonstrated by the way European artisans turned to farming on their arrival in the United States. The basic pattern would undoubtedly continue to be the exchange of "our staple commodities" for manufactured goods. Yet surely this pattern could be ameliorated to the American advantage. During 1788, he had agreed with Jefferson that "the introduction of anything which will divert our attention from agriculture must be extremely prejudicial if not ruinous

---

* Among the documents Humphreys collected for his projected biography of Washington are notes on Adam Smith's *Wealth of Nations*. In Humphreys's handwriting, they may well have been prepared for Washington's use. A typical entry: "Volume 2nd, page 27. An excellent sentiment, respect the effort natural to all men to endeavor bettering their condition—'It is this effort, protected by law and allowed by liberty, to assert itself in the manner that is most advantageous, which had maintained the progress of England towards opulence and improvement in all former times.' "

to us."[39] But within the last year he had become interested in further-ing American manufactures.

Washington had recognized a way of signalizing this concern when he had happened to see a newspaper advertisement offering woolen cloth manufactured in Hartford, Connecticut. He wrote General Knox to procure for him enough such cloth "to make me a suit of clothes." His intention was to wear the American-made suit at his inauguration. However, since all woolen cloth of any quality had always been imported from Europe, he urged Knox to proceed cautiously. If the dye proved not to be well fixed or the cloth not "very fine," Knox was to order "some color mixed in grain" that would make imperfections less visible. When the cloth arrived, Washington was delighted to find that it "exceeds my expectation."[40]

To arguments that manufacturing would weaken America by taking men off the farms, Washington replied that much of the work could be done by women and children. Spinning wheels could be placed in homes, and machinery either invented or imported that would do the work of many hands.[41]

What Washington visualized was the local processing of American staples: wood, flax, cotton, hemp, wool, leather, iron, furs, etc. Such a movement towards "the useful arts" had already been encouraged by the collapse of American credit in Europe: "The number of shoes made in one [Massachusetts] town and nails in another is incredible." Washington had been persuaded by an Englishman who called at Mount Vernon of the "extensive utility" of cotton cloth and the possi-bility of growing "that new material" in the deep south with "almost infinite consequence to America."[42]

Although Washington wrote the Hartford weaver of his suit that he did not see why such manufacturers needed "any extraordinary *legal* assistance," in his undelivered address he urged that Congress study not only what "proficiency" America was capable of, but also what encouragement should be given.[43]

Washington expressed pride that American ships were threading the seven seas and that in exotic ports "our new constellation has been received with tokens of uncommon regard." The more energetic gov-ernment would, of course, increase the respect abroad for American shipping, thus connecting us "with the rest of mankind in stricter ties of amity." However, he saw encouraging foreign trade as less within the federal province than the fostering of inland commerce. He was always eloquent on the utility of roads and canals. In his undelivered address, he argued also the importance to national unity of postal communication. Newspapers should be carried free.[44]

Perhaps because ostentatious profiteers had during the war contributed to the starving of the army, perhaps because of his personal financial difficulties at Mount Vernon, surely because he envisioned that "fine articles" would continue to be purchased abroad, adversely affecting the balance of trade, Washington saw an antithesis between luxury and prosperity. He even asked one of his female correspondents whether "your sex . . . are not capable of doing something towards introducing federal fashions and national manners. . . . Is it not shameful that we should be the sport of European whims and caprices? Should we not blush to discourage our own industry and ingenuity by purchasing foreign superfluities and adopting fantastic fashions which are, at best, ill-suited to our stage of society?" In his undelivered address he set up as an ideal for the whole nation the "primeval simplicity of manners and incorruptible love of liberty" that characterized the western settlers.[45]

The American people, Washington warned, should "guard against ambition as against their greatest enemy. We should not, in imitation of some nations which have been celebrated for a false kind of patriotism, wish to aggrandize our own republic at the expense of the freedom and happiness of the rest of mankind." He pointed out that as long as Americans did not themselves engage in aggression, the ocean, "a singular felicity in our national lot," exempted them from supporting any considerable martial establishment. An active merchant marine, seconded by some government-supported arsenals and shipyards that would permit a rapid warlike outfitting of civilian vessels, would supply the naval defense that would be the main bulwark of the nation.[46]

But supposing an invader did break through and land an expeditionary force on American soil? Should a professional army stand ready to defend? Washington knew that establishing a strong standing army would make the people smell tyranny and would also force heavy taxation, thus encouraging disunity. His conclusion was that civil unity was militarily more important than martial preparedness. The Revolution, he wrote, had demonstrated that an invader could not conquer America as long as the states remained united. And thus the General who had suffered so much during the war from the incompetence of the militia, urged present reliance on that clumsy arm. In the recesses when Congress was not meeting, Washington would be glad to review militia companies to help revive "the ancient military spirit." However, the really important matter was "to train our youths to such industrious and hardy professions as that they may grow into an unconquerable force."[47]

Every effort would have to be made to keep the government as cheap as possible, since a clear requirement for general acceptance was not "touching the purses of the people too deeply." Washington hoped that expenses and also the interest on the national debt would be paid with no further levies than "a general, moderate impost upon imports, together with a higher tax upon certain enumerated articles."[48]

Congress having been entrusted with setting up the system of federal courts, Washington urged in his undelivered address that in the process they demonstrate "supreme regard for equal justice and the inherent rights of the citizens." They should furthermore "make men honest in their dealings with each other by regulating the coinage and currency of money" and establishing "just weights and measures upon an uniform plan." As public and private men, the legislators should "use your best endeavors to improve the education and manners of a people; to accelerate the progress of arts and sciences; to patronize works of genius; to confer rewards for inventions of utility; and to cherish institutions favorable to humanity."[49]

In none of his letters, not even in those he wrote to the men he would call on (when the time came) to be his major assistants, did Washington make the slightest mention of how the executive branch of the government should be organized. If he discussed the matter in his undelivered address, that passage is lost. However, he did make it clear that he did not visualize the President as an initiator of policy, a prime mover: "The election of the different branches of Congress by the freemen, either directly or indirectly, is the pivot on which turns the first wheel of the government, a wheel which communicates motion to all the rest."[50]

III

Experiments in Government

14

A Frightening Triumph

NEVER was the election of a President so much a foregone conclusion and yet so tortuous in consummation. The Electoral College met on February 4, 1789, but its unanimous vote for Washington could not be official until a President of the Senate, temporarily elected for the purpose, opened the ballots in the presence of both Houses. Congress was due to convene in New York on March 4. On the 5th, Knox wrote Washington that only eight senators and seventeen representatives—pitifully less than a quorum—had appeared.[1]

As the most unpleasant season of the farming year moved slowly by, Washington waited at Mount Vernon in a frustration that was increased by the non-arrival of some promised grain seed, which prevented him from carrying out that year's step in his long-range plan for the rotation of crops. "£500 would be no compensation," he wrote, "for this disappointment."[2]

The continuing word was that legislators were dribbling into New York—now a senator, then a representative—but a quorum was still unachieved on March 30, when Knox notified Washington that the delay had already cost the new government the spring imposts, estimated at £300,000. Washington replied that he was sorry about the imposts, but more worried over "the stupor or listlessness" being displayed by the men on whom the success of the Constitution would depend.[3] The high-spirited anticipation he had so recently savored shredded rapidly into such gloom that he wrote as darkly as he ever had during the blackest hours of the Revolution:

"My movements to the chair of government will be accompanied by feelings not unlike those of a culprit who is going to the place of his execution, so unwilling am I, in the evening of a life nearly consumed in public cares, to quit a peaceful abode for an ocean of difficulties, without that competency of political skill, abilities, and inclination which is necessary to manage the helm. . . . Integrity and firmness is all I can promise; these, be the voyage long or short, never shall forsake me although I may be deserted by all men. For of the consolations which are to be derived from these (under any circumstances) the world cannot deprive me."[4]

Washington was not cheered when he faced up to the fact that if he were not to leave debts behind him in Virginia, he would have "to do what I never expected to be reduced to the necessity of doing" and, indeed, regarded as the most disastrous of all financial steps for farmers: borrow money at interest. After he had finally steeled himself to borrow over a thousand pounds, he discovered to his dismay that his credit was not considered good enough. Businessmen were not willing to lend. Finally, he tried a personal connection, appealing to "the most monied man I was acquainted with." But Charles Carroll of Carrollton also refused, explaining that he could not collect interest on the money he already had out on loan.[5]

A wealthy inhabitant of Alexandria, Richard Conway, finally accommodated Washington to the extent of less than half what he needed—£500—at 6 per cent interest. The money in hand, Washington paid the most pressing of his debts—and then found there was nothing left. He had to beg from Conway another hundred pounds so that he could pay his expenses to New York and the Presidency.[6]

The still-unorganized government of the United States had set up no Presidential residence. Governor George Clinton of New York, who, although an old friend, was a conspicuous anti-Federalist, asked Washington to stay with him. Washington replied that it would be wrong "to impose such a burden on any private family." He also put off Clinton's request to be kept informed on when to expect Washington's arrival. "No reception," Washington explained, "can be so congenial to my feelings as a quiet entry devoid of ceremony."[7]

Applying to Madison, Washington wrote that if lodgings could not be hired which were "tolerably convenient (I am not very nice), I would take rooms in the most decent tavern." His mind was surely running on his financial situation when he specified, "I am not desirous of being placed *early* in a situation for entertaining." He was, however, eager "to conform to the public desire and expectation with respect to the style proper for the chief magistrate to live in," and hoped that Madison would advise him concerning what the public wanted.[8]

Washington made a quick trip to Fredericksburg to visit his eighty-one-year-old mother, who seemed to be dying slowly and painfully of cancer of the breast. Then he returned to his waiting at Mount Vernon.[9]

Martha made no secret of her great bitterness at the impending destruction of her domestic life. She blamed fate, it is true, rather than her husband. She was willing to admit that he had to follow what his conscience told him was his duty.[10] Yet Washington found it both kind and prudent not to push her any harder than was absolutely necessary. She would have, of course, to apply in the end her superlative social gifts to the role of First Lady. But there was no need for her to keep packed while the dilatory government dithered.

Since, as he put it, "delay must be very irksome to the attending members," Washington intended to set an example of promptness by setting out as quickly as possible after he had been notified that the government had pulled itself together far enough to certify his election. However, Martha, with Nellie and Little Washington, could follow at their leisure.[11]

On April 14, at about noon, Charles Thomson, the Secretary of Congress, stood at Mount Vernon's door. After Washington had greeted his old acquaintance, they walked together into the high-ceilinged banquet hall that was the most formal available room. The two men stood there, facing each other, in the quiet of a Virginia afternoon. After Thomson had made a little speech, he read a letter from John Langdon, president pro tempore of the Senate, which stated that Washington had been unanimously elected President of the United States: "Suffer me, sir, to indulge the hope that so auspicious a mark of public confidence will meet your approbation."

Washington replied by reading aloud from a paper he had prepared: "Whatever may have been my private feelings and sentiments," he could not "give a greater evidence of my sensibility for the honor" done him by his "fellow citizens . . . than by accepting the appointment." He was conscious of his inability but would seek to do as much as could be "accomplished by an honest zeal."[12]

Concerning April 16, 1789, Washington wrote in his diary, "I bade adieu to Mount Vernon, to private life, and to domestic felicity, and with a mind oppressed with more anxious and painful sensations than I have words to express, set out for New York in company with Mr. Thomson and Colonel Humphreys, with the best disposition to render service to my country in obedience to its calls, but with less hope of answering its expectations."[13]

Since he believed that the future of the government depended so tremendously on its acceptance by the people, Washington was, of course, much concerned with the way his progress through the states to the Presidency would be received. But his first stop, Alexandria, was not so much a test for the future as a parting from the past.

His neighbors entertained him at a dinner studded with congratulatory toasts and affectionate speeches. He finally rose and made a brief acknowledgment, which ended: "All that now remains for me is to commit myself and you to the protection of that beneficent Being who, on a former occasion, has happily brought us together after a long and distressing separation. Perhaps the same gracious Providence will again indulge us with the same heartfelt felicity. But words, my fellow citizens, fail me: *Unutterable sensations must then be left to more expressive silence: while, from an aching heart, I bid you all, my affectionate friends and kind neighbors, farewell!*"[14]

As Washington advanced beyond home ground, the explosion of enthusiastic strangers into his presence seemed all that the most ardent Federalist could have desired. There was a perpetual bowing and clanking beside his carriage. Delegations of local dignitaries awaited him at each town, and relays of horsemen, relieving each other every dozen miles or so, formed a continuous guard of honor. Washington could hardly see the countryside, so thick were the clouds of dust thrown up by many hooves. As an observer noticed, the dust that had settled on Washington's clothes made it impossible to distinguish the true color of his coat or trousers.[15]

In Baltimore, Washington was kept up late at a dinner by an endless succession of toasts and speeches. He was off at about five-thirty the next morning, but not too early to be piped out of town by a roar of cannon and accompanied by another company of leading citizens on horseback. After seven miles, he alighted and managed to persuade the young gentlemen to go home. Then for two days, as he advanced through sparsely settled country, there were gaps in the chain of ceremony, and he could distinguish, in the sparser crowds that awaited him in towns, the emotional faces of soldiers he had last seen years before in bloody campaigns. But things hotted up again at Wilmington: another dinner, horsemen who accompanied him to the Pennsylvania line where Pennsylvania horsemen were waiting, headed by the ever suavely smiling General Mifflin.[16]

At Chester, some fifteen miles from Philadelphia, Washington alighted from his carriage and mounted a white horse. A parade of other horsemen gathered behind him. As he advanced along the familiar road towards the Schuylkill River, he saw waiting at every crossroads a new detachment of riders. He would stop, the whole procession coming to a halt behind him, for another round of ceremonial greetings. Then the newcomers fell in at the end of the ever-lengthening line.

Finally, there came into Washington's view the pontoon bridge across the Schuylkill at Gray's Ferry. It now resembled most surprisingly a grove of laurel and cedar growing out of the water. Green boughs hid all the woodwork and, at either end, tall arches of laurel rose, gaudy with banners and devices. Washington could have guessed (had he not been told) that this was the work of that indefatigably ingenious painter Charles Willson Peale. However, as he admired the effect which, according to one spectator, "even the pencil of Raphael could not delineate," he could not guess all that Peale had in store for him.

Riding under the first arch, he saw peering at him from the shrubbery a handsome fifteen-year-old girl, whom he perhaps recognized as Peale's daughter Angelica. She seemed to be encrusted with laurel. He had started to bow to the young lady when she set in motion what the *Pennsylvania Packet* called "certain machinery." Something separated from the arch above and, before Washington could duck, landed on his head. Raising a startled hand, he found that he was now crowned with laurel. (The idea was that the hero, in his modesty, would have refused the wreath if offered in a more conventional manner.) According to Peale family legend, Washington pushed off the wreath but kissed Angelica.[17]

Between the bridge and the city, twenty thousand citizens—so estimated the *Packet*—"lined every fence, field, and avenue. The aged sire, the venerable matron, the blooming virgin, and the ruddy youth were all emulous in their plaudits." At the city limits, more infantry

An East View of GRAY'S FERRY, near Philadelphia with the TRIUMPHAL ARCHES, &c. erected for the Reception of General Washington, April 20th 1789.

Charles Willson Peale's own drawing (as engraved by the *Columbia Magazine*) of his decorations for the bridge across the Schuylkill. In one of the arches he hid a machine that dropped a laurel wreath on Washington's head.
Courtesy of the Library of Congress

wheeled and more artillery set matches to their cannon. Then these new units fell into the line behind Washington, as did squads of citizens at every block "until," exclaimed the newspaper, "the column swelled beyond credibility itself." The parade finally reached the City Tavern, where Washington was tendered "a very grand and beautiful banquet." The evening was topped off with fireworks.

When the next morning dawned rainy, Washington grasped the opportunity of requesting the city troop of horsemen not to accompany him out of town: "He could not, he said, think of traveling under cover while others get wet." Whatever may have been Washington's secret relief at being able to get off quietly, his act sent the editor of the *Packet* into the stratosphere concerning the modesty of an elected leader as contrasted with the pride of European kings.[18]

As Washington crossed the Delaware opposite Trenton, his mind ran on his "situation" there during the darkest days of the Revolution, when he had struck out in utter despair: an icy river—sleet and wind—shivering, starving men—cannon and musket fire—bloody humps staining new-fallen snow—an incredible victory that had helped turn the tide.

On reaching the New Jersey shore, Washington was supplied with a fine horse. He led a noisy procession towards the bridge across the Assunpink Creek, behind which his army had taken refuge from a superior enemy before he set off on the wild and dangerous inspiration of his circuitous march to Princeton. When Washington saw that the bridge, across which his artillery had once so desperately fired, was now surmounted with a triumphal arch built of evergreens, his first thought may well have been, "What—again?" But soon his eyes were brimming with tears.

"A numerous train of white-robed ladies leading their daughters" stood where Washington had seen men die. Above them, on the top of the arch, a dome of flowers bore, pricked out in blossoms, the two bloody dates "December 26, 1776–January 2, 1777," and also a legend that brought a sob to Washington's throat: "THE DEFENDER OF THE MOTHERS WILL BE THE PROTECTOR OF THE DAUGHTERS."

The procession stopped, and Washington advanced alone. Thirteen young ladies stepped out to meet him. They were dressed in white, decked with wreaths and chaplets of flowers, and held in their hands baskets filled with more blooms. They sang:

[177]

"Virgins fair and matrons grave,
Those thy conquering arms did save,
Build for thee triumphant bowers.
Strew, ye fair, his way with flowers—
Strew your hero's way with flowers."

They threw their flowers under his horse's feet.

Writing formally in the third person, Washington thanked the ladies "for the exquisite sensation he experienced in that affecting moment. The astonishing contrast between his former and actual situation at the same spot, the elegant taste with which it was adorned for the present occasion, and the innocent appearance of the *white-robed choir* . . . have made such impressions on his remembrance as . . . will never be effaced."

No knight of ancient legend ever felt more chivalrously toward the fair sex. In wartime, Washington had done everything in his power—even to the detriment of the cause—to prevent women from becoming involved. The memory of the mothers and daughters on the bridge near Trenton would remain with him as an emotional high point, till his dying day.[19]

The contrast with this hushed, almost sacred occasion made Washington become more and more unpleasantly conscious of the hysterical notes in the plaudits which hour after hour beat continually around him. Did the rantings of the orators, the passionate handshakes, the throat-tearing cheers signify an affectionate welcome and reasoned approval of the government about to be established? Or was it all the senseless frenzy of the mob giving a complete loose rein to uncontrolled emotions? Whatever the fact, Washington had to roll on in his carriage, bow out the window, emerge to shake hands whenever there was a delegation, change to horseback whenever there was a parade to lead.

Finally, he was across New Jersey and at Elizabethtown Point, where he was to embark for the fifteen-mile trip by water that would take him past Staten Island, out into the Upper Bay, and then through the inner harbor to the tip of Manhattan Island.

He found awaiting him a sumptuous barge which had been built especially for the occasion at the expense of forty-six leading citizens.

It was forty-seven feet long at the keel, and over the elegantly appointed deck stretched an awning festooned with red curtains. There was a mast and a sail, but the main reliance was to be on the oars, thirteen on each side, which were manned by a picked group of New York harbor pilots, all identically dressed in white smocks and black-fringed caps.

Onto the deck there trooped, after Washington, representatives from the state and city governments, from the Senate and the House of Representatives. The vessel had hardly started to move before a naval parade began to form behind it. Among the first to fall in were the New Haven and Rhode Island packets. Washington was pleased to see in another boat two familiar faces: Jay and Knox. For the rest, there were ever more vessels and mostly strange faces.

As Washington's barge came opposite a battery on Staten Island, cannon began firing a thirteen-gun salute. At this signal, all the boats broke out, like so many suddenly opening flowers, into a splurge of banners. Then, from closer to Manhattan Island, there spoke out a tremendous voice. A Spanish warship was echoing the salute with larger guns than the infant republic possessed. And the stranger from Europe also had more flags: her rigging bloomed, to applause, with the ensigns of twenty-seven—or was it twenty-eight?—different nations.

Now, as the pilots rowed with perfect rhythm down the bay, a sloop under full sail slipped gracefully alongside. Two gentlemen and two ladies stood facing Washington and, as the water scudded between, they sang new words to "God Save the King":

> "... *Joy to our native land,*
> *Let every heart expand,*
> *For Washington's at hand,*
> *With glory crowned."*

Washington had hardly taken off his hat and bowed to acknowledge the compliment when another musical boat appeared directly alongside the first. The singers leaned over to exchange music, and then all rendered an ode in elaborate parts. "Our worthy President," one witness exulted, "was greatly affected with these tokens of profound respect."

As if Nature herself wished to join in the adulation, a number of porpoises frolicked briefly in front of Washington's barge. Then Washington's eyes were suddenly caught by an even more remarkable sight. The anti-Federalist journalist Philip Freneau was bowing to Washington from a vessel, "dressed and decorated in the most superb manner," but featuring on its deck "Dr. King from South Africa with a collection of natural curiosities." Washington's startled look was answered by the cold stares of "a male and female orangoutang," a species, so the newspaper paragrapher continued, "remarkable for its striking similitude to the human species."

Washington (who was in the end to be given more pain by Freneau than by perhaps any other man) had no time to meditate on what this strange sight portended, for his barge was now approaching the tip of Manhattan Island. He could see (as another observer noted) from the fort in the harbor to the place of landing and on into the city, "although near half a mile," little else on board every vessel, along the shore, and jamming the streets "but heads standing as thick as ears of corn before the harvest."

Handling their twenty-six oars "flawlessly," the thirteen pilots brought the barge into a perfect landing on Murray's Wharf at the foot of Wall Street. Here carpeted steps, flanked with railings upholstered in crimson, descended to the level of the deck. Washington mounted to be met by Governor Clinton and a pack of other dignitaries. Clinton's words of welcome were made almost inaudible by earsplitting huzzahs.

The carpeting led to a carriage, but Washington announced that he would walk to the house which the new government had hurriedly procured for him on Cherry Street. It took him half an hour to traverse the half-mile, since all the efforts of city officers with staves and also of some soldiers could not hold back the crowds that wished, screaming or tearful, to touch the tall gentleman in his cocked hat, blue suit, and buff underdress. "The General," one spectator wrote, "was obliged to wipe his eyes several times before he got to Queen Street."

As soon as he was indoors, Washington had to receive, despite his fatigue, a flood of dignitaries and former Revolutionary officers. There was no time to change his clothes before he was rushed off to a banquet given by Clinton. And then, although the evening was "very wet," he had to move through the streets and admire the illuminations in the windows. There were still tight crowds and many ululations.[20]

Washington's experiences since he had left Mount Vernon were a shocking contrast to his life among his own fields. His days and his nights had been characterized by the explosive assassination of all privacy, by a total, gleeful, self-congratulatory intrusion of the populace into his existence.

The journal Washington kept of his trip to New York has disappeared, probably another casualty of Jared Sparks's desire to oblige his friends with autographs. However, Washington's first biographer, John Marshall, copied out a comment on the final leg of the journey that is, in its clumsy phrasing, revealing of Washington's exhaustion as well as of his emotions: "The display of boats which attended and joined us on this occasion, some with vocal and some with instrumental music on board; the decorations of the ships; the roar of cannon; and the loud acclamations of the people which rent the skies as I passed along the wharves, filled my mind with sensations as painful (considering the reverse of this scene which may be the case after all my labors to do good) as they were pleasing."[21]

15

The President Is Inaugurated

WASHINGTON arrived in New York on April 23, 1789, but was not inaugurated as President until the 30th. The intervening week was a stormy one in Congress and in the drawing rooms and taverns where men discussed politics. The issues that so agitated minds seem to modern eyes at first glance trivial, since they concerned etiquette and nomenclature. Washington would appear before Congress to take his oath. How should he be received so as to preserve a proper balance between the dignities of the Presidency and the legislature? John Adams was in anguish concerning where, as presiding officer of the Senate, he should meet Washington, where each of them should sit.

An even more grievous issue involved how the President should on all formal occasions be addressed. A committee of the House of Representatives wished him to be called merely, as in the Constitution, "the President of the United States." The Senate rebuffed the committee's report. Although, as presiding officer, John Adams was not supposed to get into the debates, he could not restrain himself. "What," Adams asked, "will the common people of foreign countries, what will the sailors and soldiers say" when asked to speak of "George Washington, the President of the United States? They will despise him. This is all nonsense to the philosopher, but so is all government whatever." Adams plumped for "His Most Benign Highness," while a Senate committee voted for "His Highness the President of the United States of America and Protector of the Rights of the Same."[1]

Washington, who saw little but foolishness in John Adams's point of view,* was upset at this squabble which so soon endangered unity. The Comte de Moustier, the French minister, reported to his government that it was the fear of offending Washington that kept the Federalists from establishing titles, and Madison remembered Washington's annoyance at the efforts "to bedizen him with a superb but spurious title." It was, indeed, Washington's friend Madison who led the continued resistance in the House which finally forced the Senate to topple the whole dream of aristocratic nomenclature by agreeing that the chief executive should have no fancier appellation than "the President of the United States." Washington's associates continued to refer to him in the pre-Presidential manner as "the General."[2]

Washington's most immediate political problem was to make a final determination on his inaugural address. He decided (if he had not previously done so) to scrap the seventy-three page detailed speech on which he had spent so much labor. Instead, he perfected an address so short that it was, when read at the inaugural ceremony, to occupy less than twenty minutes.[3]

To the Constitutional provision that he recommend measures he judged "necessary and expedient," Washington responded by outlining only the most general principles. The legislature should avoid "local prejudices or attachments," "separate views," "party animosities." It should "watch over this great assemblage of communities and interests" with a "comprehensive and equal eye" and lay the foundations of policy "in the pure and immutable principles of private morality."† He went on to state what he profoundly believed and had often himself exemplified in his role as Commander in Chief: "There exists in the economy and course of nature an indissoluble union between virtue and happiness, between duty and advantage, between the genuine maxims of an honest and magnanimous policy and the solid rewards of public prosperity and felicity."

His text went briefly into the matter of amending the Constitution:

---

* The name George Washington rang more nobly in the fields of America and the capitals of Europe than any title the new nation could bestow, but luster would have been added to the name "John Adams" by some elegant epithet. That Adams was not, however, completely wrong about an American yearning for titles is revealed by the extralegal habit which has grown up to call all government officials, from senators to sewer commissioners, "the Honorable _____."

† "Private morality" could be interpreted by conservatives as referring to the sanctity of contracts (and this was probably what Washington meant), but others could interpret it as keeping usurers from foreclosing on the unfortunate.

Congress would, he was sure, avoid any changes that would weaken the government or which "ought to await the future lessons of experience." However, he endorsed the Bill of Rights, although not specifically by name, when he urged Congress to expedite amendments reflecting "a reverence for the characteristic rights of freemen and a regard for the public harmony."

For the rest, the speech Washington polished during his first week in New York was concerned with matters personal and religious. He had accepted the call to the Presidency with reluctance. In insisting on his own inadequacy, he went surely beyond what he really felt when he added to his statement that he was "unpracticed in the duties of civil administration" that he was conscious of "inheriting inferior endowments from nature." He wished to be exempted from whatever salary was established for the Presidency, merely being reimbursed for "actual expenditures."

The most remarkable aspect of what Washington wrote is the depth of its religious tone. He had often in the past expressed gratitude for the assistance of Providence to the American cause and had expressed hope that the boon would be continued. But never before had he devoted so much—more than a third—of a complicated pronouncement to religious considerations. That he was not just striking a popular attitude as a politician might is revealed by the absence of the usual Christian terms: he did not mention Christ or even use the word "God." Following the phraseology of the philosophical Deism he professed, he referred to "the invisible hand which conducts the affairs of men," to "the benign parent of the human race."*

In the speech he was preparing, Washington appealed for a celestial guidance which he undoubtedly felt the need of now more than he had ever done previously in his public career. As Commander in Chief, he had had an earthly superior which he consulted and obeyed to a point which his critics considered extreme: the Continental Congress. As president of the Constitutional Convention he had been, if the presiding officer, one of a team. But now, although Congress flanked him on one side and an as yet unestablished judiciary would on the other, in the powerful duties that had been assigned to him he stood

---

* That Washington intentionally avoided the word "God" is strongly indicated by his first Thanksgiving Proclamation. Having quoted Congress's request that he establish a day for thanking "Almighty God," in the part of the proclamation he himself wrote he used other designations.[4]

alone, with no superior to turn to but the heavens. That some people believed that he himself belonged in those heavens,* added to his plight a frightening *hubris*. No wonder he looked upwards imploringly to "that Almighty Being . . . who presides in the councils of nations and whose providential aids can supply every human defect."[5]

Fortunately the ceremonial aspects of Washington's inauguration required of him few decisions, since they had, after long debate, been established by Congress.

The morning of April 30 came in fair. If he was not already awake, he was roused at dawn by thirteen cannon shots. After that, there were church bells and the moving (with much staring) of crowds in front of his house, but, hour after hour, nothing positive to pull Washington from the meditations and memories that undoubtedly flowed through his mind.

With the approach of noon came the need for purposeful action. Washington donned the suit made from the brown Connecticut cloth he had purchased to encourage American manufactures and which he had had brightened by adding silver buttons decorated with spread eagles. He pulled on white silk stockings, stepped into shoes with silver buckles, and made sure that his dress sword with its steel scabbard lay ready. Since he believed in never keeping people waiting, his preparations were surely finished in time for him to sit again, now more nervously. He found suspense, as he often wrote, most unpleasant.

Finally there were steps in his hallway. The delegation from Congress had arrived. Washington buckled on his sword, grasped his hat, went into the parlor, bowed, shook hands—and then he was sitting alone in a ponderous state coach which Congress had procured for the occasion. Manned by lackeys he did not know, the unfamiliar coach moved slowly behind strange horses through a phantasmagoria of cheering faces. Bowing to the left and then to the right, Washington now and then paused to look behind him, for he could glimpse through the back window his own horses pulling the now somewhat

---

* Boston's Ancient and Honorable Artillery Company sang of Washington:
"Fill the bowl, fill it high,
Firstborn son of the sky,
May he never, never die:
Heaven shout, Amen."[6]

battered coach from Mount Vernon, in which he knew were his two old friends, his aides Humphreys and Lear.

Bands appeared and shrank into the distance, militia companies wheeled and fired. Surely, as he rode in solitude amidst all the jubilation, Washington's mind dwelt (as did the minds of many old patriots who in tears watched him pass) on contrasts. How, when the British and Hessians had invaded Manhattan, the militia and even the Continentals had fled like ghosts, deaf to his shouts, avoiding his sword, until at last he turned, in despair, to defy the enemy as a solitary horseman, and would, had not his aides intervened, have been captured or killed. And then, so much sorrow and bloodshed later, after the city was repossessed, he had ridden through these very streets, to see broken houses sag around him and listen to the thin cheers of a few emaciated citizens.

Now the city blossomed and the well-fed citizens lived in peace. The wild experiment he had reluctantly espoused and diffidently led had thus far—up to this climactic moment—brilliantly succeeded. The eyes of the whole world, the hopes of all posterity were fixed, so to speak, on this occasion which, if its promise were properly improved, would demonstrate for all time the ability of men to govern themselves. If properly improved! Washington knew that the triumph against ancient evil, against the darkness in the hearts of men, against despots and cringing followers, had not yet been truly won. And again on his own shoulders, older and less resilient now, rested the weight of leading the endlessly continuing campaign. Surely his silent supplications rose to "the invisible hand which conducts the affairs of men"![7]

The carriage stopped. Washington alighted and walked through ranks of militiamen into Federal Hall. Followed by dignitaries, he mounted a flight of stairs, passed through a door that was thrown open at his approach, and entered the Senate chamber. He bowed to the senators and to the envoys of foreign powers who stood on his right, to the members of the House of Representatives on his left, and saw ahead three windows, curtained in crimson damask, that opened onto a balcony. In front of the central window was a crimson canopy, a dais, three chairs, and John Adams looking both nervous and constrained.

Adams stepped down, bowed to Washington, conducted him to the central chair, and then took his own seat on the right. Speaker Muhlenberg of the House slipped into the seat on the left. There was a moment of complete silence, and then Adams rose. He made as if to speak but was unable to do so. Finally, he said, "Sir, the Senate and House of Representatives are ready to attend you to take the oath required by the Constitution. It will be administered by the Chancellor of the State of New York."

"I am ready to proceed."

Adams led the way through the central window onto a small porch that jutted out over the street at the second-story level. In front of Washington was an armchair, and on a small table draped in red, resting upon a red cushion, was a large Bible. Beyond the low railing—down the long, receding vistas of the streets, filling every window, on every rooftop—there reappeared the endless movement and cacophony of cheering faces. Washington bowed and bowed again, with his hand on his heart, and then sat down on the chair. By now, the portico was jammed with dignitaries.

Washington rose once more, and approached the railing so as to be visible to as many of the onlookers as possible. A complete silence fell on the crowd. Chancellor Robert R. Livingston faced Washington and between the two tall men a "small, short" dignitary held up the Bible on its crimson cushion. Washington put his right hand on the book. "Do you solemnly swear," asked Livingston, "that you will faithfully execute the office of President of the United States, and will, to the best of your ability, preserve, protect, and defend the Constitution of the United States?"

"I solemnly swear," said Washington and repeated the oath. Although the small dignitary was holding it up as high as he could, Washington had to bow down to kiss the Bible.

Livingston turned to the crowd. "It is done." Then he shouted, "Long live George Washington, President of the United States!"

Taken up by the multitude, the cry rose thunderously. Echoing among the buildings, it came to Washington's ear as an almost incoherent roar. From the harbor rose the booming of cannon, the Spanish frigate again making the most noise. A faint, almost drowned-out tinkling was the massed voices of all the church bells. Washington bowed and bowed and then, when the sounds gave no indication of ceasing, he walked indoors and sat down in his chair.[8]

It took some time before the dignitaries could get back into their seats and sink into quiet. Then Washington stood up with his speech in his hand. The audience also rose. His aspect, wrote a senator, was "grave, almost to sadness." His simple words of modesty and faith, his few broad recommendations were delivered in so low a voice—"deep and a little tremulous"—that all had to lean forward to hear. "This great man," so wrote another senator, "was agitated and embarrassed more than ever he was by the leveled cannon or pointed musket. He trembled, and several times could scarce make out to read."

As he proceeded, Washington moved his manuscript from his left to his right hand and put several fingers of his left hand into his breeches pocket. Soon he pulled out his left hand, again shifted the manuscript, and put his right hand into his pocket. Then he extracted his right hand and made with it what a witness considered "an ungainly impression."

The famous orator Senator Fisher Ames watched entranced, and yet with some resentment—he later described himself as sitting there like a "pilgarlic" (peeled bit of garlic)—at the effect of this simple delivery that so denied the importance of the elocutionist's art: "It seemed to me," Ames wrote later, "an allegory in which virtue was personified, and addressing those whom she would make her votaries. Her power over the heart was never greater." The whole audience, even the man most passionately jealous of Washington—Vice President Adams—gave way to tears.[9]

When Washington sat down, his twenty minutes of talking over, he looked old and tired. "Time," Ames noted, "has made havoc upon his face."[10] But his duties of the day were far from done. After much shaking of hands, Washington walked between walls of saluting militiamen to Saint Paul's Chapel, where the Episcopal Bishop of New York strung out at length his petitions to the Almighty. However, there was no sermon, and Washington was allowed to have his dinner quietly at home. Then out again in his carriage to attend a pair of receptions, to see the illuminations and the fireworks. His horses moved more and more slowly as ever-tighter crowds engulfed them in human quicksand. Finally, Washington had to abandon his carriage and walk.[11]

After the church service, while Washington was wooing rest in preparation for the evening's festivities, the Senate had reconvened in the chamber where he had so recently moved all present to tears. A squabble instantly erupted, made the more heated, probably, by reaction to the previous emotion.

FEDERAL HALL

The Seat of CONGRESS

Printed & Sold by A. Doolittle New-Haven 1790

Washington taking his oath of office as President. The architectural embel-
lishments, an American version of classicism, were designed by L'Enfant.
Engraving by Amos Doolittle after a drawing by Peter Lacour. Courtesy
of the New York Public Library

The object of the session was to prepare a reply to Washington's speech; the angry issue, whether it should be referred to as his *"most gracious speech."* To this—the wording traditionally used by Parliament in replying to addresses of the British king—so many objections were raised that the debate had to be continued on the next day. Then it was decided to strike out the phrase lest the people consider the words "the first step of the ladder in the ascent to royalty."[12]

The successful campaign against that sinister adjective "gracious" had been led by the hypochondriacal and suspicious senator from western Pennsylvania, William Maclay. Some historians have considered Maclay, although his personal character was very different from Jefferson's, a prophetic figure who took what was to be the Jeffersonian stand long before Jefferson himself had dreamed of leading an opposition.

Because of a documentary freak, Maclay plays a major role in historical literature. Determined to protect its proceedings from the vulgar eye, the conservative Senate kept no detailed journal, thus inadvertently (suppression almost never pays) throwing the ball to its most radical member. Maclay filled the gap by jotting down from day to day a voluminous diary. Not only do his pages supply the only indications of what took place at many sessions, but, being in a perpetual rage of disapproval or indignation, he wrote a spirited style that begs for quotation. Since Maclay's attitudes were shared at that time by only a few extremists, his diary, however prophetic it might be of later feelings, distorts the record of Washington's first year as President.

Maclay viewed the Virginian with awe, suspicion, and resentment. Before the inauguration, he wrote in his diary, "This day . . . General Washington, the greatest man in the world, paid me a visit." Yet during the debate over titles, Maclay could not doubt that Washington had sparked the aristocratic agitation because of a secret lust to be addressed as "your Majesty." And in describing how the Senate called on Washington to deliver their reply to the inaugural address, Maclay exhibited a gleeful urge to find "the greatest man" a clumsy fool.[13]

The President had prepared an acknowledgment of the Senate's reply. Maclay noted that, when his turn came, he took the paper "out of his coat pocket. He had his spectacles in his jacket pocket, having his hat in his left hand and the paper in his right. He had too many objects for his hands. He shifted his hat between his forearm and the left side of his breast. But taking his spectacles from the case embarrassed him. He got rid of this small distress by laying the spectacle case on the chimney piece. . . . Having adjusted his spectacles, which was not very easy, considering the engagements on his hands, he read the reply with tolerable exactness and without much emotion." Maclay commented that Washington should have received the Senate with his spectacles on, "which would have saved the making of some uncouth motions."[14]

Maclay's gleeful mockery might well seem, as the first President of the United States grasped the wheel of state to almost universal cheering, a sour note so minuscule as not to be worth recording. Yet had Washington been conscious of what was happening in Maclay's mind, he would have been alarmed. The enthusiasm which had accompanied his inauguration had not calmed the anxiety engendered by his triumphal progress from Mount Vernon to New York. "I fear," he wrote an old Virginian associate, "if the issue of public measures should not correspond with their [the public's] sanguine expectations, they will turn the extravagant (and I may say undue) praises which they are heaping upon me at this moment, into equally extravagant (though I will fondly hope unmerited) censures. So much is expected, so many untoward circumstances may intervene, in such a new and critical situation, that I feel an insuperable diffidence in my own abilities. I feel . . . how much I shall stand in need of the countenance and aid of every friend to myself, of every friend to the Revolution, and of every lover of good government. I thank you, my dear sir, for your affectionate expressions on this point."[15]

16

The President as a Social Leader

T HE storm over Presidential etiquette, which created the first controversy in the new government, was to blow ever harder as the years passed, causing in the end Washington's greatest anguish. The explosive power of arguments concerning his social stance—even over personal behavior and tastes that might have seemed nobody's business but his own—grew out of the fact that the new government had no traditional focus at all, nothing concrete and established that the people could visualize when thinking of their nation, except George Washington and, through him, the office of President. There was no permanent national capital; there were no venerable institutions; there were no precedents on which to lean. The gaggle of arguing men who made up the brand-new legislature was hardly inspiring; and it was difficult to reverence a Constitution which all admitted was imperfect, which had just been adopted over much opposition, and which had not yet been tried.

Not just a different cut in a pie traditionally sliced up between kings, the United States was, in the modern sense, the world's first new nation. There have been many subsequent national births, and these have demonstrated again and again that the symbol of their identity which a new people most naturally seek is a man, what sociologists like to call a "charismatic personality." In the late eighteenth century this universal tendency was further strengthened (and made more frightening) by the still almost totally dominant tradition of royalty. And, to top all, America possessed a man who had been the symbol of national unity for fourteen years, ever since he had been elected by an illegal junto representing thirteen mutually jealous and independent sovereignties, the Commander in Chief of a common "Continental Army," in which he was, at that moment, the only soldier. The older crisis had willed to the new government a charismatic personality of awe-inspiring dimensions. George Washington was, so Madison wrote, the only aspect of the government which had really caught the imagination of the people.[1]

If this made Washington supremely useful, it also made him seem, to men who feared for democratic institutions, extremely dangerous. Not so much in his own person—few still believed (as had many during the Revolution) that he was susceptible to the seductions of a crown—but in his extraordinary influence over the people and his power to establish precedents. It seemed as if Washington were a great boulder rising in the stream of American institutions, which could, by the position it occupied, deflect the waters, thus determining the whole future flow of the American government. And entirely apart from his own personal behavior, there was the question of what opportunities a Presidency shaped around him would leave for his successors. The office might fall into the hands of a tyrant who would use its powers for sinister ends.

Washington's instinctive sense that the adulation with which he was being received had its ominous side could not have been more accurate. He was an emotional part of every man's life, and the emotions were warped with contradictions. A feeling of dependence brought not only comfort but resentment among naturally self-reliant Americans, and also the dread a child feels both of the power and the caprice of a father. Furthermore, Washington's role as a national symbol made every man wish him to symbolize the nation as that man visualized it.

Washington was eager to please, but how to do so was no simple matter. In each citizen's preference concerning Presidential behavior, political theory was entangled, in an unanalyzable snarl, with nationalistic, aesthetic, and moral considerations.

All intelligent supporters of a strong central government agreed that a first essential was to secure the respect and acceptance of the people. The lessons urged by history and existing European example were that such popular support was, to an important extent, gained through titles and trappings which externalized the position of rulers to command and be obeyed. No one knew for sure whether or not, given the human animal in all his frailty, this was an essential aspect of leadership. On the whole, those Americans were inclined to believe it was who had the least faith in their fellowmen and who were thus predisposed all down the line towards a tight holding of the governmental reins. On the other hand, men who believed in trusting the reasoning power of the people smelled behind pomp and circumstance the autos-da-fé of tyranny.

A second line of cleavage concerned the importance of European tradition versus the possibility—nay, the glorious duty!—of American originality. Reflecting European aristocratic behavior seemed to some an influx of sophisticated institutions into a raw land, to others the importation of decadence into a fresh Eden that was evolving newer and purer institutions which the whole world would eventually follow.

The creation of this contemporary Eden was considered of transcendent importance because few American political leaders believed any more in the ancient Eden where Adam and Eve fell. If sin had not been brought into the world by the eating of forbidden fruit, if man was (as romantics and democrats believed) naturally good, the manifest existence of evil needed to be explained in other terms. Man, it was postulated, was shaped nobly or ignobly by his environment. If he grew up under evil institutions, dedicated to brutal or decadent manners, he would become evil. But in a beneficent social climate, his natural goodness would flower. Every responsible American wished the social institutions of the United States to nurture such a society as he personally most admired and desired. This gave social behavior a definite political cast. Those who feared the brutishness of the mob wished to expose the people to elegance and refinement. Those who feared aristocratic institutions saw a protection in simple manners.

Mixed in with such political theory there were, of course, aesthetic and moral predilections. Some individuals were naturally attracted by fine teams of horses, gleaming drawing rooms, and fashionably dressed women, while others preferred rural quiet and found more beauty in a neat milkmaid than a painted belle. And there was the nagging question whether luxury (particularly the variety of it that other men practiced) was not by its very nature a forcing bed for immoral behavior: greed and lust in men, lust and vanity in women. One of the arguments in the Senate was over whether an official statement should refer to the "power and splendor" or the "power and respectability" of the new government.[2]

Washington wanted to do what was expected of him, but he was, in fact, not a bloodless symbol, not a demigod. He was thrown into this maelstrom of myth, of religion and philosophy, of social and economic preconception and prejudice as a living man, with all the desires and tastes of a powerful individual habituated to controlling his own environment. That strain should result was inevitable.

On his arrival in New York, Washington had discovered instantly and unpleasantly that the door of the Presidential mansion supplied him with no protection whatsoever. "From the time I had done breakfast and thence till dinner and afterwards till bedtime I could not get relieved from the ceremony of one visit before I had to attend to another." Every person of the least self-importance felt he had a right to come in and stare, assess the furnishing of the house to see whether it was too grandly aristocratic or too squalidly republican (the French minister considered it "chetive," i.e., mean),[3] to compliment himself as well as Washington with orotund expressions of admiration and congratulation, and then assess Washington's reply on his own personal gauge for the right mixture of democratic warmth and charismatic grandeur. Seeking some method of escape that would not only preserve his sanity but enable him to get some work done, Washington hoped to find precedents for self-protection in the behavior of his partial predecessors, the Presidents of Congress. He learned that, far from disentangling themselves, they had become entrapped to such an extent that they had reduced their office to "perfect contempt," having been "considered in no better light than as a maître d'hôtel . . . for their table was considered as a public one and every person who could get introduced conceived that he had a *right* to be invited to it." This underlined the lesson that, however much the broad hospitality Washington had practiced at Mount Vernon might suit a rural landowner, being at everyone's beck in a capital city was no "way to preserve the dignity and respect that was due to the first magistrate."[4]

Two days after his inauguration, Washington published in the newspapers that he would receive "visits of compliment" only between the hours of two and three on Tuesdays and Fridays. He would return no visits and accept no invitations "to entertainments."[5]

Maclay, instantly up in verbal arms, wrote that the former leader of a desperate military cause "stood on as difficult ground as he had ever done in his life." Even admitting that the President had somehow to find time to do business, "for him to be seen only in public on stated times, like an eastern Lama, would be . . . offensive." The backwoods senator sent a message to Washington to this effect.[6]

Washington's reaction was to distribute queries to Madison, Hamilton, Adams, and Jay "on a line of conduct most eligible to be pursued by the President of the United States." The precedents he now established, Washington noted, might continue for a long time, materially affecting not only the popularity but the nature of the government. The first requisite, of course, was for the President to get his work done. He needed, in addition, to avoid "the inconveniences as well as reduction of respectability by too free an intercourse and too much familiarity." On the other hand, it was essential that he avoid giving the impression of "an ostentatious show of mimicry of sovereignty." And Washington did not wish by stopping "the avenues to useful information from the many" to make himself "more dependent on that of the few."[7]

One of Washington's specific queries was pitiful: could he sometimes slip out inconspicuously to have tea with a friend? The cashless planter also expressed worry lest Congress, in providing for the Presidency, underestimate the cost of the necessary entertaining. If he were granted too little, he could not, without demeaning his office, ask for more, but should the appropriation prove too large, he could either leave the superfluity in the Treasury or "sacredly" apply it "to the promotion of some national objects."[8]

Although Adams and Hamilton both recommended more rigorously withdrawn behavior, the conclusions Washington decided on did not allay the outrage of republicans of the Maclay stripe. Washington established two occasions a week when any respectably dressed person could, without introduction, invitation, or any prearrangement, be ushered into his presence. One was the President's "levee," for men only, every Tuesday from three to four. The other was Martha's tea party, for men and women, held on Friday evenings. Washington would also stage dinners on Thursdays at four o'clock in the afternoon. To avoid any charges of favoritism or any contests for invitations, only officials and their families would be asked to the dinners, and these in an orderly system of rotation.

However much Washington might consider it now necessary, formalized social intercourse did not root comfortably in the easygoing traditions of Virginia entertaining with which he was familiar. His levees exhibited none of the joviality of entertainments at Mount Vernon, or of the ancient relaxations in army camps. The occasions could hardly have been stiffer. Exposed, as he put it, to "foreign characters, strangers and others who from motives of curiosity . . . or any other cause are induced to call upon me," Washington suffered from the same rigid embarrassment which made him for portrait painters so frustrating a sitter.[9]

As aristocracies had learned by long experience, only ceremony can give satisfactory content to altogether formal occasions. However, Washington squashed the efforts of Humphreys, who had been received in the best courts of Europe, to import some of their style. Jefferson was told that at the opening of an early levee, Humphreys led Washington through an antechamber to what the aide called the "presence chamber," where the guests were already assembled. Humphreys threw open the door, entered first, and shouted, "The President of the United States!"

Washington, so Jefferson's account continues, was so disconcerted that he did not recover his composure during the whole time of the levee. After it was finally over, he told Humphreys angrily, "Well, you have taken me in once, but by God, you shall never take me in a second time!" From then on, Washington, wearing his most formal clothes, with a hat (designed to be thus carried) under his arm, with the white leather scabbard of his dress sword peeping out from under his black coat, was standing uneasily in the room when the door was thrown open to allow in that week's jostle and craning of callers.[10]

That he was not at ease, that he did not exude the joviality which more modern politicans have learned to assume, disappointed his guests and sent rumors flying that he was snubbing good republicans with the hauteur of aristocratic behavior. Notified that such was the gossip in Virginia, Washington replied that he could not imagine "what pomp there is in all this. . . . Perhaps it consists in not sitting." However, he had been supplied with no room large enough to contain a third of the chairs that would be required.

"Gentlemen," Washington continued, "often in great numbers, come and go, chat with each other, and act as they please. A porter shows them into the room, and they retire from it when they please and without ceremony. At their *first* entrance, they salute me and I them, and as many as I can talk to I do." That he was not "able to make bows to the taste of poor Colonel Bland . . . is to be regreted, especially too as . . . they were indiscriminately bestowed and the best I was master of." Would it not have been more charitable to ascribe his awkwardness to the stiffness of age or the unskillfulness of his teachers, rather than to pride of office? He would rather, Washington burst out, "be at Mount Vernon with a friend or two about me than to be attended at the seat of government by the officers of state and the representatives of every power in Europe."[11]

"Domestic arrangements" were the province of Lear. Washington waited until everything was "well fixed" in the new house before he summoned Martha. She arrived, with the two grandchildren, almost a month after her husband had been inaugurated.

The President's wife had been much feted on the road. She wrote concerning her grandson, "Dear Little Washington seemed to be lost in a maze at the great parade that was made for us all the way we come." Concerning her own reactions, she was more grudging: she wrote that since what she interpreted as demonstrations of affection for her husband "came from the heart, I cannot deny that I have taken some interest and pleasure in them."

She must have stared nervously from her carriage to see what kind of house had been prepared for her. Since it proved to be three stories high and have a five-window front, she concluded it was "a very good one." On entering, she was pleased to discover that it was "handsomely furnished all new for the General." But yet, how she did miss Mount Vernon!

"As my grandchildren and my domestic connections made up a great proportion of the felicity I look for in this world," she wrote, "I shall hardly be able to find any substitute." It was, indeed, unfortunate that "I, who had much rather be at home, should occupy a place with which a great many younger and gayer women would be prodigiously pleased."[12]

Yet the fact remained that, even though she was separated from two grandchildren and from the family of her double-niece Fanny Bassett Washington, her two favorite grandchildren were at her side. Lear had found them a good school "which they are both very much pleased at." The old spinet Washington had imported from England before the war for Martha's dead daughter, which had been brought with other heavy pieces from Mount Vernon by water, was turned in now for a more modern "piano forte," and ten-year-old Nellie was receiving lessons not from some peripatetic Virginia dancing master, but from Alexander Reinagle, an English immigrant who was writing the finest American instrumental music of the eighteenth century. Martha, who loved to give presents, now could send home sophisticated gifts: a fashionable silk handkerchief, a beautifully crafted child's chair.[13]

Martha was, in fact, healthier than she had been for some time. As her strength mounted and her spirits returned, she yearned for more social life and became irked by the restrictions that her husband was conscientiously placing on their social activity: "I live a very dull life here and know nothing that passes in the town. I never go to any public place. Indeed, I think I am more like a state prisoner than anything else. There is certain bounds set for me which I must not depart from. And, as I cannot do as I like, I am obstinate and stay at home a great deal." Yet there was no harm in her making herself look as pretty as she could. "My hair," she wrote Fanny, "is set and dressed every day, and I have put on white muslin habits for the summer. You would, I fear, think me a good deal in the fashion if you could but see me."* [14]

Perhaps under Martha's urging (which certainly agreed with his own preferences), Washington gradually and inconspicuously loosened his rigorous avoidance of private society—and at the public entertainments, Martha shone. She not only soothed the men, but charmed the ladies, even the most intellectual and captious.

Abigail Adams had also arrived late at the capital. Having been told by her husband John—who sarcastically referred to Washington as "*His Majesty*"—that hauteur and false grandeur now characterized the Washingtons, she must have been surprised, when she called on Martha, to be received with great "ease and politeness." Martha, she noted, "is plain in her dress, but the plainness is the best of every article. . . . Her hair is white, her teeth beautiful." Abigail even admired Martha's plump figure, considering it better than her own.

"Mrs. Washington," the Boston bluestocking summarized, "is one of those unassuming characters which create love and esteem. A most becoming pleasantness sits upon her countenance, and an unaffected deportment which renders her the object of veneration and respect."[15]

---

* Martha spent about fifty dollars a year on the hairdresser and a hundred and fifty for jewelry.

Although Washington's levees were usually dull (as well as criticized for being aristocratically stiff), Martha's weekly tea parties were gay (and criticized for being aristocratically splendid). The General, who on these more informal occasions appeared without hat or sword, was a different man. He relaxed in the presence of the fair sex. Female elegance appealed to him, and the ladies of New York (as later in Philadelphia), having no more elaborate Presidential parties to attend, did not spare the milliners and hairdressers. They wore their hair low, with pearls and bandeaux, *à la greque,* or rolled moderately skyward, *à la Pompadour.* It was noted that when his duties as a host left him free to circulate, Washington passed the men by and spent all his time with the ladies.[16]

Throughout her tea parties, Martha remained seated. Because he did not personally like the Vice President, Washington was all the more meticulous in honoring the office; he saw to it that the seat at Martha's right was assigned to the Vice President's lady. If another lady happened to be sitting there when Abigail Adams arrived, Washington got the interloper to move with a tact that made Abigail comment, "This same President has so happy a faculty of appearing to accommodate and yet carrying his point, that, if he was not really one of the best-intentioned men in the world, he might be a very dangerous one." She then launched on a panegyric about Washington that would, had he seen it, have irritated her husband: "He is polite with dignity, affable without familiarity, distant without haughtiness, grave without austerity, modest, wise and good."[17]

Servants who stood at the door announced the guests' names. Then Humphreys or Lear escorted the ladies to Mrs. Washington. After making "a most respectful curtsy" and engaging in a moment of conversation with Martha, each lady was conducted to a chair where she was supposed to sit "without noticing any of the rest of the company" until the President came up to her. When Washington approached, it was—so noted Abigail, who had been at the Court of St. James's—"with a grace, dignity, and ease that leaves Royal George far behind him." The lady was then free to go into the other room, where there were refreshments: ice cream, tea and coffee, cakes, candy, cold fruit drinks in summer.* [18]

---

* One late July, Martha ordered, at a cost of £25.40.4, one hundred oranges, a dozen pineapples, six coconuts, a fourteen-pound cheese, and assorted sweetmeats.[19]

Martha was capable of breaking up a reception at nine-thirty by stating her husband usually went to bed at nine and that she usually preceded him. Such homey notes (and the lack of liquor) did not keep Martha's teas from figuring luridly in many minds. Newspaper editors who yearned for a high, monarchical society, reported the occasions in inflated terms, even referring to the female guests not as "Mrs. ———" but as "Lady This" and "Lady That." Republican editors viewed with the utmost alarm: that the servants who ushered in the guests had their hair powdered seemed to threaten the very fabric of the nation.[20]

The Washingtons often went to the theater, on one occasion taking Senator Maclay, who was horrified that the chief magistrate should countenance the exposure of "ladies of character and virtue" to such an "indecent representation" as Sheridan's School for Scandal. Maclay also had his turns at Washington's dinner parties.[21]

Despite the restriction of the invitations to officials the dinners could be gay, since such of Washington's favorite friends as Knox and Robert Morris held office. He often tried to leaven a lump and create a party more like those at Mount Vernon by inviting (as he did with the John Adams family) not only the elders but grownup sons, daughters, and daughters-in-law.[22] However, there were unsuccessful dinners and one of these Maclay—who was enough by himself to put a damper on almost any party—reported angrily and gleefully for posterity.

As he dressed in preparation, Maclay warned himself that he had to be wary lest his pure republicanism be undermined by the seductions of Washington's environment. Thus, he was relieved, shortly after his arrival, to fortify his immunity with the conclusion that one of the couples who had come in together were in all probability not legally married.

The President and Mrs. Washington sat opposite each other in the middle of the dinner table, the ladies being ranged on both sides of Martha, the gentlemen opposite them on both sides of George. The seduction that Maclay feared then approached in a form that endangered his resolutions: food. The dinner began with "soup, fish, roasted and boiled meats, gammon, fowls, etc. . . . . The dessert was first apple pies, pudding, etc., then iced creams, jellies, etc., then watermelons, muskmelons, apples, peaches, nuts." Unable to deny that the meal was "the best of the kind" he had ever experienced, Maclay was nonetheless able to find some soothing dissatisfactions: the room was "disagreeably warm," and the food was eaten in solemn silence, "not a health drunk."

After the cloth had been removed, the pendulum swung the other way, and there were too many toasts. To Maclay's disgust, the President "drank to the health of every individual by name round the table." The guests then imitated him, "and such a buzz of 'Health, sir' and 'Health, madam' never had I heard before." Silence, according to Maclay, sank again until the ladies withdrew. Then the President told an anecdote—about "a New England clergyman who had lost a hat and wig in passing a river called the Brunks"—which Maclay did not consider funny. Another guest delighted and horrified Maclay by refering to Homer when he should have said Virgil.

"The President kept a fork in his hand," but instead of using it to open nuts, as Maclay suspected he would, he "played with the fork, striking on the edge of the table with it." Maclay assumed that the President was being pompous and dull, but perhaps Washington was hearing yearningly in his mind's ear laughter on the banks of the Potomac.[23]

Congress decided that it would make a bad precedent to accede to Washington's request that he be paid expenses but not a salary; they set the Presidential stipend at $25,000 a year. Although they seemed to be brushing aside his self-sacrifice, the decision would have been to Washington's advantage only if his expenses had been less than the $25,000.

Lear kept the most meticulous accounts. He held the private purse from which, when asked, he doled out sums to the President and his lady. Yet it was no more possible for Washington to keep his expenses down in office than on his plantation. He had to supplement his salary with some $5000 annually. Fortunately, this was not more than he could afford, since the expenses at Mount Vernon were so much reduced. Washington's total financial position moved upward. True, he still possessed little fluid cash, but he was no longer dunned for unpayable debts.[24]

In New York, Washington spent about 7 per cent of his Presidential salary on the liquor he served and, to a moderate extent, himself drank. With some difficulty (he drew a blank at Bordeaux) he searched out the proper French shipping center from which to procure a sparkling beverage called champagne. When Gouverneur Morris went abroad, Washington asked him to procure either in Paris or London (wherever they could be got more cheaply) silver-plated wine coolers with provision for ice at the bottom. The eight he needed at dinner should be light enough for ladies to handle and have space for two pint decanters, one of madeira and the other of claret. After dinner he required four man-sized coolers, with apertures large and numerous enough for "a *quart* decanter or quart bottle" of four different kinds of wine. "It often happens," Washington explained querulously, "that *one* bottle moves, *another* stops, and *all* are in confusion."

Washington also asked Morris to procure a set of mirrors that would make the center of the Presidential table sparkle. When all combined, they should flatly cover an area of ten feet by two, but they should fit together in different ways, so that they could be adapted to various table sizes.[25]

He further wished "neat and fashionable, but not expensive, ornaments" to sit on the mirrors and be reflected by them. Gouverneur Morris should remember the statuary they had both admired at Robert Morris's and get something similar. Washington eventually received twelve porcelain semi-nudes representing the arts and sciences with, as a centerpiece, a large group entitled *Apollo Instructing the Shepherds*. The mirrors and figures became standard features of Presidential entertaining.[26]

In 1789, Washington kept fifteen servants around the house, with six more assigned to the stables. He had brought with him seven slaves. However, probably because of the northern objections and his own uneasiness concerning slavery, the fourteen hired white servants occupied all the positions that came in contact with the public. They included the coachman,* two footmen, and the housemaids. Washington's steward, a well-known tavern owner in New York called Samuel Fraunces, came from the Indies and must have had a dark complexion since he was known as "Black Sam." He stood at attendance at the

---

* A glimpse into domestic disagreements is provided by a letter from Washington to Lear about coachmen. "Dunn" had demonstrated "such proofs of his want of skill in driving" that "we were obliged to take him from the coach and put him to the wagon. This he turned over twice, and this morning was found much intoxicated. He has also got the horses into a habit of stopping."

A replacement being necessary, Mrs. Washington had expressed a strong predilection for Jacob, whom Washington seems previously to have discharged. Stating that his "prejudices and fears" remained "great," Washington suggested that Lear nonetheless "ask something concerning Jacob."[27]

dinner table, dressed in a wig and small clothes, superintending the service. Washington also had a French confectioner and for a time a valet who was probably French, since his name was Julian L'Hoste.[28]

French valet or no, the Washingtons felt most at home with habitual servants who, despite their closeness to their masters remained, in the Virginia pattern, slaves. Martha had brought her veteran attendants Mollie and Oney, while Washington had replaced Will with a younger body-servant named Christopher.[29]

Will had fallen down on two occasions, each time breaking a knee-cap. He had become a cripple. Washington, who had sent him to Philadelphia for treatment, now wrote he hoped Will would return to Mount Vernon. However, if the slave wished to come to the Presidential mansion, he was too old a servant to be refused. Will came on.[30]

While in office, the French valet bought powder for the Presidential hair, black silk bags to hold the Presidential queue, and the narrow black ribbons known as "solitaires" that held the queue in place by being passed around the Presidential neck and tied behind. Although Washington wore black velvet on formal occasions, his favorite suit color was brown. He also wore gray and gray-mixtures. For trousers that were too tight at the seat and thigh to pull on with ease, he had "an utter aversion." He never appeared in military costume except to receive the Cincinnati or review militia. To the blue and buff uniform he had designed for his own militia company before the Revolution, he added epaulettes given him by Lafayette and a diamond-studded emblem of the Cincinnati presented him by the French fleet.[31]

Washington tried to take advantage of the superior skills presumably available in New York by hiring still another dentist, John Greenwood, who applied to his empty gums a complete set of new false teeth. The upper portion was a solid piece of sculpture carved from hippopotamus tusk; the base of the lower was made of the same material, but had attached to it by gold pivots (in a manner said to have been invented by Greenwood) actual human teeth. The utility was moderate, the comfort small; and this was far from the end of Washington's dental hegira that remained forever unsatisfactory.[32]

To defend her husband, who brought opprobrium down on his own head by continuing to argue that titles and politically inspired elegance were essential aspects of strong government, Abigail Adams insisted that the idolized Washington lived in great splendor. She

Washington's waistcoat. Courtesy of the Mount Vernon Ladies' Association

A suit and pair of underdrawers worn by George Washington.
Courtesy of the Mount Vernon Ladies' Association

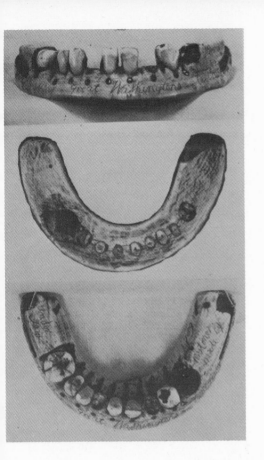

Lower denture made for Washington in 1789 by John Greenwood of hippopotamus ivory, originally containing eight human teeth retained in place with gold screw rivets. The hole was to permit Washington's one remaining tooth to slip through. The base was covered with red sealing wax. *Top:* Front view. *Middle:* Under view showing the curved surface to fit the gums. *Bottom:* View from above. Courtesy of the New York Academy of Medicine

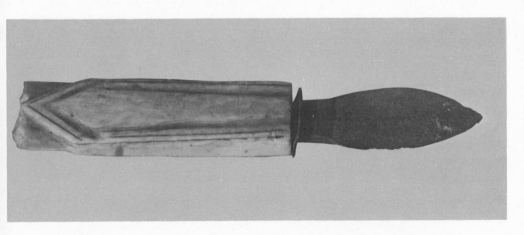

Washington's steel eraser, much worn down with correcting the Presidential prose. The handle is of ivory. Overall length 3½ inches. Courtesy of the Mount Vernon Ladies' Association

pointed in particular to his highly decorated coach that was drawn by six horses and attended by four servants in livery, with two gentlemen up behind. What Abigail—and also critics of different politics who saw the coach grinding under its wheels American democracy—did not realize was that this was no new vehicle Washington had acquired to make the Presidency dazzling. It had, indeed, been given to Martha during the Revolution by the government of Pennsylvania, and had often been seen on the roads around Mount Vernon with just as many liveried servants and just as many horses.

Perhaps because in his impoverished youth he had been forced to make such a poor appearance in comparison to his richer friends and relations, Washington had a passion for fine equipage. It had probably been this emotion which had induced him to accept (on the technicality that the gift was to Martha) this coach despite his rule against receiving expensive presents as governmental rewards. The coach had been made by a celebrated London carriage maker for the pre-Revolutionary lieutenant governor of Pennsylvania, John Penn. It featured paintings of the four seasons on the front and back doors. When in 1790, Washington had to have the vehicle repaired, he urged that the paintings be "freshened" if "a masterly hand can be employed." He then added piously that he would rather have the elaborately decorated vehicle look, when it was returned to him, "plain and elegant than rich and elegant." On another occasion, he explained the "extravagance would not comport with my own inclination nor with the example which ought to be set."[33]

However, it would have sunk his spirits when he went to his stables to find the stalls inhabited by ordinary nags. His twelve to sixteen horses were a joy to the eye. There was a matched set of six coach horses, cream-colored with white manes. There were two white saddle horses. Most of the rest were bays. He would as soon walk out with unpolished shoes as ride out with horses whose hoofs had not been blackened. It was natural for him, when he moved around on horseback, to use his pretty housing: the silver-mounted saddle rested on a leopardskin, the whole made brighter by seven yards of gold binding.[34]

In accepting the Presidency, Washington had not promised to make himself over into a new man. He could, indeed, reasonably conclude that the nation had come to him because of the kind of man he was. A personal and Virginian brand of elegance had become for him second nature, and thus, although untempted by titles and uneasy with such ceremony as would not be at home in a private setting, he felt that his normal way of life was correctly aimed "to support propriety of character without partaking of the follies of luxury and ostentation."[35]

Although Washington knew that some republicans thought he was being too aristocratic and Europeanized, he saw on the faces of European aristocratic visitors that they considered his way of life surprisingly plain.* Martha's and his desires, he wrote, were "limited," and he felt confident, after he had set up his schedule of levees and teas and dinners, that "our plans of living will now be deemed reasonable by the considerate part of our species."[36]

For the time being, public objections were, indeed, muted. Washington could not foresee that when the political sky turned truly stormy, and it became to the interest of a powerful party to discredit him, he was to suffer from passionate and wounding charges of extravagance and aristocratic living.

---

* Not only did the French minister consider the Presidential residence squalid, but the secretary of the Dutch legation reported home on Washington's "simple and frugal mode of living."[37]

17

Fleshing Out the New Government

P ROBABLY because there was so much disagreement at the
Constitutional Convention on matters of detail, the Constitution,
as established there, was little more than a skeleton in need of
flesh. How the government would function in a thousand different
particulars remained to be worked out at its beginning. Only general
boundaries were, for instance, charted between the three great divisions: executive, legislative, and judicial. The government could have
ended up not in its present form, but much closer to the British
parliamentary system, with the executive departments subservient to
the legislature. Or, had Washington lusted for power, the legislative
might have become subservient to the executive.

The first session of the new government was thus almost as important to the American future as the Constitutional Convention had
been. In some areas, indeed, the problems were greater, since it was no
longer possible to postpone specific decisions on issues that portended
disagreement. Although the judicial function was at the start in
abeyance, since the courts could not exist until set up by the legislature, the Congress and President Washington had to determine their
respective pulls and invent their harnesses while at the same time
dragging along the coach of state.

Fortunately, the historical landscape through which, as they learned
to work together, they had to move the United States, could not have
been more smiling. If, as Washington liked to believe, Providence was
watching over the daring American experiment in popular rule, surely
that benign power made no greater gift than a summer of tranquillity,

commercial prosperity, and bountiful harvests during which the government could find internal agreement with no outside interference beyond a few Indian raids on restricted frontiers.

In Europe, it is true, there exploded on July 14 one of the most crucial events in all modern history: the storming of the Bastille. However the news did not reach America until the autumn. Washington wrote that the happenings in France seemed as far away as if they were "of another planet."[1]

Meditating on these faraway events, Washington proved amazingly prescient. His French correspondents predicted that their nation would become, under a new constitution, "the most powerful and happy in Europe." But Washington believed the nation had only experienced "the first paroxysm. . . . The revolution is of too great magnitude to be effected in so short a space and with the loss of so little blood. The mortification of the King, the intrigues of the Queen, and the discontent of the Princes and the Noblesse will foment divisions, if possible, in the National Assembly, and avail themselves of every faux pas in the formation of the constitution. . . . To these, the licentiousness of the people on one hand and sanguinary punishments on the other will alarm the best disposed friends to the measure. . . . Great temperance, firmness, and foresight are necessary. . . . To forbear running from one extreme to another is no easy matter, and, should this be the case, rocks and shelves not visible at present may wreck the vessel."[2]

Fortunately, the worst of what Washington foresaw lay well in the future. Since the stresses which developed in America when the French boiler finally exploded came close to tearing apart a government then firmly established, it seems highly probable that, had the timetable in France been pushed ahead by three years, the union set up by the Constitution would have disintegrated before it could get going.

As it was, the new government was permitted the luxury of opening with its argument, then altogether abstract, on titles and etiquette. Before any further issues had any real chance to ripen, the strong hand was removed from the helm. Across the street near the Presidential mansion a rope was stretched to keep all vehicles from passing.* Straw

* Deplorers of modern delinquency will be interested to hear that the rope was stolen and had to be replaced.

was spread on the sidewalks to kill the sound of footsteps. The President seemed on the point of death.

On June 13, Washington had developed a high fever and a pain in his thigh. New York's leading physician, Dr. Samuel Bard, found a tumor which he diagnosed as anthrax. According to a believable anecdote, Washington asked the doctor for a frank report on his chances: "I am not afraid to die and therefore can bear the worst. . . . Whether tonight or twenty years hence makes no difference. I know I am in the hands of a good Providence."

Samuel Bard called in as a consultant his seventy-three-year-old father, John Bard (for which the old gentleman charged twenty-five pounds). Father and son agreed that Washington's only hope lay in an immediate operation.

According to the biographer of the Bards, the infection proved, when the tumor was laid open, to have spread further than had been foreseen. This was, of course, before the discovery of any effective way of relieving pain. As the son quailed at the prospect before him, the elder Bard cried, "Cut away—deeper—deeper still! Don't be afraid. You see how well he bears it!" Lear wrote that the tumor was "very large and the incision on opening it deep."[3]

The operation was so complete a success that Washington's fever was gone in five days. However, it took a long time for the incision to heal. Week after week, he lay perpetually on his side, raising himself a little on the settee when it was necessary to receive visitors. Early in July, he had an alteration made in his coach which enabled him "to extend myself the full length of it." He could then get what "exercise" was supplied his long frame by movements of the carriage.[4]

Forty days of the new government's first summer had passed before the doctors would allow the President to return to his desk, and it was four months before he felt completely recovered. This was the worst illness he had suffered since shortly after his French and Indian War service (1761). To his close friend and physician in Virginia, Dr. Craik, he confided, "The want of regular exercise with the cares of office will, I have no doubt, hasten my departure for that country from whence no traveler returns."[5]

Having been, on his election as Commander in Chief, the only member of the Continental Army, Washington was not dismayed to be, with the Vice President, the only member of the executive branch of the new government. He could make no appointments until Congress created the offices to which the appointments would be made. Pending that time, he had to assist him holdovers from the organization established, under the Articles of Confederation, by the defunct Continental Congress. Secretary of War Knox and Secretary of Foreign Affairs Jay were carrying on as "Temporary Secretaries." There were a Treasury Board and a few minor functionaries, a regular army not up to its quota of 840 men, and a smattering of clerks whose salaries were in arrears. The foreign service consisted principally of Jefferson in Paris.[6]

As one of his first Presidential acts, Washington called on the various holdovers for such an account of their departments "as may be sufficient (without overburdening or confusing the mind which has very many objects to claim its attention at the same instant) to impress me with a full, precise, and distinct *general idea*." From what he was sent, Washington (as was to remain his practice) made written abstracts—eight folio pages, for instance, being devoted to Jefferson's reports from Paris to Jay. As an assistance in such labors, he ordered from London "a terrestrial globe of the largest dimensions . . . now in use."[7]

With his acting Secretaries, Washington inaugurated at once the system of having them handle all ordinary matters. Although the Constitution stated that the President should "receive" top foreign representatives, Washington refused to discuss Franco-American relations directly with the French minister, Moustier. He did not intend to allow any official "to erect a wall between me and the diplomatic corps," yet under normal circumstances business that came to the President should have been first "digested and prepared" by the head of the relevant department.[8]

Washington's relation with the Vice President was not open to such clear definition. Although the Constitution made John Adams presiding officer of the Senate, there was nothing in the document to keep him from also becoming, in effect, the President's prime minister. This step would, indeed, have been logical, since the Constitution visualized the Vice President as the individual most admired by the Electors after their first choice—and it would be well to have him prepared to handle the tasks he would suddenly face if the President died. However, Washington had no urge for close collaboration with the politician who had made him so much trouble when he was Commander in Chief. And Adams himself was neither conciliatory nor eager to partake in the executive administration. In his own inaugural speech, the Vice President had not resisted coupling with a suitable reference to Washington's "commanding talents and virtues" a reference to Washington's "overruling good fortune." Sure that he would be made the scapegoat if things went wrong, Adams feared favoring the President with advice. Washington started out by including Adams in various executive discussions, but gradually abandoned such consultations. Before the end of the first term the Vice Presidency was established in the backwater from which it has never emerged.[9]

Although Jay and Knox were old friends, Washington did not, as he was later to do with his own Cabinet, ask these remains from the defunct government to play the role of general advisers. He turned for help primarily to the fellow Virginian who had been one of the major architects of the Constitution. He was perpetually summoning Madison, sending him written requests for advice. Although Madison never became an official spokesman for the administration, his closeness to Washington was well known. The opening of the government thus presented the anomalous picture of a member of the House of Representatives being as much of a prime minister as the President had.[10]

The provisions in the Constitution concerning what was to become the President's "Cabinet" (Washington seems first to have used the word in April 1793) were indicative of how much remained to be decided. The "Heads of Departments" were accorded no defining clause of their own but, their existence having been assumed, were referred to in more general contexts. The power given the President to appoint, with the approval of the Senate, all the important non-elective officers did not mention specifically the department heads. Furthermore, this provision did not imply Presidential jurisdiction after appointment, since among the officials included were the justices of the Supreme Court, who were clearly intended to be thereafter independent of the President. The only specific authority Washington was given in relation to the department heads was a minor one: he might require of them opinions relating to their duties. And Congress was given the power to assign directly to them (bypassing the President) the appointment of "inferior officers in their departments."[11]

To secure a single executive rather than a committee, and to have him elected by the people rather than by Congress, had been one of the most difficult tasks in the Constitutional Convention: the matter was still undecided two weeks before adjournment. There were many political leaders who still wished the executive limited to putting into effect the will of the legislative, and these saw their opportunity when Congress set up the executive departments. The controversy that developed turned on where the power to discharge an executive official should lie. Opponents of a strong President argued that the Constitutional provision that the President could only appoint with the approval of the Senate implied that he would also have to secure that approval before he could dismiss. This would mean, of course, that a department head who opposed or even blocked the President's policies could be kept in office against the President's wishes by a majority of the Senate. It was argued on the other side that the President would be hamstrung if he were prevented from being master in his own house.[12]

With Madison laboring mightily, the House of Representatives voted against supporting Senatorial interference in Presidential dismissals. But the Senate proved so evenly divided that the final vote was a tie, which Adams, as presiding officer, broke by supporting an independent executive.[13]

Since the matter was so closely contested even with the prestigious Washington in the executive chair, it is hard to doubt that if anyone else had been President, the vote would have gone the other way. This would have resulted in a very different form of government. Since the President's top assistants would have been no more accountable to him than to the Congress, he could have become—like a modern constitutional monarch—primarily a figurehead.

Foreign policy having been established in the Constitution as the President's province, Washington did not hesitate to assert his primacy in diplomatic affairs. Thus, when the French King notified "the President and Members of Congress" that the Dauphin had died, Washington, in sending condolences, pointed out that "the honor of receiving and answering" such communications no longer in any way involved the Congress; it was solely his own.[14]

However, the Constitution stipulated that the President had to seek the Senate's "advice and consent" concerning treaties. This provision, along with the need for Senatorial approval of appointments, required the establishment of lines of communication between the Chief Executive and the Senate. Washington had hardly risen from his sickbed when, with Madison advising him at every step, he set out to regularize those lines. Respecting treaties and perhaps foreign appointments, where there might be a need for "much discussion," Washington favored personal confrontations; for other appointments, written communication. Two meetings with a Senatorial committee made clear that there was such a wide variety of contingencies that the matter could not be standardized. It was decided that, since the Senate was "evidently" acting as "a council only to the President," the President should determine, for each specific case, the method of consultation.[15]

The most important precedent was soon established by a confrontation full of comic overtones. Having drafted instructions for a commission he had appointed, with Senate approval, to negotiate a treaty with the Creek Indians, Washington accompanied the Acting Secretary of War, Knox to the Senate chamber seeking "advice and consent."*

Maclay scented indignity to the legislature at the very start when the President "took our Vice President's chair" and Knox sat beside him facing the House, while Adams, although the Senate's presiding officer, joined the other senators below the dais.

Having been handed by Knox the proposed text of the treaty, Adams stood up and started to read it aloud. "Carriages were driving past, and such a noise!" Maclay noted. "I could tell it was something about Indians, but was not master of one sentence of it. Signs were made to the doorkeeper to shut down the sashes." It was now possible to hear a little, but the reading had gone on to a supplementary document. This finished, Adams asked for "advice and consent" to the first section of the treaty instructions.

Robert Morris suggested that the section be read again. It was. Adams asked again for "advice and consent." Maclay then rose to say, "The business is new to the Senate. It is of importance. It is our duty to inform ourselves." He requested the reading of some additional papers which had been mentioned. Washington, he considered, was surveying him with "stern displeasure."

The reading of the documents began; various members asked to hear others; there was the usual confusion of random discussion; and Washington finally agreed to postponing consideration of the first

---

* In an indicative manner, Indian relations were entrusted not to the Secretary of Foreign Affairs but the Secretary of War.

article. On to the second! A matter came up of crucial interest to Georgia, and a member from that state asked that it be postponed till Monday. Maclay was gleefully putting his shoulder to the wheel of confusion, since "I saw no chance of a fair investigation . . . while the President of the United States sat there, with his Secretary of War to support his opinions, and overawe the timid and neutral part of the Senate." However, it was Washington's own crony Morris who moved that the papers brought by the President be submitted to a committee for study.

Washington started up in what Maclay described as "a violent fret." He cried, *"This defeats every purpose of my coming here!"* He had brought Knox with him to present all the necessary information, "and yet he was delayed and could not go on with the matter!"

Maclay described Washington cooling "by degrees." The President finally agreed to a postponement till Monday. Then he departed "with a discontented air. Had it been any other man than the man whom I wish to regard as the first character in the world, I would have said with sullen dignity."

On Monday, Washington reappeared, well in control of himself. "He was placid and serene and manifested a spirit of accommodation." Although in the end he achieved his purpose—only minor changes were made in the treaty instructions—Washington had to sit hour after hour, listening to an inconsequential and boring debate. As he finally departed from the Senate chamber, he was overheard to say he would "be damned if he ever went there again!"[16]

Washington probably got himself into what proved a ridiculous situation by thinking in Revolutionary War terms. When appointed Commander in Chief, he had been ordered by the Continental Congress to consult with his general officers even as the Constitution ordered him to get the advice and consent of the Senate. Consent after the event meant nothing in war. And to get advice, all Washington had to do was to lay before his generals the very latest facts. Being all absorbed in the same campaign, they were already familiar with the background. He did not, till he tried it out, recognize that the Senate, being concerned with a wide variety of matters, would have to study before they could not make up their minds.

The British system, in which the Prime Minister defends his policies before Parliament, demonstrates that it is possible so to set up a government that there can be effective personal confrontations between the chief executive and the legislature. But in the United States, Washington forever slammed the door: he never again consulted the Senate in person. No President has ever taken part, in the British manner, in parliamentary debates.

Washington still sometimes sent the Secretaries of War or Foreign Affairs to meetings of Senate committees bearing documents that would help them "advise,"[17] but the idea seems to have already been growing in his mind that if there were to be any effective foreign negotiations, the prior advice of the Senate would have to be skimped in favor of ultimate consent. Otherwise, the negotiators' hands would be tied before the negotiation started. They might, indeed, be further embarrassed by what seemed a public commitment, since the senators could not be counted on not to leak decisions to the newspapers. Concerning the most important foreign negotiations he faced—those with England—Washington resolved to proceed in an unofficial manner which would obviate the necessity of consulting the Senate or of seeking the necessary funds from a Congress that had already hesitated to authorize suitable expenditures in the foreign service.

England had never fully recognized the victor of the Revolution by appointing a minister to the United States. Since America had retaliated in 1788 by calling John Adams home, official relations between the two nations were in abeyance. However, a British consul, Sir John Temple, appeared in New York and handed to Jay a series of questions from his government concerning American foreign trade, produce, population, and whether a new system of justice would aid "the recovery of British debts according to treaty."

In response, Washington decided to inquire informally, through "a private agent," whether the British were willing to change their legislation aimed at curbing American commerce, and would also evacuate the western posts they were holding in violation of the peace treaty. Since no money had been appropriated for the envoy's expenses, the mission would have to be assigned to someone already in Europe, who could combine it with his private business.

Acting Foreign Secretary Jay agreed to the scheme and suggested Dr. Edward Bancroft. Washington could not know that Bancroft had, when secretary to the American Commissioners in Paris during the Revolution, served as a British spy, yet he did not accept Jay's suggestion. It seemed to him more natural to select as a personal envoy a personal friend—and one of his closest friends was abroad. Perhaps at the suggestion of Hamilton (Washington's diary reference is ambiguous) he proposed to his advisers the name of Gouverneur Morris.[18]

When during 1776 Washington was trying to prepare in New York for the impending onslaught of British might, he had first met Morris, who was sent to him by the local congress as a member of a "secret committee." Later at Valley Forge, Morris had appeared as a representative of the Continental Congress and proved immensely helpful in straightening out the desperate situation of supply. By then, the New York patrician had moved to Philadelphia to become a partner of Robert Morris (who, despite the similarity of names, was no relation). As inflation threatened to wash the cause under, the two Morrises established a little bank which did something to stem the tide. They became Washington's first mentors on the sophistications of finance, and were also the original teachers of this subject to a much more eager pupil, Alexander Hamilton.

During the Constitutional Convention, Washington had again found himself in close collaboration with Gouverneur Morris. Possessed of a brilliant mind and a voice "of much compass, strength, and richness,"[19] Morris was a powerful exponent of federal power and a strong executive. The Constitution as adopted was (and is) largely in Morris's words, since he had drafted the final document for the Committee of Style.

Now, in connection with the British mission, Washington consulted Hamilton, Madison, and Jay. All agreed that Morris had "superior talents," but only Hamilton agreed to his appointment. Jay argued that Morris's "imagination sometimes runs ahead of his judgment," and that his manners created a bad impression.[20]

Morris was arrogant, intolerant of fools, and possessed of such a reputation for licentiousness that it was generally believed that the leg he had lost in a carriage accident had come off as the result of an injury he received when jumping out of a lady's window as the husband unexpectedly came upstairs. Boasting that he "never knew the sensations of fear, embarrassment, or inferiority," Morris was as cocksure as he was arrogant. An inveterate prankster, much too elegantly dressed for the taste of simple republicans, he never hesitated to use his quick wit to humiliate men less brilliant than he. Josiah Bartlett of New Hampshire wrote that Morris was "for brass equal to any I am acquainted with."[21]

When Morris had started his business trip to Europe in 1788, Washington had showered him with letters of introduction. To Jefferson, Washington wrote, "You will find [him] full of affability, good nature, vivacity, and talents." To Chastellux: "Only let him be once fairly presented to your French ladies, and I answer for it, he will not leave the worst impression in the world of the American character for taciturnity and improper reserve."[22]

He was so close in stature to Washington that Houdon used his body as a model for his full length of the hero.[23] However, Morris gave a much less ponderous impression. He was always in rapid motion, his blue eyes asparkle, his queue of light brown hair swinging perpetually from side to side. Observers, even those who recognized Morris's intellectual brilliance, were amazed to see two men so different in temperament often closeted together in gleeful conversation. No more then than now was it part of the Washington legend that he had a taste for scapegraces who could keep him amused and make him laugh. The seeming incongruity of the Washington-Morris association may explain the existence of two parallel anecdotes—neither of which saw print until long after both men were dead—which depict Morris as making too free with Washington and being devastatingly squelched.[24]

The best-known of the stories, which was originally published during 1874 by James Parton in his life of Jefferson, is laid at the Constitutional Convention. Hamilton, so the story goes, said in the presence of a large group that Washington "was reserved and aristocratic even to his intimate friends, and allowed no one to be familiar with him." When Morris objected that he could be "as familiar with Washington as with any of his other friends," Hamilton replied, "If you will, at the next reception evening, gently slap him on the shoulder and say, 'My dear General, how happy I am to see you look so well,' a supper and wine shall be provided for you and a dozen of your friends."

The "reception evenings" when (according to the anecdote) Washington kept open house for the delegates to the Convention, did not actually exist, but let us go on with the story: Morris is said to have done what Hamilton had dared him to do. Washington thereupon stepped back and "fixed his eye on Morris for several minutes with an angry frown, until the latter retreated abashed, and sought refuge in the crowd. The company looked on in silence. At the supper which was provided by Hamilton, Morris said, 'I have won the bet, but dearly paid for it, and nothing could induce me to repeat it.' "[25]

Although made suspect by its late date of publication and internal inaccuracies, this anedote does not conflict with Washington's known character as long as it is assumed that he guessed, from eager and amused faces turned towards him, that he was being made the butt of a public joke. Whatever was the situation in private, Washington had, in relation to his public image, a thinness of skin that reflected the shyness and diffidence which so strangely accompanied his self-confidence and power. An effort to make of him visibly a fool would have filled him with rage.

However, if he had been angry with Gouverneur Morris, that anger quickly passed. Despite the objections of Jay and Madison, he entrusted to his mercurial friend the most difficult diplomatic mission of the new government, thereby bringing into the American foreign service (if through the back door) one of the most picturesque characters it was ever to boast. Washington did not notify the Senate. The Constitution did not require him to do so.

"Few who are not philosophical spectators," Washington wrote, "can realize the difficult and delicate part which a man in my situation had to act. . . . I walk on untrodden ground. There is scarcely any part of my conduct which may not hereafter be drawn into precedent."[26]

Among Washington's very most important contributions to the emerging government was his restraint in exerting his great power beyond what he considered the legitimate province of the executive. Although he felt entitled to express, like any other citizen, his personal opinions to his friends, even if they happened to be legislators, he did not, in any official or concerted way, use his charisma or his office to influence legislative debates. Nor did he attempt to achieve by executive order any matter which the strictest interpretation of the Constitution could regard as within the legislative domain. The separation of powers has never known a more devoted champion.[27]

Having obeyed most sparingly the Presidential duty to make recommendations to Congress, Washington cracked no whip to get his program through. Congress did as it pleased. Among Washington's suggestions to which they agreed were amending the Constitution with a Bill of Rights, making the regular army official under the new government, drawing up plans for a uniform militia system, and calling out Virginia and Pennsylvania militia for protection of the Ohio frontier from the Wabash Indians. Other matters, such as the establishment of a mint and of uniform weights and measures, were postponed.[28] And Washington saw one of his favorite projects defeated.

Washington had always considered it a major argument for the establishment of the Constitution that a powerful centralized government would be able to retaliate against British shipping for British customs laws aimed at the Americans. When Congress defined the customs duties with which the federal government was to be supported, Washington wished them not only to favor American shipping but to discriminate against countries which, like Britain but not France, had entered into no commercial treaties with the United States. Under Madison's leadership, the House agreed, but the Senate balked so determinedly at discrimination against British trade that the bill which finally reached Washington for signature contained no such provision.

Washington was informed that the Senate had been motivated by "conciliatory considerations" and the hope that the British, knowing that America now had the power to retaliate, would voluntarily change their laws. Yet he continued to find this knuckling under to his former military enemies greatly "adverse to my ideas of justice and polity."[29]

Since setting customs duties was obviously within the legislative province, Washington made no gesture towards vetoing the bill. But he did consider registering a protest by allowing it to become law without his signature. In the end, he did not even go this far. He signed the bill, explaining that he had been assured by some members of the Senate that they would prepare another to achieve his purpose.[30]

Hamilton had explained in *The Federalist* that the veto power was essential to enable the President to protect his office from legislative usurpation.[31] Washington found no such need. Perhaps because he himself so religiously avoided encroaching on the legislative, the effort in the two houses to curb the Presidency collapsed with the effort to give the Senate a hand in executive dismissals. From then on, Congress showered on the President powers and responsibilities. Not only did the Senate forgo its Constitutional right to appoint secondary administrative officials, but it threw even such minor appointments as lighthouse keepers (with the power to build lighthouses) to the chief executive. Washington became so busy he could find no time to deal with his personal correspondence, even letters on so fascinating a subject as inland navigation.[32]

"To a man who has no ends to serve," he wrote, ". . . nominations to office is the most irksome part of the executive trust." Before any offices at all had been created by Congress, the flood of applications stormed in; it crested to between twenty-five hundred and three thousand appeals. Washington did his best to avoid interviews—"all that *I* require is the name and . . . testimonials with respect to abilities, integrity, and fitness"—but men would appear at his levees and add verbal pleas to the hard-luck stories that roared in with every mail. Many applicants, otherwise obviously unsuitable, were veterans who had fought at Washington's side; many more were old friends or sons of old friends.[33]

As a young soldier in the French and Indian War, when he was trying to make his way into the British military establishment, Washington had been blocked by his lack of "interest" with important individuals or families. Such interest was basic to the aristocratic way of life. Washington spurned it to an extent by no means always imitated by later politicians: he made practically no appointments that were based on friendship or family connection. Washington's criteria were personal merit; services and sacrifices rendered during the Revolution; a claim to an office due to having been the incumbent when the new government was established; and three matters of great moment to the general acceptance of the Constitution: geographic distribution,* sympathy with the Federal Union, and local popularity.[34]

In a nation as large as the United States, at a time when travel was so much rarer than now and communications so slow, to identify in a distant state the right man for an office required endless interviews and correspondence. Even John Adams admired Washington's industry and impartiality: "He seeks information from all quarters and judges more independently than any man I ever knew."[35]

Prevented by his sense of propriety from approaching any man before the office involved had been created,† and then suddenly pre-

---

* Washington appointed, for instance, Supreme Court justices from Massachusetts, New York, Pennsylvania, Maryland, Virginia, and South Carolina.
† In 1868, Alexander Hamilton's son wrote that Washington had told his father to expect the Treasury at so early a date that Hamilton was encouraged to play an active part in the creation of the office. Since (as we shall see) Washington

sented by Congress with vacancies to be filled, Washington was placed in the ticklish position of having to make formal offers without knowing whether they would be accepted. And every refusal brought anxiety: he feared that the prestige of the federal government would be lowered.

As the summer advanced, Congress laid at the Presidential door one batch of offices after another. The largest crop of appointments was created by the customs bill, which provided for collectors, naval officers, and other officials attached to every major port. In connection with one of these unimportant posts, the Senate made its only use of its right to refuse consent: they would not have Benjamin Fishbourne as naval officer of the port of Savannah. Maclay noted that at this turn-down, "the President showed great want of temper." It is most improbable that Washington, as has been rumored, marched personally to the Senate chamber to protest, but he did write a letter suggesting that when a nomination appeared "questionable to you," the Senate notify him so that he could give his reasons. He then, as an object lesson to the senators, outlined Fishbourne's many qualifications. However, in the same letter, he appointed another man.*36

The various great departments were set up in separate bills. Revealing how little the new government, behind its ocean, was concerned with diplomacy, the title of Secretary of Foreign Affairs was changed to Secretary of State, and the duties of the office expanded to include all domestic operations except war and finance. The War Department was set up much as before. An Attorney General was to receive a retaining fee for serving on a part-time basis as legal adviser for the executive. It was with establishing the Treasury that Congress went into the most detail. Revealing a typical eighteenth-century respect for the power of the purse, the legislature established connections with the Secretary that bypassed the Presidency. The Secretary should be directly responsive to Congress for information and should, at the request of the House, "digest and prepare" plans for the improvement

---

demonstrably did not discuss the Secretaryship of State with Jay until the post had been established, the report concerning Hamilton seems most improbable. Washington was then personally closer to Jay than Hamilton.[37]

* Although the evidence is not clear, historians have assumed that this situation was the first example of "Senatorial privilege": the Georgia delegation objected to Fishbourne.[38]

and management of revenue. These provisions were intended to enable the Congress to lead the Treasury; it was not foreseen that they would work just the opposite way.[39]

Washington reappointed Knox as Secretary of War. Since the functions of the Attorney General were so limited, he felt he could use the office to satisfy his desire to have at his side a man with whom he had "habits of intimacy."[40] He appointed Edmund Randolph, whom he had known since the younger man was a boy, who had served briefly as one of his military aides, and who, after first refusing to sign, had come round to the Constitution and helped make Virginia ratify.

Jay, as Secretary of Foreign Affairs, was the obvious choice for the enlarged office of State. However, when the post had been officially established and he was at last consulted, Jay expressed a preference for the Chief Justiceship of the Supreme Court. After a hurried conference with Madison, Washington agreed to give Jay what he wanted.[41]

And so Washington offered the Secretaryship of State to his friend and Madison's intimate and the only important official in the foreign service: Thomas Jefferson. Jefferson could not be immediately reached as he was on the ocean returning from France for a visit to Virginia. In a note to be delivered on Jefferson's arrival, Washington explained delicately that he had forborne to nominate his "successor at the Court of Versailles until I should be informed of your determination."[42]

Robert Morris was, as a senator, unavailable for the Treasury; Gouverneur Morris was abroad. The obvious man was the two Morrises' graduated disciple, Alexander Hamilton. His appointment was not only widely recommended by the business community but urged by Madison. No one foresaw that he would get into a feud with Jefferson from which would spring America's first political parties.[43]

Congress adjourned on September 30, 1789, bringing to a close the initial session of the new government. It had been a time of endless creativity achieved with a minimum of turbulence. That, as compared with the Constitutional Convention, the session plays so minor a role in the history books is a measure of how easy everything was; of how far sentiment had coalesced and how effective had been the leadership.

To the British historian Catherine Macaulay Graham, Washington wrote, "So far as we have gone with the new government (and it is completely organized and in operation), we have had greater reason than the most sanguine could expect to be satisfied with its success." To Gouverneur Morris he added that, "as far as my information goes," the session had been carried through "to the satisfaction of all parties: That opposition to it is either no more or hides its head." Of the two states that had held back, North Carolina had come into the new federation during November, and Washington believed that even in Rhode Island, where the majority had "bid adieu long since to every principle of honor, common sense, and honesty," a change for the better was taking place.[44]

After Jefferson had finally reached Virginia and then traveled to the capital, he expressed amazement to find that "the opposition to our new Constitution has almost totally disappeared. . . . If," he added, "the President can be preserved a few more years, till habits of authority and obedience can be established generally, we have nothing to fear."[45]

18

Death and Doldrums

O N September 1, 1789, Washington was enjoying a convivial dinner at which his military crony Knox was shaking his three hundred pounds with mirth, as Knox had done when he had weighed only two hundred and eighty and had kept the headquarters table at a roar. Suddenly Fraunces appeared with a letter from Fredericksburg. Washington's mother had died.[1]

Mary Ball Washington had been eighty-one and painfully ill of cancer, but still possessed of enough spirit to stage "a small battle every day" before she would take her medicine. Washington, on his last two visits to her, had each time felt he was saying a final good-by.* Mother and son had long been at odds with each other, but her death revealed on both sides deep emotion. Washington's letter to his sister contained one of his very few references to the possibility of an afterlife: "Awful and affecting as the death of a parent is, there is consolation in knowing that Heaven has spared ours to an age beyond which few attain, and favored her with the full enjoyment of her mental faculties. . . . Under these considerations, and a hope that she is translated to a happier place, it is the duty of her relatives to yield due submission to the decrees of the Creator."[2]

Despite her endless complaining that her eldest son had, in chasing after matters outside the family circle, neglected her, Mary Ball Wash-

---

* More than a month before, Washington's sister, Mary Lewis, had written him concerning his mother's illness: "I dread the consequence. She is sensible of it and is perfectly resigned—wishes for nothing than to keep [her breast] easy. She wishes to hear from you. She will not believe you are well till she has it from your hand."[3]

ington made George her principal heir, leaving him, among more valuable things, her most personal possessions: her "best bed" and the "best looking glass" which had so often reflected back her face.[4]

As the member of the family who had the least need, George was embarrassed at being preferred in her will. Concerning the personal possessions she left him, he wrote that were they not "mementos of parental affection in the last, solemn act of life, I should not be desirous of receiving or removing them."* As his share of the Negroes, he was willing to take only the one who had long lived at Mount Vernon and had a family there, "in order that the fellow may be gratified." He forgave his mother's debts to him, which ran to many hundreds of pounds.[5]

For £5.13.10, Washington bought mourning cockades, sword knots, and armbands to be worn by himself and his servants. This was, so the *Gazette of the United States* remembered, in keeping with a resolution to reduce extravagance adopted in 1774 by the First Continental Congress, in which Washington had sat.[6]

Mary Ball Washington was buried by the Lewis family on a high knoll overlooking the Rappahannock where she had often taken her grandchildren to enjoy the extensive view. She had, by her complaints that had made her seem a Tory, so disassociated herself from her son's charisma that it was not until she had been long dead, and her living presence had been completely eroded away by the Washington legend, that any marker was placed on her grave.[7]

When Congress adjourned, the government sank into doldrums. Washington planned a trip through New England. To his sister he described his purpose as being "by way of relaxation from business and re-establishment of my health" after his long bout with anthrax. To governmental officials, he stated that he wished to acquire knowledge of the country and of its attitude towards the new government. If he also believed that his presence would cement allegiance, he was too modest to say so.[8]

Martha preferred to stay in New York with her grandchildren. On October 15, 1789, Washington set out in his chariot with two aides and six servants. For his trip north, through Connecticut (Fairfield, New Haven, Hartford); Massachusetts (Springfield, Worcester, Boston,

---

* A year later Washington still had not sent for the mementos.[9]

Newburyport); and New Hampshire (Portsmouth)* he sent his itinerary ahead.

Washington's diary reveals that he was much more confident and
relaxed than when he had traveled from Mount Vernon to New York
seven months before. Then the adulation of the crowds had frightened
him, as presaging a catastrophic comedown if the new government did
not please the people. Now he interpreted the galloping of horses, the
delegations of grave officials, the cheers, and the jerry-built triumphal
arches as demonstrations that the people *were* pleased. He commented
in particular on the attention paid him by the ladies. At a ball given in
his honor at Portsmouth, "there were about seventy-five well dressed
and many of them very handsome ladies, among whom (as was also
the case at the Salem and Boston Assemblies) were a greater proportion with much blacker hair than are usually seen in the southern
states."[10]

During his travels in the old days, Washington had made extensive
notes on crops and the fertility of the land. He still did so to some
extent, but the most significant aspect of his journal is a new emphasis
on non-agricultural economics. He is much concerned with the nature
of exports, with the numbers of ships which cleared various ports. He
sought out and described the infant factories along his route. Concerning a sail manufactory in Boston, he noted that it could produce in a
week "thirty-two pieces of duck of 30 or 40 yards. . . . They have
twenty-eight looms at work and fourteen girls spinning with both
hands (the flax being fastened to their waist). Children (girls) turn
the wheels." The operatives worked hard, as they were paid by the
piece. "There is no other restraint upon them but to come at eight
o'clock in the morning and return at six in the evening. They are the
daughters of decayed families, and are girls of character; none others
are admitted. . . . This is a work of public utility and private advantage."†

A member of Washington's party wrote that at the sail manufactory,
"His Majesty made himself merry . . . telling the overseer he believed
he collected the prettiest girls in Boston."[11]

---

* Washington avoided Rhode Island, as the state was not in the Union.

† In those days, farmers commonly worked from dawn to dusk, and farm
children automatically labored in the fields. Few (if any) of Washington's contemporaries would have failed to agree that it was a social gain to enable impoverished girls to make respectable livings in clean surroundings.

In Boston, a Constitutional crisis struck. When that advocate of state supremacy John Hancock, who was now Governor of Massachusetts, had asked Washington to stay with him, Washington had seen an effort to establish the principle that the President visited a state not as supreme executive but as a guest of the local administration. He chose to interpret the invitation as a personal one between friends,* refusing on the grounds that he had determined "to avoid giving trouble to private families." He did agree to dine with Hancock, but on the assumption that, before dinnertime, the Governor would acknowledge the subordinate position of governors by paying a duty call on the President. However, word awaited Washington that Hancock was too crippled with gout to leave his mansion, although he still expected Washington.

Washington sent a refusal to Hancock, eating dinner at his lodgings, "where the Vice President favored me with his company." Later that night, the Lieutenant Governor and two members of the Massachusetts Council called to express Hancock's "concern" at being too ill to call on Washington. "I informed them in explicit terms that I should not see the Governor unless it was at my own lodgings."

The next day there was a great bustle in the street outside Washington's lodging. Hancock, copiously swathed in bandages, was being lifted out of his coach by husky servants. They carried him into Washington's drawing room. It must have been hard for the President, who suspected that the histrionic Governor was perfectly well, to receive him without smiling. In any case, the constitutional point had been settled. Washington (as he noted) "drank tea with Governor Hancock."[12]

After visiting Portsmouth, New Hampshire, the northern terminus of his trip, Washington considered his official duties over: he announced no itinerary for his return to New York. He looked forward to traveling through the countryside like an ordinary man, but found the inconveniences—"intolerable" roads and "indifferent" accommodations—extremely annoying. At one tavern, the President was turned away because the landlord was absent and his wife sick. After being misdirected in Massachusetts, he burst out, "The roads in every part of this state are amazingly crooked to suit the convenience of every man's

---

* Washington was making careful distinctions between his roles as President and as individual citizen. He refused to review the Cambridge militia, which was under state jurisdiction, "otherwise than as a private man."

fields; and the directions you receive from the people equally blind and ignorant."[13]

"It being contrary to law and disagreeable to the people of this state [Connecticut] to travel on the Sabbath," he found himself trapped for a long, boring Sunday in the hamlet of Ashford. The tavern was "not a good one. . . . A meetinghouse being within [a] few rods of the door, I attended morning and evening service, and heard very lame discourse, from a Mr. Pond."[14]

On November 13, Washington "arrived at my house at New York, where I found Mrs. Washington and the rest of the family all well."[15]

The temporary capital was still half asleep. One snowy afternoon, the President waited with his dress sword buckled on and his hat under his arm, but not a single gentleman appeared for his levee. Concerning Christmas, he noted, "The visitors to Mrs. Washington this afternoon were not numerous but respectable." New Year's Day was another story, since the government was again assembling. Washington had many callers between twelve and three o'clock, and later in the afternoon "a great number of gentlemen and ladies" visited Mrs. Washington. Abigail wrote that Martha's drawing room was "as much crowded as a birth night as St. James's and with company as brilliantly dressed, diamonds and great hoops excepted."[16]

Washington studied the situation with the Creek Indians, whom he suspected of negotiating to see whether they could profit more from an alliance with the Spanish colonies than the United States. He worried whether he would have to let the Spanish minister return home without a discussion of policy, since the Senate was not sitting to advise. Most willing to take a strong lead in his ancient military province, he drew up a plan for a national militia and asked Knox to work it into a bill which could be furnished to Congress. He wrote a much-belated letter to the Emperor of Morocco, his "Great and Magnanimous Friend," in which he combined flattery with a request for help in reducing the attacks by Algerian pirates on American shipping. And he wished he had a Secretary of State.[17]

When Jefferson had landed at Norfolk, Virginia, on November 23, he had been informed of his appointment. However, he decided to send no answer until he had received the official notification. That was slow in catching up with him as he traveled around Virginia. He had been back in the United States for twenty-one days before he wrote to

Washington. Then he stated that he was happy as Minister to France and had "gloomy forebodings" concerning the Secretaryship of State, since it embraced, in addition to foreign affairs, "domestic administration" at which he did not feel himself competent. He would accept if the President wished it, but added two provisos which Washington must have found disturbing.

"Having no motive to public service but the public satisfaction," Jefferson would, he wrote, "certainly retire the moment that satisfaction should appear to languish." To receive "criticisms and censures of a public" would be "disagreeable to me." Probably because his admiration for Washington was so overwhelming, Jefferson (so it seems) did not consider that the hero could need his help, might find it disagreeable to be deserted if the going got rough.

Jefferson's second proviso was that, since he had many private affairs to attend to, he could not, should Washington require his services, "set out on my journey northward till the middle of March." This would mean that for at least another three months Washington would lack a Secretary of State.[18]

However, Alexander Hamilton was at Washington's side in New York. Hamilton was eager to answer any questions or offer any assistance. In his official role as Secretary of the Treasury, he was hard at work preparing a report, for which he had been asked by the House of Representatives, on how best to build up the public credit.

Concerning January 2, Washington noted laconically in his diary, "Exercised in the carriage with Mrs. Washington. Read the report of the Secretary of the Treasury respecting the state of his department and proposed plans of finance. Drank tea at the Chief Justice's of the United States." It had seemed a tranquil day. Washington could not realize that Hamilton's paper would be opening gun in a controversy that would in the end blow his administration apart.[19]

19

Debts, Credit, and the National Capital

ALEXANDER HAMILTON had a fair complexion; almost rosy cheeks; dark, deep-set eyes that sometimes seemed violet; a massive, symmetrical head with firmly cut features; reddish hair that was turned back from his forehead, powdered, and collected into a queue.* "Graceful and debonair," so wrote Claude Bowers, "elegant and courtly, seductive and ingratiating, playful or impassioned, he could have fitted into the picture at the Versailles of Louis XV."[1]

Twelve years before Hamilton became Secretary of the Treasury, on March 1, 1777, General Washington had appointed him aide-de-camp. Thus Washington brought into his military family and his life a fiery youngster of twenty, whose equivocal background (Hamilton's birth in the West Indies had been illegitimate) only made the youth more courtly, determined, and ambitious. Hamilton had already served the patriot cause as a brilliant political pamphleteer, and, after the fighting had broken out, had shown gifts as an artillery officer. Washington, with that flair for smelling out ability which was one of his major gifts, soon made Hamilton, although both in age and service one of his junior aides, in effect his chief of staff. And, acknowledging the social charm of the elegant, intense stripling, Washington normally placed Hamilton at the head of the headquarters table, sitting himself at one side.[2]

---

* Among the overlooked trivia of history is that fact that Washington, Jefferson and Hamilton were all, although none to an extreme degree, redheads.

Valuable as Hamilton then was to Washington, historians have tended to exaggerate his functions as military aide. There exists, for instance, a belief that Hamilton was at that time Washington's adviser on financial matters. Firm evidence disproves this. When asked in 1781 whether Hamilton would make a good Superintendent of Finance, Washington replied, "How far Colonel Hamilton, of whom you ask my opinion as a financier, has turned his thoughts to that particular study I am unable to answer, because I never entered upon a discussion on this point with him."[3]

The letters that went out from headquarters over Washington's signature were in many autographs. It is assumed that to those in Hamilton's hand Washington contributed nothing but the signature. This is wildly unlikely, since Washington enforced a rigid routine by which he initiated, supervised, and corrected, thus keeping complete control of the letters his aides executed and he signed. He was, indeed, so extremely master in his own house that Hamilton was steamrollered into mounting resentment.

Concluding that Washington was "neither remarkable for delicacy nor good temper," Hamilton rebuffed (as he later explained) Washington's cordial advances, making it clear "that I wished to stand rather on a footing of military confidence than of private attachment." He tried again and again to secure preferment that would take him out of Washington's military family, but the General found him too useful to let him go. Finally, Hamilton forced a breach with Washington by responding to an irritable remark with his resignation. Nor would he accept from Washington what was in effect an apology. The whole matter was made more unpleasant because Hamilton induced Washington to agree that nothing would be said about the particulars of their breach—and then talked and wrote about it himself in a manner highly critical of Washington.[4]

Washington had little connection with Hamilton during the ensuing campaigns but could not forget that he owed the youth a debt of gratitude for four years of invaluable personal service. Knowing that Hamilton's fondest vision of himself was as a romantic warrior, he indulged his former aide with the command of a party which captured a redoubt at Yorktown.

Hamilton's next important appearance in Washington's affairs was in 1782, when the army was angry at not being paid, and the business community was trying to inspire the troops to terrify the civilian governments. Although Hamilton took upon himself the task of seducing Washington, whom he boasted (as it turned out fatuously) he knew how to handle, Washington blamed the movement (which he indignantly blocked) less on Hamilton than on Robert and Gouverneur Morris.[5] Inclined to take people as he found them, Washington forgave all three, but remained closer to the Morrises than to Hamilton.

After his return to Mount Vernon, Washington's contact with Hamilton practically ceased. Although he often sought the advice of Jefferson and Madison, during the three and a half years of his retirement he wrote only one letter to Hamilton. It urged the decontamination of the New York State Cincinnati by various reforms including the abolishment of the hereditary principle.[6] Hamilton not only ignored Washington's advice but became a leader in opposing it.

Washington met Hamilton again at the Constitutional Convention. He made no mention in his diary of their having dined or gone on any excursion together. From the floor of the Convention, Hamilton made a quixotic plea for a government on the British model—the executive to be elected for life and to have, like a king, an unalterable veto on all legislation—that was so extreme it was not even discussed.* Then, being perpetually outvoted in a New York delegation opposed to central government, Hamilton went home. From New York, he wrote Washington that a revolution was going on in the minds of the population towards federalism. "Not having compared ideas with you, sir," he added revealingly, "I cannot judge how far our sentiments agree."[7]

That, in his reply, Washington urged Hamilton to return to the Convention has been widely regarded as a demonstration of dependence.[8] What Washington actually sought was to have present as many supporters of strong government as possible. In the end, Hamilton's signature alone indicated any New York support for the proposed Constitution.

Although impressed with *The Federalist*, Washington, who was so intimate with Madison, could not have given Hamilton all the credit. When Hamilton sent Washington an exhortation to accept the Presidency, Washington expressed polite gratitude for the advice. Then he added that he had already sought the opinions of "my best friends," a

---

* As Washington listened, undoubtedly in some puzzlement concerning the purpose of this wild gesture, he could not possibly have foreseen how much trouble this speech, which lurked in the memories of democrats, was to make for him when, as President, he supported financial measures proposed by Hamilton.

Alexander Hamilton, the elegant financier. Courtesy of the Chamber of Commerce, State of New York. Photograph by Pach Brothers

Thomas Jefferson, the rangy philosopher: a detail from John Trumbull's
The Declaration of Independence. Courtesy of the Yale University
Art Gallery

statement which implied that Hamilton did not belong in that category.[9]

Shortly after he had arrived at New York, Washington asked Hamilton in conversation what etiquette he should observe as President. To Washington's pleasure—"the manner chosen for doing it is most agreeable to me"—he received Hamilton's advice in the form of a brisk, well-expressed letter. Although he did not accept Hamilton's suggestions (which would have isolated him too much), he was encouraged to ask that the opinions of Madison, Jay, and Adams be also sent him in writing.[10]

Washington must have discovered, during the early months of his Presidency, that his former aide had mastered those recondite matters of finance which his business friends told him were extremely important, but the detailed working of which he could not understand. When Congress finally established the Treasury, Hamilton was recommended not only by moneymen like Robert Morris but also by political advisers like Madison.[11] Washington was surely pleased to have the post so obviously easy to fill. It seemed also fortunate that Congress had established its own direct line of communication with the Treasury, taking so much of the responsibility from the President that he felt it unnecessary for him to do more than watch benevolently while Hamilton prepared the reports and plans he had been asked for by the House.

Washington's First Annual Address, delivered in the Senate chamber on January 8, 1790, was brief and general. He urged in short paragraphs consideration of such matters as organizing the militia and providing a small regular army; encouraging manufactures with particular emphasis on those needed for defense; setting up a uniform system of weights and measures; taking a census; encouraging inventions and also communication through better roads and post offices. But the heart of the message was concerned with the support of education.

The self-taught leader, who remained conscious of his own "defective" training, wished the legislative to consider "affording aids to seminaries of learning already established" or "the institution of a national university. . . . Knowledge is in every country," he pointed out, "the surest basis of public happiness." In America, where "the measures of government receive their impression so immediately from the sense of the community," knowledge was doubly important.

Washington was not trying to enable the people to advise the government on specific measures, but rather saw education as "the security of a free Constitution." Officials who presided over an informed electorate would realize that "every valuable end of government is best answered by the enlightened confidence of the people." Education would, furthermore, teach "the people themselves to know and to value their own rights; . . . to distinguish between oppression and the necessary exercise of lawful authority; . . . to discriminate the spirit of liberty from that of licentiousness." Education would unite "a speedy but temperate vigilance against encroachments with an inviolable respect to the laws."[12]

The financial report which Hamilton presented to Congress had, as its obvious aim, the solving of the problem which had been to Washington, when he served as Commander in Chief, a major worry, and then, during his retirement, had caused a lingering sense of guilt because he was not dealing with it more actively. Hamilton was proposing means for paying off the debts which had been incurred by the American government during the Revolution.

Washington surveyed Hamilton's efforts with admiration as he was only too conscious that there was an Augean stable to clear out. Fighting a war without any effective access to revenue, the Continental Congress had used almost every method of going into debt known to governments in the eighteenth century. The size of the foreign debt was well recorded—$10,000,000 plus $1,600,000 in interest arrears—but no one knew for sure how much was owed on certificates that had been issued locally: Hamilton guessed $27,000,000 plus some $13,000,000 interest.[13] Washington's commissary and quartermaster departments had, to take one example, spread a snowstorm of unrecorded paper when requisitioning supplies for which they had no other method of payment. Furthermore, the claims of the states against the federal government had never been determined.

There were those who thought that the whole debt ought to be canceled, since everyone had profited from independence, but this would have made a mockery of the promises Washington had made to the army when he had persuaded the soldiers to go home carrying certificates of indebtedness instead of back pay. "Repudiation" would also have penalized those who had patriotically loaned money to the government, or had later given veterans or farmers some money for their certificates.

Probably, Washington did not completely understand the long-range implications of the methods—known as "funding"—Hamilton recommended for raising the money to pay the debt. Only the financial community understood, and they raised no questions, since Hamilton's objectives were also their own. Agrarians, it is true, were worried that Hamilton did not intend to wipe out the debt as quickly as possible, yet they did not realize that Hamilton's methods for funding were aimed at grafting onto a farming society the self-reproducing cells of capitalism.

Far from having any sympathy with schemes (like that proposed by Senator Maclay) to liquidate the obligations at once through the sale of western lands, Hamilton provided that only 2 per cent of the principal could be retired in one year. The rest of the obligations were to be met, with some reduction in the back interest due, through the distribution of government bonds. The bonds that would handle what was owed abroad would take the form of new foreign loans, which would surely be procurable when it was clear that the American financial house had been set in order. Bonds issued to meet local debts would be sold in the United States. They would attract purchasers because they would be guaranteed by a fund, usable for only this purpose, to which stated amounts of tax money would be annually allocated.

Being guaranteed investments, the bonds which remained in American hands would expand the national financial resources by circulating more or less at par, as if they were currency. The interest payments would further increase what the United States was desperately short of—namely, fluid capital. Should the bonds issued domestically prove attractive enough to attract foreign investors, that would bring in even more capital. Thus, the very means of meeting the debt would, by loosening the credit structure, facilitate business exchanges and the establishment of new enterprises, which would in turn encourage the prosperity that would keep the payments on the debt structure from being onerous.

The agrarians looked somewhat cross-eyed at these measures but did not seriously oppose them. Concerning another aspect of Hamilton's plans, however, there exploded a controversy which marked the first split in Washington's team. Madison led the opposition. Hamilton was shocked into saying that, if he had known that Madison would go against him, he would not have accepted the Treasury.[14]

The basis of the controversy was that the simple soldiers and farmers, who had been given governmental certificates in return for services or produce, had usually been unable to hold on to the paper in the hope that it would someday be cashable at full value. To meet immediate needs, they had sold their certificates to speculators for a few cents on the dollar. Since Hamilton's plan involved making payment to the existing owners of the certificates, those individuals who had contributed to the cause and sold out would get nothing, while speculators were enriched.

To make this situation more painful, news of what Hamilton intended leaked to his intimates, and then, with presentation to Congress, became common knowledge in New York. Speculators were taking advantage of inside knowledge and the slowness of normal communications to reap a final harvest at the expense of the poor. Boats were flying along the coast and horsemen galloping through rural roads to buy up as many certificates as possible before those who had earned them discovered that they would suddenly become valuable.[15]

The scheme which Madison presented to the House and which came to be known as "discrimination" provided that some of the value be paid to the present holder of the certificate and the rest to the individual to whom it was originally issued. Against this plea for human justice, Hamilton's supporters presented a series of objections. The certificates had printed on them that the amount was owed to the bearer: did not this make them as much the holder's property as "their hats or their coats"?[16] Furthermore, having been assured by the Continental Congress that the certificates would be paid at face value, Dutch bankers had invested in them heavily. If this promise were broken, would not that be the end of the United States' credit and ability to borrow abroad? In Hamilton's opinion, the clinching argument was that to identify the original holders would in many cases be impossible and, where possible, would be murderously expensive. Madison's proposal was voted down by a large majority.

Resentments were, however, far from being quieted: Hamilton later wrote that the controversy had "laid the foundation for the great schism which has since prevailed."[17] As word of the debates spread across the farmlands, the question appeared to have been whether the government would support the poor man or the rich, the noble veteran or the wicked speculator, the honest farmer or the city shyster. As for Hamilton and his urban friends—although this they did not publicly argue—they had what they considered sound fiscal reasons for preferring not to have the money sprinkled across the countryside into the pockets of little people. Achieving the fluid capital necessary for an active business society required, they believed, making the payments not to those who would dribble the money out on small purchases, but to aggressive capitalists—call them "speculators" if you please—who, being congregated in commercial centers, would venture what they received in new enterprises. Their activities would, by continually priming the pumps of industry and commerce, create prosperity which would in the end (so the argument went) help the farmer more than if he had received and expended a lump sum on a few more acres or new furniture for his parlor.*

Having defeated "discrimination," the House faced an even thornier issue: "assumption." As urged by Hamilton, assumption meant that the federal government would assume the war debts, which he estimated at twenty-five million, still unpaid by the states. Such debts were almost altogether in the hands of speculators, which exacerbated that issue; and assumption seemed unfair to those states which had sacrificed to pay off what they owed. They would now be taxed to meet the debts of states that had made no sacrifices. New England, where Shays's Rebellion had frightened away the collection of heavy taxes, and also North Carolina, had their obligations largely intact and thus were enchanted to hand them over to the nation. On the other hand, Virginia, having cleared up most of her debts, was outraged by the proposition.

---

* An enthusiast urged the history painter John Trumbull to depict Madison "pleading the cause of justice and humanity in Congress, an angel whispering in his ear, and a group of widows and orphans and decrepit soldiers contemplating him with ineffable delight." But Hamilton should be shown, surrounded with jackals and other beasts of prey, loading wealth on his favorites, while behind him lurked the sinister figures of a king and some lords.[18]

Historians who perpetuate such metaphors overlook the fact that the controversy in which Hamilton and Madison were opposed was not the first occasion in which "discrimination" had been urged but voted down. This had also happened six years before, in the absence of Washington, Hamilton, and Madison, when the Pennsylvania legislature had acted to pay that state's debts.[19]

Also involved was the old, angry issue of state versus federal power. "The leading objects" of assumption, Hamilton later explained, "were an accession of strength to the national government, and an assurance of order and vigor in the national finances by doing away with the necessity of thirteen complicated and different systems of finance." The federal government would collect the lion's share of the taxes. And, believing that it was "ambition and avarice" which bound individuals to a government, Hamilton concluded that "if all the public creditors receive their dues" from the central authority, "their interest" would be to support that central authority.[20]

Perhaps because he was a Virginian, Madison, although a strong supporter of central authority, would not go along. He threw a new diversion into the hopper. He moved that, in order to keep some states from profiting over others, the federal government, in addition to paying the debts of delinquent states, reimburse those states which had paid their debts for what they had expended. This would almost double the obligations Hamilton was willing to assume. The House was thrown into a deadlock that lasted for five months.

During much of this period, Washington remained without a Secretary of State. Having received, during the previous December, Jefferson's letter stating that he could accept the office reluctantly and only if Washington insisted, Washington deputized Madison, who was going to Virginia for Christmas, to discuss the matter with their mutual friend. Madison's return to New York was delayed by illness, and thus it was late January before Washington was in a position to write Jefferson again. He urged the importance of the office and Jefferson's fitness for it. Since Madison had reported that the nominee feared the weight of domestic duties, Washington wrote that should these prove in fact too onerous, the office could be divided, leaving Jefferson the foreign part. He begged Jefferson (who was enjoying himself in Virginia as Washington would have loved to do) to reach an immediate decision and, if it were favorable, postpone all private business and hurry to the capital. "Many things are required to be done," he explained, "while Congress is in session rather than at any other time. . . . Your presence might doubtless be much better dispensed with" when the session was over.

This letter convinced Jefferson that he had no choice. If, despite what Washington had written, he continued as minister to France, that "would have exposed me to the danger of giving disgust, and I value no office enough for that." And so, after what he himself described as "three months parleying," he agreed "to sacrifice my own inclinations." On February 14, he wrote Washington that he would accept. However, he could not get off until the end of the ensuing week, "and then I shall have to go by the way of Richmond, which will lengthen my road."* [21]

On March 21, when Congress had already been in session for almost three months, Washington was able to note in his diary, "Received Mr. Jefferson, Minister of State, at about one o'clock."[22] The man who came into his office was as tall as Washington, but where the President stood like a rock, Jefferson gangled. The new arrival was loose-jointed and somewhat awkward in his movements. He sprawled rather than sat, and even some of his friends felt that he abused the philosopher's privilege of negligence of dress.

As compared to the tensely held and perfectly turned-out Hamilton, Jefferson could have been judged to be the more provincial, but only by an observer of little perception. For Jefferson had a more widely cultivated mind than Hamilton, and as a birthright Virginia aristocrat, he was much more sure of himself in the role of a gentleman than the illegitimate immigrant from the West Indies. Jefferson lolled in the great world the way a man lolls in his own house.

Where Hamilton sparkled in conversation like a soldier swinging a sword, Jefferson poured out information and inspiration like a farmer wielding a watering can. Both ministers were more brilliant talkers than the President, whose "colloquial talents" Jefferson considered "not above mediocrity, possessing neither copiousness of ideas nor fluency of words."[23] However, although Jefferson could criticize Washington, he stood before him in awe. He had arrived in New York with the primary determination to be a loyal supporter of the man he considered very great.

Washington and Jefferson knew each other very well and also hardly at all. Very well, because, as Virginia planters, they shared a similar background, and because they had been in contact for more than twenty years, ever since they had met as fellow members of the Virginia House of Burgesses. Hardly at all, because they had never been

---

* He explained to Madison that he had to attend his daughter's wedding and work out the marriage settlement with her future father-in-law.[24]

intimately associated. Their connection in the Burgesses had been no more than mutually appreciative and pleasant; Jefferson had entered the Continental Congress as Washington left to become Commander in Chief; Jefferson had spent most of the war in Virginia whence, as Governor, he had corresponded cooperatively with the General, who was serving up north. After Washington's retirement and before Jefferson went off to France, their letters had been more frequent and confiding, yet Washington's diary never puts Jefferson among the stream of guests at Mount Vernon. However, the two men now greeted each other as old friends.

So far as anyone knows, Jefferson and Hamilton had never met before that March of 1790. They were undoubtedly encouraged into mutual confidence by Madison, who loved Jefferson and who, although he was opposing some of Hamilton's ideas in the House, had not yet begun to suspect the motives of the Secretary of the Treasury. Wishing Washington's administration to succeed, Jefferson looked forward to cooperating amicably with his fellow Secretary.

The late-arriving Secretary of State was still trying to find his way around when a shattering blow descended. Washington was taken so ill with pneumonia that on the fifth day, May 15, he was, as Jefferson wrote, "pronounced by two of the three physicians present to be in the act of death. . . . You cannot conceive of the public alarm on this occasion. It proves how much depends on his life." Jefferson was "in total despair." Even the extreme democrat Maclay was moved. Calling at the President's house, he found "every eye . . . full of tears."[25]

However, at four o'clock that afternoon, so Jefferson reported, "a copious sweat came on, his expectoration, which had been thin and ichorous, began to assume a well-digested form, his articulation became distinct, and, in the course of two hours, it was evident he had gone through a favorable crisis." Less than a week later, Washington was able to ride out in his carriage, although for a month he felt too weak to write in his diary.[26]

In the presence of Martha, who had lost so many of the people she most loved, Washington kept up a cheerful face, but to his male intimates he admitted, more than ever he had done as a soldier, that he felt he was dangerously risking his life for his country. He wrote Stuart, "I have already had within less than a year two *severe* attacks, the last worse than the first. A third more than probable will put me to sleep with my fathers. At what distance this may be, I know not. Within the last twelve months I have undergone more and severer sickness than thirty preceding years afflicted me with, put it all together." His physicians, he confided to Lafayette, advised "more exercise and less application to business. I cannot, however, avoid persuading myself that it is essential to accomplish whatever I have undertaken (though reluctantly) to the best of my abilities." One comfort was that "by having Mr. Jefferson at the head of the Department of State, Mr. Jay of the Judiciary, Hamilton of the Treasury, and Knox of that of War, I feel myself supported by able coadjutors who harmonize extremely well together."[27]

As Hamilton's financial plans failed of legislative enactment month after acrimonious month, the speculators who had invested heavily in the certificates the value of which was being jeopardized were thrown into consternation. Responding to rumor, they bought and sold in alternating frenzies, thus further exacerbating agrarian disgust at money sharks. On five occasions, the funding-assumption bill was narrowly defeated in the House. The suggestion that the issues be postponed until the next session made Hamilton cry out that if that happened, the public creditors would sell in despair, creating a total financial crash. Finally, the House sent to the Senate a funding bill which made no provision for taking over the state debts.

If the Senate agreed, assumption would be forever lost. Reports circulated that should this happen, New England and South Carolina would be so enraged that they would withdraw from the Union. And if continuing controversy kept any bill from being passed, there was the danger that the credit of the new government would crash, perhaps bringing the Federal Union down with it.

Jefferson was suffering from headaches and, when he felt well enough, he was busy preparing a report for which Washington had asked on weights and measures. He wrote concerning the crisis over finance: "My duties prevent me from mingling in these questions. I do not pretend to be very competent to their decision." However, he was worried by the controversy, which seemed to him to have risen to greater heights than he had ever seen. "I think it necessary to give as well as take in a government like ours."[28]

As the deadlock continued, the Secretary of State was accosted outside the Presidential mansion by the Secretary of the Treasury.

Jefferson was shocked to see Hamilton not as usual dapper and cocky, but "sober, haggard and dejected beyond description, even his dress uncouth and neglected." With great earnestness, Hamilton insisted that assumption was necessary to keep New England, which had made such great sacrifices during the war, from seceding. If assumption were voted down, Hamilton himself would resign. Was not the success of the administration a common concern towards which all the Secretaries should make common cause? The situation could be saved if Jefferson would use his influence with his friends from the south.

Jefferson, as he remembered three years later,* replied that he had not put his mind on fiscal matters. Yet he was disturbed by the rise in bad feelings. He would think the matter over.[29]

Although this fact has often been suppressed, Jefferson was already committed to Hamilton's program since he had, when representing the United States abroad, assured Dutch bankers that there would be no discrimination and that the federal government would assure the payment of the states' debts.[30] Deciding to act as a mediator, he asked Madison and Hamilton to dinner. He presided benignly over the consummation of a deal.

Even if temporarily shouted down by the clamor over finance, another matter of long-range importance and emotional disagreement pended before the Congress: Where would the permanent capital settle? More was involved than issues of local prosperity and pride. As Madison put it, "Those who are most adjacent to the seat of legislation will always possess advantages over others."[31] This was particularly true at a time when news moved so slowly.

Agrarians were opposed to financial centers such as New York or Philadelphia, where day-by-day living would bring government officials under the influence of moneymen and their high-flying women. Southerners, recently made uneasy by a Quaker petition demanding the abolition of slavery, wished to move the capital south. But the financial community wished the government to stay in an environment favorable to their ideas, and northerners as a group distrusted southern influence.

The stakes were present for a swap. Hamilton agreed to throw away "the dearest interest of New York," although the city had spent heavily

---

* A second account of what happened, which Jefferson wrote in his old age, is obviously less reliable.[32]

to make the federal government so comfortable it would not go away. It was decided that Pennsylvania should be placated by having the capital move to Philadelphia for ten years, after which the government would settle in a new city to be created for that purpose on the banks of the Potomac. Madison was so committed he could not agree to change his own vote, but he and Jefferson promised that in return for having the permanent capital in the south, they would procure enough southern votes to please the northeast by carrying both funding and assumption.[33]

The compromise worked perfectly. Funding and assumption were passed, as was a bill ordering the establishment on the Potomac of a ten-mile-square district to house the permanent capital.

Several years later Jefferson was to start his lifelong complaint that he had been "duped" by Hamilton: "Of all the errors of my political life, this has occasioned me the most regret." However, for the moment he was very pleased with the compromise. "In this way," he explained to Monroe, "there will be something to displease and something to soothe every part of the Union, except New York, which must be content with what she has had." It had been necessary to yield "to the cries of the creditors in various parts of the Union, for the sake of the Union and to save us from the greatest of all calamities: the total extinction of our credit in Europe."[34]

Washington had taken no public part in the great financial controversy of 1790, yet a word from him, addressed however scrupulously only to a friend, had a way of reverberating. It has always been believed that he agreed with Hamilton, and this seems, indeed, to have been the case. When Hamilton's schemes began to produce the results the Secretary of the Treasury had foreseen, Jefferson and Madison were frightened,[35] but not Washington.

The General's experiences in leading an army perpetually in want because there was no way to concentrate the national resources, had taught him the importance of fluid capital, of trading on a large scale. He had, indeed, been shocked into making, as the war ground discouragingly on, a statement that was a complete denial of the agrarian point of view in which he had been raised. He wrote to his brother Jack that he realized his continuing desire "to have my property as much as possible in lands," rather than investing it in bonds or business enterprises, "is not consistent with national policy."[36]

[248]

Washington had hoped, when he accepted the Presidency, that it would only be necessary to release the resources of the country to solve the economic problems of the nation. Hamilton's plan for "reviving the dead corpse of the public credit" seemed to fit in with this belief since it did not involve upsetting the electorate by establishing any taxes beyond the customs duties which had already been voted. To Lafayette, Washington wrote happily that although "anxiety and perplexity" had been created by the new fiscal schemes, yet "our revenues have been considerably more productive than it was imagined they would be." He specified plentiful crops, "great prices" paid for American grain in Europe, and a rate of exchange "much in our favor." Duties on extensive importations of European goods were flooding money into the Treasury. "Our trade to the East Indies flourishes. The profits to individuals are so considerable as to induce more persons to engage in it continually; a single vessel just arrived in this port pays $30,000 to government. Two vessels fitted out for the fur trade to the northwest coast of America have succeeded well. The whole outfits of vessels and cargoes cost but £7000. One is returning home loaded with India produce, the other going back to the coast of America; and they have deposited $100,000 of their profits in China."[37]

Washington's natural predilections must have been for discrimination. When he had sent his soldiers home bearing not money but certificates of debt, he had mourned that they would be "considerable sufferers" since "necessity will compel them to part with their certificates for what they will fetch" to "unfeeling, avaricious speculators." He had been forced to do just that with some certificates he had himself received. However, his only recorded comment on discrimination, which was made after the proposal had been voted down, expressed regret at the controversy it had inspired. He was convinced that Madison had been actuated "by the purest motives and most heartfelt conviction, but the subject was delicate and perhaps had better never been stirred."[38]

To his Virginia correspondent Stuart, he wrote that, "though it is a sentiment I have not made known" in New York, he favored assumption. With Hamilton's desire not to have thirteen financial systems competing with the federal he was in such complete agreement that he had, in 1789, drawn up a "Plan of American Finance" which (however unsophisticated in its specific working) envisioned having all taxes collected by the Union. As for Hamilton's belief that a man's loyalty was largely determined by his interest, Washington had expressed it (using Hamilton as his amanuensis) in 1778 when arguing that the Continental Congress should set up a system of pensions for the Revolutionary officers. There was a limit to the sacrifices men would make for patriotism. No institution would succeed that was "not built on the presumptive truth" that, "with far the greatest part of mankind, interest is the governing principle."[39]

Furthermore, Washington believed that assumption was just. He wrote Stuart without any injunction that the letter be not shown around in Virginia, "The cause in which the expenses of the war was incurred was a common cause. . . . If then some states were harder pressed than others, or from particular or local circumstances contracted heavier debts, it is but reasonable" that all should help. "Had the invaded and hard-pressed states believed the case would have been otherwise, opposition in them would very soon, I believe, have changed to submission, and given a different termination to the war."[40]

As for the other half of the Hamilton-Jefferson-Madison compromise, Washington's personal desires were certainly greatly gratified by the decision that the permanent capital should be near his beloved Mount Vernon. Now, whether the Potomac Canal succeeded or not, a great city would rise on the banks of the river—and it would be by definition the national center. Perhaps because the project was so dear to his heart, not one word about it appears in his writings until after the bill had been passed. Even then, he took so seriously a technical objection raised by a pamphleteer that he did not sign the bill until Jefferson had sent him a many-page memorandum establishing its constitutionality. Yet, however much he leaned backwards, no one could doubt that Washington was delighted.[41]

Washington did not, in the manner of one school of modern historians, view the controversies over Hamilton's schemes as disagreements between economic classes. He saw the cleavages as primarily regional, reflecting the old forces of disunion. This was not only because Hamilton's proposals would in themselves strengthen the federal government. There was also the fact that the agrarian southerners distrusted the moneymen to the north of them. Even the issue of discrimination, where differences of interest between the rich and the poor seemed most obviously involved, was given an important regional angle by the fact that southerners, even well-to-do planters like Washington, had commonly sold their certificates to men who had carried them north.*[42] It was, indeed, all down the line, northerners who would most profit from Hamilton's schemes. It was no coincidence that the compromise which brought agreement mediated not between economic but between regional interests.

Presiding over a government which he realized "depends so much in its first stages on public opinion," Washington had been bothered by all the acrimony. Although he admitted that "long, warm and animated debates" were necessary to reconcile the different areas to what he considered the general welfare, he nonetheless felt that Congress had sunk into "a warmth and intemperance, with prolixity and threats, which, it is to be feared, has . . . decreased that respect which was once entertained for it." He greatly regretted that congressmen had ascribed in their letters to their respective states "the worse motives for the conduct of their opponents . . . by which means jealousies and distrusts are spread, most impolitically, far and wide."

Disunion, Washington feared, would "injure our public affairs, which if wisely conducted might make us (as we are now by Europeans thought to be) the happiest people upon earth. As an evidence of it, our reputation has risen in every part of the globe; and our credit, especially in Holland, has got higher than that of *any* nation in Europe (and where our funds are above par). . . . But the conduct we seem to be pursuing will soon bring us back to our late disreputable condition."[43]

The rancor raised by the first set of Hamilton's schemes did not spare Washington himself. An angry note, still muted but nonetheless audible, brought new touches of discord into the old chorus of praises. Despite the conscientiousness with which he had avoided entering the controversy, it was inevitable that he would be blamed.

In the *Boston Independent Chronicle*, "Old Soldier" recalled the General's promises to his troops and asked whether they had not been betrayed. And the *New York Journal* considered that placing the capital on the Potomac had been "a political trap set for the integrity of the executive . . . tempting our Saviour into sin." The indomitable Maclay assumed, of course, that Washington's "great influence" had

---

* In 1785, Massachusetts received $300,000 in interest on United States securities, Virginia only $62,000.

been behind linking the Potomac and assumption: "Alas, that the affection, nay almost adoration, of the people should meet so unworthy a return. . . . The President had become in the hands of Hamilton the dishclout of every dirty speculator, as his name goes to wipe away blame and silence all murmuring."[44]

But whatever was published or whispered, Washington was delighted that the squabbles in Congress had been settled. "The two great questions of funding the debt and fixing the seat of government," he wrote, ". . . were always considered by me as questions of the most delicate and interesting nature which could possibly be drawn into discussion. They were more in danger of having convulsed the government itself than any other points. I hope they are now settled in as satisfactory a manner as could have been expected." And in reply to an address from the state of South Carolina he exclaimed, "If there be for me any peculiarly just subject of exultation, and with an honest pride I avow the fact, it is in being the citizen of a country whose inhabitants were so enlightened and disinterested as to sacrifice local prejudices and temporary systems for the sake of rendering secure and permanent that independency which had been the price of so much treasure and blood."[45]

Nootka, Yazoo, and the
Southwest Frontier

A CROSS the ocean, the French Revolution seemed to be pursuing a moderate course, with Louis XVI and Marie Antoinette still (if uneasily) occupying their thrones. Washington's disciple Lafayette was more or less in control. In a grand gesture, he sent Washington the "main key" of that destroyed "fortress of despotism," the Bastille and also a picture of the destruction in progress. The gift, Lafayette wrote, "is a tribute which I owe as a son to my adoptive father, as an aide-de-camp to my general, as a missionary of liberty to its patriarch."[1]

In his reply, Washington expressed his happiness that Lafayette had shown the "address and fortitude" to steer his political ship "hitherto safely through the quicksands and rocks which threatened instant destruction on every side, and [that] your young king in all things seems so well disposed to conform to the wishes of the nation." He admitted that the accounts in the English newspapers "caused our fears of a failure almost to exceed our expectations of success." But, so he added in a letter to Rochambeau, "We remembered how our own armies, after having been all slain to a man in the English newspapers, came to life again and even performed prodigies of valor against that very nation whose newspapers had so unmercifully destroyed them."[2]

Although Washington's anxiety over French happenings had not yet been given substance, the confusion in that country loosened an important strand in the intricate net of European power politics. Con-

The key to the Bastille, which had been presented to Washington by Lafayette, and the case in which he hung it, first at the Presidential mansion and then in the front hall at Mount Vernon, where it still hangs. Courtesy of the Mount Vernon Ladies' Association.

Representation of the destruction of the Bastille, also presented to Washington by Lafayette, which hung beside the key. This is an engraving of the lost original. Courtesy of the Mount Vernon Ladies' Association

The engraving of Louis XVI which Washington hung with the key and
engraving of the Bastille in order to ward off an impression of political bias.
After the King had been dethroned the picture came down, leaving a display
which shocked visiting French aristocratic refugees. Courtesy of the Mount
Vernon Ladies' Association

cluding that France was too absorbed in her inner affairs to support her old ally Spain, England decided that the time had come to challenge a situation which had persisted since the lifetime of Columbus, when, at the Treaty of Tordesillas (1494), the Pope had given Spain exclusive sovereignty over the Pacific Ocean. Now England established a fur trading station on North America's Pacific Coast, in Nootka Sound (Vancouver Island). Spain seized the British ships. Convinced that she could blow the unaided Spanish navy from the seas, Britain set the war tocsins of Europe ringing. It seemed inevitable that the two powers whose colonies were neighbors of the United States would be at each other's throats.

The Spanish could hardly mount an offensive from their weak holdings at the mouth of the Mississippi and in the Floridas. However, the British in Canada had potentially the strength to move. Washington was deeply concerned to be told (he could not know that the rumor was false) that the man he most hated, "the traitor Arnold," was at the British-held post of Detroit and had, in his role as a general in the British army, "viewed the militia . . . twice." On August 27, 1790, Washington sent a secret communication to the heads of his departments and the Vice President: "There is no doubt in my mind that New Orleans and the Spanish posts above it" would be attacked by an "operation from Detroit." What should the United States do, he asked, if the British, with or without prior request for permission, should march through western forests claimed by the United States?

It was "obvious," Washington wrote, that an English takeover of Spain's North American possessions would be misfortune. With "so formidable and enterprising a people as the British on both our flanks and [the] rear, with their navy in front," the United States would be surrounded. But he agreed with his advisers that no immediate action should be contemplated beyond protests and negotiation.[3]

The most important consideration, Washington believed, was not to convulse the growing national unity with any anticipatory mobilization that would raise again fears of a strong, centralized army and force stringent new taxation. At the height of the Nootka crisis, he repeated to Lafayette that it should be "our policy . . . to observe a strict neutrality" as long as "circumstances and events will permit us so to do. . . .

"Gradually recovering from the distresses in which the war left us, patiently advancing in our task of civil government, unentangled in the crooked politics of Europe, wanting scarcely anything but the free navigation of the Mississippi (which we must have and as certainly shall have as we remain a nation), I have supposed that, with the undeviating exercise of a just, steady, and prudent national policy, we shall be the gainers, whether the powers of the Old World may be in peace or war, but more especially in the latter case. In that case, our importance will certainly increase and our friendship be courted."[4]

Great Britain was already doing some courting, however tentatively. Having never accorded official diplomatic representation to the United States, she had long relied on the secret activities of Major George Beckwith, who had in 1787 spent six months in New York observing the American government. When during 1789 discrimination against British trade was being considered by Congress, Beckwith had reappeared to warn that the British would retaliate. Since Jefferson had not yet made his entrance, there was no Secretary of State. Beckwith got in touch with Hamilton, whom he found delightfully sympathetic and who, in his turn, did not notify Washington of his conversations with a man presumed to be an altogether private British gentleman. In March 1790, Beckwith came again. Now he admitted to the title of aide to Lord Dorchester (the former Guy Carleton), Governor of Quebec, although he claimed that his presence in New York was purely accidental. Again he made overtures to Hamilton. In this instance, Hamilton decided to consult Jefferson, and the two carried to Washington Hamilton's memorandum of what Beckwith had said.[5]

The burden of the message proved to be that Gouverneur Morris's mission to England had produced no results, not because the government was unfavorable to the United States, but because "Mr. Morris had not produced any regular credentials" and had been absent "on a trip to Holland." In fact, "the Cabinet of Great Britain entertained a disposition not only towards a friendly intercourse but towards an alliance with the United States" which would certainly, as a commercial nation, "find it to be their interest to take part with Great Britain rather than with Spain." Washington's sour summary of this communication was that the British were not inclined to give satisfactory answer to Morris, who was *"officially* commissioned," until by "this unauthenticated mode" they discovered whether America would enter into an alliance against Spain. They then would enter into a commercial treaty "and *promise perhaps* to fulfill what [according to the peace treaty] they already stand engaged to perform."[6]

It was agreed that since Jefferson was the official Secretary of State, he could in no way countenance Beckwith's backstairs embassy. Jefferson was not, indeed, present when Washington, in conference with Hamilton and Jay, decided that Hamilton should engage in further conversations with Beckwith, gaining all information he could without making any commitments.[7]

Since Spain obviously needed help, this seemed the time for renewed efforts to open the Mississippi. Wishing to take advantage of Lafayette's powerful role in the French government, both Washington and Jefferson urged him to put pressure on Spain. Why, Washington asked, should not the Spanish "be wise and liberal at once? It would be easy to annihilate all causes of quarrels between that nation and the United States at this time." Jefferson instructed an American envoy to threaten Spain: If the United States could not secure navigation down the Mississippi by negotiation, so the word was to run, she would use force, perhaps in alliance with the British.[8]

In no area beyond the Alleghenies was the sovereignty of the United States as undisputed as it appeared to be on maps. Not only did thousands of Indians move beneath the unending canopy of trees, but there were two spheres of white influence: the British coming down from the north and the Spanish coming up from the south. During 1790, the Spanish sector seemed to Washington the more troubled.[9]

Spain's policy was aimed at compensating for the weakness of her North American colonies. Since she had so recently acquired them—at the end of the French and Indian War—there were practically no nationals of her own among the inhabitants. Most were French. And the total population of allegiance, about twenty-five thousand, was hardly half the number of the wild American settlers on the river above. It was Spain's desire to keep her potential enemies from becoming more numerous that induced her to try to strangle the economic life of the American frontier by blocking the Mississippi.

Capturing New Orleans would not, unless Europe was at war, open navigation from the American West to the great world. The United States was not a naval power; Spain was. But, as the Nootka crisis emphasized, there was always a chance that Spain would lose control of the seas. And unruly American frontiersmen were threatening that, whatever was dictated by reason or the policy of Washington's government, they would express their emotions by taking New Orleans. Spain wished to keep the American settlements—at present attackers would have to drift downriver a thousand miles—as far away as possible. She also labored to have the intervening Indian nations protect her territory as active allies.

On the face of it, the Indians should have been the dominant force in the southwest. The Creeks boasted some six thousand warriors, the Cherokees two thousand, the Choctaws five thousand, and the Chickasaws five hundred—huge forces in forest warfare. The basic attitude of all the tribes towards the United States and Spain was, of course, "a plague on both your houses." However, they lacked self-sufficiency. They had become dependent for not only luxuries and clothing, but also guns and ammunition, on the exchange of furs for white man's goods. Finding it necessary to deal with some white nation, the tribes tried to play the United States and Spain against each other for their own advantage. But they could not act effectively, since they were conglomerations of clans and villages whose central government was vague. The white powers—Spain, the United States, and various states acting separately—took advantage of this vagueness to procure, as soon as the Revolution was over, contradictory treaties in which presumed representatives of all four tribes acknowledged their nations under the protection of whoever supplied the liquor and the presents.

In trying to make the imperfect treaties stick, Spain had the major advantage that her economic interests were the same as the Indians'. She had no excess population, lusting for Indian hunting grounds, but preferred to encourage Indian hunters; the fur trade, which brought the Indians prosperity, also contributed to the prosperity of Spain. However, the treaties negotiated for the United States usually included large cessions of land. The Indian nations instantly repudiated these treaties as having been agreed to by only a few of their nationals. But settlers swept into the disputed territories (and beyond). Fighting ensued.

When vainly trying to defend the Virginia frontier during the French and Indian War, Washington had considered the Indians "butchering" monsters imbued with "savage fury." Now he described them as "poor wretches." Although he had once himself ordered secret surveys to be made in lands legally assured to the Indians, he now saw the white men who stole Indian land as the villains of the forests. It was *they*, not the savages, who were "diabolical." How could anyone, the President asked, expect peace "so long as the spirit of land jobbing prevails and our frontier settlers entertain the opinion that there is not the same crime (or indeed no crime at all) in killing an Indian as in killing a white man"? The Indians could not be expected to "govern their own people better than we do ours." That the tribes had no newspapers in which to report the atrocities committed on them did not make the atrocities less dreadful.[10]

One of the administration's main tasks was to determine the actual validity of the treaties that had been made during the disorder of the Confederation both by the national government and the various states. The only way to keep the frontier from being perpetually aflame, Washington stated to Congress, was to foster the "happiness" of the Indians which "materially depends on the national justice and humanity of the United States." Land should be purchased fairly and only as it was required by orderly expansion. It was essential to make sure that until each new sector was honestly secured, no white man encroached.[11]

There was always the danger that incidents on the frontier would detonate an Indian war which could spread until it embroiled the United States with England or Spain. That fighting might become necessary, Washington did not deny, but "if extremities are at any time to ensue, it is of the utmost consequence that they should be the result of a deliberate plan, not of an accidental collision." Washington knew all about the danger of accidental collisions since, as a very young officer operating for Virginia over the frontier in partial disregard of his orders, he had fired the first shots in a worldwide conflict: the Seven Years' War.[12]

As long as the United States applied to the great central valley the virtues of "circumspection, moderation, and forbearance,"[13] she had an invisible ally who every day was fighting her battles as resolutely as Kipling was to hope "the stars in their courses" would support the British Empire. That ally was time. Every day there climbed over passes through the mountains, there floated down the connecting rivers, additional American settlers, more and more weights in the wilderness balance of power. The gradual absorption of the Indian hunting grounds was inevitable and sooner or later, although not specifically foreseeable, there would be a European war that would shake down for the United States to catch one or both of the foreign territories under dispute.

Washington's policy was to hold on, soothe wounds with whatever poultices came to hand, cut out an abscess only when the operation would not be more than local, be forever patient and watchful as intrigue in the forests seethed with the slow rhythm of almost unpopulated places.

Washington had to handle not only Spain and the Indians, but opposition in those states that were encouraging and profiting from land-grabs. Such conflict between central authority and local speculators was built into American history. In his desire to view the frontier as a whole, to negotiate fair treaties and fairly to enforce them, Washington was playing the role that had, before the Revolution, been played by the British Crown. Indeed, fear that this pattern would repeat itself had encouraged, in some states, opposition to the Constitution.

The United States, and specifically the state of Georgia, claimed much land also claimed by Spain. While the federal government was still forming, the Georgia legislature sold to three companies, which included important politicians and soldiers, fifteen and a half million acres, mostly in the disputed area. The tract, so Washington's government reported to Congress, comprised almost the whole of the land of the Choctaws and Chickasaws and part of the Cherokees'.[14] Since much of this territory lay between the Mississippi and Yazoo Rivers, the scheme is designated in history by the picturesque name of Yazoo.

Georgia, having authorized this settlement, made no effort to govern or control it. The speculators chose as their general agent an Irish adventurer, James O'Fallon. He offered to Spain the establishment of an independent buffer nation, and at the same time offered Washington military might with which to attack Spain.

The Yazoo scheme, which was in 1790 ripening towards consummation, might well, as Washington saw it, embroil the United States not only with Indians but with Spain. If Spain, by sponsoring a separate white nation in the Yazoo, tried to take so great a bite out of the United States, that obviously could not be borne. And if, on the other hand, Spain decided to protect her territorial claims and her Indian alliances by forcibly expelling the settlers, frontier sentiment would dictate intervention by the United States. Washington felt it necessary to squash Yazoo—but how?

That Georgia had not ceded her western lands to the Union created constitutional issues which Washington considered it prudent not to raise. But enforcing Indian treaties was definitely in the federal power.

Washington wondered whether, since the Yazoo grants violated various treaties, he had the right to place the federal authority in opposition to Georgia's official acts. After the matter had been formally called to his attention by Knox, he consulted Attorney General Randolph on the constitutional considerations. Next, he asked Hamilton whether he should denounce Yazoo in a proclamation. Hamilton doubted that he had the right, under the Constitution, so Washington put the matter to Jefferson. Hamilton in the meanwhile, discussed the question with Rufus King of the Senate and reported back that the Senate would probably take up the matter and that, in his opinion, it would be better to let action originate there. Jefferson considered Georgia's behavior unconstitutional, but felt that the state and the Indian tribes should be further consulted before Washington acted. Washington, however, decided to go ahead with his proclamation. On August 26, 1790, he announced, without even mentioning Georgia or her legislation, that the proposed settlements were contrary to various treaties with the Choctaw and Chickasaw nations. He therefore required all officers of the United States and all citizens to observe the treaties, "as they will answer the contrary at their peril."[15]

This was all very well, but Washington had no way of enforcing his decree. Like everyone else who wished to achieve anything in that wilderness, he thought of Alexander McGillivray.

McGillivray's father had been a Tory, a Scotch fur trader whose property was expropriated by Georgia. McGillivray's mother was the daughter of a Frenchman and a Creek. Since in the female progression his ancestry was pure Indian, McGillivray was considered by the matrilineal Indians just as much a tribesman as any other Creek. Although now living with his tribe, he had resided in Georgia as a white man, and he knew the white man's two-tongued ways. This combination, joined with natural gifts for leadership, enabled him to dominate Indian council fires far beyond the confines of the Creek nation. A statesman who ruled the forest in his own right, he was nonetheless dependent on his partnership in a Spanish fur trading company and on a subsidy from the Spanish crown. His way of life was extravagant. Deep in the Indian country, he maintained an estate that might have graced the tidewater: a mansion house, extensive plantations, a horde of black slaves.[16]

Washington's appearance before the Senate which had resulted in the eternal abolition of such confrontations between the chief executive and the legislature, had been to secure "advice and consent" concerning a negotiation with McGillivray and his nation, who were threatening a border war with Georgia. The issue concerned three treaties (1773, 1785, 1786) in which Georgia claimed the Creeks had made tremendous sales of land, and which the Creeks claimed had been perfidiously set up by Georgia with stray Indians of no authority. Washington secured in the end Senate approval for a federal commission that would "judge impartially" the validity of Georgia's treaties and, if necessary, negotiate a new one.[17]

On learning that the commission was on its way, the Spanish authorities became upset. They admonished McGillivray and presented the Creeks with ammunition. McGillivray took advantage of a tactless remark by one of the United States negotiators, Washington's old friend Humphreys, to break up the conference.[18]

Enter James O'Fallon. By offering to give McGillivray a sizable share of Yazoo stock, he sought the Indian leader's support for the scheme. (While taking land from other nations, Yazoo would not damage the Creeks.) If McGillivray agreed, the scheme was as good as launched. However, the Indian statesman was being given second thoughts about relations with Washington's government by the news, which had filtered to him through the trees, of the Nootka crisis.

His own prosperity and that of his followers depended on the fur trade. The goods the Indians received were not manufactured in Spanish America or even in non-industrial Spain, but imported into New Spain from England. Therefore, a war between Spain and England would, McGillivray recognized, create the need for a new source of supply. In reply to a personal invitation from Washington, he agreed to visit New York.

On horseback and by wagon, McGillivray and twenty-nine headmen moved northward from Georgia, receiving in the towns through which they passed as flattering welcomes as the federal government could

[263]

engineer. Curiosity helped things along by drawing to the Battery, when the Indians sailed up to New York City from New Jersey, the largest crowd that had been seen there since Washington had arrived to be inaugurated. The braves were conducted by "some uniform[ed] troops" and the Society of Saint Tammany "in their proper dresses" to the President's house where Washington, so the *New York Journal* continues, "received them in a very handsome manner."[19]

Washington, whose first military mentor had been an Iroquois called the Half-King and who had, as a stripling, matched wits (not to his advantage) with the great French Indian agents in the days of French Canada, must have studied with interest the ruler of the southwestern forests. He saw a frail man in slovenly Indian dress, who was much lighter-skinned than his companions. Marks of debauchery were evident on a countenance which Humphreys described as having "nothing liberal and open in it." It was an intelligent face, combining, so Humphreys continued, "the good sense of an American, the shrewdness of a Scotchman, and the cunning of an Indian." Although Washington left the actual negotiations to Knox, he had occasion to see that McGillivray could get roaring drunk without losing "his recollection and reason."[20]

The Treaty of New York, which Washington and McGillivray signed with much ceremony on August 7, 1790, procured for Georgia much but not all of the land in dispute.* The Creeks acknowledged the sovereignty of the United States insofar as the Indian towns lay within her boundaries. A provision that the Indians would expel all unauthorized intruders was, so McGillivray confided to Spain, aimed at the Yazoo speculators (whom the federal government thus effectively blocked). Of the two secret provisions, one was a pension for McGillivray three times that paid him by Spain; and the other provided that should the fur trade by way of Spanish possessions be stopped by war, fifty thousand dollars' worth of goods might annually be imported to the Creek country through the United States without duty.

---

* James Jackson, a member of the House of Representatives, fulminated that the treaty had given away "three million acres guaranteed to Georgia by the Constitution." Washington tried to soothe outraged Georgians by stating that the land returned to the Indians was "reported to be generally barren, sunken, and unfit for cultivation," though covered with a fine stand of trees.

The Treaty of New York was a triumph for Washington's government, all the more so (since peace was the objective) because Spain was not really displeased. The matter of McGillivray's pension and the allegiance he swore to the United States were comfortably handled by Spain's upping the pension she gave him until it became much the larger. Spain was as pleased as Washington to have toned down the threats of warfare involved in the Yazoo speculation and in the controversies between Georgia and the Creeks.[21]

In raising the specter of a separate white nation appearing beyond the Alleghenies, Yazoo had followed a pattern now familiar. Ever since the migration that had followed the Revolution, there had existed the possibility that, under the aegis perhaps of Spain or perhaps of England, settlements would secede. Washington had expressed this worry when beyond the Alleghenies in 1784.[22] Since then, he had not been over the mountains. However, frightening reports had come in to him. Jay's ancient offer to accept the closing of the Mississippi, although so rapidly dropped, had made many frontiersmen suspect that the eastern seaboard plotted to strangle the west. Furthermore, the rapidity of migration often outran the ability of the eastern areas, which theoretically ruled the territories, to expand their governmental organizations. The frontiersmen had to set up their own illegal legislatures, create their own armies. Perhaps most disturbingly of all, they were supplied no effective facilities for registering and adjudicating land claims.

Spain was happy to encourage any confusion. A promise to open the Mississippi to frontiersmen who would cross the river into her territory and swear allegiance to her brought hysterical reports to Washington that the American forests would be "depopulated."[23] However, Spain's autocratic Catholic government could not be adequately modified to suit settlers enamored of freedom and Protestantism. Then the word went round that Spain would be happy to open the river to areas that formed, under her aegis, independent nations. There were mysterious comings and goings; special trade concessions to the friends of Spain put money in privileged hands for everyone to see; and oratory, soaring loud in the wilderness stillness, promised wealth and freedom if only the ties with the United States were broken.

As Washington waited, in March 1789, for Congress to certify his election as President, both verbal and written information concerning

[265]

the "Spanish Conspiracy" (as historians have called it) came to Mount Vernon. Washington asked his correspondents to keep him informed, sending them ciphers to use since "a miscarriage of letters on such delicate subjects might be attended with very disadvantageous consequences." In response to one particularly flamboyant letter he wrote that he was "greatly alarmed," but as a matter of fact he was less alarmed than he had been when over the mountains in 1784.[24]

At the earlier date Washington, who was himself trying to find some European religious group that would take over his extensive Kanawha lands, had assumed that the settlers of the west would primarily be foreigners whose lack of "particular predilection for us" would encourage their having "different views, different interests."[25] Actually, the post-Revolutionary migration had proved to be overwhelmingly from the eastern states. The pioneers had not emigrated because of any dissatisfaction with American institutions; they wished to re-create those same institutions with themselves nearer the top.

The Spanish Conspiracy was thus very similar to one Washington had lived with at a much more dangerous time. During the Revolution the inhabitants of Vermont, who had previously been engaged in a local war with New York, simultaneously offered to enter the United States on their own terms (which New York would not accept) and intrigued with the British enemy. Washington had cautioned against trying to use force against them, even when they declared themselves an independent nation. They were still in their limbo of semi-independence, still negotiating with the British as well as Congress—and nothing dreadful had happened.

As he prepared to step into the Presidency, Washington wrote that the solution to the intrigues on the Mississippi was to establish "such a system of national policy as shall be mutually advantageous to all parts of the American republic." A healthy nation would quickly throw off the Spanish contagion.[26]

Extending governmental institutions across the mountains required much fitting and adjusting both in the parent areas and in the new territories, but it was important that there be no stagnation to inspire rebellion or despair. Progress was primarily dependent on the legislative branch. However, Washington did what he considered suitable to encourage the ever-perceptible flow that was carrying Kentucky and Vermont to statehood. South of Kentucky, on land finally ceded to the

Union by South Carolina, Congress established in 1790 the Southwest Territory.*

It was up to Washington to appoint the official who would administer the Southwest Territory. For this ticklish task, which was made more ticklish by the fact that much of the land involved was also claimed by Spain, he could either designate individuals (perhaps necessarily outsiders) who had not been involved in the previous tumults, or he could entrust federal power to local leaders who, sharing the growing pains of the area, had speculated not too scrupulously in disputed land titles and even flirted with the Spanish Conspiracy. Eager not to exclude dissidents but to bring them within the national pale, Washington secured recommendations for office from John Brown, a congressman from the Kentucky area who he knew had been accused of plotting with Spain. As Governor of the Territory and Superintendent of Indian Affairs for the Southern Department, he then appointed a notorious land speculator, William Blount, and around Blount he placed various men who had in various ways engaged in scheming. It was a gamble, but it paid off handsomely. Although Blount was to get into hot water with new plots during Adams's administration, he served Washington faithfully as did the other appointees.[27]

In August 1790, Washington wrote Lafayette that the summer's labors "will leave us in peace from one end of our borders to the other, except where it may be interrupted by a small refugee banditti of Cherokees and Shawnees, who can be easily chastised or even extirpated if it shall become necessary." To do the chastising he ordered Brigadier General Josiah Harmar to advance from Port Washington (Cincinnati) into the valleys of the Maumee and the Wabash.[28] He did not foresee that what he considered a minor operation would uncover extensive and dangerous malignancy in the forests where British influence prevailed.

---

* Following the provisions by which the Continental Congress had in 1787 established the Northwest Territory, the bill furnished immediate government by appointment and defined steps by which areas, as they became more populous, would take over their own administration and eventually enter the Union as separate states.

CHAPTER

21

Vacation Time

THE time had come for the government to move to Philadelphia
for a ten-year stay until the new Federal City was prepared.
Washington wrote an agent in Philadelphia, requesting that
his letter be burned "as soon as you have read it." He had seen an
advertisement offering for sale three farms near the new temporary
capital. He would like to secure one of these, in exchange for "valuable
lands, improved, in the counties of Fayette and Washington in the
state of Pennsylvania. . . . I shall candidly declare that to pay money
is out of the question with me. I have *none* and would not, if it was to
be had, run in debt to borrow."

He wanted one of the properties, preferably the largest (284 acres),
"for the amusement of farming and for the benefit arising from exercise." It was "my own opinion, strengthened by those of my physicians,
that my late change from active scenes, to which I had been accustomed and in which the mind has been agreeably amused, to the one
of inactivity which I now lead and where the thoughts are continually
on the stretch, has been the cause of more illness and severe attacks of
my constitution within the last twelve months than I had undergone in
thirty years preceding put together. A deviation therefore is necessary."[1]

Who can doubt that Washington wanted his request kept secret
since he knew that, should it become public knowledge, he would
receive an offer of a farm at someone else's expense? He accepted
without complaint that fact that his western holdings, although one of
them consisted of three thousand acres within sixteen miles of Pitts-

burgh, were not considered fair exchange for as little as sixty acres within easy distance of Philadelphia. The President was not to ride from his tasks to any friendly fields.

Before his pneumonia struck, Washington had sought a change of scene in a five-day exploration of Long Island. There being no manufactures there to engage his mind, he had reveled in agricultural observations. His pneumonia was less than a month behind him when he took Hamilton and Jefferson out with him on a three-day fishing expedition off Sandy Hook. The President caught "a great number of sea bass and blackfish." After Congress had adjourned on August 12, he found an excellent reason for another jaunt: Rhode Island, which he had skirted during his New England trip as outside federal jurisdiction, had at last joined the Union. It should receive a Presidential visit.

At Newport, the recovered if elderly athlete "completely fatigued the company" by walking briskly from nine in the morning until one in the afternoon. He strode all over town; went out to the college where he climbed to the roof to see the view; explored a shipyard and went on board a large Indiaman that was in the stocks; returned to town, dropped in at four houses to drink wine and punch.[2]

For real relaxation, Washington intended to go to Mount Vernon, staying until Congress was ready to reconvene on the first Monday in December. He ordered that thirty-six dozen bottles of port be sent ahead, and notified his Cabinet ministers that, since he wished "to have my mind as free from public care as circumstances will allow," he wanted to have all public matters that needed attention disposed of before he left.[3]

New York (which, as it turned out, would never see him again) would not let George Washington go without an "affectionate farewell," which featured a parade, cheering crowds, firing cannon. According to the newspapers, many spectators wept; the President "seemed sensibly moved" and Mrs. Washington "greatly affected." Wherever the famous travelers passed, there were other celebrations including "an elegant *fête champêtre* in Gray's Gardens on the banks of the Schuylkill" near Philadelphia, attended by two hundred ladies and gentlemen.[4]

At Mount Vernon, Washington did his best to exclude the cares of the world, but he did not pull in the latchstring. Now he could entertain as he preferred, and those who had complained at his constraint at levees and official dinners would have been amazed. The grandson of one of Washington's old friends thus described a two days' visit: "I have been treated as usual with every most distinguished mark of kindness and attention. Hospitality, indeed, seems to have spread over the whole its happiest, kindest influence. The President exercises it in a superlative degree, from the greatest of its duties to the most trifling minutiae, and Mrs. Washington is the very essence of kindness. Her soul seems to overflow with it like the most abundant fountain, and her happiness is in exact proportion to the number of objects upon which she can dispense her benefits."⁵

Domestic arrangement always supplied amusement to the designer of Mount Vernon. Now Robert Morris's mansion in Philadelphia, which had been rented to serve as the President's house, needed fitting up. When Washington had stayed there during the Constitutional Convention, it had seemed palatial, but his new needs made it small and inconvenient. He launched with enthusiasm into instructing Lear, who was on the scene in Philadelphia, concerning the building of additions, redecorating, organizing the staff. As on his farm he concerned himself with a single bush, so no domestic detail proved too minor to catch his eager attention. He was worried lest an exchange of mangles with Mrs. Morris should turn out to her disadvantage. What servants to hire or fire, which to bring over from New York or up from Mount Vernon occupied thousands of words of Presidential prose. Since "the principal entertaining rooms in our new habitation" had a view into the kitchen, Lear should leave Mrs. Lewis and her daughter in New York: Their "dirty fingers" would not be "a pleasant sight." Washington would import from Mount Vernon to staff the kitchen his slaves Hercules and Nathan, although this involved bringing along Hercules's incompetent son, because the cook insisted on it.⁶

Washington varied his vacation with a twelve-day trip up the Potomac, during which he added to his old interest of inspecting the ever-lagging canal works a substantial new excitement. In its decision concerning the national capital, Congress had decided that the federal area, which could be as large as a hundred square miles, was to be located on the Potomac somewhere between the Eastern Branch, less than fifteen miles from Mount Vernon, and the confluence of the Potomac and the Conococheague, near the Pennsylvania border some sixty-seven miles upriver from the lower limit. That the specific choice was left to Washington gave the former surveyor and land speculator as important a task of land location as was ever in history entrusted to one man.

On his first surveying trip to the wilderness, when he had been a stripling of sixteen, Washington had been followed around by German squatters whose illegal farms his activities menaced: he had smiled in his diary over their "antic tricks." Now, whenever he paused on his journey to examine any terrain, he was followed around by "the principal citizens of this town and neighborhood," each blatantly or subtly trying to influence Washington's judgment to the advantage of his own holdings. The old fox, who had fabricated ruses to fool British generals and who now wished to avoid informing land speculators, amused himself in encouraging false conclusions that sent hysterical rumors charging up and down the river. It was only after his vacation had ended and he had returned to Philadelphia that he announced a decision. He had selected the most southerly part of the authorized tract, that nearest Mount Vernon, and wished indeed (Congress quickly agreed) to move the boundary a little further south so that the proposed city would achieve the scenic and economic advantages of including within it the Eastern Branch of the Potomac.[7]

Almost no public business that he found bothersome obtruded into Washington's vacation. Although Hamilton could not resist sending this and that to Mount Vernon, Jefferson, who was on his own vacation at Monticello, disturbed Washington with no problems of state. Knox, it is true, reported that the punitive expedition against the Indians northwest of the Ohio seemed stalled, but there was nothing Washington could do about it. His next foreseeable task was to prepare his Second Annual Address to Congress. He asked Hamilton, Jay, and Knox to send him ideas, not necessarily limited to their own departments. He did not ask Jefferson, perhaps because he did not wish to disturb his fellow agrarian's vacation.[8]

Having stayed away for forty-one days, Washington returned to the government, now located in Philadelphia, with his health, as he boasted "perfectly re-established." He ceased expressing concern lest a third serious illness were hovering nearby to carry him to "the gloomy mansion of my fathers."[9]

IV

The Great Schism Opens

22

The Bank of the United States

W ASHINGTON delivered his Second Annual Address before both houses of Congress on December 6, 1790. Those
historians who wish to demonstrate him a perpetual slave
to Hamilton point out that he had admitted himself "somewhat at a
loss to frame . . . a paragraph" in connection with the loan in Holland,
and had asked Hamilton to send him a "model" (which he had used).[1]
However, in two major respects Washington flew directly in the face
of Hamilton's desires.

Hamilton urged Washington to state that "the measures heretofore
adopted for the support of public credit" had lifted prosperity high.
However, Washington chose to attribute "the progress of public credit"
not to Hamilton's measures but to what Hamilton had mentioned as a
less important consideration: abundant harvests which "blessed our
country with plenty and with the means of a flourishing commerce."
That commerce had raised customs duties beyond expectations. Washington praised the patriotic "punctuality" with which merchants had
paid the imposts.[2]

Since news had not yet arrived that the Nootka crisis had quieted in
Europe,* Washington spoke of the threat a naval war would pose for
American commerce. In their preliminary consultations, Hamilton had
pressed Washington not to go beyond urging Congress to do nothing
rash. However, Washington recommended "such encouragements to
our own navigation as will render our commerce and agriculture less

---

* Spain, finding she could secure no help from France, had knuckled under to
England.

dependent on foreign bottoms, which may fail us. . . . Our fisheries and the transportation of our own produce offer us abundant means for guarding ourselves against this evil."[3] Washington's sentiments were extremely unsatisfactory to Hamilton, who was convinced that sound economics and sound international relations involved no interference with the prevailing trade pattern that carried American goods in British bottoms. Hamilton was alarmed. In one of those private conferences with Beckwith which he failed to report to his own government, he warned the English agent that this session of Congress would probably put the same restrictions on British boats as the British kept on American.[4]

As Hamilton watched disapprovingly, Washington and Jefferson gave repeated encouragement to the movement to curb British shipping during the early months of the Congressional session. In a report on New England's cod and whale fisheries, Jefferson argued that the British policy of "mounting their navigation on the ruin of ours," was greatly damaging this important industry. He urged a bounty for American fishermen and reprisals against the British. An argument for encouraging the use of American bottoms was, he pointed out, that during the eighteenth century England had been at war three years out of every eight. While she fought, the cost of using her boats had mounted alarmingly.[5]

Washington presented to Congress a French protest: as former allies of the United States they complained that, although they had signed a commercial treaty, they were given no trade advantages over America's former enemy, which had refused to sign a treaty. Jefferson added a gloss in which he urged various special concessions to the French.[6]

Washington's personal envoy in London, Gouverneur Morris, had been sending such unfavorable reports concerning British actions that during the previous September Hamilton had used information, which in this instance he frankly admitted had come from Beckwith, in an effort to discredit Morris: the envoy had been treated coldly not because of any anti-American sentiment but because he had consorted with the leaders of the opposition and the French ambassador. The French ambassador was none other than Luzerne, who had represented France in America during the Revolution, and with whom Washington himself corresponded. When Washington expressed suspicions that Beckwith was lying to serve his government's policies,

Hamilton, probably because he did not wish to emphasize his bias to his chief, was too prudent to argue.[7]

Having received from Jefferson a compendium of Morris's reports, Washington held it for two months and then sent it to the Senate as if to reinforce Jefferson's tirade on the fisheries. Although Hamilton assured Beckwith that "the President had not a thought of timing reports to help the French party," there is no doubt that Washington was acting in close collaboration with Jefferson. Washington's letter to the Senate introducing the Morris compendium incorporated alterations made by the Secretary of State.

In this covering letter, Washington spoke out strongly: the British, so Morris's evidence revealed, had declared "without scruple" that they did not intend to fulfill their remaining obligations under the old peace treaty (delivering surrendered western posts and paying for property—mostly slaves—which had been carried off) unless the United States carried out certain clauses (concerning payments to Tories) which, so Washington continued, the British delay made "now impracticable." Furthermore, Britain would not enter into a treaty of commerce unless the United States would agree to join her, "in the event of a rupture," in fighting Spain.

England's one concession had been to indicate that they would officially recognize the United States by sending a minister. Washington pointed out that even this act had been grudging: "They made excuses in the first conference, seem disposed to it in the second, and in the last express an intention of so doing." Washington was so little mollified that he closed his message: "Their views being thus sufficiently ascertained, I have directed Mr. Morris to discontinue his communications with them."

When Hamilton heard that a British minister was to be appointed, he told Beckwith, "I think I can assure you that nothing will take place during this session to the injury of your trade." Hamilton knew his cohorts. Although indirectly supported by Washington and directly by Jefferson in his reports and Madison on the floor of the House, a bill that was an exact imitation of the British navigation laws failed, as similar bills had at previous sessions. Hamilton had won again.[8]

For the Treasury Department, Hamilton presented Congress with a two-pronged program: He proposed a tax expansion to cover the cost of funding and also the establishment of a national bank.

Since duties on imports had been adequate, no internal taxes had so far been levied by the federal government. Now Hamilton recommended a tax on spirituous liquors. This was eventually to cause an armed insurrection on the frontier, where whiskey was a major asset. (Distilling grain so reduced bulk that the produce of isolated farms became exportable.) Albert Gallatin, a new member of the House from western Pennsylvania, protested violently against Hamilton's proposal, but almost no one listened to his warnings. Colonel Edward Carrington, Virginia's tax collector, was soon to assure Washington that the tax "may be executed without difficulty—nay more, that it will become popular in a little time." While regretting that a direct levy should be necessary, Madison felt that a liquor tax was of all the least objectionable. To this Jefferson agreed, although he expressed worry that in framing its policies the Treasury did not pay enough attention to public opinion. In sum, the tax on liquor passed both houses without difficulty, to be cheerfully signed by the President.[9]

Hamilton's principal proposal to this legislative session was that Congress charter an institution to be known as the Bank of the United States. Washington undoubtedly approved. Although he did not understand all the intricate financial machinery comprised in Hamilton's plan,[*] the conception was not new to him and experience had taught him its value. When in 1780–1781 the money that the Continental Congress had printed had become so worthless that Washington could not buy food for his army, the businessmen of Philadelphia had helped out by establishing the Bank of North America, which had, on the basis of funds deposited in its coffers, issued notes that had circulated more or less at face value.[10]

The Bank of the United States would be, according to Hamilton's proposal "a great engine of state" but not actively controlled by the state. The Secretary argued, and the experience of the nation during the Revolution seemed to shout agreement, that the people's money should not be at the mercy of governmental action, since a government—and particularly a democratic government—always resorted, when pressed, to devaluation. By seeking mutual prosperity, private interests would keep the economy healthy.

---

[*] During 1794, when he was considering for the first time the possibility of borrowing personally from a bank, Washington wrote, "I know nothing of the rules and regulations by which the banks are governed, having no interest in or the least concern with any one of them."[11]

Three-fifths of the bank's ten-million-dollar capital was to be in the form of government securities, the other two-fifths in gold and silver. The government would be assigned a fifth of the stock, on a basis advantageous to it,* and would appoint five of the twenty-five directors. The Secretary of the Treasury would be authorized to examine the books; and the bank would, in any case, have to remember the public interest since it would have to be rechartered by the government after a period of years.

Hamilton did not envisage an ordinary bank of deposit and discount. The Bank of the United States would service the national debt; it would make loans to the government and on a large scale to private individuals; its paper would circulate as currency;† through its creation and control of credit it would stabilize inflation and deflation and force its policies on local banks. And it would enrich its stockholders.[12]

Concerning Hamilton's bank bill, a later opponent was to write, "It was one of those sly and subtle movements which marched silently to its object: The vices of it were at first not palpable."[13] In contrast with the funding and assumption bills, the bank bill made little stir outside Congress, as no one felt directly affected except the businessmen who favored the legislation. The proposal passed in the Senate almost casually, by a voice vote. When the House considered it in a committee of the whole, no objection was raised. It was only after the representatives had reported the bill out favorably to themselves sitting in their full capacity that, to Hamilton's amazement, Madison rose in opposition. He talked for a whole day.

Madison's objection was one that Hamilton, who had tried in his report to forestall all negative arguments, had not foreseen. The Constitution, Madison insisted, did not give the federal government the power necessary to incorporate a bank. However, the bill passed the House by a vote of thirty-nine to twenty. It would become law if Washington signed it.

Washington, so Madison remembered, was "greatly perplexed" by the question of constitutionality. "He held several free conversations with me on the subject in which he listened favorable, as I thought, to

---

* The bank would lend the government, at a lower interest rate than the stock would yield, the money to buy the stock.

† This was all the more important since Congress, despite Washington's urging, had delayed in establishing a mint. What specie circulated, was a ragtag and bobtail collection of gold or silver coins minted abroad.

my view, but certainly without committing himself in any manner."
Madison reminded Washington that giving Congress power to incorporate institutions had been discussed at the Constitutional Convention and laid aside. When Washington pointed out that the Continental Congress had in 1781 incorporated the Bank of North America,
Madison replied that this was no valid precedent since the earlier act
had been a child of necessity. There was no necessity now.[14]

Washington consulted the two Virginians in his Cabinet: Jefferson
and Attorney General Randolph. They backed Madison in his basic
contention: Powers not specifically granted to Congress were forbidden to it. As Jefferson saw it, under the Constitution, Congress
could only exert such authority as was necessary to keep functions
specifically granted from being "nugatory." Madison, admitting that
Congress had the right to regulate trade, asked rhetorically, "Would
any plain man suppose" that a bank had *"anything* to do with trade?"[15]

In opposing what has come to be known in constitutional parlance
as "implied powers," both Jefferson and Madison were contradicting
previous stands. Jefferson had argued in his correspondence for implied powers, and, according to Dumas Malone, "It may be claimed
that the doctrine of implied powers really originated with Madison."
He had stated it in a report he had made to the old Congress in 1781,
and reaffirmed it in *The Federalist,* writing, "There must necessarily be
admitted powers by implication unless the Constitution descended to
recount every minutia. . . . No axiom is more clearly established in
law or in reason than that wherever the end is required, the means are
authorized; wherever a general power to do a thing is given, every
particular power for doing it is included."[16]

That Jefferson and Madison thus reversed themselves reveals that
their concern was not really with the interpretation of the Constitution.
They were seizing an impediment to throw across a path they considered dangerous. As Malone points out, they envisioned as the
greatest danger the individual who was leading the procession down
the path. Their real concern was Hamilton's rising influence. Had not
Hamilton in the Constitutional Convention proposed what was in
effect a monarch elected for life? Was he not a city man, unconcerned
with the best way to plant a field, who found the scratching of pens in
business ledgers more fascinating than the rustling of the wind? An
upstart and a foreigner, Hamilton was encouraging the rise of a

nouveau riche class of city traders, just the kind of men who descended on farmers after a disastrous harvest and seized their land for debt. And, to top everything, were not his supporters northeasterners whose economic interests were different from those of the agrarian south?

This dossier would not have been so frightening had Hamilton been a man of ordinary charm and skills. To menace the state, a villain had to be more than some little devil capable only of souring the milk on a few governmental doorsteps. He had to have the greatness of Milton's Satan, and this greatness, alas, it seemed that Hamilton might well possess.

Madison was, of course, Washington's trusted adviser on constitutional matters, and usually when they had disagreed it had been because Madison had wanted to go further than Washington had thought politic in strengthening federal power. This made doubly disturbing Madison's contention that the bank bill stretched federal power illegally far. That Jefferson and Randolph agreed with Madison further increased the dilemma.

Washington himself sympathized with the intentions of the bill, and, in his concern with the separation of powers, he had happily avoided up to this moment using his veto on any legislation. However, he felt himself faced with a responsibility he could not shirk. In those years, before the Supreme Court had taken the prerogative to itself, Washington believed that a major function of the Presidential veto was to protect the Constitution. If the bank bill actually violated the Constitution, he would have no choice but to veto it.

The letter Washington now wrote Hamilton seems in its cold impersonality to indicate irritation at having been placed in such a situation. The constitutionality of the bill, Washington stated, had been objected to by the Attorney General and the Secretary of State. "That I may be fully possessed of the argument *for* and *against* the measure before I express any opinion of my own, I give you an opportunity of examining and answering the objections contained in the enclosed papers. I require the return of them, when your own sentiments are handed me (which I wish may be as soon as is convenient); and further, that no copies of them be taken."[17]

Amazed by Madison's constitutional about-face, Hamilton seems to have assumed that the President would brush the objections aside. Now he recognized a severe crisis, not only for the bank bill but for the whole federal structure. He worked passionately on his rebuttal, but he wished to make it masterly, and time passed.

If Washington did not act on the bill within ten days of its submission to him, it would become law without his signature. As he awaited Hamilton's reply, he summoned Madison and asked him to summarize the objections to the bill in preparation for a veto message.[18]

The President's hesitation, which threatened to torpedo all their plans, terrified everyone who had moored his financial boat to the federal government. Listening to talk in New York City where he was visiting, Madison suspected that Hamilton's supporters were preparing to turn on Washington: "The licentiousness of tongues exceeded anything that was conceived." Senator Fisher Ames, indeed, recorded the suspicion that Washington was motivated by fear lest the bank make Philadelphia so powerful that it would of necessity supersede the area near Mount Vernon as the national capital. [19]

Hamilton's argument, which finally reached Washington on February 23, is generally conceded to be one of the greatest state papers in American history. Jefferson's biographer Malone and Madison's biographer Brant agree that Hamilton was right and their men wrong. For Hamilton pointed out that the federal government would sink to incompetence if its action were limited to enumerated powers. For one thing, the Constitution admittedly contained no more than the foundations on which the government was to be built. For another, any hard and fast document could not be adapted to reality as history changed. Strict interpretation would, in the long run, destroy the central authority, since the states, not being so bound, would keep up to date while the federal government became increasingly obsolete.[20]

On receiving Hamilton's report, Washington wrote him to ask how much more time there was before the bill would become law without his signature. It was, he noted, Wednesday noon. Hamilton replied that he had until Congress's adjournment on Friday.[21]

Washington had already begun to read, and, as he read, his decision became inevitable, all the more because Jefferson, tempering his disapproval of the bank with his belief in the primacy of the legislature, had conceded that should Washington find the contrary arguments on constitutionality about even in force, he ought not to negate a decision of Congress. Washington signed the bill that created the Bank of the United States.

After Congress had adjourned on March 3, 1791, Washington wrote a summary of the winter's events to Humphreys, whom he had sent to Portugal as United States Minister. Indian affairs had gone badly because Harmar's expedition to the northwest of the Ohio had "not been productive of the consequences which were expected from it." (It had, indeed, been driven back with considerable loss.) Since the Indians were continuing hostilities, further military steps would be necessary.

However, "our public credit is restored, our resources are increasing, and the general appearance of things at least equals the most sanguine expectation that was formed of the effects of the present government." Congress had voted the admission of Vermont and Kentucky. Washington hoped a mint would soon be established. Having stated that the legislative session was characterized "on all occasions, with great harmony and cordiality," Washington added that "in some few instances, particularly in passing the law for higher duties [the tax on liquor] mentioned above and more especially on the subject of the bank, the line between the southern and eastern interests appeared more strongly marked than could have been wished." Then he could not resist returning to his optimistic note: "But the debates were conducted with temper and candor."[22]

Maclay had been defeated for re-election to the Senate. What was his surprise to receive an invitation to dinner from the President whom he had so consistently opposed! And despite the fact that he no longer had any power!

He accepted, but went in no conciliatory mood. When the President edged over on a sofa to make room for the grouch to sit beside him, Maclay, being (as he boasted) not "a true courtier . . . sat on the opposite settee or sofa with some New England men."

Then came dinner. "After my second plate had been taken away, the President offered to help me to part of a dish which stood before him." However, Maclay had "just before declined being helped to anything more," and "had, of course, for the sake of consistency, to thank him negatively." Washington tried again with some pudding, and this time Maclay submitted to being helped.

"He soon after," the retiring senator continued, "asked me to drink a glass of wine with him. This was readily accorded to, and, what was remarkable, I did not observe him drink with any other person during dinner."

Maclay was puzzled. Surely Washington knew that he was retiring and had drawn on himself "the resentment of all speculators, public creditors, expectants of office and courtiers." Thus, "to the score of good nature must I place these attentions. Be it so. It is at least one amiable trait in his character."

Maclay then launched into a description of the President he might never see again: "In stature about six feet with an unexceptional make but lax appearance. His frame would seem to want filling up. His motions rather slow than lively, though he showed no signs of having suffered from gout or rheumatism. His complexion pale, nay cadaverous. His voice hollow and indistinct, owing, as I believe, to artificial teeth before his upper jaw, which occasioned, a flatness of. . . ." (The next sheet of Maclay's diary is lost.)[23]

Journeys and Bad News

G EORGE WASHINGTON was in mortal danger, perhaps drowned. He had vanished on Chesapeake Bay.

The Governor of Maryland, a flock of dignitaries, and a corps of artillerymen summoned to fire salutes waited on the Annapolis waterfront. The President was already very late and darkness was falling when a great southeast storm began to roar in. There were two hopes: one, that the President had not actually left the Delaware shore some twenty miles away; the other, that he would arrive before the cataclysm broke.

A sailboat was seen dashing for the harbor. On arrival, it proved to contain the President's horses. The grooms reported that Washington had set out in another small sailboat at the same time they had. The vessels had become separated.

The storm now struck with full force. In the most seaworthy vessel they could find, the Governor and several other gentlemen set out in search of the President. They were beating into the teeth of the gale when they saw through the driving rain a vessel stuck on a sandbar at a considerable distance from shore. The *Maryland Journal* was to report, "She made signals of distress." The rescue party tried to get to her, but the wind was now so strong that they were driven backward. The ship that might well contain Washington grew fainter and fainter until it disappeared into the storm.[1]

Washington had never shown fear during a battle, but he was less at home on water. As he had set out that day—March 24, 1791—in a hired vessel from the Delaware shore, he was uneasy. He commented in his diary on "the unskillfulness of the hands and the dullness of her sailing." For two hours, the sluggish craft advanced slowly, beating into a light headwind. Then the wind died and the boat rocked with aimless monotony. "After which," so Washington noted, "the wind sprung up at southeast and increased until it blew a gale."

But at least they were now able to move. They sped along under reduced sail until, in the deepening twilight made more impenetrable by rain, Washington could see ahead dim lights which he assumed were Annapolis. However, his feeling of relief was short-lived. With a shudder and a shock, the boat struck an underwater sandbar. Cargo was shifted, everyone pushed with oars and spars, and at last, "with much exertion and difficulty, we got off." Again towards the lights which were now often completely blocked out by the increased fury of the storm. Another shock! They had struck a second sandbar, and this time "all efforts [were] in vain."

"In my greatcoat and boots, in a berth not long enough for me by the head, and much cramped," Washington did his best to sleep. He was no longer sure about the lights he had seen. He did not know "where we were" or "what might happen."

At daylight, the wind died and the water was suddenly alive with bounding boats. Climbing into another craft, Washington moved to the Annapolis shore. The now dried-out artillerymen fired a salute to which Washington listened with pleasure—not the traditional thirteen but fifteen shots. The Union, with Vermont and Kentucky added, was on the march across the continent.[2]

Congress being in recess, Washington was on his way to Mount Vernon. Thence he undertook a tour of the southern states similar to his New England tour of the previous summer. The territory he would now visit would be altogether new to him, since he had never been south of his native Virginia.

He instructed Lear to offer Martha money periodically during his absence "as she is not fond of applying." Although he could not foresee that, due to confusions of roads and mails, he would be out of touch with his government for almost two months, he wrote his Secretaries of State, Treasury, and War to meet together, consulting the Vice President if he happened to be in Philadelphia, should any occasion arise.

Washington would "approve and ratify" what this council decided, or return post haste if summoned.[3]

Washington's cavalcade was to consist of his light coach drawn by four horses, a baggage wagon, four extra coach horses and one saddle horse. In addition to the men necessary to handle the horses, Washington's only attendant would be a valet. Jefferson was worried by the arrangement, but not because of the absence of guards and secret service men. The President, so the Secretary of State warned, would encounter extremely bad roads. He should lower "the hang of your carriage" and exchange his coachman for postilions, riding ahead of the coach one on each pair of horses. In his reply, Washington made no comment on the hang of the carriage, but dismissed the idea of postilions by stating that his usual one, Giles, "is still too much indisposed to ride the journey."[4]

On April 7, 1791, Washington set out for North Carolina, South Carolina, and Georgia. Traveling south along the coast—Halifax, Newbern, Wilmington, Charleston, Savannah—and back again close to the fall line—Augusta, Camden, Salisbury, Winston-Salem—he was amazed at the poverty of the land: "From the seaboard to the falls of all the rivers which water this extensive region," he encountered "with but, few exceptions neither more nor less than a continued pine barren very thinly inhabited." Even on the road between Charleston and Savannah, he saw only a few gentlemen's seats that had "anything of an elegant appearance." The rest of the buildings were "altogether of wood and chiefly of logs. Some, indeed, have brick chimneys, but generally the chimneys are of split sticks filled with dirt between them." As for the inns, they were "extremely indifferent, the houses being small and badly provided either for man or horse. . . . It is not easy to say on which road—the one I went or the one I came—the entertainment is most indifferent." He blamed the quality of the taverns on "the kind of travelers which use them, which with a few exceptions only on the upper road are no other than wagoners and families removing [going west], who generally take their provisions along with them."[5]

During his New England tour, he had been bothered by an endless succession of ceremonial greetings and by militiamen accompanying him on horseback. Now word that the President was coming did not consistently precede him. Innkeepers were amazed when a little cavalcade, appearing suddenly in their dooryards, proved to include The Greatest Man in the World.

April 16 was one of the more annoying days. Starting out in the morning (as was his wont) "a little after five o'clock," he crossed from Virginia into North Carolina. At first, he "traveled through a cloud of dust." Then a rainstorm created a dramatic transformation: "My passage was through water, so level are the roads." "The uncomfortableness of it for men and horses" made him resolve to "put up," should a possibility arise, before they reached Halifax. Finally, a clumsily painted sign indicated a tavern. Washington gladly called a halt. But the coachman, having set out to investigate, soon reappeared to say that there were "no stables in which the horses could be comfortable." The house proving to offer no better accommodation for people, "and everything else having a dirty appearance, I was compelled," Washington wrote, "to keep on."

Through thirty more miles, the horses splashed and the rain fell. As they neared the Roanoke River, Washington wondered how his equipage would get across to Halifax. He was relieved to find that the flatboats which served as ferries were big enough to "take in a carriage and four horses at once." No one seems to have expected him in the town, since the inevitable group of gentlemen did not call till the following morning.[6]

Washington attended a ceremonial dinner and was off the next day at six A.M. Two days later he was delighted to happen, just at breakfast time, on what seemed a startlingly well-appointed tavern. His arrival created a great scurrying of servants, and soon he was led to a table groaning under young pig, turkey, fried chicken, country ham, sausages, eggs in every style, waffles, batter cakes, and hot soda biscuits. Marveling idly at this abundance, he ate a hard-boiled egg and drank some coffee with rum in it. Only when, as he wrote, it was "too late to rectify the mistake," did Washington discover that the money his servants had offered had been refused. He had been entertained in a private house belonging to Colonel John Allen.[7]

Of all the places he saw, Washington was naturally most impressed by Charleston: "It lies low with unpaved streets (except the footways) of sand. There are a number of very good houses of brick and wood, but most of the latter. The inhabitants are wealthy, gay, and hospitable." The gardens and trees interspersed with the houses added "much to the beauty of the prospect."

At Charleston, Washington was accorded "the first honor of the kind I had ever experienced, and it was as flattering as it was singular." He was called on, at about two o'clock in the afternoon, "by a great number of the most respectable ladies." The next evening, he was guest of honor at "a very elegant dancing assembly at the Exchange, at which were 256 elegantly dressed and handsome ladies." (Washington did not comment on how much these ladies had sacrificed to honor him. They had killed the subtle effects of their azure, mauve, and maize costumes by adding red, white, and blue ribbons; and had laid aside their usual elaborate hairdresses decked with feathers to arrange their tresses around the portraits of Washington which every hand, professional or amateur, that could hold a brush had worked for days to furnish.)

Washington was wearing his suit of black velvet. Gold buckles gleamed on his knees and on his shoes. Under his arm he held a cocked hat with a cockade, the edges adorned with black feathers. His hair, profusely powdered, was gathered behind in a black silk bag. At his left hip, he dangled a long, slender sword, the finely wrought hilt made of steel, the scabbard of white polished leather. He wore yellow gloves. All this grandeur, however, did not keep him from dancing, a sport which he had always enjoyed. And his eyes were perpetually roving over the ladies.[8]

Notes on the number of ladies who attended the various receptions given to him ("about seventy" at Newbern, "sixty-two" at Wilmington) were standard in his diary. The climax was reached at a concert tended him at Charleston the night after the ball. Washington was surrounded by "at least four hundred ladies, the number and appearance of which exceeded anything of the kind I had ever seen." He was later to send his "grateful respect" to the "fair compatriots" of Charleston who had so "flattered" him.[9]

Having found amusement in keeping careful track, Washington was able to report that during his absence from Philadelphia, he had traveled 1887 miles. He expressed pride that "the same horses performed the whole tour and, although much reduced in flesh, kept up their full spirits to the last day." He had himself "rather gained flesh."[10]

Although Washington's principal political objective had been to make the federal presence at its highest level visible in the south, he gathered what information he could. He was most concerned about

[289]

the excise tax on homemade spirits. At the time the law was passed, he noted, "it was vehemently affirmed by many that such a law could never be executed in the southern states, particularly in Virginia and North Carolina." He did his best to find out. Although, communications being what they were, he could not route his return journey through the frontier rather than just below the fall line, he made it a point to visit western Pennsylvania on his way back from Mount Vernon to Philadelphia. And throughout his travels he did not frequent solely the drawing rooms of the correct; he often stayed at cheap inns where his fellow guests were simple people.

Had Washington's investigations revealed that the gravest warnings concerning the liquor tax were well justified, his future administration would have been much smoother and political parties would have appeared more slowly on the American scene. However, he reached the following conclusion: "As this law came in force only on the first of this month, little can be said of its effects from experience, but . . . there remains no doubt but it will be carried into effect not only without opposition but with very general approbation in those very parts where it was foretold that it would never be submitted to by anyone."

Some of Washington's misunderstanding undoubtedly grew from the natural difficulty of communication, even over the meanest tavern table, between the humble and one so obviously great. Perhaps Washington did not try too hard to bridge the gap, since it was his conviction that the common people did not decide for themselves but followed the persuasion of leaders. In judging leaders, the aging hero revealed a mounting tendency to believe that those opposing federal policy could be dismissed as "demagogues." He shrugged away as unimportant that "some demagogue" might "produce and get signed some resolutions" denouncing the tax.[11]

In Georgia, Washington had assayed attitudes towards federal action concerning Indians and the wilderness. He recognized that opposition still existed to the Treaty of New York and that there was still support for the Yazoo land-grab, yet he expressed hope that "the good sense of the state will set its face" against the unprincipled "land jobbers."

"Little," Washington noted, "was said of the banking act." On the whole, the people "appeared to be happy, contented, and satisfied with the general government under which they were placed. When the case

was otherwise, it was not difficult to trace the cause to some demagogue or speculating character."[12]

Washington was back in Philadelphia on July 6, 1791. This was two
days after stock in the Bank of the United States had been put on
public sale.

The offering was of scrip that would eventually enable the holder to
buy stock at par. To circumvent the charge that he was favoring the
rich, Hamilton had priced the scrip at twenty-five dollars per share.
The cost was so low that once secured, the scrip could instantly be
sold at a profit. Foreseeing a bonanza, rapacious moneymen filled
Philadelphia. They set the streets and taverns abuzz with financial talk
which shocked agrarians. When the doors were finally opened, there
was a near riot as the crowd of spectators "rushed in like a torrent."
The stock was oversubscribed by four thousand shares. Many of the
lucky applicants started at once to hawk their scrip from tavern tables
or even on street corners. Speculators borrowed money to buy, and
then sold again. By August 10, the value of a piece of scrip had risen
from twenty-five to three hundred and twenty-five dollars. This orgy
was already in full swing when Washington reached Philadelphia.

A newspaper paragrapher wrote, "The men who had resigned their
lives in the war, or who had parted with their patrimonies or hard-
earned estates to save the public liberty, stood at a distance and with
astonishment beheld the singular and unexpected phenomenon."
Washington may well have found distasteful the speculators who
whispered about money at his levees, yet he considered the total
phenomenon "pleasing. . . . Our public credit stands on that ground
which three years ago it would have been considered as a species of
madness to have foretold. The astonishing rapidity with which the
newly instituted bank was filled gives an unexampled proof (here) of
the resources of our countrymen and their confidence in public measures." Considering that "the establishment of public credit is an
immense point gained in our national concerns," he began ending his
letters to Hamilton, as he had long done his letters to Madison and
Jefferson, by sending his "affectionate regard."[13]

Washington could only stand back and admire Hamilton's achievements. However, in Jefferson's field of foreign affairs, he knew enough

to take a strong hand and was further involved personally because Lafayette still led in France.

Washington hesitated to send specific advice to his former disciple, being "well aware that it is impossible to judge with precision of measures, the motives of which are sometimes unknown and the necessity of them not always understood." But sometimes, as during the previous March, he did break his resolve of silence: "I find it difficult to suppress an anxious wish that the present National Assembly may not protract their own existence so long as to beget any uneasiness on that score. The confirmation of their decrees will be best made by a second representation of the people."[14]

Back in Philadelphia after his southern tour, Washington received from Lafayette the disturbing news that the National Assembly had broken the existing commercial treaty with the United States by placing a duty on American tobacco and whale oil.

Washington replied that he foresaw no hasty countermeasures. Americans expected that the French would, on calmer deliberation, reconsider, "for we have never entertained a doubt of the friendly disposition of the French nation."

In the same letter, Washington again expressed forebodings: "I assure you I have often contemplated with great anxiety the danger to which you are personally exposed. . . . The tumultuous populace of large cities are ever to be dreaded. Their indiscriminate violence prostrates for the time all public authority and its consequences are sometimes extensive and terrible. In Paris, we may suppose these tumults are peculiarly disastrous at this time, when the public mind is in a ferment and when (as is always the case on such occasions) there are not wanting wicked and designing men whose element is confusion, and who will not hesitate in destroying the public tranquillity to gain a favorite point. But until your constitution is fixed, your government organized, and your representative body renovated, much tranquillity cannot be expected; for until these things are done, those who are unfriendly to the Revolution will not quit the hope of bringing matters back to their former state."[15]

To Gouverneur Morris, Washington wrote that new revolutionary governments, not prejudiced by memories of how weak the United States had formerly been, would be more ready than their predecessors to recognize the nation's present strength. However, the United States should be very careful not to take "undue advantages," in any treaty negotiations, of any "nation whose circumstances may not at this moment be very bright. . . . For unless treaties are mutually beneficial to the parties, it is in vain to hope for a continuance of them beyond the moment when the one which conceives itself to be overreached is in a situation to break off the connection. And I believe it is among nations as with individuals: the party taking advantage of the distresses of another will lose infinitely more in the opinion of mankind and its subsequent events than he will gain by the stroke of the moment."

In more general terms, Washington expressed the hope that "the change of systems," the "disorders, oppressions, and incertitude . . . will terminate very much in favor of the rights of man."[16]

It was mid-August and Washington was bowing repeatedly to the circle of gentlemen at one of his levees when Jefferson appeared, his face working with emotion. Washington stepped aside to receive the news that Louis XVI and Marie Antoinette had dramatically ruptured their connection with the government that was seeking reform in France. They had fled in a secret effort to join the foreign armies of the Prussian King and the Austrian Emperor which were preparing to invade over France's northern border. The royal couple had been intercepted and, by Lafayette's orders, brought back as virtual prisoners to Paris.

The legitimacy of the French Revolution had been shattered. Jefferson remembered that he had never seen Washington "so dejected by any event."[17]

The Northern Frontier

T HE news from France might be "gloomy," but the ocean was still wide, and America was experiencing, as Washington wrote, no more than "suspense as to what may have been the consequences" of the rash act of the King and Queen. After Congress had again recessed, Washington set off "for Mount Vernon with Mrs. Washington and the children, where I shall, if possible, enjoy a few weeks of retirement."[1]

With an inefficiency previously completely uncharacteristic of him, he failed to get clear the date during October 1791 when Congress would reconvene. On the 14th of that month he wrote Hamilton frenziedly from his plantation, "It had taken such deep root in my mind that the *last* Monday in the month was the time that I never consulted the law or made any inquiry about it." He had no more idea that it was the 23rd "than I had of its being doomsday." He bundled off to Hamilton for tailoring into his Third Annual Address to Congress suggestions he had received from Jefferson and Madison and also his own ideas. On receiving Hamilton's draft, Washington sent it on to Madison for checking.[2]

Appearing before both houses of Congress on the 25th, Washington first alluded to "the prosperous situation of our common country," which he attributed to an abundant agricultural year and "the happy effects of that revival of confidence, public as well as private, to which the Constitution and laws of the United States have so eminently contributed." Again he did not single out, as specific causes, Hamilton's financial measures. However, instead of attacking speculation, he cited the enthusiasm with which the bank stock had been received as "among the striking and pleasing evidences which present themselves not only of confidence in the government but of resource in the community."[3]

The sanguine impressions concerning the whiskey tax Washington had imbibed during his southern tour had been belied by the tarring and feathering of two tax collectors. Having assured the Congress that the community as a whole realized "the propriety and necessity of the measure," and that opposition vanished when the situation was carefully explained, Washington went on to urge that if some concessions could be made to remove "any well-intentioned objections . . . it will consist with a wise moderation to make the proper variations."[4]

After announcing that no new taxes were needed, he urged on Congress several measures which he had vainly proposed before: provisions for a uniform militia; the establishment of arsenals and the fortification of "important and vulnerable" places; the organization of a post office and of post roads that would, through "diffusing a knowledge of the laws and proceedings of the government," contribute to the security of the people and also "guard them against the effects of misrepresentation"; the final establishment of a mint that would remove "the scarcity of small change, a scarcity so peculiarly distressing to the poorer classes"; the determination of uniform weights and measures (Jefferson's famous report on this subject had not been adopted); and "a provision for the sale of the vacant lands of the United States" that were "pledged as a fund for reimbursing the public debt."[5]

Washington dealt at much greater length than he had devoted to any other matter to the problems raised by the northern Indians.

That trouble was proving so much more difficult to keep tamped down on the northern frontiers than farther south implies the existence of a more crucial key to wilderness strife than Spain's highly publicized stranglehold on the lower Mississippi. This key Washington did not mention at all in his message to Congress, and when he referred to it in writing his friend Humphreys, he made a gesture towards discretion by omitting letters in the significant word. The United States, he wrote, would either awe the Indians into submission "or make them feel the effects of an enmity too sensibly to provoke it again unnecessarily, unless, as is much suspected, they are countenanced, abetted, and supported in their hostile views by the B——h."6

While Spain was operating in the south from weakness, Britain was operating in the north from strength. Louisiana and the Floridas were vulnerable outposts, but Canada had proved uncapturable during the Revolution. Spain's surrender in the Nootka crisis had been an acknowledgment of Britain's control of the seas, and the whole western world knew that Spain's power was sinking while Great Britain's was on the rise. The Spanish foreign office felt it wise to walk softly in the wilderness, using Indian allies more as a threat than a weapon, lest their whole North American holding be overwhelmed; the British suffered from no such fears.

The defeat of General Harmar's expedition against the Indian raiders north of the Ohio had induced Washington to suggest that Jefferson protest to the "Governor of Canada." It could be pointed out that "certain information has been received of large supplies of ammunition being delivered to the hostile Indians from British posts." Having gone this far, Washington added, "These are my sentiments on this subject at the present moment; yet so unsettled do some circumstances appear that it is possible you may see a necessity either to treat it very delicately or to decline acting on it altogether. The option is therefore left to your judgment."7

The reasons for caution were several. Since the United States had no way of enforcing her demands short of a war with Great Britain which she wished to avoid, protests which revealed that Washington was conscious of English interference in American forests might merely encourage them to operate more openly. And any public charges which incited the frontiersmen to blame the English for Indian atrocities might stir up incidents that would set off the undesired war. That the British Indian agents were operating from the posts held in violation of the peace treaty strengthened Washington's legal position but made it more difficult to hold the American people to a pacific line. Washington felt it necessary to assure Governor Clinton, in an extremely carefully worded letter, that "I feel a due concern for any injury, inconvenience, or dissatisfaction which may have arisen or may arise, in respect to the State of New York, or any part of its inhabitants, in consequence of the detention of the posts, or the interferences which may have grown out of it. Nor has the matter failed to receive from me the degree of attention to which it is entitled. Yet in a point of such vast magnitude as that of the preservation of the peace of the Union, particularly in this still *very early* stage of our affairs, and at a period so little remote from a most exhausting and affecting, though successful war, the public welfare and safety evidently enjoin a conduct of circumspection, moderation, and forbearance. And," Washington added hopefully, "it is relied upon that the known good sense of the community ensures its approbation of such a conduct."[8]

Formal protests at the illegal holding of the frontier posts were, of course, the staple of American diplomacy concerning the northwest frontier. These posts, which controlled the major waterways—the St. Lawrence, Lake Champlain, the Great Lakes, and the level route from Lake Ontario to New York—had all been surrendered to the United States by British negotiators who knew nothing of American geography. When it became clear that a stupid mistake had been made, the British found in various American violations of the treaty excuses for holding the posts.

At issue was the fur trade to Montreal which the historian Samuel Flagg Bemis has called "the greatest and most profitable single industry in North America." The disputed posts controlled the routes down which the furs came from the north and the far west. But an even more valuable source of furs was in the area south of the Great Lakes and north of the Ohio (in and around the present state of Ohio), which the clumsy negotiators had ceded to the United States and towards which American settlement was pressing. In this area too, the British found a way to nullify the treaty.[9]

As in the wilderness further south, the Indians had regarded the Crown as their protector against American land-grabbers; they had been unhappy with the outcome of the Revolution. Thus the white man most influential in the northern forests was a Tory refugee: Sir John Johnson, the son of Sir William Johnson, who had been George III's ambassador to the Indians. Closely allied to Sir John was his step-uncle, the brother of Sir William's Indian widow, the Mohawk leader Joseph Brant.

Writing Brant in February 1791, Sir John stated the British position so subtly that the letter would create no diplomatic incident if it fell into American hands. The Indians northwest of the Ohio, Sir John

[297]

explained, were committed by the British cession of their territory to the United States only if they had "at some time or other" done more than announce themselves under British protection; had, indeed, actually invited the British to come in and govern them. "Whether or not this is the case," Sir John continued, "I know not, nor can I at present find out, but certain I am that without such a secession of power on the part of the Indians, no just right or claim to such a power can be supported [by the United States] beyond the line of 1768." This line, drawn by Sir John's father at the Treaty of Fort Stanwix, was the boundary last agreed to with the Crown before the Revolution. It reserved to the Indians all the land northwest of the Ohio.

Sir John passed lightly over the possibility that at later conferences the Indians might have ceded further land to the United States. The British, he continued piously, could not offer the Indians ammunition but would be glad to assist them in negotiation. "Upon the whole," the British agent concluded, "you understand your own rights better than I do. I shall therefore say no more than to recommend coolness and manly firmness in whatever you may determine upon."[10]

The Americans insisted that, at various conferences subsequent to the Revolution, the Indians had, indeed, ceded most of the territory northwest of the Ohio. However, there was the usual confusion as to whether the various Indian deputations had possessed official authority. The tribes repudiated the treaties, and the British, in response to American insistence that they cease to support Indian intransigence, offered their service as mediators. By early 1792, as the efforts of the United States to pacify the northern wilderness continued to flounder, the British envisioned negotiations under their aegis which would reserve to the Indians a wide strip of land between Canada and the United States that would serve as "a neutral barrier."[11]

The tribes were, of course, enchanted to seek English mediation, and Gouverneur Morris reported to Washington that the British Home Secretary was stating "that the United States had asked the mediation of Great Britain." To Morris, Washington wrote "You may be *fully* assured, sir, that such mediation *never* was asked; that the asking of it *never* was in contemplation, and I think I might go further and say that it not only never *will* be asked but would be rejected if offered. The United States will never have occasion, I hope, to ask for the interposition of that power or any other to establish peace within their own territory."[12]

When as a very young man Washington had been forced to surrender Fort Necessity, he had first learned the bitter lesson of how aggressive the elated tribes became after a victory. Now they were inspired by the defeat of General Harmar to cross the Ohio River, over from the west bank which American settlers feared to invade, and bring fire and scalping knife to the settlements which stretched for some four hundred miles along the eastern shore of that broad waterway. Some raiding parties even penetrated to the Allegheny River above Pittsburgh.

During the French and Indian War, Washington had discovered that forts, although they might serve as refuges for local inhabitants, were useless in protecting a frontier. The garrison was always cooped up, and the "posts can be insulted or avoided at the option of the enemy in a covered country."[13] The only solution was to send a new army, strong enough not to be turned back, into the Indians' own country.

Congress voted to increase the regular army by one regiment. This, plus expectations of militia levies, enabled Washington to plan an expeditionary force of two thousand. As commander he appointed Arthur St. Clair, who was Governor of the Northwest Territory and who had during the Revolution been an important general, if not an inspired one. St. Clair was to cut a road north by west from Fort Washington for 135 miles and then establish a permanent post at the site of the main Miami Village (Fort Wayne, Indiana).[14]

When Washington heard that St. Clair had sent the British assurances that his intended expedition would not attack their posts, the President had mixed feelings. From the point of view of Anglo-American relations, this was prudent, but the now informed British would surely warn the Indians. Washington warned St. Clair to beware of surprise.[15]

In his address to Congress, Washington stated that the military operations were to be conducted "as consistently as possible with the dictates of humanity. . . . Overtures of peace are still continued to the deluded tribes." His fundamental policy remained to remove the need for coercion through "an intimate intercourse . . . calculated to advance the happiness of the Indians and to attach them firmly to the United States." He reminded Congress that peace on the frontiers was impossible without an orderly progression of treaties fairly arrived at, and the enactment of laws that would protect the Indians from white violence and white land encroachment. Trade should be equitably regulated.

However, Washington realized that none of these reforms would really extricate the Indians from their dilemma. He urged that "such rational experiments should be made for imparting to them the blessings of civilization, as may, from time to time, suit their condition."[16]

As long as the Indians remained alien to white culture, they would be pushed back and back. Nor did the nature of their own culture permit them to be paid adequately for their lands, since they had no financial conceptions that enabled them to lay assets by. They had no permanent possessions except that which they at every treaty alienated—their land. The best that could be done—and this Washington urged—was to pay annual stipends in return for the territory the tribes had relinquished and also for subsequent pacific behavior.

As a young man, Washington had suffered through much personal contact with Indians. Long before the blossoming of anthropology, he had not imbibed any sense of a culture worth preserving. However, he did not regard inducing the Indians to exchange their own religions for Christianity as in itself any gain. A much more effective method to secure their attachment would be "to convince them that we are just and to show them that a proper and friendly intercourse with us would be for our mutual advantage." He wondered whether the tribes were not more hampered than helped by having a few of their young men carried off to missionary schools. What the Indians needed was "practical knowledge." He wished, for instance, that an annual stipend of fifteen hundred dollars to the Iroquois be used to buy clothing, domestic animals, and farming tools, and to encourage white artisans to settle in their villages.[17]

Towards the end of his second term, Washington made a detailed offer to the Cherokee Nation. The growth of settlement around them, he pointed out, was destroying the game on which their hunting economy depended. They should keep cattle and hogs. They should grow wheat, flax, and cotton. The government would supply the necessary tools and give medals to the best farmers. A woman would be hired at public expense to teach Indian wives and daughters to spin and weave. "What I have recommended to you," the President then stated, "I am myself going to do. After a few moons are passed, I shall leave the great town and retire to my farm."[18]

Washington may have been as upset early in the December of 1791 as legend reports. The news revived in his memory that day in 1755 when, sick and helpless, he had seen a great army massacred by Indians firing invisibly from surrounding woods. He was now notified that Braddock's defeat had been re-enacted on only a slightly smaller scale. St. Clair's expeditionary force had suffered a loss, in killed and wounded, of 950, almost two-thirds of the men engaged. The survivors had fled in their haste, throwing away their arms. St. Clair's army had ceased to be.[19]

Further reports indicated that every kind of organizational confusion had preceded the defeat. Supply and recruiting had moved so slowly that the grass on which the horses were supposed to feed had already withered when the army began its advance. The troops soon found themselves in the old Revolutionary situation of being unpaid. And the army had been lost in the forest, not sure where they were when they had stumbled into ambush.

The House of Representatives, having ordered an investigation, decided not to entrust it to the President but to appoint a committee of their own. The committee called on Washington for relevant War Department documents. Since this was the first legislative request for executive papers, Washington recognized that an important precedent would be established. He summoned one of the first meetings of his full "Cabinet." He opened it by stating, so Jefferson noted, that "he neither acknowledged nor denied nor even doubted the propriety of what the House were doing, for he had not thought upon it, nor was acquainted with subjects of this kind." However, he pointed out the possibility that at a future time the House might ask for papers "of so secret a nature as that they ought not to be given up." The Secretaries replied that "we were not prepared and wished time to think and inquire."[20]

At another meeting two days later, the Secretaries urged that such requests should be made directly to the President, rather than to individual ministers, and that he should in each instance use his discretion. Despite Hamilton's agreement to this principle, Jefferson sensed in Hamilton an uneasiness which Jefferson assumed grew from a fear that some future investigation would reveal how far he and his governmental backers "had been dabbling in stocks, banks, etc."

At that very moment, indeed, the Hamiltonians seemed to be in trouble: Knox, who as Secretary of War had been responsible for St. Clair's expedition, was one of Hamilton's allies, and there were whispers of dishonesty among the army contractors, who included Hamilton's assistant Duer and many of the Treasurer's close supporters. However, Hamilton agreed that no papers relevant to the defeat should be withheld. In the end, the investigation blew over, probably because the fissures in Washington's government had not yet gone so far as to make any officials really wish to open up a public scandal.[21]

Privately, Washington blamed St. Clair's defeat on "his want of information" and "not keeping his army in such a position always as to be able to display them in a line behind trees in the Indian manner." Publicly, he ascribed the catastrophe to untrained militia on short enlistment, and thus finally got through Congress the authorization for a uniform, federally supervised militia which he had since he entered the Presidency vainly sought.[22]

To meet the immediate need, Congress authorized three new regular regiments. Since only one major general was provided for, St. Clair could not be tried by a court-martial of his peers, and had, as Washington pointed out to him, to resign so that someone else could be appointed.[23]

In preparation for a meeting of his department heads, Washington wrote down, with a completely unsentimental candor towards his former companions in arms, his opinion "of all the general officers now living and in this country, as low as *actual* brigadiers." Significantly, considering the charges that were made during the Revolution by Washington's critics concerning drunkenness among his general officers, he had much in mind whether or not the candidates were addicted to the bottle. On the whole, the list, as Washington presented it, was far from encouraging. Only three full major generals were still above the sod. Of these, Lincoln was "infirm"; Moultrie, whose service had been in the south, was little known to Washington but seemingly dull; and Steuben, although an excellent officer, was not to be trusted. Washington dismissed the German immigrant, who had favored a King of the United States, as "ambitious and a foreigner."

Four major generals by brevet—Weedon, Scott, Hand, and Huntington—were without enterprise and the first two of these no enemies to the bottle. The fifth such major general, Anthony Wayne, had too much enterprise. Washington characterized him as "more active . . . than judicious and cautious. No economist, it is feared. Open to flattery, vain, easily imposed upon, and liable to be drawn into scrapes. Too indulgent (the effect perhaps of some of the causes just mentioned) to his officers and men. Whether sober or a little addicted to the bottle I know not."

Washington saw the full brigadiers, all six of them, as a sorry lot, even the rifleman Daniel Morgan. Morgan, although he "has been fortunate and has met with éclat," was dishonest, intemperate, and illiterate. The best of the entire boiling was at the very bottom of the seniority list as a brigadier by brevet. Charles Cotesworth Pinckney had failed of advancement during the Revolution because he had become a prisoner of war at the fall of Charleston. Although Washington considered Pinckney's lack of rank an unfair result of chance, he feared that if Pinckney were appointed, "it would be a fruitless attempt and a waste of time to propose to those officers who have been his seniors to engage again subordinately." To make the situation even more discouraging, Washington's other preference was not even on the list of general officers. Although now Governor of Virginia, Henry (Light Horse Harry) Lee had in the army never risen above colonel.[24]

After making seemingly casual inquiries, Washington reluctantly reached the conclusion that there was no way to get around the appointment of one of the major generals, either full or brevet. He selected the least unpromising: Wayne.

In his unhappiness with the choice, Washington wrote out in his own hand (thereby bypassing his secretaries) the first really indiscreet letter he had so far dispatched during his Presidency. It was to Lee, in answer to a bitter complaint at not having been given the command.

"I have no hesitation," Washington wrote, "in declaring to you that the bias of my inclination was strongly in your favor." However, investigation revealed that even if senior officers were persuaded "grudgingly" to serve under Lee, "the seeds of sedition would be coeval with the formation of the army, such [so commented the retired soldier] being the nature of military pride." The alternative would be to staff the army with "junior characters." However "excellent" these officers might in fact prove, "if any disaster should befall the army, it would instantly be ascribed to the inexperience of the principal officers . . . thereby drawing a weight upon my shoulders too heavy to be borne."

Concerning the man whom he had appointed commander in chief and towards whom public confidence was therefore required, Washington confided, "G. W. [General Wayne] has many good points as an officer, and it is to be hoped that time, reflection, good advice, and above all a due sense of the importance of the trust which is committed to him will correct his foibles or cast a shade over them."[25]

The tiny military establishment of the United States had been shattered by St. Clair's defeat. Wayne had to organize a new army. Arriving at Fort Pitt (Pittsburgh) in June 1792, he was soon bogged down in a replay of the difficulties Washington had faced during the Revolution. The recruiting officers brought in, the President complained to the Secretary of War, *"boys* in *many instances,"* and in others, "the *worst miscreants,"* who promptly deserted. Supply was bogged down awaiting a decision as to whether an official commissary or private contractors (whom Washington favored as in the end cheaper) should be employed.[26]

While Wayne's forces accreted haltingly, terror swept the northwest frontier. Washington could be jocose on the fear inspired by the Indians—"the *hair* must have stood on Major S——'s *head,* and a *stake* full in his view, when his letter of the 8th of July was writing"[27]—but the former Indian fighter understood the desperate cruelty of Indian raids. He did his best with the only weapon he at present had: negotiation.

Washington undertook what was probably the most extensive effort to conciliate hostile tribes ever engaged in by any United States government. Council fires glowed in countless forest shades. Belts of wampum were flung to the endless droning of the oratory the Indians so enjoyed. Federal officials knocked the heads off innumerable kegs of rum, and silver medals bearing Washington's image were distributed to brighten many a chief's plumage. Negotiators reported back that the British were bolstering the Indians' repudiation of all land grants made since the Revolution. Yet, so writes the historian of the frontier William L. Stone, something was accomplished to make the raids less frequent, the opposition to the United States less unanimous.[28]

There remained forests that Washington could not reach. Envoys

Medal given to a Shawnee chief to encourage peace (see discarded toma-hawk and the pipe passing from hand to hand) and also the practice by the Indian of agriculture (see background). Courtesy of the Museum of the American Indian

who tried to carry their flags of truce into the embattled territory of the Miamis were fired on and some killed. With the active support of Sir John Johnson's British Indian department, Brant was trying to weld the tribes along the Canadian frontier into a confederation that would repel the claims of the United States. The chiefs involved refused to attend any council with Washington's emissaries.

However, the other Iroquois nations did not share the extreme hostility of Brant's Mohawks. In June 1792, Washington "with some difficulty indeed" lured to Philadelphia what he called—despite Brant's absence—"a full representation of the Six Nations." They departed so fully convinced of the justice and good dispositions of this government" that, as Washington happily reported, they had promised "to send a deputation of *their* tribes to the hostile Indians with an account of all that has passed, accompanying it with advice to them to desist from further hostilities."[29]

The conference had, in fact, been so successful that Brant, after making "*still* greater" difficulties, finally agreed to come to Philadelphia and talk to Washington. Secretary Knox expected Brant's visit to "be productive of great satisfaction to himself by being made acquainted with the humane views of the President of the United States." Brant did promise to carry back to his allies Washington's offer of limited insistence on boundary expansion paid for by additional money annuities. However, so he informed Sir John Johnson, he intended, when the council fires were actually lit, to oppose any acceptance of Washington's terms.[30]

So the warfare, which the tribes could not in the long run win, continued. Would the Indians be better off today if not isolated in those limbos, their reservations, but gathered, as so many other ethnic groups have been, into the American melting pot? If so, they should have listened to Washington's siren song. However, accepting the white man's civilization would have involved a reversal of the basic Indian conviction that a brave who engaged in any occupation but hunting and war was bringing disgrace on himself, his clan, and his ancestors by turning himself into a woman. Had such a cultural revolution been in any situation possible, the times did not favor it. There was little in the behavior of the frontiersmen the Indians encountered to encourage emulation. Furthermore, if they were to begin to wade in the American mainstream, those self-reliant people would have to accept an intermediate period of persecution and dependency. They had no reason to trust the white man's integrity or mercy. However much Washington and his ministers might promise and insist, the conception of justice for Indians was laughed at on the frontier and by many a legislator. What use could the Indians make of Washington's invitation that they appeal to the federal courts when they neither bred or were in a position to hire lawyers?

In any case, no surrender seemed required of them. Having turned back two armies Washington had sent against them, they could confidently expect to drive away any others that would follow. And the British were assuring them that should further American armies be "decisively defeated," mediation by the Crown would assure to their descendants forever extensive hunting grounds.[31]

In August 1790, Washington had believed that he was negotiating from strength, needing to use force only to make an example of a few irresponsible "banditti." However, the lack of military preparedness on which Congress had insisted had snatched out of his hand the sword of triumph, giving it to the tribes. Until this situation was reversed, until the United States won in the forests a major military victory, diplomacy would almost certainly achieve little. Washington admitted that he continued the parleys not out of any true prospect of success, but from a determination not to give up until conciliation had been proved utterly hopeless.[32]

Fortunately, the wilderness was now so far from the seaboard that the United States could, as long as no European war widened the conflicts, go about her major business while sections of the frontier flamed and settlement in the northwest was blocked. Wayne's slowly augmenting army was to remain at Fort Pitt until after the close of Washington's first term.

25

Philadelphia High Life

T HE Congressional session which opened with Washington's
Third Annual Address and closed in May 1792, is principally
known for having been the stage upon which Hamilton presented his Report on Manufactures. This was in response to a request
of the House that the Treasury prepare a plan for encouraging "such
manufactures as will tend to render the United States independent of
other nations for essentials, particularly for military supplies."[1]

Treating the subject as broadly as possible, Hamilton included a
summary of the existing state of American manufactures; an argument
that industrialization was the road from economic colonialism to world
power; a demonstration that northern industries processing southern
staples could unite the nation into a coherent economic unit; and a
plan for encouraging American manufactures through tariffs, bounties,
subsidies, and premiums. As his biographer John C. Miller wrote, the
"Report on Manufactures contained the embryo of modern America."
It was too far ahead of its time to receive from Congress serious
consideration.[2]

Before he had re-established close connections with Hamilton,
Washington had demonstrated his concern with American manufactures by ordering American-woven cloth to wear at the inauguration.
That the company which manufactured the cloth subsequently went
bankrupt[3] underlined the basic problem.

In his eagerness to get factories going, Washington had in 1791
violated his usual concern with obeying the law. As President of the
United States he could not (so he wrote the Governor of Virginia)

help smuggle out of England a mechanic and machinery which "it is felony to export." However, since such smuggling was needed to establish a woolen manufactory, he wished Virginia to proceed. He was happy that "my agency is not *absolutely necessary* to the completion of this object."[4]

The Secretary of State was administering the newly passed patent law. Washington referred to Jefferson the inventor of a loom with a warm letter of recommendation[5]—yet he did not back Hamilton's report.

Washington made no public statement; since Hamilton had responded directly to a legislative request, he considered the matter (unless a bill should be sent to him for signature) outside the Presidential province. However, he wrote Hamilton privately, "The advantages which would result to this country from the produce of articles which ought to be manufactured at home is apparent, but how far bounties on them come within the powers of the general government or it might comport with the temper of the times to expend money for such purposes is necessary to be considered—and without a bounty is given, I know of no means by which the growth of them can be *effectually* encouraged."[6]

Subsidies in the form of bounties would be required since protective tariffs (which were more clearly within the federal province and also did not involve the government in any financial outlay) could not create industries from the ground up. To attempt this would create intolerable shortages and cruelly high prices. Not until there were enough domestic producers potentially to supply the national market and to keep prices down by competition would tariff barriers be effective.

Eager to demonstrate how industry could be got going under existing conditions, Hamilton steered through the New Jersey legislature a charter for the Society for Useful Manufactures, which was to be capitalized at a million dollars—more than the total assets of all the joint stock companies in the United States. The factory city of Paterson was to rise where, at a rare relaxed moment during the Revolution, Washington had picnicked beside the Falls of the Passaic River. Wheels were to be turned by the highest waterfall Washington had at that time ever seen.[7]

No American in those days was concerned with preserving scenic beauties—there seemed plenty on the vast continent to last out millennia—but southern agrarians and western pioneers were viewing all of Hamilton's ideas and works with outrage and fear.

Much was visible in Philadelphia to cause concern. The city had long been the largest and richest in America. During the Revolution, it had been the national capital: there Congress sat and there profiteers had congregated. While New York was suffering under perpetual enemy occupation, Philadelphia had been touched by the British as with an enchanter's wand. For a single winter, the city had entertained the royal army. That had been the most resplendent, gayest winter America had ever seen. Prosperous patriots who had felt it necessary to flee had often left their women behind to protect their property, and lukewarm families had stayed. Night after night, the young ladies of Philadelphia had danced with British aristocrats. Thus was established a tradition of great belles.

After the Continental Congress had moved away in 1782, the gaiety had gone on but without any official center. What was the jubilation at the return after eleven years of a government become more resplendent and with as its leader the world's greatest hero! "You have never seen anything like the frenzy which has seized upon the inhabitants here," one commentator wrote. "They have been half mad ever since this city became the seat of government."[8]

At the very center of the revels was the most celebrated beauty (perhaps) in all American history: Mrs. William Bingham. She was the daughter of Robert Morris's senior partner, Thomas Willing, and had at the age of sixteen married a man who had mysteriously made a great fortune during the Revolution as government purchasing agent in the Indies. They had spent some five years abroad, where Mrs. Bingham had sparkled at The Hague and in the courts of Louis XVI and George III. Abigail Adams considered her "taken altogether . . . the finest woman I ever saw. The intelligence of her countenance, or rather, I ought to say, its animation, the elegance of her form, and the affability of her manners convert you to admiration: and one has only to lament too much dissipation and frivolity of amusement, which have weaned her from her native country, and given her a passion and thirst after all the luxuries of Europe."[9]

Before they returned home, the Binghams made a special study of domestic architecture in London and Paris, deciding that the plan of the Duke of Manchester's mansion would do for their Philadelphia residence, if it were considerably enlarged. The result was thus described by an English visitor to Philadelphia: "I found a magnificent house and gardens in the best English style, with elegant and even superb furniture. The chairs in the drawing room were from Seddons's in London of the newest taste: the back in the form of a lyre, adorned with festoons of crimson and yellow silk; the curtains of the room a festoon of the same; the carpet one of Moore's most expensive patterns. The room was papered in the French taste after the style of the Vatican at Rome."[10]

François René Chateaubriand, who was to become famous as a Napoleonic statesman, expressed amazement at the "elegance of dress" and "the profusion of luxury" displayed by rich Philadelphian "wives and daughters." However much their men might try to shush them, these wives and daughters did not hide their desire to have reproduced in Philadelphia the British royal system. Another Frenchman, the Duc de la Rochefoucauld, complained that "the English influence prevails in the first circles and prevails with great intolerance;" while an English visitor noted that "nothing could make them happier than that an order of nobility should be established."[11]

Jefferson admired luxury as conceived of in Virginia plantation terms—fine horses and houses, all the products (if not the institution itself) of slavery. Yet he did not look kindly on the pleasures and vices of urban societies and the European aristocrats. Unable to ignore the charms of Mrs. Bingham, he wrote her a long letter in which, though preserving a flirtatious tone, he lectured her on the advantages to womankind of American domesticity over European gadding.[12]

Even in New York, Jefferson had been made uneasy—or so he remembered as an old man—by the aristocratic talk in some Federalist circles. Observing the social scene in Philadelphia, he gave way to concern lest monarchical corruption and decadence might come to dominate American life. He was not reassured to remember that Mrs. Bingham, in countering his praises of American domestic females, listed among the superiorities of their French sisters that women in France "interfere with the politics of the country and often give a decided turn to the fate of empires."[13]

When he went to Mrs. Bingham's, Jefferson found, interlarded with the ladies in their decolletage and huge headdresses, senators and representatives and directors of the bank. He often saw the militarily erect and beautifully belaced figure of Hamilton, frighteningly at home, always popular and conspicuous, lightly flirtatious one minute (to the consternation of uneasy husbands) and then in serious conference with important leaders.

If the cosmopolitan Jefferson was upset by Philadelphia society, how much more so the less-traveled republicans from the south or across the mountains! Were not "the whole legs" of Mrs. Bingham's daughter sometimes in view "for five minutes together"? To hear references to bearing (and even conceiving!) children come from the same shapely female lips that had just praised kings made hearts beat with alarm. Although Senator Maclay had returned to backwoods Pennsylvania, his spirit was marching on.[14]

Visiting Philadelphia during the Revolution, Washington had been horrified by the ostentatious luxury of the profiteers—but then he had commanded an army that was freezing and starving on dangerous hillsides.[15] Now there were still dislocations (particularly on the frontier) but no major crisis loomed. Washington liked an elegantly groomed woman, good food and wine, a well-appointed house. He observed the society around him benevolently, not thinking of it as a shoot-the-chute towards decadence, but as another symbol of the overall prosperity which he believed his administration was bringing to all ranks and classes.

What dangers Washington saw stemmed not from the existence of aristocratic manners but from the impression they made on some minds. Thus in 1788, he had written that he did not find in the practice of heraldry, the use of coats of arms, etc., "any tendency unfriendly to the purest spirit of republicanism." Had not Congress and all the states "established some kind of *armorial devices* to authenticate their official instruments"? However, political sentiments were various, and some men, "possibly from turbulent or sinister views," were trying to persuade people that the government "is pregnant with the seeds of discrimination, oligarchy, and despotism." It was not wise "to stir any question that would tend to reanimate the dying embers of faction." The objections to the Cincinnati had been a warning. It made no difference whether charges were true or false, as long as they were believed.[16]

Although he was unconcerned to the point of complete ignorance with the English background of his family, Washington could not

resist using the coat of arms which had been dug up by an aristocratically minded Virginia relation. He did have a crest, "a flying griffin,"
emblazoned on his carriage,[17] but he felt that even less than in New
York was he setting an example of ostentation. The Morris house
which he inhabited, was, despite enlargements, cramped and inconvenient. The bow windows he had added on the downstairs dining
room and parlor did not make these chambers really spacious. The two
other public rooms occupied only the front of the second floor. Behind
them, and extending into a back building, were accommodations for
"Mrs. Washington, and the children, and their maids." He also managed to squeeze in here his own private study and, since he shared his
wife's bedroom, a personal dressing room.

On the third floor, there was a chamber for Mr. and Mrs. Lear, two
rooms crowded with beds for the Presidential aides, and "a public
office." Washington lamented that people coming on business "have to
ascend two pairs of stairs and to pass by the public rooms"—but there
was no space for the office lower down.

The servants' quarters were in the garrets of the main house and the
back building, in a smokehouse remodeled for that purpose, and over
the stables. These stables, which stood in a garden shaded by lofty
trees and enclosed with a brick wall, Washington had enlarged, although Morris's coach house had proved adequate.[18]

Washington conspicuously displayed in his parlor the key to the
Bastille and the drawing of the fortress being destroyed, which
Lafayette had sent him. He also hung, in his desire to be nonpartisan, an engraving of Louis XVI. After the king disappeared, that
portrait came down, but the rest of the display remained, to the horror
of French aristocrats who had fled to the United States. However, the
Frenchmen saw nothing at Washington's levees or Martha's tea parties
to make them regard the President as a radical. Those citizens who
took advantage of the almost completely free entry to the President's
home were the better dressed, more prosperous citizens.[19]

Washington's formal invitations continued to be sent in rotation to
the correct officials, which meant that foreign courts and the electorate
did much to establish the President's invitation list. On a more personal plane, the Washingtons' taste in friends ran to families of sophis-
tication and wealth. Their intimacy with the Robert Morrises was
usually attributed to Martha's affection for Mrs. Morris. However, a
similar motivation could not be ascribed to their relationship with the

Samuel Powels, since there the closest affinity was between the President and Mrs. Powel.[20]

Elizabeth Willing Powel (Eliza) was no such "girl" as Washington had once wondered whether, should he become a widower, he would be imprudent enough to fall in love with. She was only ten years Washington's junior. In December 1790, Abigail Adams wrote, "Mrs. Powel I join the general voice in pronouncing a very interesting woman. . . . She looks turned of fifty, is polite and fluent as you please, motherly and friendly."[21]

Motherly or no, Mrs. Powel was many times as intellectual and worldly as Martha Washington. Her father, Charles Willing, had earned wealth by establishing in Philadelphia a branch of his own father's English mercantile firm; her brother, Thomas Willing, was Robert Morris's senior partner. She was Mrs. Bingham's aunt and first cousin to Peggy Shippen, the socially correct wife of the traitor Benedict Arnold.

At the age of twenty-seven Eliza had, after flirtations with John Dickinson, Richard Henry Lee, and Mr. Beverly of Virginia,[22] married Samuel Powel. It had been a combination of fortunes; Powel was considered the richest young man in Philadelphia. He may also have been the most sophisticated. He had just returned from six years in Europe, where he had traveled in such style that he was received by crowned heads everywhere. One of his companions had been Dr. John Morgan, the most brilliant scientific physician and medical teacher the American colonies produced.[23] Powel was among those Philadelphians who changed the history of American painting by subscribing to send Benjamin West abroad for Italian studies. He was a member of the American Philosophical Society of Philadelphia and the Royal Society of London.

Powel had been the last mayor of Philadelphia under the Crown. Although after the Revolution he became also the first mayor under the city's new charter, he and his wife had not been conspicuous for republican ardor. They had stayed in Philadelphia during the British occupation. The enemy authorities complimented their establishment by quartering there the head of the British peace mission, the Earl of Carlisle. The nobleman considered the mansion "perfectly well furnished" and enjoyed talking politics with the Powels: "They are agreeable, sensible people, and you never would [want to be] out of their company," Samuel Powel was to invest £5000 in the Bank of Philadelphia which was helping to supply Washington's army, but this may well have been more a financial than a political act.[24]

During their stay in Philadelphia after the victory at Yorktown, the Washingtons had lived next door to the Powels, and, while attending the Constitutional Convention, the General had seen much of his former neighbors. Samuel shared his interest in a strong central government and in scientific agriculture. Washington found things to say to Eliza; he noted in his journal that he had drunk tea with her in her husband's absence.[25]

When the Powels visited Mount Vernon in the fall of 1787, Washington, who usually kept away from that sad spot, took his friends "to view the ruins of Belvoir." Why? Was it that he felt some affinity between Eliza Powel and Sally Fairfax, the love of his youth who had once inhabited the wrecked rooms?[26]

Held in abeyance when the capital was in New York, the friendship between the Washingtons and the Powels flared up again in Philadelphia.

Despite Abigail Adams's praises and Washington's predilection, Eliza's character was by no means to everyone's taste: she inspired both annoyance and ridicule. That cultured Frenchman, the Chevalier de Chastellux, wrote: "She talks a great deal. She honored me with her friendship and found me meritorious because I meritoriously listened to her." When this passage appeared in the private edition of Chastellux's *Travels,* Eliza (with a sensitivity to criticism as great as Washington's own) was so upset that Chastellux, to the amusement of Philadelphia society, deleted the sentences from his public edition.[27]

Eliza's letters are full of quirks and contradictions. They mix pretentiousness with intelligence and humor, gaiety with morbid gloom. She could attack the male sex for keeping women uneducated, and then define such education as being aimed at fitting "the female character . . . for receiving and communicating happiness." When, on a visit to Mount Vernon, she felt that her presence was depressing the company, she departed, and only confided, in her thank-you letter to Martha, that she had been upset over the misfortunes of a sister.[28]

Describing herself in 1784, Eliza wrote that she rarely went to public entertainments because of "a total disinclination to blend with brilliant circles. My disposition is by no means dissipated, though it is naturally gay. It is true, I have necessarily seen a great deal of company in our own house. Extensive connections and supposed large fortunes have their consequent appendages, though not always of the most agreeable sort. My health has been more delicate this winter than I ever before experienced it. I have sometimes thought even my ideas were frozen."[29]

Eliza, who sent a young man a pair of fur gloves on the assumption that he had not written her because his "Herculean hands" were cold,[30] had her saucy side, and this particularly appealed to Washington. She coquetted with the President in a gay and bantering manner he enjoyed; she teased him; she inspired him to sallies of wit; she kept him amused. And her way of life gave Washington pleasure. As far back as 1774, John Adams had described dining at the Powels': "A most sinful feast again. Everything which could delight the eye or allure the taste. Curds and creams, jellies, sweetmeats of various sorts, twenty sorts of tarts, fools, trifles, floating islands, whipped syllabubs," etc. When in the cool of the evening, Washington stepped out of her door with the lady, he was in a Willing family enclave, an extensive formal garden in which four mansions—one was the Binghams'—were embedded. Compared to the elegance here, Mount Vernon was simple, rural. The decorative walks were bordered in an Old World manner with statuary. Washington felt botanical as well as aesthetic admiration for Samuel Powel's "profusion of lemon, orange and citron trees, and many aloes and other exotics."[31]

Martha, who had been for so long dragged in the wake of the overwhelmingly able and energetic husband who was in fact younger than she, seems to have observed without any jealousy his friendship with Eliza—she had, indeed, nothing specific to be jealous about.* What uneasiness she felt came from a fear that compared with Mrs. Powel, she herself was naïve and clumsy. She was so naïve—or so pure of heart—that when she had to prepare a letter to her husband's knowing friend, she got him to write a draft which she copied out, word for word. As a doting grandmother, who wished the three Custis girls to be great belles, Martha had got into the habit of humbly asking Mrs. Powel's advice. In November 1787, the Philadelphian had sent to Mount Vernon collars which "may be raised by means of a screw" to force the girls to keep their heads up. "I have made a little ornament of ribbon which may be worn over them as a disguise when the young ladies are dressed and go without a vandyke. It is a pity that a fine

---

* In one of her most flirtatious letters, Eliza teased Washington about his continence with the ladies.[32]

[316]

Martha Washington in 1795, by Charles Willson Peale. Courtesy of the
Independence National Historical Park Collection

Martha's niece, Fanny Bassett, who married Washington's estate manager and favorite nephew, George Augustine Washington. Painted in 1785 at Mount Vernon, where for many years she made her home, by Robert Edge Pine. Courtesy of the Mount Vernon Ladies' Association

Mrs. Samuel (Eliza) Powel, President Washington's favorite female friend.
Portrait by Matthew Pratt. Courtesy of the Pennsylvania Academy
of the Fine Arts

Mrs. William Bingham, the most famous beauty of what was sometimes called Washington's "Republican Court." An unfinished portrait by Gilbert Stuart. Privately owned. Photograph courtesy of the Frick Art Reference Library

form be spoiled by a child's not holding herself erect. Indeed, I think it is essential to health and beauty to hold up the head and throw back the shoulders. It expands the chest and prevents those ridiculous distortions of face and eyes" produced by "a foolish bashfulness."[33]

The portrait Matthew Pratt painted of Eliza is an enigma. She is shown wearing a silk dress with a V-neck that sinks to a deep decolletage. Her hair, powdered to a dull, wool gray, is raised high on her head, with a heavy loop hanging down the back of her neck, and a long corkscrew curl lying on her right shoulder. Her round face, with its high forehead, placid eyebrows, blue eyes, long, shapely nose, and firm, full mouth is composed, sure, good-looking, determined. Disillusionment and a touch of melancholy are, it is true, marked in the face, but her pose epitomizes negligent self-confidence. The assertive air of the entire image seems strangely out of key with the inscription on the urn which tops the fashionable classic pillar against which Eliza leans. Only partially visible, the inscription reads: "DEAR PLEDG . . . OF CHASTE & . . . FAREWE . . ."

Since the picture seems to have been painted about 1793, the year when Samuel Powel died, one may assume that the inscription refers to that melancholy event.[34] Yet, this admitted, the broken message remains equivocal.

Mrs. Bingham would have approved of the way her aunt argued politics, eagerly and passionately, with the President. And the President enjoyed verbal battles with one so bright, who (as an English visitor wrote) "had improved her mind with reading." In thanking her for sending him a pamphlet, which she had viewed with alarm, the President assured her gaily that "the sentiments and charges therein contained have not given me a moment's painful sensation." He then signed himself, "with very great esteem, regard, and affection."[35]

Washington's close friendship with conservatives like the Morrises and the Powels (to say nothing of General and Mrs. Knox and Colonel and Mrs. Walter Stewart) worried Lear into expressing to Jefferson "extreme regret" that Washington was surrounded with people who assured him that the opposition to Hamilton's policies represented "just a little faction." Washington, himself conscious that he was in danger of being misinformed, called on Lear to help. In a letter to his aide, he pointed out that Lear's opportunities of "mixing with people in different walks, high and low, of different descriptions and of different political sentiments must have afforded you an extensive

range for observation and comparison; more so, by far, than could fall
to the lot of a stationary character who is always revolving in a particular circle."[36]

As later events were to reveal, many a republican breast was beginning to harbor concern and resentment at the way Washington accepted and participated in Philadelphia high life. Open criticism,
however, blamed the extravagance on Hamilton and his financial
measures which stoked in the fuel on which the sexual-monarchical
juggernaut ran. Since it is hard to object to prosperity, the level of
public opposition was somewhat muted as long as the new financial
dispensation worked well. But, despite Hamilton's efforts to put on the
brakes, by February 1792 the price of government securities and bank
scrip had reached untenable heights. On March 9, William Duer, who
had been Hamilton's Assistant Secretary of the Treasury and who was
the most daring speculator of all, had to suspend payments. This set in
motion what was to be the first of America's financial panics. Although
the plummeting of the prices of scrip and government bonds was
hardly felt outside the financial community itself, Hamilton's reputation was wounded by the backlash of the claim that the high prices
paid for his paper demonstrated the wisdom of his schemes.

"Faction," one observer wrote, "glows within like a coal pit." Argu-
mentative tongues linked support for Hamilton with worship of the
British and of monarchy; opposition to Hamilton with French revolutionary principles and a desire to dismember the Federal Union.
Hamilton, it was argued on one side, was trying to corrupt the
government so that "the well-born few" could trample under foot "the
free citizens of America." To which the answer was that Jefferson
(who was coming more and more to the fore as the leader of the
opposition) was cultivating "vulgar prejudices" in order to destroy
credit and through it the sinews of the government.[37]

Increasingly, the personalities of the leaders became legislative
issues. On the question of who should succeed if the President and
Vice President both died, the popular branch, the House, plumped for
Jefferson by designating the Secretary of State. But the conservatives
who dominated the Senate were determined that Jefferson should
never be "King of the Romans." They forced this sequence: first the
President pro tem of the Senate and then the Speaker of the House.[38]

In the House, the anti-Hamiltonians moved to push the Treasury a large step away from their deliberations by providing that the Secretary could not communicate directly with them, but must send all messages through the President. Hamilton said angrily that Madison, in supporting the change, knew that if the bill passed he would resign. It did not pass. However, the vote was so close—thirty-one to twenty-seven—that Jefferson wrote gleefully that the Treasury had been "deeply wounded."[39]

Ignoring all personal animosities, still not thinking in terms of conflicts between economic classes, Washington continued to diagnose the controversy as basically geographical. The enactment of Hamilton's first program—funding and assumption—had been accompanied by a sop to the south in the form of the location of the national capital. No such sop had accompanied the bank. In his eagerness to encourage fluid capital, Hamilton eschewed possible direct benefits to farmers. The bank's charter forbade it to invest in land or buildings; Hamilton turned a deaf ear to suggestions that loans be made on warehouse certificates for stored tobacco.

The paper Hamilton had created did not, by circulating there, ameliorate the currency shortage at a distance from commercial centers. This was true in all regions, but politically determining in the south, where the governmental leaders and the most affluent citizens were not drawn into the financial circle Hamilton fostered. The planters had no urge to risk their assets in machinations they did not understand, and, in any case, slaveholders had their capital tied up in their labor force. When in 1779 Washington had considered buying loan certificates and "collecting the interest," he had realized that this would involve a complete change in his way of life. From the point of view of conscience, he would have been very glad to abandon slaveholding, but his tastes and training were so much those of a planter that he had not seriously contemplated the switch.[40]

That Washington hurried to Mount Vernon whenever his governmental duties allowed; that he was happy to have the nation's capital placed (so to speak) in his backyard, indicated that his emotions were still tied to his native soil. But on an intellectual level, he considered such local attachments contrary to the public interest. Thus, he was inclined, as Jefferson's notes on "reapportionment" reveal, to overcompensate.

Reapportionment was a necessary reconstituting of the House of

Representatives. Although the size of each state's delegation was supposed to be based on population, no census had existed when the government began; representation had been based on guesses. Now a census had been completed. It gave the total population as 3,893,000. That the 697,000 slaves were rated at three-fifths their actual number produced the corrected figure of 3,614,000. Equally divided, this number authorized 121 representatives, an increase of 52. If, however, the constitutional figure of 30,000 was divided into the population of each state there would be only 103 representatives, because of the fractions left dangling. Congress decided to achieve a total of 120 by assigning to various states the additional members authorized by adding up all the fractions. An outraged south insisted that this mathematical magic had given three times as many seats to the north as to them.

Such was the bill which Washington had to countenance or veto. His Cabinet proved equally divided. The southerners, Jefferson and Randolph, insisted that the bill was unconstitutional. The northerners, Hamilton and Knox, urged that the Constitution was capable of such interpretation, and that Washington would do well to accept the judgment of the legislature. Washington, who had so far never used his veto power, kept postponing his decision.

At last he could hesitate no longer, since the bill was about to become law without his signature. After what was undoubtedly a sleepless night, he appeared at Jefferson's lodgings before the Secretary had had breakfast. He explained that one reason he was loath to intervene was "that the vote for and against the bill was perfectly geographical, a northern against a southern vote, and he feared that he should be thought to be taking sides with a southern party."

"I admitted this motive of delicacy," Jefferson remembered, "but that it should not induce him to do wrong."

After much discussion, Washington stated that he would negative the bill if Madison agreed with Randolph and Jefferson that he should. Madison agreed, and Washington finally used his veto. The upshot was that Congress forgot the fractions and established a House in which all state populations were treated alike.[41]

26

The Great Columbian Federal City

S INCE the original plan for Washington, D.C., is considered one of the great masterpieces of city designing, and since Jefferson is revered as an architect, it is generally assumed that the majestic plan resulted from the cooperation of Jefferson with the actual designer, Major Pierre Charles L'Enfant. Washington, who is not commonly credited with aesthetic gifts, is pictured as looking on benevolently. This conception reverses the actual situation. Washington hired L'Enfant and worked with him to perfect the plan while Jefferson looked on disapprovingly. Jefferson was pleased when, despite Washington's extreme efforts, L'Enfant forced his own discharge.

L'Enfant, born at Paris in 1754, was the son of a painter, six of whose battle scenes are in the museum at Versailles. Having studied under his father, the son drifted into the French colonial army. At the age of twenty-two, he became one of the first French volunteers to join Washington. Before being wounded and captured at the siege of Charleston, he was a light infantryman, an engineer, an aide to drillmaster Steuben—but the attention he attracted was for artistic abilities. "Monsr. Lanfang" (as the Commander in Chief then wrote the name) first entered Washington's presence with pencil, paper, and a commission from Lafayette to draw the General's portrait (now lost). He designed the pavilion for the grandest party Washington attended during the Revolution—the French ambassador's celebration of the birth of a Dauphin—and he created the insignia for the Society of the Cincinnati in a manner he claimed to be entirely original: not a geometric medal but a cutout silhouette of an eagle. The hall where

[325]

Washington had been inaugurated had been rebuilt by L'Enfant in a classical style using American symbols, and he had been the architect for other houses which Washington had admired in New York.[1]

Almost a year before the bill establishing a federal city had passed Congress, L'Enfant wrote Washington asking to design the city. As subsequent events demonstrated, Washington was impressed by L'Enfant's conviction that "the plan should be drawn on such a scale as to leave room for the aggrandizement and embellishment which the increased wealth of the nation will permit it to pursue at a period however remote." L'Enfant stated that "no nation perhaps had ever before the opportunity offered them of deliberately deciding on the spot" and the "design" of a great capital city.* He wished to grasp "so great an occasion for acquiring reputation."[2]

Washington already knew that the architect was not an easy man to handle. When representing the Cincinnati in France, L'Enfant had run up huge and unauthorized bills which revealed that his conceptions of suitable grandeur inspired in him a kind of financial madness. However, from the very first, Washington was convinced that L'Enfant was better qualified than anyone he himself knew of or could hope to procure "for projecting public works and carrying them into effect." L'Enfant possessed what Washington admired: a combination of the practical and the visionary. He was "a scientific man . . . who added considerable taste to professional knowledge."[3]

Washington had selected the area for the federal district without consulting L'Enfant, but that area, being a hundred square miles, offered a wide choice of actual city sites. Two seemed most promising: the land around Carrollsburg, where the East Branch of the Potomac (now the Anacostia) joined the main river, or that farther north in the vicinity of the more thriving village of Georgetown. The former site offered a magnificent terrain but was in the hands of stubborn landowners; the latter had the practical advantages of more available land and better existing communications. Still, seeking cheaper purchases by keeping owners and speculators off balance, Washington insisted, even to his confidential agents, that he had not made up his mind between the two areas. Yet there is a clear indication that he had

---

* The only preceding opportunity since ancient times had been supplied by St. Petersburg in faraway Russia.

already decided to prefer picturesqueness to utility: he assigned a competent surveyor, Andrew Ellicott, to plot the Georgetown terrain but sent the brilliant L'Enfant to the area around the Eastern Branch. On January 29, 1791, Jefferson noted, without expressing any opinion of his own, that Washington "thought Major L'Enfant particularly qualified to make such a draft of the ground as will enable him to fix on the spot for the public buildings."[4]

As Secretary of State, Jefferson was supposed to be the executive officer for the new capital. Under him and entrusted with active supervision were the three commissioners Washington had been required by the enabling statute to appoint. He selected David Stuart, his friend and the stepfather of Martha's grandchildren; the distinguished Marylander Thomas Johnson, another old friend who had, indeed, nominated him for Commander in Chief; and the largest landholder in the Federal District, Daniel Carroll.[5] However, the existence of these subordinates did not at the start keep Washington from running everything himself.

The most pressing problem was financial. Since Congress had refused to appropriate any money for the capital and since the sums being contributed by the most interested states, Maryland and Virginia, were hardly adequate even for a beginning, the venture would have to be made self-supporting through intelligent use of the way the city would increase the value of the land on which it was located.

In late March 1791, on his way to Mount Vernon and his subsequent southern tour, Washington stopped off at Georgetown. Calling the local landowners together, he told them that by squabbling among themselves and seeking high profits, they might lose the entire opportunity: Pennsylvania was scheming to keep Philadelphia the capital. She would take advantage of every confusion on the Potomac.[6]

Washington, so he notified Jefferson, succeeded in persuading the proprietors at both Carrollsburg and Georgetown to give the government free of charge every other lot in an area a mile and a half wide. The owners were to receive twenty-five dollars an acre in return for land taken "for public use, for squares, walks, etc.," but they were not to be reimbursed for "streets and alleys." Washington had insisted on "the right to reserve such parts of the wood on the land" as might serve "ornament." His intention was to support the venture by selling for city prices the alternate lots of farmland the government had got for nothing.

Washington notified Jefferson that he had commissioned L'Enfant to lay out the city. However, he failed further to confide that he and the architect had agreed that the public buildings should occupy the picturesque terrain near Carrollsburg. Washington had, indeed, pointed out to L'Enfant as the best site for the President's house the hill on which the White House now stands.[7]

L'Enfant also sent a letter to the absent Jefferson. Impeded by bad weather, he stated, he had been able to show Washington only rough drawings, but the President's "indulgent disposition" had recognized the difficulties under which he had labored. From Jefferson, L'Enfant wished to learn "the nature and number of the public building." He would also be grateful for any plans Jefferson could send him of major European cities. Then, as if embarrassed at asking for such sources, L'Enfant explained that advantages could be got from comparison, even if only the discovery of faults to be avoided. He intended, L'Enfant continued, to copy from no source, but rather "to delineate on a new and original way the plan, the contrivance of which the President had left to me without any restrictions soever."[8]

Jefferson, who disapproved of urban life, was not pleased with the scale on which Washington and L'Enfant were envisioning the capital: he would have preferred a town two or three times smaller, an enlarged Williamsburg. On the other hand, Washington was disappointed at being unable to get even more land. Philadelphia (which Jefferson regarded as a sink of iniquity) occupied, so Washington pointed out, an area of three miles by two: "If the metropolis of *one state* occupied so much ground, what ought that of the United States to occupy?" Washington instructed L'Enfant to acquire as much more ground "as there is any tolerable prospect of obtaining." Selling off the government's share of the extra blocks would increase the revenue, and "the plan will be enlarged and thereby freed from those blotches which otherwise result."[9]

The semi-apology with which L'Enfant had accompanied his request for European sources must have seemed outlandish to Jefferson, who had happily modified the Roman temple at Nîmes into the Virginia Capitol. When Jefferson responded by sending L'Enfant a large number of city plans, he proudly explained that they had been "procured by me when in those respective cities myself." He went on to say that, "having communicated to the President before he went away such general ideas on the subject of the town as occurred to me, I make no doubt that, in explaining himself to you on the subject, he has inter-woven with his own ideas such of mine as he approved. For fear of repeating therefore what he did not approve, and having more confi-dence in the unbiased state of his mind than in my own, I avoid interfering with what he may have expressed to you."

But Jefferson could not refrain from adding, "Whenever it is pro-posed to prepare plans for the Capitol, I should prefer the adoption of some one of the models of antiquity which have had the approbation of thousands of years. And for the President's house, I should prefer the celebrated fronts of modern buildings which have already received the approbation of all good judges."[10]

If Jefferson thought it unsafe to count on Washington's having repeated this advice, he probably guessed correctly. The President's attitude on such matters was revealed when Jefferson wrote the Presi-dent that he had selected while in Europe a dozen or two plates "of the handsomest fronts of private buildings." Would it not, Jefferson asked, be a good idea to distribute copies of these examples of good taste to the inhabitants of the new town? Washington answered unenthusiastically that the scheme "may answer a good purpose" if it could be "carried into effect at a moderate expense." Washington, indeed, regarded the traditional rules of architecture as restrictions one had to follow as far as was necessary to avoid criticism. In his own efforts, such as the designing of Mount Vernon, he obeyed (as he put it) no guide but his own eyes.[11]

Now that he had actually commissioned L'Enfant, Washington forwarded to him a sheaf of suggestions from his files: "Although I do not conceive that you will derive any material advantage from an examination of the enclosed papers, yet, as they have been drawn by different persons and under different circumstances, they may be compared with your own ideas." The rough sketch by Jefferson had been done when the Secretary believed the owners of Carrollsburg could not be moved. It was thus "accommodated to the grounds about Georgetown."* [12]

Jefferson's plan placed the President's house and the Capitol a short distance apart and connected them with a broad mall. The immedi-

---

* Jefferson's plan would have placed the governmental area in what is now called Foggy Bottom, the Capitol being near Pennsylvania Avenue near Tenth Street, and the President's house near the Naval Hospital.[13]

ately surrounding area was designed as an unvaried grillwork of streets. Any further extension of the small city he had envisioned could be, Jefferson noted, "laid out in the future."[14]

L'Enfant, the ever impulsive and tactless, wrote in a memorandum (which it is generally assumed Jefferson saw) that such a regular plan "must, even when applied upon the ground best calculated to admit of it, become at last tiresome and insipid, and it never could be in its origin but a mean continuance of some cool imagination wanting a sense of the real grand and truly beautiful only to be met with where nature contributes with art and diversifies the objects."[15]

After Washington had returned from his southern trip, L'Enfant appeared at Mount Vernon with a draft of his city plan. Preferring to concentrate on the overall design, the architect had not made drawings of any specific buildings or plazas. His first consideration had been the natural features of the terrain. He had selected the points he wished to emphasize with major buildings or monuments and laid out broad avenues which, meeting at various focal points, cut at angles through an overall pattern of rectangular squares. He visualized the avenues as grandly broad: "eighty feet for a carriageway, thirty feet on each side for a walk under a double row of trees, and allowing ten feet between the trees and the houses." The avenues would offer handsome vistas, both because of their length and location; they would provide elegant sites for mansions, and they would facilitate communication sideways across the city.

On "the western end of Jenkins's Heights," which "stands really as a pedestal waiting for a superstructure," L'Enfant intended to put the Capitol. The effect would be made more grand by letting a small river called the Tiber, which was to supply water for a canal, "return to its proper channel by a fall which, issuing from under the base of the Congress building, may there form a cascade of forty feet high and more than a hundred wide."*

The "Presidential Palace" (as L'Enfant called it) was placed to obtain "an extensive view down the Potomac with a prospect of the whole harbor of Alexandria." In the foreground would be a big park

---

* This canal, connecting the Tiber with a good harbor in the Eastern Branch of the Potomac, would achieve what Washington had long sought by differently planned works: a water route around the Great Falls of the Potomac. Washington was happy to conceive that the plans for the Federal City made the whole Potomac Canal scheme both more necessary and more practical.[16]

including a garden which, as it sloped towards the canal, overlooked one end of "the vast esplanade." This esplanade, going off at a right angle, eventuated at a considerable distance in the "Congress House." At the intersection of the lines of sight from the Presidential windows and those of Congress, L'Enfant wished to place an equestrian statue (preferably the one of Washington voted by Congress in 1783 but never executed) which, "with proper appendages and walks adequately managed, would produce a most grand effect."[17]

Even Washington's intimate Stuart was shocked by the size of the intended Presidential park. "It may suit the genius of a despotic government," Stuart wrote, "to cultivate an immense and gloomy wilderness in the midst of a thriving city . . . I cannot think it suitable to our situation." Washington replied good-humoredly that he saw at present no necessity to diminish the park: "It is easier at all times to retrench than it is to enlarge a square."* [18]

For the plazas where grand avenues came together L'Enfant imagined monuments: a column commemorating some future historical event which, by being exactly a mile from the Capitol, would double as a basic measure "for the geographers of the whole nation"; a naval column awaiting victories to be emblazoned; an interdenominational church where the bodies of national heroes, either military or otherwise, would be interred by act of Congress. L'Enfant had not needed Washington's urging to carry his plan far out into fields and marshes. It covered fifty square miles, providing for a city of eight hundred thousand, the size of eighteenth-century Paris.[19]

Arguments continue on the question of how far the plan was derived, how far original. That Jefferson's sketch had placed the President's house back from the esplanade that ran to the Capitol is supposed by some writers to have inspired L'Enfant's much more extensive but somewhat similar arrangement. Perhaps, to a lesser or greater extent it did; perhaps L'Enfant had reacted on his own to the geographical situation.[20]

William T. Partridge, consulting architect for the National Park Commission, stated in 1930 that L'Enfant's plan was "exactly what he

---

* Although now largely open to the public, most of the Presidential park still remains in front of the White House as one of the pleasures of the city. The obelisk-like Washington Monument stands close to the spot where L'Enfant had wished to put an equestrian statue of the hero. The projected canal is now Constitution Avenue.

Lat. Capitol.____38: 53, N.
Long._____0: 0.

GEORGE TOWN

PART OF VIRGINIA WITHIN THE TERRITORY OF COLUMBIA

POTOMAK RIVER

President House

OBSERVATIONS
explanatory of the
Plan.

I. THE positions for the different Edifices, and for the
several Squares or Areas of different shapes, as they are laid
down, were first determined on the most advantageous ground,
commanding the most extensive prospects, and the better susceptible
of such improvements, as either use or ornament may hereafter
call for.

II. LINES or Avenues of direct communication have been devised,
to connect the separate and most distant objects with the principal,
and to preserve through the whole a reciprocity of sight at the same time.
Attention has been paid to the passing of those leading Avenues over the
most favorable ground for prospect and convenience.

III. NORTH and South lines intersected by others running due East and
West, make the distribution of the City into Streets, Squares, &c; and those
lines have been so combined as to meet at certain given points with those
divergent Avenues, so as to form on the Spaces "first determined," the different
Squares or Areas.

SCALE OF POLES.

100   200   300   400   500   600 Poles.

A masterpiece of city planning created over the opposition of Jefferson by
L'Enfant in cooperation with Washington. Courtesy of the New-York
Historical Society

claimed": an "original plan," an "entirely unique" response to the nature of the land. Some architectural historians insist, however, that in his overall design L'Enfant imitated Versailles. That there are similarities between the American and French plans is clear, but it is not clear how far one copied the other, how far they were independent results of creative minds operating within the same broad aesthetic conceptions. The American city was, like Versailles, conceived of as an outdoor palace in which the viewer moved out from major centers harmoniously through one visual experience after another.[21]

Define the inspirations as you will, the fact remains that President Washington, as he examined the plan L'Enfant was submitting to him, held in his hands a great work of art. He made a few suggestions and then, without waiting to consult Jefferson, gave L'Enfant his official approval.

On his way back to Philadelphia in June 1791, Washington spent four nights at Georgetown. He cleared up some difficulties with the owners of the land which the commissioners had been unable to handle, and stood by while the necessary deeds were signed. Walking the terrain with L'Enfant and Ellicott, he decided on a small westerly move for the President's house and to reduce somewhat the number of diagonal avenues. Finally, he laid the plan of the city before the proprietors and observed "with much pleasure that a general approbation of the measure seemed to pervade the whole." Then Washington went on to Philadelphia, leaving L'Enfant to set, in consultation with the commissioners, actual operations in motion.[22]

Finally, Jefferson notified L'Enfant that Washington wished to discuss "some matters which have occurred to him." L'Enfant came to Philadelphia, arriving on August 27. Now at long last Jefferson saw the city plan Washington had approved.[23]

Jefferson's worst fears were certainly realized by the grandeur of the conceptions. This was no capital for a modest agricultural nation tilling its fields quietly in a corner of the world. There is, indeed, evidence that L'Enfant, who admitted to a conscious intention of fostering a nation dedicated to "magnificence," was an active ally of Hamilton's.

In a memorandum which L'Enfant prepared in 1800 when seeking belated compensation for his services, the planner stated that "particular companies" had agreed to give him, had his plan for the capital gone through as intended, the supervision of erecting, as the start of a more extensive project, "houses to the amount of a million dollars." Hamilton had personally stated his intention of providing "as many pounds sterling as I at that time computed dollars wanted." This, L'Enfant continued significantly, would have given "greater certainty to the attainment of the political end." He blamed the defeat of "the dearest interests of the city of Washington" not only on "the passion and weakness of its most esteemed supporters [including the President?]" but on "the infatuation" of those who wished to have the "seat of government stand a mere contemptible hamlet."[24]

Washington could not have been unconscious that democrats were worried by the environmental implications of L'Enfant's plan. However, he shrugged such worries off, as he had Stuart's complaints concerning the size of the Presidential park. Fear that luxury and grandeur would corrupt had never been among his natural fears—and he was willing to face what political risks there might be in order to obtain the beauty.

Jefferson was far from convinced of the beauty, but he did not openly oppose L'Enfant's schemes as he was opposing Hamilton's. Regarding the capital as a particular concern of the President's, he acted as an altogether loyal assistant, only enunciating his own ideas when consulted. In answer to questions from Washington, he urged that, as in Paris, houses be limited to a given height—this would keep the streets light and airy while reducing the danger from fires—and opposed, as fostering monotony, having all the houses an equal distance from the street. It was only after Washington had been forced to dismiss L'Enfant that Jefferson put on paper his rebuttal to L'Enfant's statement that he had a mean, cool imagination because he wished an unvariegated grillwork of streets. At angular intersections between streets and avenues, Jefferson believed, the houses could not be got close enough to the corners to be visible in the vistas L'Enfant intended. In any case, the structures on the triangular lots "may probably be offensive to the eye" unless the "deformity" was "obviated" by some such device as "terminating the house at that end with a bow window, with a semicircular portico, and with other fancies."[25]

Although, as L'Enfant and Washington collaborated, Jefferson held in his disapprovals and resentments, it remained a fact that, should difficulties develop, the city planner would not find a supporter in the Secretary of State.

The first explosion had been presaged when Washington visited Georgetown in June. L'Enfant had objected to the method which had been decided upon for financing the project. The intended immediate sale of lots, he argued, would prevent fluidity in the application of his plans, and, in any case, lots would bring more when the work was further advanced. Washington should procure a loan, putting up the land as security.

Washington replied that to secure such a loan would be time-consuming and perhaps impossible, while no time was to be lost or prestige hazarded, since Pennsylvania was engaged in trying to keep the capital by actually erecting buildings for the federal government in Philadelphia. Washington instructed L'Enfant to have a plan of the city engraved as quickly as possible so that purchasers could identify choice property and pay accordingly. L'Enfant continued to protest, but Washington had no doubt that he would obey.[26]

Jefferson and also Madison having now been brought up to date on plans, Washington's two friends undertook the next step as part of a trip they were making to Virginia. They met with the commissioners at Georgetown. This conference determined official designations: what was sometimes called the Great Columbian Federal City was named Washington; the area, the District of Columbia. It was also decided that the first sale of lots should be held in mid-October, and that L'Enfant was to have his plan engraved in time to be distributed at the auction.[27]

L'Enfant's disapproval of such a sale had been increased by a suspicion that the commissioners were plotting with their local friends to snap up the best lots before any vendue could be conducted on a national basis. He went through the gestures of having his plan engraved—but the plate failed to be ready.[28]

Washington contributed the prestige of his presence to the gathering of the bidders. However, he had to hurry back towards Philadelphia before the auction commenced. At five-thirty the next morning, from Bladensburg, Maryland, he expressed to Stuart his eagerness to hear the results: "I am now writing by candlelight, and this is the only piece of paper the landlord is able to procure for me."[29]

The news was that the sale had been far from brilliant—thirty-five lots sold for $8756, of which little more than $2000 was in cash. This poor showing was partly because of bad weather, but more because

L'Enfant had refused to obey the commissioners' orders that he exhibit at the sale his map of the city.[30]

Washington reacted to L'Enfant's behavior "with a degree of surprise and concern not easy to be expressed." He burst out, "It is much to be regretted, however common the case is, that men who possess talents which fit them for peculiar purposes should almost invariably be under the influence of an untoward disposition, or are sottish idle, or possessed of some other disqualification by which they plague all those with whom they are concerned. But I did not expect to have met with such perverseness in Major L'Enfant."

Washington went on to comment that, being himself convinced that L'Enfant was irreplaceable, he did not doubt that the city planner considered himself in the same light. It seemed natural to Washington that the artist "would be so tenacious of his plans as to conceive they would be marred if they underwent any change or alteration." Perhaps the commissioners had not given L'Enfant, and also Ellicott, adequate chances to express their ideas: "The feelings of such men are always alive, and where their assistance is essential . . . it is policy to humor them or to put on the appearance of doing it." Yet it was certain that L'Enfant should not have interfered in the sale of the lots.[31]

Trying to move as gently as possible, Washington did not himself sign—it was signed by Lear—a letter to L'Enfant in which he incorporated "sentiments of admonition . . . with a view also to feel his pulse under reprehension." L'Enfant, the letter stated, had "laid the foundation of his grand design," but "the superstructure" depended on the commissioners. The architect had to obey the commissioners. Washington was confident that they would listen to suggestions that were "properly offered and explained."[32]

To the commissioners, Washington wrote of his continued belief in the abilities of L'Enfant, and of his conviction that the city planner was not hostile to them personally: "His pertinacity would, I am persuaded, be the same in all cases and to all men." L'Enfant had intended to act for the best, "but I have caused it to be signified to him that I am of a different opinion."[33]

Before L'Enfant's plan had become known, a local landowner, Daniel Carroll of Duddington, had begun to build a house which proved to encroach on an intended street. This brought him into angry controversy with L'Enfant. Washington was taking time from his other

[337]

duties to write the contestants calming letters when L'Enfant struck out. All the more gleefully because this Carroll was a nephew of the commissioner of the same name, L'Enfant, in flat contradiction of orders from the commissioners, ordered out workmen who pulled down the house.

On being notified, Washington sent his file of correspondence with L'Enfant to Jefferson, asking advice on "how far he may be spoken to in decisive terms without losing his services, which, in my opinion, would be a serious misfortune. At the same time, *he must know* there is a line beyond which he will not be suffered to go . . . or we shall have no commissioners."[34]

Jefferson sent Washington the draft of a possible letter to L'Enfant. Washington copied, grammatical mistake and all, into his own letter Jefferson's statement that the architect had to obey the commissioners, "to whom, by law, the business is entrusted, and who stands between you and the President of the United States." Then Washington added to Jefferson's draft two paragraphs of sympathetic reasoning. "Having the beauty and regularity of your plan only in view, you pursue it as if every person and thing was *obliged* to yield to it; whereas the commissioners have many circumstances to attend to, some of which, perhaps, may be unknown to you."[35]

L'Enfant, had decided to do some admonishing himself. "I doubt not," he wrote the President, "you have as much at heart the speedy advancement of the great work on hand as I have. I trust you will see the propriety of your never interfering with the process of execution but in [a] case when an appeal to you from individuals may be justly grounded." He continued to deny the authority of the commissioners, and he insisted that in all his acts he had been right.[36]

Again appealed to by Washington, Jefferson found L'Enfant completely at fault, nor did he in this (or in any other communication on the subject) indicate that he considered L'Enfant's services worth preserving. "To render him useful," Jefferson stated, "his temper must be subdued." He must be made to "submit to the unlimited control of the commissioners."[37]

Washington wrote L'Enfant that it was "painful" but nonetheless necessary to reiterate that he must obey the commissioners, who had "every disposition that can be desired to listen to your suggestions." To the commissioners, Washington wrote, "His aim is obvious. It is to have as much scope as possible for the display of his talents." If "he will bear the curb" of obedience, "I submit to your consideration whether it might not be politic to give him pretty general and ample powers for *defined* objects, until you shall discover in him a disposition to abuse them. His pride would be gratified and his ambition excited by such a mark of your confidence." If L'Enfant "should take miff and leave the business, I have no scruple in declaring to *you* (although I do not want *him* to know it) that I know not where another is to be found who could supply his place." Washington then launched into an argument to show that in the recent dispute Carroll had been as much to blame as L'Enfant, who had "many objects to attend to and to combine, not on paper merely but to make them correspond with the *actual* circumstances of the ground. This required more time than the patience, perhaps the convenience, of Mr. Carroll would admit."[38]

L'Enfant came to Philadelphia to draw up specific plans for the next few years, leaving behind his roommate and assistant, Isaac Roberdeau, to whom he had given, without consulting the commissioners, instructions for the winter's work. The commissioners decided to save money by discharging the workmen and waiting till spring. Roberdeau defied the commissioners; they had him imprisoned for trespass; L'Enfant screamed with outrage. He openly accused the commissioners of fraudulent collusion with speculators. The commissioners wrote Washington that they would resign unless L'Enfant were controlled. L'Enfant wrote Washington that he would resign rather than take orders from such venal commissioners.* [39]

As the controversy ground on, L'Enfant did not temporize with existing difficulties. He boldly proposed "grand machinery" that would lift, "as if it had been magically, a ready-built city out of the earth." In the dawning year of 1792, he wished to employ a thousand workmen and spend more than three hundred thousand dollars. He estimated that a loan of a million dollars, which he told Washington to raise in Holland, would, with grants from Maryland and Virginia, support expenditure at this rate for four years.[40]

History was to prove that L'Enfant had a right to be worried at the piddling rate at which the project was proceeding. When in 1800 the government finally moved in, the city was more characterized by mud and empty lots than magnificence. Yet L'Enfant's efforts to dictate

---

* No evidence exists impeaching the commissioners' honesty.

financial and political planning were as harmful as they were impractical. He had, by keeping his map hidden, dampened the first auction, creating a bad commercial precedent; he frightened moneymen away by seeming likely to bankrupt the operation before it got really started; and, in overlaying the whole project with a miasma of controversy, he increased fears of investors that the city never would rise.

The million-dollar loan L'Enfant wished Washington to raise would have been one-tenth of the entire foreign debt incurred by the thirteen states during the Revolution. The President saw much less chance of getting Congressional authorization for such a sum than of having Congress decide to scrap the whole project in favor of continuing to occupy that already-built city, Philadelphia.*

Washington dictated to Lear, for dispatching over his secretary's signature, a letter to Samuel Powel, who, in addition to being the husband of the lady the President found so attractive, was a leader in Philadelphia's efforts to keep the capital. In supporting a bill in the Pennsylvania legislature to build a house for the President, Powel was making the statement (based undoubtedly on his intimate knowledge of Washington's household) that Washington was dissatisfied with the Morris house, where he was quartered. The letter to Powel stated (untruthfully) that the President "felt himself perfectly satisfied with the house in which he resides." The President, so the letter continued, "further observed that if the house in question was even now finished, he should not go into it." The President's sentiments had already been repeated not only to Powel but to other Pennsylvania leaders. It was hoped that the matter was now entirely clear.[41]

According to the compromise Washington was trying to work out, L'Enfant would handle the artistic and engineering aspects while the commissioners balanced income with outlay and dealt with other worldly problems. The commissioners were willing to agree, but not so the artist. He continued to insist that unless he could have complete

---

* The question of why, if Hamilton was actually encouraging L'Enfant, he did not edit the architect's financial dreams, is worthy of speculation. It may be guessed that Hamilton was not eager to save the city of Washington, since he may well have preferred, if given the choice, to keep Philadelphia as the national capital rather than labor to make a new city accord with his ideas. Furthermore, when Hamilton came to employ L'Enfant to design the new industrial city of Paterson, New Jersey, he proved no more successful in controlling the visionary than Washington had been.

control of everything, he would resign. His possessiveness had reached a point where he not only continued to block the engraving of his map but implied that the President was guilty of theft when he allowed drawings entrusted to him to be copied so that they could be hung, as propaganda for the new city, on the walls of Congress.[42]

Washington was mightily puzzled. Was L'Enfant motivated by "self-importance and the insolence of office" or was he engaged in some "unworthy" intrigue?* However, the President was still determined not to lose the services of the brilliant artist. On Washington's sixtieth birthday, Jefferson wrote L'Enfant, "I am charged by the President to say that your continuance would be desirable to him." However, the law required submission to the commissioners.[43]

L'Enfant replied with a long, hysterical screed attacking the commissioners and refusing any compromise with them. Washington sent the letter on to Jefferson with the suggestion that he show it to Madison and Randolph, after which he hoped "that all three of you would be with me at half after eight o'clock tomorrow." They would have to reach "a final decision."[44]

What that final decision would have to be was so clear that Washington decided on an extreme expedient. Laying aside the dignity of the Presidency, he sent Lear to L'Enfant's lodgings to plead in the President's name. After a while, Lear returned with no smile on his face. The President's emissary had been rebuffed. L'Enfant had silenced him, shouting that "he had already heard enough of this matter." Washington's anger flared. He felt himself "insulted."[45]

The next morning's conference eventuated in a letter to L'Enfant over Jefferson's signature. L'Enfant was discharged.[46]

To various correspondents, Jefferson expressed satisfaction. "I am persuaded the enterprise will advance more surely under a more temperate direction." He was to insist that L'Enfant's city plan "mixed conjecture with fact," whole blocks of lots being actually in the river.[47]

---

* In a letter to Humphreys, his fellow intimate with Washington, Lear tried to explain L'Enfant's behavior. The Frenchman's powers had, most unfortunately, not been defined at the start. "He felt himself great in the business," and the commissioners, being new on the job and reposing great confidence in him, allowed him to do as he pleased. Those concerned with the project who had not read the enabling law came to agree with L'Enfant's own belief that he was independent of the commissioners. However, when he proved so extravagant, the commissioners, who feared that they would be blamed as the authority was legally theirs, felt required to intervene. L'Enfant's outrage was encouraged by owners of the land who had a personal dislike for the commissioners.[48]

Washington, on the other hand, found difficulty in reconciling himself to L'Enfant's dismissal. Among Jefferson's papers is a note in Washington's hand asking, "Would it be advisable to let L'Enfant alter the plan if he will do it in a certain given time?" However, it remained evident that any move Washington made to re-employ the architect would be interpreted as abject surrender. The President's hope was that L'Enfant would himself reopen the negotiation.[49]

According to Lear, L'Enfant told an intimate friend "that he would give the universe if he possessed it" to be back where he had been before he fought the commissioners, but now he was so far along that his pride would not permit him to recede a single step.[50]

Since L'Enfant would make no conciliatory move, Washington could only urge that Ellicott, who had undertaken the supervision and the publication of the map, should again be "asked in strong and explicit terms" whether the plan he was exhibiting was "agreeable to the designs of Major L'Enfant."*[51]

Washington had felt obliged to write L'Enfant a personal letter justifying the discharge he so regretted. Among other points, he stated that "five months have elapsed and are lost by the compliment which was intended to be paid you in depending *alone* upon your plans for the public buildings instead of advertising a premium to the person who should present the best, which would have included yourself equally."[52]

No time was now lost in establishing competitions for the President's house and the Capitol.

Jefferson himself undertook two designs for the President's house. The most ambitious—in which he tried to combine "the celebrated front" of the Hotel de Salm, with flanks adopted from the Garde-Meuble, and a main entrance reduced from the central colonnade of the Louvre—got out of hand and had to be abandoned. The other design, based on the conceptions of Palladio, Jefferson submitted anonymously.[53]

Perhaps because he did not wish to judge his own design, Jefferson

---

* Although down the years L'Enfant's design has been blunted and cheapened in many ways, while the more extreme features—such as the great cascade charging downward in front of the Capitol—have been entirely eliminated, the spirit of the great designer still presides over the center of the city of Washington, giving that metropolis a green and variegated charm which makes it potentially one of the world's most delightful cities.

was not present when in July 1792, Washington met with the commissioners at the District of Columbia to go over all submissions. Washington chose for the President's house a design submitted by James Hoban.

Hoban was a recently arrived (1789) Irishman who had received some professional training as an architect in Dublin. For the President's house, he sought inspiration—as Virginia gentlemen did when designing their mansion houses—from English architectural books. The outside of the well-proportioned box derived from plates 52 and 53 in James Gibbs's *A Book of Architecture* (1728). Washington, who expressed less enthusiasm with the choice than satisfaction at having got the matter settled, made clear that he had been influenced by the architect's ability himself to supervise the erection of the building. Not only did Hoban seem "a master workman" but he possessed his own corps of artisans. (Actually, Hoban moved, as did everything else in the city, with monumental slowness.) [54]

If Jefferson felt disappointment that Washington had thrown out his anonymous plan, and if he would have preferred something in the French rather than the British taste, he must nonetheless have found (so wrote Fiske Kimball in his book on Jefferson as architect) Hoban's design "at least partially acceptable." After all, it was based on "respectable precedent."*

While L'Enfant had still been officially the architect of the government buildings, Jefferson had begun discussions on the design for the Capitol with Stephen Hallet, a French architect who had reached the United States in 1789. Jefferson told Hallet that the temple form was "the model for cubic architecture." Since the drafts Hallet was producing with Jefferson's help were considered more promising than any other submissions, Washington postponed decision on the Capitol. However, Hallet proved unable to get the temple form large enough. Jefferson agreed that something else would have to be tried, turning to what had been, while he was still in Paris, the most recent achievement of French classical architecture: the Pantheon. Hallet developed the plan of that structure into a central dome with balancing wings for the

---

* Jefferson's passion to base American art on the best European sources was to be typical of the post-Revolutionary generation. In painting, it swayed Allston, Vanderlyn, Morse. In his greater reliance on American-bred experience and emotions, Washington belonged to an older generation: the generation that in painting produced West, Copley, Stuart, Charles Willson Peale.

two branches of the legislature. However, tinker as he would, he failed to translate the conception into an effective design.

Enter William Thornton, an English-trained physician with a taste for architecture. Adopting the Jefferson-Hallet conception, Thornton re-created it in a spirited drawing which (although it later proved impractical) enchanted both Jefferson and Washington. Among the papers of both men is a letter to the commissioners exulting in identical words over "the grandeur, simplicity, and beauty of the exterior; the propriety with which the apartments are distributed, and the economy in the mass of the whole structure." Hallet's just claims were a problem, but Washington felt that they could be met (as they were) by paying him for the services he had already performed and also to supervise the actual erection of Thornton's building.[55]

As the year 1792 approached its close, the city of Washington consisted of little more than some holes and stakes in the ground and some drawings on paper. Its enemies were saying, so the President complained, "that the accomplishment of the plan is no more to be expected than the fabric of a vision, and will vanish in like manner."[56]

An effort to secure in Boston a loan on the capital property had ended in complete failure. Afraid to raise the issue, Washington did not dare seek funds to carry out Congress's responsibility of having the boundaries of the district surveyed. Few of the lots that were put on the market sold. Although Washington had urged that competent craftsmen be recruited in Europe and imported as indentured servants, there was hardly any labor force to carry through what few operations there was money to pay for. And to top everything, all business in the district drooped under wobbly laxness because of inadequate supervision.

Those who were scheming to keep the capital in Philadelphia, led by Eliza's husband Samuel Powel, smiled with an infuriating satisfaction when the matter was mentioned. "I am very apprehensive," Washington wrote the commissioners, that "if your next campaign in the Federal City is not marked with vigor, it will cast such a cloud over this business, and will so arm the enemies of the measure as to enable them to give it (if not its deathblow) a wound from which it will not easily recover."[57]

An effective superintendent was needed, "a man of fertile genius and comprehensive ideas. . . . But where, you may ask, is the character to be found who possesses these qualifications? I frankly answer, I know not!" How Washington wished that Major L'Enfant "could have been restrained within proper bounds"; that "his temper was less untoward!" The discharged genius remained "the only person with whose turn to matters of this sort I am acquainted that I think fit for it."[58]

V

The Desire to Escape

27

Jefferson Begins to Doubt
Washington

SEVENTEEN NINETY-TWO was Presidential election year. In
the early months, Washington notified Jefferson, Hamilton,
Knox, and Madison—but no one else—that he hoped to refuse
a second term.[1]

That Washington's withdrawal would create a crucial situation only
a fool could deny. The dangers inherent in a changeover of power had
been so eloquently presented by history that in monarchies it was
considered infinitely preferable to accept a sadistic, half-witted legitimate heir rather than throw the crown open to the rivalry of pre-
tenders, however able. Whether it was possible for a republic peace-
ably to replace one chief executive with another remained to be
determined. Yet the American experiment, which Washington hoped
would point a glorious future for all mankind, could not be ruled
successful until such a changeover was attempted and achieved without turmoil.

. Eager to make the transition as mild as possible, Washington
confidently expected that his top aides would provide continuity
during the period of change.* [2] They should remain in office, without
any flouncing visible to the public, at least until the will of the new
President was known. Washington may well have assumed that his

---

* At that time, there were hardly any of the career employees, none of the
civil service bureaucrats, who were at a later date to carry on the government
during (and sometimes despite) changes at the top.

successor (as was eventually to prove to be the case) would find it wise not to upset, at least until he had solidified himself in office, the makeup of the great departments.

At the very end of February, Washington received a severe shock. The occasion started out routinely enough as a consultation with the Secretary of State about post riders: Jefferson had a scheme for increasing their daily ride from fifty to a hundred miles. Washington, who regarded information disseminated by post as a cement for the Union, was pleased and enthusiastic. Jefferson then argued that the post office should be changed from the jurisdiction of the Treasury to his own department. The Treasury already possessed "such an influence as to swallow up the whole executive powers." Future Presidents, backed by less "weight of character" than was Washington, "would not be able to make head against this department."

Washington was opening his mouth to make a conciliatory reply when Jefferson dropped his bomb. He stated that in trying to increase the power of his office, he could not be accused of seeking personal power, since he intended to retire when Washington did, and "the intervening time was too short to be an object."

Washington was still speechless when a servant announced that he was needed at one of his levees. "He desired me," so Jefferson's notes continue, "to come and breakfast with him the next morning."

At breakfast, conversation was held to social chitchat. After "we retired to his room," Washington discussed the matter of the post office, and then asked Jefferson to commit his views to writing. Finally, Washington said "in an affectionate tone that he had felt much concern at an expression which dropped from me yesterday, and which marked my intention of retiring when he should. That, as to himself, many motives obliged him to it. He had through the whole course of the war, and most particularly at the close of it, uniformly declared his resolution to retire from public affairs." He had reluctantly gone back on his word when it had been represented to him, first in relation to the Constitutional Convention and then to the Presidency, that his participation would help persuade the people to accept a government "of sufficient efficacy for their own good."

"Were he to continue longer," Washington went on, "it might give room to say that, having tasted the sweets of office, he could not do without them; that he really felt himself growing old, his bodily health less firm, his memory—always bad—becoming worse; and perhaps the other faculties of his mind showing a decay to others of which he was insensible himself. That this apprehension particularly oppressed him; that he found, moreover, his activity lessened. Business, therefore, [became] more irksome, and tranquillity and retirement became an irresistible passion."

Washington then stated that he "should consider it as unfortunate" if his retirement "should bring on the retirement of the great officers of the government, and that this might produce a shock on the public mind of dangerous consequence."

"I told him," so Jefferson's memorandum continues, "that no man had ever had less desire of entering into public offices than myself." Jefferson had become Governor of Virginia in response to public crisis. He had departed from that office "with a firm resolution never more to appear in public life." He had only accepted the appointment to France because the death of his wife "made me fancy that absence and a change of scene for a time might be expedient for me." He had not intended to stay long, but "the Revolution in France coming on," he had become so interested in what would be the outcome that he had resolved to put off his "final retirement" until he had seen it through. As Washington knew, he had accepted his present position with great reluctance and only because he was assured "that I might be more serviceable here than in France."[3]

When, during the summer of 1791, Washington had written Jefferson that he would never occupy any of the governmental buildings to be erected in the Federal City,[4] Jefferson had "instantly" made up his mind to retire when Washington did.* But Washington need not fear that there would be no one to carry on, so Jefferson continued in what could only have been an angry or sarcastic tone of voice. The Secretary of the Treasury surely had no intention of retiring. Hamilton had schemes which it would take years to mature.

Washington thereupon tried to soothe Jefferson by stating that the Department of State was much more important than the Treasury, since it embraced "nearly all the objects of administration" while the

---

* Since the Federal City would not be occupied by the government until 1800, Jefferson, who had been opposed to having the Constitution allow the President more than one term, seems to have assumed that Washington's administration would go on at least into a fourth. This was, of course, a hangover from monarchical thinking. During April 1790 the President's cousin and former estate manager, Lund Washington, wrote him "No person has any idea but that you must remain at the head of the government as long as you live."[5]

Treasury was only concerned with revenue. It followed that Jefferson's retirement "would be more noticed." Although the government had at first earned general good will, "symptoms of dissatisfaction had lately shown themselves far beyond what he could have expected; and to what height these might arise in case of too great a change in the administration could not be foreseen."

"I told him," Jefferson noted, "that in my opinion there was only a single source of these discontents." Although the debacles in Indian fighting had spread criticisms to the War Department, the troubles were "generated" by the Treasury.

In his previous communications with Washington, Jefferson had never (so the evidence indicates) expanded his arguments against various of Hamilton's policies into an all-out attack on the Treasury. But now, although he still did not use Hamilton's name, Jefferson was fairly launched. Washington, who liked to fool himself into believing that the disagreements in his Cabinet were cracks, not fissures, must have listened in consternation as his Secretary of State expostulated with all the heat of a man who is giving vent to long-suppressed convictions.

Jefferson stated that a system had "been contrived for deluging the states with paper money instead of gold and silver; for withdrawing our citizens from the pursuits of commerce, manufactures, buildings, and other branches of useful industry, to occupy themselves and their capitals in a species of gambling, destructive of morality, and which had introduced its poison into the government itself. That it was a fact, as certainly known as that he and I were then conversing, that particular members of the legislature, while those laws were on the carpet, had feathered their nests with paper, had then voted for the laws, and constantly since lent all the energy of their talents and instrumentality of their offices to the establishment and enlargement of this system. That they had chained it about our necks for a great length of time, and, in order to keep the game in their hands, had from time to time aided in making such legislative constructions of the Constitution as made it a very different thing from what the people thought they had submitted to. That they had now brought forward a proposition far beyond every one ever yet advanced, and to which the eyes of many were turned as the decision which was to let us know whether we live under a limited or an unlimited government."

Washington "asked me to what proposition I alluded.

"I answered to that in the Report on Manufactures" (which was still pending). Jefferson burst into a passionate argument that if the payment of bounties to industries were accepted under the public welfare provision in the Constitution, no limit would remain on Congress's powers.[6]

Washington not only agreed with Jefferson on this but had told Hamilton so.[7] He could have calmed Jefferson by stating his opposition to bounties and confiding that he would in all probability veto as unconstitutional any bill that authorized them. But Washington kept his counsel. He remained determined to keep above all squabbles, to take no part in arguments beyond listening to what everyone had to say and finally, if that became necessary, announcing his decision. Washington allowed Jefferson to go away disconsolate.

Then the President took what steps he could to soothe his Secretary of State. He felt that he could not reverse the decision to give the post office (as a revenue-collecting body) to the Treasury, but he did assign to State a just-established agency which by all logic should have gone to the Treasury. Jefferson was to have the mint. And now that Washington realized how great were Jefferson's suspicions of Hamilton, he sometimes went out of his way, when discussing a matter of foreign affairs, to assure the Secretary of State that "no other person" had been consulted.[8]

Probably because of a desire to iron out in advance the disagreements to which his advisers were becoming more prone, Washington had, some three months before, established the precedent for the Cabinet meetings that were to continue through American history. As a substitute for his previous method of consulting his Secretaries singly, and in whatever order suited his immediate needs, he called the department heads together, requesting the Secretary in whose department the business to be discussed "more immediately" lay to bring a written statement of "the several points on which opinions will be asked."[9]

If Washington hoped that face-to-face discussion, under his own nonpartisan eye, would dampen the fires in his Secretaries' breasts, he hoped vainly. Since Hamilton did not keep detailed memoranda, we do not in most cases know his reactions to specific meetings, but Jefferson's notes reveal him as perpetually aglow with distrust. He sifted Hamilton's every word for indications that his enemy was scheming not only to overthrow republicanism, but to undermine, in secret cahoots with representatives of Britain, American friendship with France.[10]

The newly arrived British minister, George Hammond, had gathered a mass of evidence to demonstrate that American violations of the Peace Treaty were so numerous that the British were justified in not relinquishing the western posts. Using his old training as a lawyer, Jefferson undermined Hammond's evidence and picked holes in his reasoning to create what Samuel Flagg Bemis regarded as the greatest paper Jefferson drafted as Secretary of State. Before sending his screed to Hammond, Jefferson showed it to Madison and then Randolph and then Hamilton. Hamilton, ever careful to keep an appearance of balance, particularly where Washington could see, raised only a few objections, the most important being to Jefferson's claim that some of his lawyer's arguments had justified the refusal of various states to enforce the payment of debts to Englishmen. Hamilton thought it would be more logical to say that what Jefferson had put forward was an "extenuation" rather than a "justification." The disagreement was carried to Washington, who ruled for Jefferson's stronger wording. However, Washington, as he lightly confessed to Jefferson, expected the document to have little effect.

The British could hardly be expected to give up their charges of treaty violations, which served as valuable cover for keeping the frontier posts that enabled them to stalk larger game. But Hamilton took no chances; in secret conferences with Hammond, he labored to vitiate the State Department paper. He told Hammond that Jefferson's "intemperate violence," which he himself lamented, by no means expressed the views of the administration. He revealed that Washington had not seen the actual paper, but had approved it only on the basis of a précis given him by Jefferson.

Malone, the ever judicious, writes, "One would have to search far in American history to find a more flagrant example of interference by one high officer of the government with the policy of another which was clearly official policy, and the attempt to defeat it by secret intrigue with the representative of another country."[11]

The appearance of Hammond as British minister had been accompanied by the arrival of a minister from France. This enlargement of diplomatic relations had involved reciprocity on the part of the United

States: America's two equivalent ministries needed to be filled, and there was also reason for stronger representation in Holland.

Although Washington consulted Jefferson, he made the appointments himself. To England, he sent a South Carolinian whom Jefferson had never met: Thomas Pinckney. Ever since Jefferson had come home from Paris, American business had been transacted there by his secretary and protégé, William Short. Although seemingly too young and inexperienced to succeed to the position of minister, Short wanted desperately to do so, or at least be appointed to Holland. Jefferson had written him the previous year that it was better not to press the matter with Washington: "To overdo a thing with him is to undo it. I am steering the best I can for you."[12] Now Washington was willing to indulge his Secretary by sending Short to Holland. But for the important post in France he made a most controversial choice: Gouverneur Morris.

Morris's appointment was strongly opposed in the Senate. James Monroe, the radical senator from Virginia, charged that Morris was a "monarchy man," and had gone to Europe "to sell lands and certificates." But the final vote did not break on party grounds: the opposition included, indeed, the two conservative senators from Massachusetts.[13] After the appointment had squeaked through by a narrow vote, Washington wrote his appointee a remarkable letter:

Having stated that he had nominated Morris "with *all my heart*," Washington launched into a summary of the debate in the Senate. Morris's abilities and knowledge and disposition to serve his country were admitted, but he was charged with "imprudence of conversation and conduct. It was urged that your habits of expression indicated a *hauteur* disgusting to those who happen to differ from you in sentiment, and among a people who study civility and politeness more than any other nation, it must be displeasing; that in France you were considered as a favorer of aristocracy and unfriendly to its Revolution (I suppose they meant constitution). That under this impression, you could not be an acceptable public character. . . . That the promptitude with which your lively and brilliant imagination is displayed allows too little time for deliberation and correction and is the primary cause of those sallies which too often offend, and of that ridicule of characters which begets enmity not easy to be forgotten, but which might easily be avoided if it was under the control of more caution and prudence. In a word, that it is indispensably necessary that more circumspection should be observed by our representatives abroad than they conceive you are inclined to adopt.

"In this statement you have the pros and cons. By reciting them, I give you a proof of my friendship if I give none of my policy or judgment. I do it on the presumption that a mind conscious of its own rectitude fears not what is said of it, but will bid defiance to and despise shafts that are not barbed with accusations against honor or integrity. And because I have the fullest confidence (supposing the allegations to be founded in whole or part) that you would find no difficulty . . . to effect a change and thereby silence, in the most unequivocal and satisfactory manner, your political opponents.

"Of my good opinion and of my friendship and regard, you may be assured."[14]

Washington, who had so effectively learned to control his own passions, clearly felt that, if admonished to follow the right path, Gouverneur Morris could make himself over. But even so, the President realized that the appointment might not be a proof "of my policy and judgment." Why did he take the risk?

That Morris was extremely brilliant even his enemies did not deny: Washington could have found no one abler. True, the envoy had in letters to Washington made clear his lack of enthusiasm over the reforms in France; he had written that the new constitution was "good for nothing." But on the other hand, when he had been Washington's personal representative to England, he had demonstrated—to the irritation of Hamilton and Beckwith—that he was not pro-British. In the political alignment developing in the United States, Morris had no part; in the lineup developing in Europe, he had no emotional ties except to the United States. Years later, in repelling a charge by Monroe that he had appointed a monarchist to revolutionary France, Washington wrote, "Whatever may have been his [Morris's] political sentiments, he pursued steadily the honor and interest of his country with zest and ability, and with respectful firmness asserted its rights." This was more, Washington added, than could be said of the subsequent embassy of the pro-French Monroe.[15]

Perhaps the determining factor was that Morris was Washington's intimate friend. This had practical as well as emotional advantages. Suspecting that the game in France had only started, Washington saw the tremendous importance of keeping in touch. Any informant was sure to have some bias. Had Washington appointed Jefferson's protégé

Short, that bias would have been pro-revolutionary, but to what extent and in what particular ways Washington would not have known, since he did not know Short. But from his understanding of Morris's character and convictions, he could correct the news Morris sent him.

Partly because Morris's appointment had been accompanied by a post for Short, partly because of his continuing deference to Washington, Jefferson had not made any major protest. But Jefferson was beginning to become conscious of a worry. Although he himself had been greatly upset by the flight of the French King and Queen, it had disturbed him to see Washington greatly upset. Did this mean that the man he had always so revered suffered from a conservative and unworthy lack of faith in the ability of the French people to govern themselves?[16]

In early 1792 the Terror was hardly more than a year away, but Jefferson continued to believe that France was proceeding with adequate smoothness down a rosy path to freedom. It bothered him to have Washington state that, judging from the English newspapers and other sources, the affairs of France were "going into confusion." Preferring not to blame the President for a lack of noble republican confidence, Jefferson charged that Morris, "a high-flying monarchy man, shutting his eyes and his faith to every fact against his wishes and believing everything he desires to be true, has kept the President's mind constantly poisoned with his forebodings."[17]

It was comforting thus to blame Morris, but surely Washington should not have been so susceptible to the influence of misguided men like Morris and most especially that villain Hamilton. What about that conversation Jefferson had had with Washington concerning the proposed annual bribe to keep the Algerian pirates from attacking American ships? Advising with the executive on this foreign policy matter was, under the Constitution, solely the province of the Senate. Yet the money would have to be appropriated with the concurrence of the House. In replying to the suggestion that the House be consulted before the diplomatic commitment was made, Washington (so Jefferson remembered) referred to the direct popular election of the House. He said "that he did not like throwing too much into democratic hands." If the House tried to violate the Constitution by interfering with foreign affairs through the power of the purse; if, Washington said, the House "would not do what the Constitution called on them to do, the government would be at an end and must *then assume another form.*"

Jefferson was drawn rigid by a fear that Washington was referring to an American monarchy. "I kept silence to see whether he would say anything more in the same line, or add any qualifying expression to soften what he had said, but he did neither."[18]

Jefferson walked off at last with his mind spinning.

28

Determination to Retire

A FTER Washington had failed to veto the bill for the Bank of the United States, Jefferson and Madison faced the fact that they would probably have to fight for their ideas outside the administration as well as within. They got in touch with an editor, the very Philip Freneau who had greeted the arriving President in New York Harbor from a boat on which there capered a pair of orangutans.

Freneau had been a classmate of Madison's at Princeton, was a poet of ability, and a radical journalist of great fire and effect. Jefferson offered him a post as translator in the State Department, pointing out tactfully that the office, while paying a salary, would leave plenty of time for other pursuits. It was Madison who put in writing the wish that Freneau should publish from the capital a national newspaper. This was to be an answer to John Fenno's *Gazette of the United States,* a strongly Hamiltonian biweekly that received advertising from the Treasury. Freneau hesitated for a while, but arrived in Philadelphia during August 1791 to accept the governmental salary Jefferson offered and to launch in October the *National Gazette.*[1]

In February 1792, Freneau opened a sustained attack on Hamilton's financial measures as increasing unnecessarily the national debt, encouraging speculation, and leading to monarchy. "Artifice and deception," Freneau charged, had created "one revolution in favor of the few. Another revolution must and will be brought about in favor of the people."[2]

The Hamiltonians were caught by surprise, but they soon mounted a counterattack in the *Gazette of the United States.* Jefferson was accused of employing Freneau in the government in order to overthrow that government. The traitorous Secretary of State should resign!

Washington's comment on the whole newspaper war was that the gazettes "are *sur*charged and *some of them* indecently communicative of *charges* that stand in need of evidence for their support."[3]

In May, Washington demonstrated that however much Hamilton's policies might seem to dominate his administration, he still felt closest to Madison. It was his old friend whom he called in to give him advice on "the *mode* and *time*" most proper for announcing that he would not accept another term. According to Madison's memorandum of the conversation, Washington said that he had consulted no one else on the strategy of his retirement, although he had made his intention known to Jefferson, Hamilton, Knox, and more recently Randolph.

Washington reported that Randolph, Hamilton, and Knox had been "extremely importunate" against his retiring and that Jefferson "had expressed his wishes to the like effect." However, Washington did not himself believe that his continuance "could be of so much necessity or importance as was conceived; and his disinclination to it was becoming every day more and more fixed." He wished to find the mode of announcement that "would be most remote from the appearance of arrogantly presuming" that he could be re-elected. He wished to pick "such a time as would be most convenient to the public in making the choice of his successor."

Madison replied that "the aspect which things had been latterly assuming" forced him to insist that Washington's retirement "ought not to be hazarded." It was true, Madison admitted, that when he had first urged Washington to accept the Presidency, he had said that Washington could protect himself from the charge of ambition by "a voluntary return to private life as soon as the state of the government would permit." The state of the government did not now permit. Washington would have to trust that should he die before he could voluntarily retire, his friends would "do justice to his character" by "in some way or other" presenting evidence that he had been motivated throughout not by ambition but a sense of duty.

Far from accepting a necessity of his further service, Washington stated that "he had from the beginning found himself deficient in many of the essential qualifications, owing to his inexperience in the forms of public business, his unfitness to judge of legal questions and questions arising out of the Constitution. . . . He found himself, also [he had just passed his sixtieth birthday], in the decline of life, his health becoming sensibly more infirm and perhaps his faculties also; that the fatigues and disagreeableness of his situation were, in fact, scarcely tolerable to him." He added "that his inclination would lead him rather to go to his farm, take his spade in his hand and work for his bread, than remain in his present situation."

The unpleasantness of this situation was being augmented by "a spirit of party" in his own government. "Discontents among the people . . . were also showing themselves more and more." Although none of the public attacks were pointed directly at him, in some he was "the indirect object." It was thus becoming clear that since his presence was not fostering harmony, "his return to private life was consistent with every public consideration."

Madison assured Washington that, "however novel or difficult the business might have been to him," his judgment had been as "competent in all cases as that of anyone who could have been put in his place, and in many cases certainly more so." Furthermore, his services had been "essential" in uniting all groups. Madison admitted a renewal of party spirit, but regarded this as an argument for Washington's staying on "until the public opinion, the character of the government, and the course of its administration should be better decided, which could not fail to happen in a short time, especially under his auspices."

The parties did not appear to Madison as formidable as some believed. He admitted that in one party (his own and Jefferson's) there might be a few who retained their original opposition to the federal government and would like to destroy it. However, insofar as they expressed such views, these individuals "would lose their weight with their associates." He considered it "pretty certain" that the other party was "in general unfriendly to republican government and probably aimed at a gradual approximation of ours to a mixed monarchy." Yet their attitude was so contrary to public sentiment that the party could not long continue its "dangerous influence." Thus, in another four years of "temperate and wise administration," both types of enemies of the government should fade away.

As Washington listened, he must have noticed that Madison foresaw the entire abolition of the Hamiltonian party and, in the case of his own and Jefferson's, purification which would leave them in undisputed control.

Continuing his arguments, Madison asked who, if Washington refused to run again, would be the candidates? He mentioned neither Hamilton nor himself. The possibilities were Adams, Jay, and Jefferson. Adams would be widely opposed because he had expressed monarchical principles. Jay was believed to agree with Adams; he was charged with having espoused claims of British creditors at the expense of his fellow Americans; and it was not forgotten that he had tried to bargain away the navigation of the Mississippi. As for Jefferson, his "extreme repugnance to public life" made it doubtful that he would accept the Presidency, and it might well be that he would be barred by "local prejudices in the northern states" and by Pennsylvania's resentment at losing the national capital. The lack of an adequate substitute, Madison concluded, made it the more clear that "another sacrifice" was "exacted" by Washington's "patriotism."

Washington "turned the conversation to other subjects." However, before Madison withdrew, the President stated that he had not changed his mind about retiring.[4]

When Congress adjourned in May 1792, they had acted favorably on five of the seven suggestions Washington had made to them in his Annual Address; they had postponed two, but not opposed anything he was known to favor.* The President's actual power seemed in no way to have diminished when he set out, without Martha, for a quick trip to his private world of Mount Vernon.

In the golden sunshine of a Virginia summer, riding his fields, sitting on his porch as the Potomac moved below him, Washington "again and again revolved" in his mind "with thoughtful anxiety" Madison's insistence that he accept an additional four years of service, power, exile. He was surrounded by such weather—neither too hot nor too cold, too wet nor too dry—as farmers dream of but rarely see. He was "much pleased to find the appearance of crops of my own farms more flattering than I had known them for many years past. . . . The country generally exhibited the face of plenty."[5]

---

* Congress had acted favorably on excise revision, apportionment, the creation of a uniform militia, the improvement of the post office, and the establishment of a mint. They had done nothing positive on weights and measures and the disposal of vacant land.[6]

On May 20, he wrote Madison that he had not been able "to dispose my mind to a longer continuation in the office I have now the honor to hold. I therefore still look forward to the fulfillment of my fondest and most ardent wishes to spend the remainder of my days (which I cannot expect will be many) in ease and tranquillity.

"Nothing," he continued, "short of conviction that my dereliction of the chair of government . . . would involve the country in serious disputes respecting the chief magistrate, and the disagreeable consequences which might result therefrom in the floating and divided opinions which seem to prevail at present, could, in any wise, induce me to relinquish the determination I have formed—and of this I do not see how any evidence can be obtained previous to the election. My vanity, I am sure, is not of that cast as to allow me to view the subject in this light."

He wished Madison to prepare a draft of "a valedictory address from me to the public, expressing in plain and modest terms" that he had reached the age of retirement and that "a rotation in the elective officers" contributed to the "liberty and safety" of the government. He wished to impress on the citizenry "that we are *all* the children of the same country" which promised "to be as prosperous and as happy as any the annals of history have ever brought to our view. That our interest, however diversified in local and smaller matters, is the same in all the great and essential concerns of the nation." The economic proclivities of the various regions could be made to key together to "render the whole (at no distant period) one of the most independent in the world."

He further wished his statement to point out "that the established government, being the work of our own hands, with the seeds of amendment engrafted in the Constitution, may by wisdom, good dispositions, and mutual allowances, aided by experience, bring it as near to perfection as any human institution ever approximated; and therefore the only strife among us ought to be who should be foremost in facilitating and finally accomplishing such great and desirable objects by giving every possible support and cement to the Union." Was there an oblique comment on Jefferson's tirade against Hamilton in Washington's next point? He said: "That however necessary it may be to keep a watchful eye over public servants and public measures, yet there ought to be limits to it; for suspicions unfounded and jealousies too lively are irritating to honest feelings, and oftentimes are productive of more evil than good."

Washington doubted that he should suggest specific changes in the Constitution. Other matters that ought to be brought up might occur to Madison—and he still wished his friend to advise him concerning the time when the announcement should be made.[7]

Returning to Philadelphia late in May, Washington received there a letter from Jefferson that had been forwarded from Mount Vernon. The Secretary's explanation of why he had put his sentiments thus on paper illustrates how difficult it was for even Washington's intimates to discuss with him grave matters not of his own choosing. Jefferson explained that he had been unable to find "a good occasion of disburdening" himself "in conversation."

When Washington had first spoken of retirement, Jefferson had been "in a considerable degree silent" because he had felt that the public mind was "calm and confident" enough to permit the experiment of changing leaders. But now, "from causes in which you are in no ways personally mixed," the public was dangerously agitated. Jefferson then launched indirectly (he did not mention Hamilton by name and he stated that he was reporting "general beliefs" that could be "real or imaginary") into a renewed argument to demonstrate that all the troubles stemmed from Hamilton's misbehavior.

An "artificially created" public debt had caused a "habitual murmuring against taxes and tax gatherers." Furthermore, the excise on liquor had committed "the authority of the government in parts where resistance is most probable and coercion least practicable." The tax would (so Jefferson wrote prophetically) eventuate in "evasion, and war on our own citizens to collect it."

Returning to his metaphor that the money market was "a gaming table," Jefferson again insisted that far from increasing the assets of the nation, the Treasury's policies reduced them by directing into speculation resources that would otherwise sustain commerce and agriculture. And then there was the vice and the idleness!

The "corrupt squadron" which the Treasury's virtual bribery had created in Congress was now in control and was trying to subvert the Constitution into a monarchy on the British model. "Public faith and right," Jefferson admitted, made impossible the undoing of much to which the government's credit was committed. "But some parts of the system may be rightfully reformed." More important still, the direction of the political current must be changed away from monarchy and towards republicanism. Unless the reform was achieved—and achieved at once as a result of the new election of an augmented House of Representatives—the Union would break up geographically into two or even more nations.

"This is the event at which I tremble, and to prevent which I consider your continuance at the head of affairs as of the last importance. . . . North and south will hang together, if they have you to hang on," giving time for wise measures to heal the widening breach.

Jefferson said again that he could not be accused of personal ambition in giving such advice since he was still determined to retire. His services contributed nothing to the public confidence. "I therefore have no motive to consult but my own inclination, which is bent irresistibly on the tranquil enjoyment of my family, my farm, and my books."[8]

Although he expressed gratitude to the President, Jefferson indicated no sense of obligation to back up his chief on whose unhappy shoulders he wished to clamp further responsibility at this difficult time. Washington could not fail to recall that Hamilton had shown, despite occasional pettish remarks that he would resign, no real desire to desert the ship.

Washington told Jefferson "that he would take an occasion of speaking with me on the subject," but postponed discussing the letter for more than two weeks. Then "he began by observing that he had put it off from day to day because the subject was painful." Having repeated his reasons for wishing to retire, he deplored "suspicions against a particular party which had been carried a great deal too far. There might be *desires* but he did not believe there were *designs* to change the form of government into a monarchy. That there might be a few who wished it in the higher walks of life, particularly in the great cities, but that the main body of the people in the eastern states were as steadily for republicanism as in the southern."

Washington, who of course knew that Freneau was employed in the government by Jefferson, now stated that "the pieces lately published, and particularly in Freneau's paper, seemed to have in view the exciting [of] opposition to the government," especially in western Pennsylvania against the excise law. Such publications, Washington continued, tended to produce the separation which Jefferson spoke of fearing, and also "anarchy." Anarchy would encourage "a resort to monarchical government."

Washington then repudiated the notion, to which Jefferson was adhering to at least in his conscious mind, that he had been no more than an innocent bystander while Hamilton made policy. The newspapers, Washington insisted, were also attacking him, "for he must be a fool indeed to swallow the little sugar plums here and there thrown out to him. That in condemning the administration of the government they condemned him, for if they thought there were measures pursued contrary to his sentiment, they must conceive him too careless to attend to them or too stupid to understand them. That, though indeed he had signed many acts which he did not approve in all their parts, yet he had never put his name to one which he did not think on the whole was eligible. That as to the bank, which had been an act of so much complaint, until there was some infallible criterion" by which to judge its success or failure, a difference of opinion must be tolerated.

"He had seen and spoken with many people in Maryland and Virginia in his late journey. He found the people contented and happy. He wished, however, to be better informed on this head. If the discontent were more extensive than he supposed, it might be that the desire that he should remain in the government was not general."

Jefferson then made observations "to enforce the topics of my letter." In reply to the charge that the legislature had been corrupted, Washington "said not a word." Washington stood up for assumption and the excise. "Finding him really approving the Treasury system," so Jefferson concluded his notes on the interview, "I avoided entering into argument with him on those points."⁹

On July 30, Hamilton wrote the President that he had been pleased to discover, during their last conversation, that Washington was "relaxing" his disposition to retire. Hamilton had inquired around, as he had promised to do, and found that everyone agreed "that your declining would be . . . the greatest evil that could befall the country at the present juncture." He added a matter on which neither Madison nor Jefferson had presumed to touch: retiring when Washington was needed would be "critically hazardous to your own reputation."

People said that the government was not yet firmly established. Equating the present opposition with the anti-Federalists who had opposed ratification of the Constitution, Hamilton stated that the enemies of the government, "generally speaking, are as inveterate as ever. . . . Their enmity has been sharpened by its success and by all the resentments which flow from disappointed predictions and mortified vanity."

Jefferson had told Washington that the election for the new enlarged House of Representatives contained the hope for an anti-monarchical future, and he wished Washington to stay on until that hope had been realized. Now Hamilton wrote that the next House, which might be dominated by opponents of federal union, was the great danger. He wished Washington to stay on until that danger had passed.[10]

29

Personal Feuds Cut Deeper

L ATE in July 1792, as the newspaper war flashed and roared
and drenched the government in Philadelphia, Knox complained to his wife, "The President is buried in solitude in
Mount Vernon."[1] Washington might have made the trip anyway, but
visiting Mount Vernon had become imperative to his personal emotions and affairs because his nephew and estate manager, George
Augustine Washington, had been struck with a return of tuberculosis.

The greatest tragedy of Washington's young manhood had been the
death of his beloved older half-brother, whom he had vainly nursed,
from the disease that was killing the young man who was now closest
to him of all his blood relations. It seemed a replay of the old tragedy
when George suffered with "a violent and copious discharge of pure
blood from them [his lungs], by which he is so reduced as to be
almost unable to speak." That George's wife, who was Martha's
favorite niece, seemed in her anguish to be coming down with her
husband's disease, contributed to the gloom by the Potomac, where
Martha wrung her hands as her husband was forced to cope with a
thousand details. He had been unable to bring himself to keep the two
aides, whom he had taken with him to Virginia, from going off again
"on visits to their friends. . . . All my business, public and private, is
on my own shoulders."[2]

A change to more sedentary and less violent interests was revealed
when a conflict arose between his affections for his deer and for his
hounds. A favorite hobby in his younger days had been importing,
breeding, and training hounds to take part in the foxhunts he so

enjoyed. As an embellishment of his estate, he had fenced in a deer park and stocked it with both imported and domestic deer. Recently his fence had broken, allowing "about a dozen" half-tame deer to "range in all my woods and often pass my exterior fence. It is true, I have scarcely a hope of preserving them long, although they come up almost every day, but I am unwilling by any act of my own to facilitate their destruction." Since they were "as much afraid of hounds . . . as the wild deer are," Washington had parted with all his hounds. Now instead of leaning eagerly forward as he rode shouting to the chase, Washington sat quietly on his porch watching the nearby woods for the shy appearance of the gentlest of forest creatures.[3]

On his way from Philadelphia to Mount Vernon and after his arrival home, Washington had anxiously questioned "sensible and moderate men, known friends to the government." They had agreed that the country was prosperous and happy, but "seem to be alarmed at that system of policy and those interpretations of the Constitution which have taken place in Congress." Now really perturbed, Washington decided to report this to Hamilton and also forward the strictures in Jefferson's letter attacking the Treasury's policies. However, not wishing to encourage disunity by letting Hamilton know that charges had been made by Jefferson, Washington engaged in some politic lying.

Having reported to Hamilton that there was concern among men loyal to the government, Washington continued, "Others less friendly perhaps to the government and more disposed to arraign the conduct of its officers (among whom may be classed my neighbor and quondam friend Colonel M[ason]), go further and enumerate a variety of matters which, as well as I can recollect, may be adduced under the following heads: viz. . . ." Washington copied the "heads" almost word for word from Jefferson's letter.

After he finished quoting Jefferson, Washington again attributed the whole to his memory of what various people had told him. He stated that he had numbered the charges so that Hamilton could answer each one by number.[4]

Hamilton's reply was much more voluminous than Jefferson's letter, since the strictures had been general and vague, while Hamilton answered specifically and in detail. Where Jefferson said that the debt was artificially created, purposely protracted, and greater than the nation could pay, Hamilton pointed out that it was not a new but an inherited debt; gave statistics to demonstrate advantages resulting from his funding system; and stated that far from being tremendous at about fifteen million sterling, the debt was no greater than the annual budget of Great Britain. Taxes were small and imposed on a very few things.* Instead of draining America dry (as charged) for the advantage of Europe, his policies brought foreign capital into the United States. Nor did the debt reduce purchasing power: those parts of the nation where the greatest number of debt certificates were held also had the most circulating capital. In the financial areas of the controversy Hamilton moved, indeed, with the ease and effect of an expert parrying the clumsy thrusts of an amateur.

With vehement outrage, he called the charge that the legislature had been corrupted "malignant and false." Why should "creditor" be equated with "enemy," support of the public credit with corruption? No facts had been brought forward to demonstrate corruption. That there had been speculation was not the fault of the government, nor should the government be deflected from important objectives thereby. The fact of the matter was that the carpers, limited by their "narrow and depraved ideas," wished to "sacrifice everything that is venerable and substantial in society to the vain reveries of a false and new-fangled philosophy."

In reply to the charge that he was seeking to establish a monarchy, Hamilton argued that the way to achieve this was surely not to build a republican government on a sound financial foundation, but rather to undermine the government as its critics were trying to do. The demagogues in the opposition, being frustrated, were enraged because "the beneficial effects of the government have exceeded expectation and are witnessed by the general prosperity of the nation."[5]

The growing season at Mount Vernon continued beneficent, crops bowing to the wind in every field. Yet disturbing news came in from east and west.

Hamilton forwarded reports that resistance to the excise tax on whiskey was rising in western Pennsylvania, and might spread to other backcountry areas. Techniques which had nurtured the Revolution

---

* Washington had written in August 1791 that he had discovered "with astonishment hardly to be conceived" the weight of taxes the English people bore. Had he read it in a less reliable source than the leading English agricultural journal, he would have *"absolutely"* disbelieved."[6]

against England were being imitated: an illegal assembly, elected from several counties, had convened at Pittsburgh, had threatened revenue officers, and had even established "committees of correspondence" to keep the rebels in touch and extend the rebellion.

When Shays's Rebellion had developed in a less well-organized manner against a less well-organized government, Washington had been greatly perturbed. He had recommended that if there were legitimate grievances, they should be righted—otherwise force would have to be used. Presiding now over a strong government, he was far less upset, although he did write Hamilton that if it were not for the sickness of his nephew he would hurry to Philadelphia. As for righting grievances, he felt this had already been done in the recent revision Congress had passed in the excise law. He wrote Hamilton that should "peaceable procedure" prove "no longer effectual, the public interest and my duty will make it necessary to enforce the laws respecting this matter; and, however disagreeable this would be to me, it must nevertheless take place." If force should prove necessary, he dreaded using the regular army, which recently had been augmented for Indian warfare, lest "there would be a cry at once, 'The cat is let out: we now see for what purpose an army was raised.'" Yet to support the Constitution and the law, he would, if necessary, accept "the dernier resort."[7]

Hamilton's suggestion, which was backed by the other members of the administration present at Philadelphia, was that Washington denounce the rebels in a proclamation which, by bringing to bear Washington's personal prestige and that of the Presidency, would make the insurgents realize the gravity of their acts. Sending a suggested text, Hamilton urged that, since speed was essential to stop the movement from spreading, time be not taken to get the approval of the absent Secretary of State.[8]

Washington, however, sent a draft by express to Monticello, ordering the messenger to track the Secretary down wherever he was, if he were not at home. "I have no doubt," so ran Washington's covering letter, "but that the measure I am about to take will be severely criticized," but nothing "in my opinion is more important than to carry the laws of the United States into effect."[9]

Jefferson urged (and Washington obliged him) the deletion of a phrase implying this particular law was necessary, but approved the rest, writing, "I am sincerely sorry to learn that such proceedings have taken place, and I hope the proclamation will lead the persons concerned into a regular line of application, which may end either in an amendment of the law, if it needs it, or in their conviction that it is right."[10]

Washington thereupon published the proclamation, which stated that the government had shown great moderation;* that Congress had made changes "to obviate causes of objection"; and that it was his duty to enforce the law. "Now, therefore, I George Washington, President of the United States do by these presents most earnestly admonish and exhort all persons whom it may concern to refrain and desist from all unlawful combinations. . . . And I do moreover charge and require all courts, magistrates, and officers" to use all their powers to enforce the law.[11]

For the moment (and in however illusory a manner) it looked as if the opposition would quiet down. Even before the proclamation was issued, Hamilton had detected "favorable symptoms."[12]

Developments in France worried Washington for the safety of the people there, for his beloved Lafayette, and for the peace of Europe, but he still did not foresee domestic repercussions. On June 22, he wrote that France's declaration of war against the King of Hungary would make the nations of Europe take sides. However, so he added optimistically, "our local situation and political circumstances guard us against an interference in the contests between the European powers." A month later, informed that French civil violence was mounting, he wrote Jefferson that he wished the Secretary of State would find it convenient to drop in at Mount Vernon as he traveled to or from Monticello. Gloomy news followed on gloomy news, but Jefferson did not appear until the very end of September.[13]

Still supported by the British, the northern Indians were continuing their depredations. They murdered a brigadier general and a major sent by Washington to treat with them. In the southern wilderness, Spain was exhibiting a new militancy, conspicuously stirring up the Creeks against the Treaty of New York. Washington was informed that "five regiments of about 600 men each, and a large quantity of

---

* Enforcement had been delayed for fourteen months in an effort to secure agreement.

ordnance and stores, arrived lately at New Orleans, and that the like number of regiments (but this can only be from report) was expected at the same place from the Havana."[14]

Washington knew that shared opposition to the French Revolution was bringing together the European neighbors of the United States who had previously felt for each other a reassuring enmity. If the reports of Spain's frontier activities were correct, "I shall entertain strong suspicions that there is a very clear understanding in all this business between the Courts of London and Madrid." He wished Pinckney, the American minister in London, "to be very attentive to the embarkation of troops for America."[15]

To meet this potentially extremely dangerous alliance against the United States, Washington's own house was far from in order. "Turbulent" settlers on the Georgia frontier were reported to be inciting hostilities with the Creeks that could set the whole wilderness aflame. In the east there was strong opposition to any warfare with the Indians. And Washington's hands were tied, since Wayne's army was still far from ready to fight.[16]

Although peace was "indispensably necessary," Washington believed that "peace or war are now in balance." He sent almost daily letters to Knox, whom he instructed to consult Hamilton and Randolph, in the absence of Jefferson. Hoping that perhaps the new Spanish militancy was not ordered from Madrid, Washington wished a protest made to the Spanish commissioners in Philadelphia against the actions of their officials in North America.* The protest, Washington pointed out, could be more effectively phrased if the Cabinet ministers who were on duty could find in Jefferson's files the previous communications with the Spanish commissioners. If, however, Jefferson had put the records "among the private transactions in his own keeping . . . no information can be obtained in time."[17]

When Washington informed the vacationing Secretary of State concerning the gravity of the situation on the frontier, he made the depressing intelligence a preamble to a lecture: "How unfortunate, and how much is it to be regretted then, that whilst we are encom-

---

* The cause of the militancy seems, indeed, to have been a new appointee in New Orleans, Hector, Baron de Carondelet. Being incapable of thought, he tinkered with action.

passed on all sides with avowed enemies and insidious friends, that internal dissensions should be harrowing and tearing our vitals. The last, to me, is the most serious, the most alarming, and the most afflicting of the two. And without more charity for the opinions and acts of one another in governmental matters; or some more infallible criterion by which the truth of speculative opinions, before they have undergone the test of experience, are to be forejudged than has yet fallen to the lot of fallibility, I believe it will be difficult, if not impracticable, to manage the reins of government or to keep the parts of it together. For, if, instead of laying our shoulders to the machine after measures are decided on, one pulls this way and another that, before the utility of the thing is fairly tried, it must, inevitably, be torn asunder. And, in my opinion, the fairest prospect of happiness and prosperity that ever was presented to man will be lost, perhaps forever!

"My earnest wish and my fondest hope therefore is that, instead of wounding suspicions and irritable charges, there may be liberal allowances, mutual forbearances, and temporizing yieldings on *all sides.* Under the exercise of these, matters will go on smoothly and, if possible, more prosperously. Without them, everything must rub; the wheels of government will clog, our enemies will triumph, and, by throwing their weight into the disaffected scale, may accomplish the ruin of the goodly fabric we have been erecting."

Washington notified Jefferson that he had sent similar observations to other officers of the government.[18] On the same day, indeed, he wrote Hamilton. His opening statement, that he had not yet been able to give "the attentive reading I mean to bestow" to Hamilton's defense of his policies, may well have been a ruse to protect him from having to make specific comments that would involve taking sides. Then he said that differences of political opinion are "as unavoidable as, to a certain point, they may, perhaps, be necessary." Yet subjects should be discussed with good temper and without impugning motives. "Regret borders on chagrin when we find that men of abilities, zealous patriots, having the same *general* objects in view and the same upright intentions" could not exercise "charity" towards each other. "When matters get to such lengths, the natural inference is that both sides have strained the cords beyond their bearing, and that a middle course would be found the best, until experience shall have decided on the right way."

Having denounced, in somewhat the same words as he had employed to Jefferson, the divisions that were tearing the union, Washington opined hopefully, "I cannot prevail on myself to believe that these measures are as yet the deliberate acts of a determined party."[19]

Jefferson and Hamilton both answered Washington's pleas for unity on September 9, the former from Monticello, the latter from his desk at the capital.

Jefferson stated that at the very beginning of his service as Secretary, he had been "duped" by Hamilton into supporting funding and assumption, being thus made a "tool" for forwarding Hamilton's evil schemes. He had never meddled with the legislature as Hamilton had. Repeating his charges that Hamilton bought votes, he insisted that all legislators who stood to profit from Hamilton's stratagems should have refrained from voting on them. Since they had not refrained, Jefferson did not consider their decisions as "the measures of the fair majority which ought always to be respected."

He had, Jefferson continued, never interfered in Hamilton's department, but Hamilton had, "by his cabals with members of the legislature" blocked the policy, which Jefferson believed (correctly) had been Washington's preference as well as his own: rewarding France in the customs laws for her liberality and retaliating on Britain for her restrictions. Hamilton had furthermore conferred privately with ambassadors and distorted his reports on those conversations to serve his own ends.

Most disingenuously (as Washington may or may not have realized) Jefferson tried to evade the charge that he had imported Freneau to start an opposition newspaper. "I cannot recollect whether . . ." when he had offered Freneau a job in his department, "I was told he had a thought of setting up a newspaper."* However, "I can protest in the presence of heaven" that he had never attempted to influence what was published in the *National Gazette*. His expectations in relation to that newspaper "looked only to the chastisement of the aristocratical and monarchical writers, and not to any criticisms on the proceedings of government." How dare Hamilton try to make capital

---

* According to Malone, Madison was the prime mover, but his object in importing the well-known journalist "was far from a secret to Jefferson."[20]

out of Freneau when the Secretary himself wrote—something Jefferson had never stooped to do—scurrilous attacks for his own servile press under an alias![21]

Hamilton's reply was much shorter. Where Jefferson had woven a dubious web to cover up his role in public controversy, Hamilton admitted his role. He stated that he had tried to abate newspaper attacks on Jefferson until he had realized that Jefferson was behind the formation of a party in the legislature "bent upon my subversion" and "the subversion of measures which, in its consequences, would subvert the government." He insisted (Washington knew that this was not true) that Jefferson and his supporters wished to undo the funding system. This would "prostrate the credit and the honor of the nation," and "bring the government into contempt with that description of men who are in every society the only firm supporters of government." Since he found his own reputation and the nation thus endangered, "I have had some instrumentality of late in the retaliations which have fallen upon certain public characters, and . . . I find myself placed in a situation not to be able to recede *for the present.*"

Hamilton expressed no yearning for retirement, but stated that, should the breaches in the administration continue, "in my opinion the period is not remote when the public good will require *substitutes* for the *differing members* of your administration. The continuance of a division there must destroy the energy of government. . . . On my part, there will be a most cheerful acquiescence" to a change of Secretaries. However, "it is my most anxious wish, as far as may depend upon me, to smooth the path of your administration and to render it prosperous and happy." Although he considered himself "the deeply injured party . . . I pledge my honor to you, sir, that if you shall hereafter form a plan to reunite the members of your administration upon some steady principle of cooperation, I will faithfully concur in executing it during my continuance in office. And I will not directly or indirectly say or do a thing that shall endanger a feud."[22]

The replies from Jefferson and Hamilton increased Washington's concern because the rancor of the two men against each other was too clear to be overlooked. Washington had (as he was to tell Jefferson) previously recognized a marked difference in "political sentiments" between his Secretaries, but had "never suspected it had gone so far in producing a personal difference."[23]

Now, when the servant he had sent to Alexandria brought newspapers up his quiet driveway, Washington perused them with a more anxious eye. If the gazettes persevered in their abuse of public officers, "and this too without condescending to investigate the motives or the facts, it will be impossible, I conceive, for any living man to manage the helm or to keep the machine together."[24]

As he meditated on whether he would have to make the attempt, Washington could find "nothing agreeable of a domestic nature to relate. . . . Intermittent fevers" [malaria?] were striking down his slaves and servants as never before in his memory; and it was clear that his nephew would either die or have to move to a warmer climate, in either case leaving Mount Vernon without a competent manager. Washington knew of no possible replacement. That his affairs were so badly in need of his personal attention gave "additional poignancy" to his mounting fear that he could not escape re-election to the Presidency.[25]

Randolph wrote, warning of "civil war." Should such a conflict arise, "you cannot stay at home."[26]

Washington replied, "I will take no measure yet awhile that will not leave me at liberty to decide from circumstances and the best lights I can obtain on the subject."[27]

Needing to discover what the "circumstances" were, Washington found frustrating what he usually so enjoyed: Mount Vernon's isolation. "The truth is, I go out nowhere, and those who call upon me observe a silence which leaves me in ignorance." When Colonel Bassett came up from coastal Virginia on a visit, Washington looked forward to news recounted by an old friend, but Bassett "was seized, hand and foot, with the gout on the road and has not been out of his bed since, nor in a condition to communicate what he knows."[28]

Washington asked Lear "to find out from conversation, without appearing to make the inquiry," whether anybody in Philadelphia preferred anyone else for the Presidency. Lear replied that "the universal desire" was for Washington to continue; any other possibility aroused only "apprehension." This, however, was only the opinion of the north. What about the south? Washington asked Jefferson, when the Secretary finally appeared at Mount Vernon on September 31. "I told him," Jefferson noted, "that, as far as I knew, there was but one voice there which was for his continuance."[29]

Firm that Washington could not retire, Jefferson felt no such call of duty for himself. He explained "that I had constantly kept my eye on my own home, and could no longer refrain from returning to it." Washington argued that Jefferson was needed as a counterweight to Hamilton: "He thought it important to preserve the check of my opinions in the administration in order to keep things in their proper channel." For his own part, Washington would not decide whether he would accept or reject a second term until "a month before the day of election. [He seems to have meant not the popular elections but the day the President was selected by the Electoral College.]

"He finished," Jefferson wrote, "by another exhortation to me not to decide too positively on retirement, and here we were called to breakfast."[30]

On November 8, 1793, when most of the voters had already expressed their preferences for the offices open to direct balloting,* Washington still had not made up his mind. This is demonstrated by a letter (previously unpublished) written to the President by his charming and political friend Eliza Powel.

Washington was in Philadelphia for the lame duck session of the Third Congress. He had that day confided to the lady his "sentiments" and "intentions." When she was again alone, she composed—with many interlineations and feminine blots and more dashes than any other form of punctuation—eight pages of passionate argument that Washington should not follow his "inclinations" and refuse re-election. To withhold the feelings that gushed up within her, "would be inconsistent with my friendship with you."

For the student of Washington's character, the greatest interest of this letter is its revelation of how an able woman, the possessor of Washington's confidence and admiration, felt she could most effectively sway her friend. In stating that Washington should not allow his "diffidence of your abilities" to obscure the fact that he is indispensable, she comments, "Be assured that I am so superior to the meanness of adulation, as you are incapable of receiving it with pleasure." However, she does point out that "your very figure is calculated to inspire confidence with people whose simple good sense appreciates the noblest qualities of mind with the heroic form, when all is embellished by such remarkable hints of mildness and calm benevolence—and such was the first intention of nature, I believe."

---

* The Electoral College was selected in some states by popular vote, in some by the state legislatures.

In arguing that his retirement would be a disaster, she writes not of its effect on any class or group but on "the repose of millions." She does not mention Hamilton or Jefferson or any controversy over issues. In her one clear political reference—"the Federalists consider you their own and glory in the possession"—she surely uses the word Federalist in the older meaning that was still current: those who favored the Constitution and the central government. As to the menace Washington's continuance in office would dissipate, that is the destruction of "the glorious fabric of liberty." Her only statement that could have any class reference is that Washington would not be able to behold with "fortitude . . . the monster licentiousness with all his horrid attendants, exalted on its [the government's] ruins."

Eliza's principal emphasis is on an argument Jefferson and Madison had avoided and which Hamilton did not pursue far. Knowing "your sensibility with respect to public opinion," a friend has to point out "that a great deal of the well-earned popularity you are now in possession of will be torn from you by the envious and malignant should you follow the bent of your inclinations." Washington's enemies—surely he knew he had enemies!—would say "that a concurrence of unparalleled circumstances had [hitherto] attended you. That ambition has been the moving spring of all your acts," and that now, when things are hard and further satisfaction for his reputation is not promised, "you would take no further risks" for the people. It would even be said that he foresaw the collapse of the government and fled to keep from being crushed by the crash. "Give free exercise to those sentiments of patriotism and benevolence which are congenial to your bosom!" exhorts the lady. "Attend to their verdict—let your heart judge the truth—Its decrees will be confirmed by posterity!"

In closing, Washington's intimate asks, "But admitting that you could retire in a manner exactly conformable to your wishes and possessed of the benediction of mankind, are you sure that such a step would promote your happiness? . . . Have you not on some occasions found the consummation of your wishes the source of the keenest sufferings? . . . May the remnant of your days be happy and actively employed in the discharge of those duties which elevate and fortify the soul! And may you until the extremest of old age, enjoy the pure felicity of employing your whole faculties for the prosperity of the people for whose happiness you are responsible, for to you their hap-

[379]

piness is entrusted. Adieu. Believe me, as ever I am, your sincere, affectionate friend."[31]

Since no written reply is to be found among either the Powel or Washington papers, Washington must have answered his affectionate friend in conversation.

30

The Shades of the Prison House

W ASHINGTON was capable of generating great drama. However, at times when conventional men would have grasped an obvious opportunity, he sought none. He had slipped so inconspicuously into Cambridge to take command of the Continental Army that historical legend, abhorring a vacuum, fabricated an impressive ceremony under the "Washington Elm." When his army recaptured Boston, when his army recaptured Philadelphia, the Commander in Chief failed to appear for any triumphal parade. His acceptance of his first term as President had taken the passive form of not refusing, and his agreement to a second term was, if possible, even more silent. Surely he could not have himself stated when the decision was reached. Every day he drifted further down the river until he found himself out on the main.

The 1792 election was accompanied by a newspaper war which today seems of unbelievable scurrility. Hamilton leapt into print under a series of aliases: Amicus, Catullus, Scourge. In his hatred, he singled Jefferson out for personal attack, thus inadvertently establishing (as Malone points out) his enemy in the popular mind as the leader of the opposition.[1]

In its mythological retelling, the Jefferson-Hamilton feud has lost an aspect which works against the accepted interpretation of a duel between the supporters of humble farmers on one hand and would-be aristocrats on the other. Born into an old, landed aristocracy, Jefferson looked down on Hamilton and his followers as *nouveaux riches* and vulgar people who wished to exalt themselves above their betters.

No attitude could have been more infuriating to the proud, self-made, illegitimate immigrant from the Indies, and he found it doubly infuriating to be scorned as socially inferior by a politician who asserted that he himself was the "plain, simple, unambitious republican." Hamilton announced that he would tear off the veil and show Jefferson for what he really was: "a secret voluptuary; . . . the intriguing incendiary; the aspiring, turbulent competitor" who wished to be another Caesar or Catiline.[2]

Jefferson was too "astute"—the word is Malone's[3]—to write anonymous articles himself, but a team made up of Madison, Monroe, and Randolph rushed to the defense, ringing the tocsin against a legislature corrupted and a monarch desired. Surely the many should be supported against the few!

In a letter to Gouverneur Morris, Washington commented, "From the complexion of some of our newspapers, foreigners would be led to believe that inveterate political dissensions existed among us, and that we are on the very verge of disunion; but the fact is otherwise: the great body of the people now feel the advantages of the general government." The press was making trouble, but, so Washington continued, when the misrepresentations were placed in the balance opposite "the infinite benefits resulting from a free press," there could be no doubt concerning the pitch of the scale. He was to urge on Congress postal regulations that would encourage "the transmission of newspapers to distant parts of the country."[4]

Washington had been determined to take no part in the campaign. He thus expressed annoyance when a candidate in Maryland for the House, George Francis Mercer, let it be rumored that he had the President's support. To Mercer, Washington communicated his conviction that for him "the exercise of an influence (if I really possessed any) however remote would be highly improper, as the people ought to be entirely at liberty to choose whom they pleased to represent them in Congress." He had observed "the most scrupulous and pointed caution . . . not to express a sentiment . . . that could be construed by the most violent torture of the words into an interference in favor of one, or to the prejudice of another."* [5]

---

* In a manner typical of the way that Jeffersonian historians torture the record, Bowers claimed that, since Mercer was a Jeffersonian, Washington's refusal of the support he refused all candidates was "probably due to the importunity of Hamilton, who did not scruple to use him without stint."[6]

The Jeffersonians welcomed the results of the election as a considerable victory: the new House of Representatives would be more according to their ideas, although no one could give any accurate statistics, since political divisions were still wavy. How wavy was revealed by the Presidential aspect of the election.

Washington later admitted that he "would have experienced chagrin" had he not been returned to the Presidency by "a pretty respectable vote."[7] The Electoral College chose him, on February 13, 1793, unanimously.

To insiders, the contest for Vice President had added importance because it had been held up to Washington as a lure that he might, if conflict abated, be able to resign before the end of his second term. The Vice President would then be elevated before another election took place. As the incumbent, John Adams was an obvious candidate. The Hamiltonians supported him—although, since he was a crotchety New Englander not easily controlled, without enthusiasm. And so, with even less enthusiasm, did Jefferson. This was because the Anti-Federalists had revealed their still uncut roots in the controversies of the past by deciding to back Governor George Clinton of New York, who had strongly opposed the ratification of the Constitution. More recently, Clinton had stolen an election in his own state.

Jefferson desired a healthily strong vote for Clinton, which would frighten the "monocrats," but believed that the strength of Adams's personal services and worth would prevail over the demerit of his aristocratic tendencies.[8] The Electoral College gave Adams seventy-seven votes; Clinton, five; Jefferson four (all from Kentucky) and Aaron Burr one.

The Congress which convened in November 1792 and adjourned on March 1, 1793, was left over from the previous election. Since the Hamiltonians proposed no further important legislation and the Jeffersonians looked forward to more power in the next Congress, the session was for the most part given over to inconclusive bickering. The single major move was an effort of the Jeffersonians to set the stage for Hamilton's future disgrace.

It was not difficult to demonstrate that various of Hamilton's followers had enriched themselves through shady deals or even actual fraud. However, the jailing of Duer, formerly Hamilton's Assistant Secretary of the Treasury, had not wounded Hamilton's power. To achieve that end it would be necessary to pin something disgraceful on the leader himself. It seemed inconceivable to Jefferson and his supporters that Hamilton would set before his followers such a feast without having spooned into it himself. But how to catch him? The most promising lead that came the way of Hamilton's opponents—the claim of an imprisoned man that he had evidence which would disgrace the Secretary—proved to reveal not financial peculation but that the married Hamilton had been sleeping with the prisoner's wife and paying hush-money. Too gentlemanly (at least for the moment) to make capital out of this personal matter, the Jeffersonians launched what seemed to them a very clever political move.

They would have the House ask Hamilton for a complete accounting of all the acts of the Treasury since the government had started. But the request would be made so late in the session that Hamilton would not have time to prepare so complicated a report before adjournment. Thus the implication of dishonesty would hang over Hamilton through the summer, increasing popular suspicions; and then the charges would be considered by the new, more anti-Hamiltonian House.

Late in January, the request for records was voted. If this was a fishing expedition, historians have considered it justified, since Hamilton had kept the House in the dark about what use he had made of funds appropriated. The only unfair aspect of the maneuver was the timing, and this Hamilton circumvented by working night and day. To the amazement of his opponents, he presented his records to the House in plenty of time for them to be examined and acted on during the current session.

The agrarians knitted their brows over Hamilton's statistics, but, stare between the lines as hard as they could, they could find no evidence of personal dishonesty. (No such evidence has ever been discovered.) It did, however, come clear that Hamilton had, upon occasion, used appropriations for purposes other than those specified. Even if one object had avowedly been to shore up credit during the recent panic, the Jeffersonians remained convinced that such legerdemain must be aimed at nefarious ends. Jefferson characterized Hamilton to Washington as a "man who has the shuffling of millions backwards and forwards from paper into money and money into paper, from Europe to America and America to Europe." Washington assured Jefferson that he did not approve of the shifting around of appropriations, but he must have regarded the sin as minor, since he was capable of doing the same thing himself: in 1789, wishing to expedite a survey that would define a border with Canada, he had spent money appropriated for treaty negotiations with the southern Indians.[9]

Making the most extreme use of what irregularities could be found in the Treasury report, and adding to them a thick sauce of rancor and suspicion, Jefferson drew up a series of resounding charges against his fellow official which would, if passed, have forced Hamilton's dismissal. Jefferson's coadjutors felt it necessary to tone down their leader's strictures before presenting them as a resolution to the House.[10] Even in this watered form, the resolution was soundly defeated.

The round was Hamilton's. Meanwhile, three thousand miles away, events were taking place that were to change utterly the complexion of American politics.

In August 1792, the lack of success of French armies, one of them led by Lafayette, in an offensive against Austria and Prussia, had touched off in Paris mass Jacobin demonstrations. The Tuilleries was stormed, the King imprisoned, the Assembly disbanded, the constitution suspended, a provisional government set up under Danton, and a large National Convention elected to meet in September. Accused of treasonable collusion with the King, Lafayette was forced to flee France. This governmental upheaval was followed by revolutionary victories over an aristocratic army led by the Duke of Brunswick.

When the news reached Philadelphia in December, cheering crowds poured into the streets. The citizens assumed that the happenings in France represented a spread of their own influence. A kindling in Europe of the "Spirit of '76" presaged, it was believed, the downfall of all aristocracies: a republican utopia was about to embrace all mankind! To revel in support of the French revolutionaries became a ruling American passion. Cannon were fired by the hundreds, feasts mounted, oceans of liquor consumed; and the French marching song, "Ça ira! Ça ira!" was sung as a companion to—or often as a substitute for—the usual anthem, set to the tune of "God Save the King," which began "God Save Great Washington!"

Jefferson and his fellow anti-Hamiltonians observed these events with enchanted fascination. They had been unable, for all their attacks on assumption and the bank and the villainous Hamilton and presumed monarchical tendencies, to raise a coherent opposition. But now

[385]

an emotional issue had appeared, even if it had little direct relevance to America or American conditions. For, while the populace enshrined the French revolutionaries, the "monocrats," as Jefferson was now calling the Hamiltonians, could not hide the distrust and, indeed, the fear engendered in their breasts by the events in France. What Washington called "factions"—and we today call political parties—began to separate the people. And the Jeffersonians seemed clearly to be on the majority side.[11]

After the Electoral College had formally doomed Washington to a second term, the trapped official heard a rumor that Jefferson's Philadelphia house had been rented to another. In sadness, Washington concluded that he was in fact being deserted by his old friend. He had till then carefully refrained from mentioning "to any mortal" that Jefferson had spoken to him about resigning. Now he asked Randolph to determine what the situation really was.[12]

Jefferson thereupon (February 7, 1793) dropped in on the President. He stated that he had not "for some time" spoken to Washington on whether he would continue, since a bill before the Senate had threatened to weaken the foreign service into a department too inconsiderable to be worth his continued attention. But the bill that finally passed had been satisfactory. Furthermore, the American reactions to the news from abroad "have shown that the form our own government was to take depended much more on the events of France than anybody had before imagined." The tide, which had seemed to flow towards "the tassels and baubles of monarchy, is now getting back, as we hope, to a just mean: a government of laws addressed to the reason of the people and not to their weaknesses." Under the circumstances, Jefferson would be willing, if Washington had made no arrangements to the contrary, "to continue somewhat longer, how long I could not say, perhaps till summer, perhaps autumn."

Washington "expressed his satisfaction at my change of purpose, and his apprehensions that my retirement would be a new source of uneasiness to the public." He had that very day received an "alarming" report from Governor Lee about "the general discontent prevailing in Virginia of which he never had had any conception. . . . He proceeded to express his earnest wish that Hamilton and myself could coalesce in the measures of the government." He had spoken to Hamilton, "who expressed his readiness."

Jefferson replied that his concurrence was of little importance, since "I kept myself aloof from all cabal and correspondence on the subject of the government, and saw and spoke with as few as I could."* Jefferson then repeated that "my wish was to see both Houses of Congress cleansed of all persons interested in the bank or public stocks." It was true, he continued, that there were great discontents in the south: they were caused by the fact that southern "judgments and interests were sacrificed to those of the eastern states on every occasion," by the "corrupt squadron of voters in Congress at the command of the Treasury."

Washington made no answer beyond saying that he had himself remained in office because of strong solicitations after his return to Philadelphia. (Was Eliza Powel's one of these?) They had persuaded him that he had no choice but to continue what he described bitterly to Jefferson as "the extreme wretchedness of his existence while in office."[13]

As Washington braced himself for further unpleasant public tasks, he was assailed by two personal tragedies. His nephew George Augustine Washington died; and word came in that his spiritual son, Lafayette, had been thrown into an Austrian prison.

In relation to George Augustine, Washington could find comfort in generosity to his family. He hoped the widow would live at Mount Vernon—Washington gave her her own carriage—and he offered to undertake both the cost and the supervision of the education of the son, Fayette.[14]

All the more because of his position as President of the United States, which made interference in French or Austrian affairs unsuitable, Washington could do nothing to ameliorate the plight of Lafayette himself. Again his thoughts flew to the wife. The Marquise de Lafayette remained as a possible object of his care—that is, if he could find her. In response to an uncertain rumor that she had fled to Holland, Washington sent two hundred guineas to a Dutch banker, with a request that he make every effort to forward it to the lady. He enclosed a letter intended to shield the Marquise from any sense that

---

* Malone accepts the statement as for this date, although only a few days later Jefferson was to draft the resolutions attacking Hamilton he wished Giles to present in the House of Representatives.[15]

she was accepting charity. The sum he was sending, Washington wrote, "is, I am certain, the least I am indebted for services rendered me by Mr. de la Fayette, of which I never yet have received the account. . . . At all times and under all circumstances, you and yours will possess the regard of him who has the honor, etc."[16]

The first official problem raised by the changes in France was whether the United States should follow the aristocratic powers of Europe in refusing to recognize a government which had illegally overthrown the legitimate monarch. On this matter, the leader of the American Revolution had no hesitations. He agreed with Jefferson that the true basis of legitimacy was "the will of the people." He even backed Jefferson in writing officially that there had been an effusion of joy in the United States on seeing French "liberties . . . rise superior to foreign invasion and domestic trouble."[17]

A more practical consideration was whether the United States should pay to the new government impending installments of the debt incurred during the Revolution to the French crown. Here (to Jefferson's outrage) Hamilton urged caution—if the monarchy were reestablished, the French might refuse to credit the payments—but even Hamilton did not argue very hard, and it was agreed to pay not only the current debt but some little in advance.[18]

As usual, the issue of greater closeness to France or to England agitated the Cabinet. Hamilton suggested that the United States should obviate the danger of England's joining with Spain on the western frontier by agreeing to a continuation of England's commercial discrimination for ten years, and giving Canada "admission to some navigable part of the Mississippi." Washington answered dryly, "The remedy would be worse than the disease."[19]

Washington's mind was moving in the opposite direction. After the French victories at Spires, Worms, and Nice, he said to Jefferson, "It was time to endeavor to effect a stricter connection with France, and that G. Morris should be written to on this subject." Should the United States face joint action by Britain and Spain, "there was no nation on whom we could rely at all times but France." In his journal, Jefferson commented, "I did not need the successes of the republican arms in France, lately announced to us, to bring me to these sentiments."[20]

Word began coming in to America of the Terror. "We have had," Gouverneur Morris reported, "one week of unchecked murders in which some thousands have perished." From his post in the Nether-lands, Jefferson's protégé William Short wrote in horror that the French people had created "the most mad, wicked, and atrocious assembly that was ever collected."[21]

Jefferson thereupon wrote Short in indignation at his lack of faith. It was necessary that "many guilty people fell without the forms of trial and with them some innocent. These I deplore as much as anybody. . . . But I deplore them as I should have done had they fallen in battle." Rather than see the failure of the cause on which the liberty of the whole earth depended, "I would have seen half the earth deso-lated. Were there but an Adam and Eve left in every country, and left free, it would be better than as it now is." Jefferson added that these were the sentiments "of ninety-nine in a hundred of our citizens."[22]

Washington could not possibly have agreed with these sentiments. He had, of course, led battles, ordered men to kill as Jefferson had not. Yet he had labored, among the passions of warfare, to protect Tories from persecution. He believed that extralegal violence, whether initi-ated by aristocrats or republicans, traveled the same road. As he had put it to Lafayette, "Cool reason, which can alone establish a perma-nent and equal government, is as little to be expected in the tumults of popular commotion as an attention to the liberties of the people is to be found in the dark divan of a despotic tyrant."[23]

Washington's "reserve," so Jefferson wrote Short, had prevented the Secretary of State from discovering how the President felt towards France since the new developments until Short's immoderate letters "induced him to break silence." Then he had made it clear that he still "considered *France as the sheet anchor of this country and its friend-ship as a first object.*" Washington wished Short to desist from conver-sation "offensive to our allies."[24]

In late February, Vice President Adams's son-in-law, Colonel Wil-liam S. Smith, returned from Europe to announce himself an unofficial representative of France, although admittedly from a fallen govern-ment, that of the Gironde. He reported that the French intended to grant the United States great commercial privileges, particularly in the Indies, which they might even set free; they intended to attack Spain's South American possessions and would have no objection if, in the confusion, the United States took the two Floridas. They were sending a new ambassador, Edmond Charles Genêt, with full powers to ar-range all this. However, they wished Washington to know that "the

[389]

French ministers are entirely broken with Gouverneur Morris, shut their doors to him, and will never receive another communication from him." Smith confided that Morris had at his own table, in the presence of guests and servants, "cursed the French ministers as a set of damned rascals; said the King would still be replaced on his throne."*

Washington's response to this information was that Morris ought to be removed: "The moment was critical in our favor and ought not to be lost." However, he did not know where to turn for a representative to France. Jefferson suggested reversing Pinckney and Morris, sending the former to Paris and the latter to London. Washington replied that if the French so distrusted Morris, they would not be satisfied to see him in London.

Then Washington made a startling suggestion which does not receive due attention in the history books. The innumerable writers who have accused Washington of keeping Morris in Paris because of his own conservative prejudices, overlook the fact that Washington sought to replace him by the most conspicuous leader of the pro-French party in the United States.

"He then observed," Jefferson noted, "that, though I had unfixed the day on which I had intended to resign, yet I appeared fixed in doing it at no great distance of time; that in this case he could not but wish that I would go to Paris. . . . I possessed the confidence of both sides and might do great good; that he wished I could do it were it only to stay there a year or two."

Jefferson "told him that my mind was so bent on retirement that I could not think of launching forth again in a new business; that I could never again cross the Atlantic; and that, as to the opportunity of doing good, this was likely to be the scene of action, as Genêt was bringing powers to do the business here." Jefferson repeated, "I could not think of going abroad."

For once Washington was goaded into pointing out "that I had pressed him to continue in the public service and refused to do the same myself."

Jefferson replied that "the case was very different." Washington was irreplaceable but "a thousand others could supply my place to equal

---

* Morris's diary shows that he connived with the royalists, but his dispatches to the American government do not seem overly intemperate when we consider the violence and horror of the upheaval he was witnessing.[25]

Gouverneur Morris (left), the obviously mercurial, and Robert Morris, the seemingly solid: two financiers, of the same name but unrelated, who were Washington's close friends. Courtesy of the Pennsylvania Academy of the Fine Arts

advantage. Therefore, I felt myself free." He again urged Pinckney, and Washington again urged him to consider the matter "maturely."[26]

The pro-French hysteria made Jefferson's followers consider even such salutations as "sir" or "madam" disgustingly aristocratic. They addressed each other as "citizen" and (oh, delightful term!) "citess." When seen from such a viewpoint, Washington's formal entertainments and "fastidious" behavior seemed to glow as balefully as any crown.

An article in Freneau's newspaper, attributed to a simple farmer from Bucks County, stated, "There appears to be a great uproar in your city about levees." The fictitious farmer had assumed that these must be "some favorite republican distinction." What was his horror to discover levees to be "the legitimate offspring of inequality, begotten by aristocracy and monarchy upon corruption." He accused Washington of attempting to "blind" the people "with the glitter of distinction. . . . There will be a monstrous revolution in the opinions of the people of this country. . . . The freemen of America understood their rights and the dignity of their character too well to surrender them for the gratification of the ambition of any man, however well he may have deserved of his country."[27]

Such direct and personal thrusts at Washington were the first he had suffered since that time, almost fifteen years before, when the effort called the Conway Cabal had been made to remove him as Commander in Chief. It would not have been so bitter had he enjoyed his official entertaining, rather than have to drag himself to the occasions like an elderly cart horse to the thill. He complained "lengthily" to Jefferson that his unhappiness in office was being compounded by "the late attacks on him for levees, etc." If he could only discover the sense of the public in relation to entertaining, he assured Jefferson, "he would most cheerfully conform to it."[28]

Jefferson wrote Madison that Washington was "extremely affected by the attacks made and kept up on him in the public papers. I think he feels those things more than any person I ever yet met with. . . . I remember an observation of yours, made when I first went to New York, that the satellites and sycophants which surrounded him had wound up the ceremonials of the government to a pitch of stateliness which nothing but his personal character could have supported and which no character after him could ever maintain. It appears now that even his will be insufficient to justify them, in the appeal of the times, to common sense as the arbiter of everything. Naked he would have been sanctimoniously reverenced, but enveloped in the rags of royalty, they can hardly be torn off without laceration. It is the more unfortunate that this attack is planted on popular ground, on the love of the people to France and its cause, which is universal."

Jefferson stated that he was "sincerely sorry" to see Washington so hurt, but he made no effort to still or abate the attacks made by his partisans and his employee on his aging chief.[29] It was hardly an auspicious beginning for what would probably be four more years of enforced public service.

VI

Conclusion

The First Term Surveyed

W HEN Washington had set out to command the Continental Army, he had seen himself as engaged in a local
cause of great concern to himself and his compatriots:
they were driving tyrants from their fields. As the war progressed, his
vision enlarged until he believed his army was fighting to establish
the right of all people to govern themselves without outside interference, for liberty envisioned as the self-determination of peoples. This
was a noble cause but left open the question of what people would do
with their liberty when they had it. As he moved towards the Presidency, Washington was concerned with trying to answer, in the most
affirmative conceivable manner, that question.

During the war, he had known that victory was possible: Although
the situation might not work out that way, there was no overriding
philosophical reason why the British could not be defeated and independence be established. But no one knew whether mankind was
capable of achieving, in modern times and on a large scale, their own
happiness through self-government. Jefferson, for whom it was an act
of faith to believe that mankind was so capable, recognized correctly
that there was doubt in Washington's mind. He rather despised Washington for the doubt, but certainly there was little in the lessons of
history to dispel it; and that he did doubt made the mission on which
Washington was engaged for him all the more grievous. Although he
would never have described himself in such terms, he was rather like
Prometheus trying to bring fire down from heaven. If the United
States conclusively demonstrated that modern man could in a republi-

can manner establish freedom, prosperity, and justice, the whole course of history—so the proponents of progress believed—might be deflected, that ancient bloody river flowing, now clear as stainless crystal, to Utopia.

The responsibility of leading the experiment that could be the last great hope of the human race hung heavy on the shoulders of the man who had intended to spend the rest of his life in retirement, who felt that he had passed his physical prime, and who had never made a profound study of government. That he had been forced to borrow the cash that would carry him to New York and the Presidency showed that although his estate had grown in size and complexity, he had not been, from a businessman's point of view, successful. He had failed in his command during the French and Indian War. The Revolution had, it is true, ended up as a victory, but only after years of such anguishing travail as his physique would perhaps no longer bear. And the new task would surely be the hardest of all, since the outcome was so transcendently important. If the experiment failed through some fault of his own, how unforgivable would be the guilt that poisoned the future of mankind!

The first problem was to make the government which had been adopted, often by the thinnest of majorities, and in only eleven out of thirteen states, happily acceptable to the overwhelming majority of the entire population. The second problem, as Washington recognized, in actuality encompassed the first: it was to make the machinery of government function with the minimum of inner friction, to carry the nation ahead towards the linked goals of prosperity, peace, freedom.

The initial year of the experiment was given over to building, from the often vague blueprint supplied by the Constitution, the vehicle that was later to be driven. This was successfully accomplished, and Washington could look back contentedly to his part in the process. He had given auspices with his prestige, and used both that prestige and his daily intelligence to build a structure that rigidly observed the separation of powers. The executive had become strong under his cultivating, partly because he had been so meticulous not to invade the prerogative of the legislative.

Washington's conception of the Presidency was, although it perfectly suited the period of the formation of the government, quite far from that which operates today. Disapproving of factions, he did not see himself as the leader of any political party. Although he insisted on

[398]

being master in his executive house, it was contrary to his principles to try to influence elections or interfere with the legislature. It was his duty to enforce the laws as passed.

Washington, indeed, did not feel he would be justified in negating a law because he considered it ill-advised. He visualized the President's power to veto as in modern times we visualize the function of the Supreme Court.

During Washington's first term, the judiciary had not developed into a third, equal arm of the government. The Supreme Court ruled on the validity of state laws in relation to the Constitution, but did not interfere with acts of the national legislature. The justices traveled on circuit nationally as judges of less jurisdiction did regionally. After Washington had been in office for a little more than a year, he referred to Chief Justice Jay as one of his "coadjutors" in the administration of the government. During his first two years or so, he consulted Jay on Cabinet decisions and in general asked him for advice which he hoped "may not be confined to matters merely judicial, but extended to all other topics." Although after that Jay stepped further away into his own function, as late as 1794, Washington thought that the Chief Justice might consider it a step up to become Ambassador to England. Washington believed that determining of the constitutionality of a Congressional act was among his duties and the correct basis for his use of the veto.[1]

Seeking the most brilliant possible help in carrying out his functions, Washington in three shots hit the bull's-eye every time. No historian would deny that the most important American statesmen in the generation after Washington were Madison, Hamilton, and Jefferson. To recognize such a constellation revealed the insight of genius; to get three such men in a single harness required both genius and the complexion of the times.

As Washington began steering the government, the major political conflict was between those who supported and those who opposed the Constitution. Although some "revisionist" modern historians argue that the Articles of Confederation was an adequate instrument and the Constitution unnecessary, one has to suspend common sense to believe that a nation covering a vast geographic area could in the long range operate effectively as an alliance of semi-autonomous political powers. When Washington took office, the leading opponents of the Constitution were almost all older men—George Mason, Patrick Henry, George Clinton, Samuel Adams, John Hancock—whose unshaken political convictions had been imbibed at the time of the Revolution. Although himself an older man, Washington was marching with the younger generation. Since the younger generation was marching with him, he was able to get together its three most fruitful leaders; all agreed that the federal government must be made to work.

Once the wheels of that government were really turning and the opposition to it as an entity had sunk to the growls and whispers and old-fogeyism, Washington's brilliant younger men began pulling not as a group but apart. This, with Washington's attempt to keep them working together, supplies the drama of the second half of his term—a drama that was far from completed as the term came to an end.

The conflict between Washington's coadjutors cannot be viewed, as is too often done, in relation to more recent Cabinet practice. As we have seen, Washington did not use the word "Cabinet" until April 1793,[2] and he did not call formal meetings of "the Heads of the Great Departments" until close to the end of his first term, when he hoped that such consultations would help him calm down disagreements already rampant.

Washington had brought to the Presidency experience gained in his last major executive post: the command of the army. He had felt even more diffident of his abilities to lead an army than he was later to feel about leading a nation. At the start of his command, he called his generals together into Councils of War; when they voted him down, he gave way to their decisions. But as he became more at home in his job, he greatly reduced the number of formal councils. He now preferred to make up his mind privately, after collecting information and advice from many sources, including, of course, his generals. Obviously, it would have been ridiculous to limit each officer to discussing his specific responsibility; the right wing could not move into battle without the left; the artillery might be brought to bear anywhere.

When in 1793, Washington offered the Secretaryship of War to C. C. Pinckney, he explained that, although the specific duties of the office were not taxing, a Secretary was "a branch of the executive and called to its councils upon interesting questions of national importance." All Secretaries should thus be possessed of "a general knowledge of political subjects." Washington wrote Hamilton, "Having no other wish than to promote the true and permanent interests of this country, I am anxious always to compare the opinions of those in whom I confide with one another, and those again (without being bound by them) with my own, that I may extract all the good I can."[3]

Washington's method for reaching a decision had been, at least since Revolutionary times, to balance arguments as on a pair of scales and then follow the direction that tipped the beam. This method gave special value to the availability of able advisers and double importance to the presence in his Cabinet, when conflict arose, of the leading exponents of the opposite points of view. But it further encouraged him to obliterate, on the higher policy levels, the divisions between the various departments. There was no need for Hamilton to hide his friendly association with the British diplomatic representatives, since Washington (who did not suspect that Hamilton was giving away Cabinet secrets) found this (even if it crossed over into Jefferson's specialty) useful to his gathering of information. As we have seen, he could even make a decision concerning foreign affairs in consultation with other Secretaries than Jefferson.

Jefferson encouraged interference in his department by absenteeism. Slow communication, but even more his own slowness in making up his mind, had brought him to the capital months after Hamilton was at his desk. And Hamilton stayed at his desk while Jefferson took long vacations at Monticello from which even Washington's appeals that he appear for consultation failed, on at least one important occasion, to budge him. As Washington was often also away, this tended to put the ship of state under the immediate command of Hamilton.

One of Jefferson's favorite charges, that Hamilton interfered in his department, has been endlessly echoed by historians. It is not so often pointed out that Jefferson interfered to the best of his ability in Hamilton's. His advice that Washington should veto the bank bill was, of course, given at the President's request, but the fact remains that had it been acceded to, that would have toppled Hamilton's financial system. Having failed in an effort to get the radical Thomas Paine appointed Postmaster General, Jefferson tried (vainly) to wrest the post office, so important because of its role in disseminating information, away from the Treasury into his own bailiwick. On another occasion, Jefferson forwarded to the President, with a suitable blank commission, the application of his own candidate, Tench Coxe, for the second post in the Treasury, although he knew that Hamilton favored Oliver Wolcott, Jr. Had Washington obliged Jefferson (which he did not) the Secretary of State would have had a hand on the steering wheel of the Treasury.[4]

For his part, Washington saw nothing unsuitable in encroachments or attempted encroachments, for he envisioned the government as a team in which, despite the disagreements and arguments on particular matters that are inherent in human endeavor, all were playing on the same side.

A variation of functions seemed to the President viable only on the lower administrative level—and even there he kept a sharp and perpetual eye on all that transpired. However much Jefferson may have at the time felt confined by Washington's practice, when he himself became President, he outlined the procedure to his own subordinates as a good one. Most letters, he explained, had come directly to the department heads. If one was addressed to Washington, he would refer it to the Secretary most concerned. Should a Secretary decide that a letter required no reply, he would nonetheless communicate it to the President "for his information." Letters which the Secretary answered were also sent, with the proposed reply attached. In most cases, Washington returned the papers without comment, "which signified his approbation. Sometimes," so Jefferson continued, "he returned them with an informal note, suggesting an alteration or a query. If a doubt of any importance arose, he reserved it for conference. By this means, he was always in accurate possession of all facts and proceedings in every part of the Union, and to whatsoever department they related, he formed a central point for the different branches; preserved an unity of object and action among them; exercised that participation in the suggestion of affairs which his office made incumbent on him; and met himself the due responsibility for whatever was done."[5]

Despite this testimony of Jefferson's, Washington was not, as many writers claim, a systematic administrator. His method of handling problems became, indeed, the less predictable the more the importance of the issue increased the intensity of his efforts. Acting pragmatically in response to the immediate situation, he would sometimes reach a decision entirely on his own; sometimes authorize his Secretaries to make decisions as a group; sometimes throw a matter altogether into the lap of one Secretary; sometimes ask that papers be drafted for him and sometimes draft a paper for a Secretary to sign; sometimes, the matter being "more immediately" in a Secretary's department, ask him to draw up a list of questions to be answered by his colleagues or in discussion; sometimes draw up his own list, or get one from a Secretary less immediately involved. When he held Cabinet meetings, he would call for a vote or would not call for one, pay attention to the tally or brush it aside. His ministers, even the transcendently able Secretaries of State and the Treasury, were never actually denied authority, but at the same time they were given no final authority that they could count upon. The top machine of government was Washington's own brain. His fundamental function as President lay, he believed, in "obeying the dictates of my conscience."[6]

In his relations with both the Continental Congress and the federal Congress, Washington never reached, in any manner that would open him to a denial, beyond his right and power to command. As he confessed on one occasion, to have his opinions disregarded "could not fail to wound his feelings."[7] A determination to be in complete control within the area across which he operated had always been for Washington a ruling passion.

During the French and Indian War, this obsession had thrown him, whenever he was not clearly the top officer, into friction with his rivals and superiors. During the Revolution, effective and ambitious men had found it difficult to get on in close association with him, although some, like Lafayette and Nathanael Greene, remained his devoted disciples. Now he had gathered around him the three ablest statesmen of the younger generation.

Madison got off easiest. Even during those initial months, when he had been Washington's closest adviser, he had had his own province as a leading member of the House. After the department heads were appointed, he was called in only occasionally. He did not, like Hamilton and Jefferson, have to struggle to keep upright in daily association with the overpowering genius who was the President.

Hamilton had faced the situation before. When, as a young man, he had been in effect Washington's chief of staff, he had at first tried to protect his personality by rejecting Washington's overtures of friendship, keeping their relationship altogether official. But at last he had picked with the Commander in Chief a fight that enabled him to present an angry resignation. Although Washington apologized and begged the youth to remain, Hamilton had had enough: He stamped away—and into relative obscurity.

Having been, while on Washington's staff, at the heart of the military effort, Hamilton had, on breaking with Washington, lost much of his power. He was no slow learner. Although years were to pass before he was again presented with the opportunity, he began a study of his own and Washington's character that would enable him not to fight against the great human force but to channel it towards the ends he himself wished to achieve.

The historian Richard Morris has written, "No doubt the subject of the Washington-Hamilton relationship would provide a psychoanalyst with opportunities to expatiate on father images and father substitutes, on inferiority complexes, narcissism, and the sense of insecurity." Without entering this haunted forest, it is possible to conclude that Hamilton got to know himself well enough to realize—although he did sometimes have resplendent visions—that he lacked the balance to occupy the very top of the political pyramid. Again and again, he was driven by a perverse integrity, a fierce self-will to extreme acts like his majestically indiscreet and utterly pointless speech in which he proposed to the Constitutional Convention what seemed very like an American limited monarchy. Although he could not peer far enough through time to know that this inflamed crack in his judgment would make him accept a challenge that would leave him dying with a dueler's bullet in his belly, he did realize that if he were to operate successfully, "an aegis" was "very essential to me."[8]

Many a historian has found a key to Hamilton's character in the fact that he did not come from the British Indies until he was in his late teens, that he was not really an American. Certainly, he became able to reconcile his tremendous pride to at least an appearance of subservience. He had no theoretical objection to monarchical forms, and in a monarchy legitimate ambition did not go beyond being the King's first minister. Hamilton was so sure that the Treasury was the first office under the President that he sometimes suspected that Jefferson was opposing him out of a personal desire to step up from State to Treasury.[9]

To use Washington as an aegis did not, in Hamilton's mind, involve more frankness than was politic. Far from repeating his old mistake of visible rebellion, he never conspicuously disobeyed an order; he professed loyalty and seemed to live up to his professions. When he felt it necessary to work at cross purposes with the demiurge he served, he receded into secret shadows. Since the Treasury had its own connection with the legislature and Washington was not, in any case, familiar with the complications of finance, Hamilton could be open enough on Treasury business. It was when he wished to control foreign policy that, skirting close to the edges of treason, he plotted with British agents.

Of Washington's three major advisers, Jefferson walked the most difficult road. Not only did the State Department have no connection with Congress which did not pass through the President, but Washington had, during his retirement after the Revolution, made a study of international affairs that enabled him, on assuming the Presidency, to act as his own foreign minister. Jefferson was allowed most autonomy in those aspects of his office—the details of internal administration—which had most induced him to hesitate about accepting the appointment.[10]

Malone tells us that when Jefferson began his collaboration with Washington, his respect for the President amounted almost to reverence.[11] Jefferson was glad to serve as an extra pair of hands for the fellow Virginian he so admired. But the very closeness of this beginning made the continuance more emotionally shattering. The story of the city of Washington is symbolic. Historians have argued that their common interest in erecting a southern capital was a bond tying Washington and Jefferson together. But it was an equivocal bond. Jefferson, who had been to Europe where Washington had never been, who professed a knowledge of architecture as Washington did not, found himself overwhelmed, not consulted on the most important aesthetic decisions. Carrying out obediently orders of which he did not approve, he was surely, although he did not complain, resentful.

Jefferson's anger over Hamilton's policies is, of course, spread across the record. Hamilton had been in full flow of those policies when Jefferson came onto the scene. Having brought with him no program of his own, Jefferson was at first caught up in the flood. He had eventually pulled himself with difficulty to shore, still dripping with what he now considered the distasteful moisture of Hamiltonianism. He now wished Washington to come ashore too, but Washington did not. And whenever there was a vote in Congress, Hamilton won.*

Jefferson's growing unhappiness during Washington's first term did not make him strike out at Washington as Hamilton had done years before. Nor did he cease to serve in his official capacity with complete obedience. He engaged in no such dark maneuverings as Hamilton permitted himself with the British agents. Although he eventually could hold back no longer from jousting with Hamilton outside the government, he could not bring himself to admit to Washington (as Hamilton freely did) that he was in part responsible for the newspaper war.

When his arguments against Hamilton's policies failed to move the President, Jefferson decided to resign. Yet he never made clear that his desire to withdraw was motivated by disagreements over policy or implied that concessions to his ideas would keep him in the Cabinet. The reasons he gave for his intended retirement were altogether personal. He spoke of his dislike for public office and his yearning for the pleasures of plantation life.

Hamilton professed loyalty to Washington, but Jefferson professed none. This conspicuous lack may have been motivated in part by a feeling that Washington was, like an all-powerful father, in himself too strong to need support. Reticence above expressing strong emotions may also have been involved. But another motivation was surely the anger of a person who feels that his affections have been betrayed.

In his later years, Jefferson insisted that he and his followers had felt "love and gratitude" towards Washington greater than "the pharisaical homage of the federal monarchists." Certainly, Jefferson's disapproval of Hamilton's policies was colored by personal jealousy concerning Washington. Jefferson and the President were old friends, fellow Virginians sharing the ties of a mutually inherited culture. Jefferson had started his service as the absolute epitome of loyalty to his chief—and yet Washington had shown, in various major matters of policy, more confidence in Hamilton. The elderly Jefferson, having expressed, in memory, admiration for the "purity" of Washington's integrity, went

---

* The interpretation that since Hamilton never lost a vote he got everything he wanted is, of course, faulty. The third major section of his program, the encouragement of manufactures, was never brought to a vote.

on to characterize Washington as "inflexible" because his justice was uninfluenced by "motives of interest or consanguinity or friendship or hatred." Washington's "heart was not warm in its affections; but he exactly calculated," so Jefferson continued, "every man's value and gave him a solid esteem proportioned to it."[12]

Jefferson came to exercise, in his sessions with Washington, what might be considered sadism. In one breath, he insisted that his elderly chief, who was yearning for rest at Mount Vernon, might not retire. In the next breath, he described the pleasures he himself would have in his own retirement at Monticello. Although Washington had, when Commander in Chief, sometimes appealed in personal terms to his subordinates not to desert him, he now went no further in trying to stir Jefferson's emotions than to describe how unhappy he was in office. Jefferson listened without sympathetic response, and then continued to describe to the President his own anticipations of relaxation. After his return to his lodgings, he noted Washington's protestations with a stony, clinical hand.

When Jefferson finally decided that he could not retire under fire and that the future looked rosier than he had expected for his policies, when he finally agreed to stay in Washington's Cabinet, he acquiesced in a new method for torturing his chief. He did not intervene to hinder his employee Freneau from assaulting Washington with virulent personal attacks.* To Madison, Jefferson expressed regret that Washington should be made unhappy, but added that infliction of pain on the President was essential. He described Washington's suffering without any warmth or sympathy.[13]

The conception, so beloved of American historical legend, that Washington became during his first term a tool of Hamilton's has been one of the few ideas on which Jeffersonian and Hamiltonian historians have agreed; it has served equally the purposes of both persuasions. On one hand, it justified Jefferson's eventual break with Washington. On the other, it augmented the importance of Hamilton. Yet the interpretation is now recognized as contrary to fact. Washington was far

---

* Freneau was, of course, his own man, but, in his note on an angry conversation he had had with Washington on May 23, 1793, Jefferson acknowledged that he could "interfere" with the acts of the journalist if he wished to. "I will not do it," Jefferson continued. "His paper has saved our Constitution, which was galloping fast into monarchy."[14]

from being any man's tool. Nor was he by any means in his own right ineffectual.

Since controversy makes exciting reading, the fracas over Hamilton's financial policies tends to occupy most space in accounts of Washington's first term. The President's quieter achievements in setting the governmental machine going are usually assigned a second place. Yet it is highly significant that the divisive forces did not pull apart the solidity of the government which had been Washington's first concern.

In the area of finance, the debate was not between alternative lines of positive action, but over whether to approve, modify, or disapprove of Hamilton's proposals. Washington went along with Hamilton, but not automatically or all the way. He hesitated as to whether he should veto the bank and continued to say that if that charter proved a mistake, it could be rescinded. And his belief that Hamilton's program on manufactures was impractical and probably unconstitutional contributed to the abandonment of that report.

In foreign policy, the President and Hamilton were at odds. During the Confederation, Washington had regarded as a major argument for a stronger federal government the need for a uniform customs policy that could be used to retaliate against British trade restrictions. As President, both before and after the arrival of Jefferson, Washington had done all that he considered within the province of his office to urge laws that would put on British ships the restrictions the British put on the American. And he backed Jefferson's pro-French recommendations to Congress. All these efforts failed. They failed because of the Hamiltonian conviction that trade with Britain was essential to American prosperity in general and particularly to the customs duties that supplied the revenue on which the government ran. Furthermore, Hamilton and his supporters nurtured an admiration for Britain which the former Commander in Chief did not share. He still felt dislike for his old enemies, and also affection for the French who had fought by his side.

Washington did not blame Hamilton for the failure of his commercial policies because he did not agree that Hamilton's influence in the Congress was excessive. He felt that he was bowing not to the will of his Secretary but to the will of the branch that was empowered by the Constitution to make the laws that the executive enforced.

Jefferson agreed that the legislature should be the mainspring of the government, and it was for this reason that he was particularly upset when he felt that Congress was being polluted by Hamilton's "corrupt squadron." He was, in fact, being perturbed by a phenomenon which he did not in its profoundest implications correctly identify: Hamilton's organization of his supporters was the first major step towards the creation in the United States of a machine hitherto unknown to government: the modern political party.

Discussions of when and how political parties arose in the United States are menaced by varieties in the use of the word. The division over whether the Constitution should be ratified is sometimes considered a conflict of parties, and, as we have seen, Madison was by 1792 describing his supporters and those of Hamilton as opposing parties. But, as the elections exemplified, these were not parties in the modern sense, not broad, cohesive alliances, with a central structure and some internal discipline, which spread across a large segment or all of the nation. Such parties belonged to the future, even in that cradle of parliamentary government, England.

As the historian William Nisbet Chambers points out, the labels Whig and Tory as then used in England "denoted general persuasions rather than distinct political formations." Political maneuvering took place not between formal organizations but between personalities and personal followings. The result was a kaleidoscope of shifting combinations and alliances which made the legislative process invisible to the electorate and thus prevented the people from influencing decisions on a national scale.[15]

When he entered the administration, Jefferson was as opposed as was Washington to those fractional precursors of true political parties which they both denounced as "factions." It was only to fight Hamiltonianism that, following the lead of Madison, he began trying to envision some combination that would extend over local lines. At the end of Washington's first term, Madison's and Jefferson's firm influence still did not go beyond Virginia. This did much to explain their about-faces on matters of governmental theory. If they failed to honor the convictions of the Virginia electorate, they would have been left without political support.

As a matter of fact, neither Washington, nor Hamilton—who was to travel the road towards true parties less far than his opponents—nor Madison, nor Jefferson clearly envisioned the complicated political forms which were to prove inherent in representative democracy. The conception of a tug of war between nationally organized groups, all equally loyal, lay so far in the future that Jefferson found in the past an explanation of why Congress—which in theory he revered—voted in a manner he considered contrary to the popular interest. He envisioned not the type of controversy with which we are now familiar—different groups competing to serve their special interests—but such a conspiracy of evil men as sometimes perverted the councils of kings.

Seen in modern terms, the extent to which Jefferson was justified in outrage depends on the line one draws between legitimate and illegitimate conflicts of interest in government. Down the years, this line has remained so imprecise that in specific instances arguments have usually turned less on abstract moral principles than on the efforts of the arguers to discredit those who stand in their way. Senator Robert Kerr of Oklahoma observed, "If everyone abstained on the grounds of personal interest, I doubt you could get a quorum in the United States Senate on any subject."[16]

Washington, for his part, shook his head sadly when Jefferson insisted that, in order to make the legislature "honest," everyone who owned securities that were involved in governmental policy—which meant in effect the whole financial community—should be prevented from voting on financial measures. Washington, who had for so many years seen so many people try to exclude so many other people from the national councils, could not help noticing that Jefferson did not suggest that no agrarians, no land speculators, no slaveholders be permitted to vote on matters of special import to them. He replied to Jefferson "that, as to that interested spirit in the legislature, it was what could not be avoided in any government unless we were to exclude particular descriptions of men . . . from all office."[17]

Since Washington believed that there were not more than ten influential men in the entire United States who desired an American king,[18] Jefferson further weakened his arguments in Washington's mind by insisting that Hamilton led a monarchical party. Washington had for more than twenty years heard charges of royalism reiterated as insults to himself and blocks across roads he considered important. No sooner had he been elected Commander in Chief than John Adams had assumed he would, unless his wings were kept clipped, soar onto a throne. The fear of an ambitious general at the head of an effective army had throughout the war damaged his efforts to create a powerful instrument with which to fight the British. And during the controversies that had preceded first the Constitution and then its ratification, the opponents of central government had perpetually conjured up the specter of a scepter and a crown.

Jefferson undoubtedly revived the old cry in part because "monarchy" was at that time—as "communism" is today—the most damaging epithet, but there was more to the matter than that. The United States had recently cast off a king and was still surrounded with kings. No one possessed the clairvoyance to realize that the capitalism Hamilton had copied from England would in the long run be history's most effective underminer of royalty. No American was able to foresee the type of tyranny which would actually be created by excessive financial power in the hands of an oligarchy. Jefferson's sensitive antennae indicated the approach of a monster, but failed to identify the beast. He called it not "capitalist exploitation" but "monarchy."

Hamilton's freely if indiscreetly expressed admiration for monarchy as an administrative system and his doubts that a republic was workable were, of course, known to Washington. Yet Washington believed that Hamilton believed (what Hamilton had told the skeptical Jefferson) that only "a depraved mind . . . would not prefer the equality of political rights, if it can be obtained consistently with order."[19] It was clear to Washington that Hamilton's schemes, by assisting order, were further dimming the already dim chances of an American monarchy. Thus Jefferson's cries of alarm did not frighten the President.

Nor was he frightened by Hamilton's warnings. He knew that Jefferson had not actually opposed the Constitution as charged: Jefferson had, in fact, welcomed it with the addition of a Bill of Rights which Washington was glad to accept. He also knew that the anti-Hamiltonians—was not that architect of the Constitution Madison one of their leaders?—were not now trying to dismember the Union. Despite Hamilton's insistence that Jefferson was determined to destroy the credit of the government,[20] Washington accepted as sincere Jefferson's admission that, since the honor of the government was involved, funding and assumption could not be recalled. Jefferson, it was true, would have liked to rescind the bank's charter, but this was a matter of judgment that in no way impugned the Secretary of State's usefulness or integrity.

Although he preferred not to encourage disagreements by commenting on them, Washington could not have been oblivious of the differences in political philosophy between Jefferson and Hamilton. The conflict seemed to Washington in no way surprising, since humans almost always started out with varying approaches to life. The need, Washington believed, was to find a road that almost all men could travel, each carrying his principles snugly on his back. It seemed to Washington that, since the charges the two Secretaries made against each other were invalid, there was no reason that they could not, by sinking suspicions and applying good will, agree on specific measures.

Washington came to this conclusion the more easily because his own mind was unconcerned with theoretical speculation. Certain broad principles came to him as revealed truth: Freedom was better than tyranny; order than chaos; kindness than cruelty; peace than war. Royalty was evil; the government belonged to the people and should be responsive to their will. The pursuit of happiness, which it was the government's duty to encourage, included the pursuit of property; no man or groups of men, rich or poor, should be allowed to steal from each other. Government should be strong enough to protect as well as foster. No nation should dominate any other, and the United States in particular should keep out of foreign quarrels.

Washington felt that trying to push directly against all obstacles as you steered by compass was no way to reach a difficult objective. The art of road building (had he not as a stripling built the first road that carried wheels across the Alleghenies into the western wilderness?) was to work out how best to get, without losing your bearings, around that cliff, across that run. Problems never appeared in Washington's mind shorn of particular circumstances; decisions always involved a choice of practical alternatives. It now seemed to him petty to engage in passionate controversy (as he himself had when an unwhipped cub) as to whether the road should run past a particular impediment to the left or the right. If the expedient decided on proved to be a mistake, you could backtrack to the last point that had been successfully reached and try the other way. That is, as long as the ultimate goal remained clear; and Washington could see no real division between his advisers concerning the ultimate goal.

He wrote Jefferson and undoubtedly said the same thing to Hamilton, "I will frankly and solemnly declare that I believe the views of both of you are pure and well meant; and that experience alone will decide with respect to the salubrity of measures which are the subject of dispute. Why then, when some of the best citizens in the United States, men of discernment, uniform and tried patriots, who have no sinister views to promote, but are chaste in their ways of thinking and acting, are to be found, some on one side and some on the other of the questions which have caused these agitations, should either of you be so tenacious of your opinions as to make no allowances for those of the other?" He hoped that "the cup which has been presented may not be snatched from our lips by a discordance of *action,* when I am persuaded there is no discordance in your *views.* I have a great, a sincere esteem and regard for you both, and ardently wish that some line could be marked out by which both of you could walk."[21]

Of his three great assistants, Washington had, at the start of his Presidency, felt warmest towards Madison, next towards Jefferson, and last towards Hamilton. Although his friendship for Madison remained alive—he turned to his old adviser to help him with his proposed farewell address—it gradually receded, in part, perhaps, through lack of propinquity.

That Washington's feelings for Jefferson should become increasingly equivocal as his first term drew to its close was inevitable under the circumstances. However, in no record from that period did he accuse Jefferson of disloyalty. Although he complained of unfair attacks, he did not make it clear (as he was later to do) that he thought Jefferson should curb Freneau. Once a hint did slip out that he suspected Jefferson of dealing with him disingenuously. After L'Enfant's successor, Ellicott, had resigned as superintendent of the capital city, blaming his dissatisfaction on Jefferson, Washington wrote his intimate Stuart that Jefferson insisted he had done nothing to offend Ellicott, "having shown me the *only* letters which (he says) he has written to him for many months."[22]

If Jefferson sank in Washington's esteem, Hamilton rose. Although both seemed equally to blame in their squabble, Hamilton was franker in admitting his part in the controversies outside the Cabinet, and Washington never suspected that he was undermining official policy in secret confidences to British envoys. Hamilton had not dawdled in accepting his appointment as Jefferson had done; he expressed no real desire to leave Washington in the lurch by resigning; and he did not go off on long vacations.

Washington needed personal support now for an irreversible reason which had not impinged on his military campaigns. It was not rhetoric that made him give as an argument for his retirement that he felt himself growing old. In 1791, his double niece, Fanny Bassett Washington, wrote, "Although the President looks better than I expected to see him . . . there are traces on his countenance of his last two illnesses which I fear will never wear off." Washington was becoming deaf, and he acknowledged in 1793, "my memory is too treacherous to place dependence on it in cases where accuracy is necessary."[23]

All during the seven long military years before the victory at Yorktown, Washington had not given himself more than two or three days of holiday. Now he felt that periods of rest at Mount Vernon were essential to his health. When he was at the capital, he usually lacked the energy to write those answers to letters about problems at his plantation which during the Revolution he had regarded as a relaxation. Lear undertook the task. It was a comfort for Washington to feel that Hamilton was almost always available. Whatever went wrong in the government, he had a competent minister perpetually ready to be relied on.

Yet Hamilton did not become one of Washington's personal intimates. None of his three great collaborators moved Washington as had his friends of Revolutionary days. He had wept unashamedly at his dinner table when describing his affection for Lafayette. One cannot imagine him doing the same in relation to Jefferson or Hamilton or even Madison.*

During their frequent interviews with Washington, his close advisers met an intangible barrier which kept them from expounding, except on very rare occasions, their angers and grievances. When they finally did express themselves, Washington listened majestically and revealed no more of his own convictions than he thought necessary to soothe contention. Jefferson had thus been permitted to believe first that Washington did not specifically approve of Hamilton's acts, and then that Washington had stupidly allowed himself to be duped (as Jefferson considered that he himself had been when he first joined the administration). Jefferson wrote in his old age that Washington had been a true republican who had been "not aware of the drift or of the effect of Hamilton's schemes. Unversed in financial projects and calculations and budgets, his approbation of them was bottomed on his confidence in the man."[24] If this conception that Washington was an innocent

---

* Of all the members of his executive department, he seems to have felt most strongly for the brilliant and indiscreet Gouverneur Morris.

dazzled by Hamilton has down the years damaged Washington's reputation, it was useful in holding Jefferson in the Cabinet.

Keeping Jefferson and Hamilton together through his first term and into his second was not the least remarkable achievement of Washington's remarkable career. Towards this public end, the individualistic exertion of power which created personal problems for his coadjutors made an essential contribution. Had Washington argued matters out with his ministers, he could have been no more than a makeweight, moving sometimes to this side and sometimes to that. As it transpired, he resembled the keystone of an arch, holding all upright and in equilibrium, while the Hamiltonians curved off to the right and the Jeffersonians to the left.

The position Washington occupied above the battle was viable because it reflected the true situation. His application of his general principles to specific issues proved to be in many ways a summation of the attitudes represented by Madison, Jefferson, and Hamilton.

In relation to Madison, Washington's position could be said to resemble the straight line which marks the actual direction of a tacking and veering ship. When the Constitution was being drafted, Madison wished to give the federal government "a negative in all cases *whatsoever* on the local legislatures," and he was willing to risk the collapse of the Constitutional Convention rather than accede to any compromise that would mollify the smaller states. Later, in attacking Hamilton's policies, Madison reversed himself (as Brant points out) on states rights to the extreme extent of in effect denying that the federal power had in itself any legitimate claim to revenue; he denounced Congress for giving away "the money of the states."[25] In each situation, Washington tried to pull Madison back towards a center course which led to a mixed government that stepped as little as possible on the interests of the large states and the small, the central and the local power.

Jefferson, who had lived in Europe and known by experience European tyrannies, was ever fearful that an aristocratic government would clasp the American people in an unbreakable stranglehold.* He

---

* The contrast between Washington's belief that the pro-Hamiltonian decisions were reversible and Jefferson's fears that they would permanently subvert republicanism reveals one context in which the President had more faith in democratic institutions than his Secretary of State.

[415]

felt that a despotism established by the people—the majority tyranniz-
ing over minorities—was not equally dangerous, since the innate virtue
of the people would eventually right the situation. Hamilton believed
that unless the people were restrained by an aristocracy of money and
brains they would wallow in blood and injustice like the beasts they
were. Washington was equally opposed to despotisms of the mob or
the aristocracy. He saw, indeed, little distinction between the two,
since both subverted personal liberty.[26]

Jefferson favored the minimum amount of governmental interference in men's affairs, while Hamilton was an advocate of powerful
control. Before Shays's Rebellion, Washington's view had been close to
Jefferson's. The positions he subsequently occupied moved between
those of his two ministers. His basic belief was that a government truly
responsive to the people and so organized through checks and balances as to protect minorities, should possess and exert the power
necessary to enforce its laws. To the questions of how much power and
how it was to be exerted he had, as he dealt with specific problems, no
theoretical answer. The most satisfactory laws were certainly those
that required the least enforcing. Laws that raised opposition should
be carefully explained and, whenever possible, modified. But in the
last analysis, the government must govern. His acts in this area remained, during his first term, so close to the center that they were
endorsed by both Jefferson and Hamilton.

Jefferson was agrarian, Hamilton urban. As his continuing passion
for life at Mount Vernon reveals, Washington had by no means abandoned agrarianism. He could still write his overseer, "There is one rule,
and a golden one it is: that nothing should be bought that can be
made or done without." He agreed with Jefferson that the American
economy would for generations to come be basically agricultural and
that no steps should be taken that would damage agriculture.[27]

However, Washington's experience, particularly during the war, had
demonstrated to him that the American economy was dangerously
lopsided. Where Jefferson saw Hamilton's schemes as an effort to rev-
olutionize the nation by elevating the city speculator on the prostrate
body of the farmer, Washington saw an essential strengthening of
weakness in an economy too overwhelmingly agrarian. He did not doubt
but that farming and personal freedom were so strong in the United
States that they could not be sunk by a bank and some financiers. Yet
general prosperity needed what the bank and the financiers supplied.

When faced with the actual responsibility after he himself became President, Jefferson testified to the correctness of Washington's analysis by not abolishing the bank as he had wished Washington to do. Jeffersonianism was sustainable, when it finally took over, partly because Hamiltonianism had established for it an adequate financial base.

Washington had once been just as much of a regionalist as any of the local politicians who seemed intent to pry the nation apart: that a Marylander should presume to command Virginians had, during the French and Indian War, set him spluttering with public indignation. He could still find particular pleasure in having the new national capital seated near Mount Vernon—it *did* have to be in some single place—but now he applied all the stupendous power of his will "to contemplate the United States as one great whole." He was so determined to escape from the southern bias of the Jeffersonians that, on the issue of apportionment in the House of Representatives, he was tempted to lean so far over backwards that he was in danger of toppling into the northeastern bias of the Hamiltonians. Fortunately, he righted himself. "My system," he stated in 1795, ". . . has uniformly been to overlook all personal, local, and partial considerations."[28]

Hamilton's statements that his measures were taking advantage of self-interest to tie a powerful group to the federal government did not upset Washington, as the President did not feel that the business community was actually gaining a menacing and irreversible power. (The menace did not develop until several generations later, when circumstances were quite different.) Washington was in favor of binding all interests to the government, and his memories of how he had been forced to put his reputation in the balance at the time of the anti-republican Newburgh Addresses made him conclude that creditors defrauded were a greater danger to the state than creditors satisfied.

In his old age, Jefferson admitted that Washington had been "no monarchist from preference." The President had, indeed, been passionately eager to make republican government succeed. However, he was "distrustful of men and inclined to gloomy apprehensions." Fearing that the United States might have to recede into something resembling British monarchy, Washington had staged, so Jefferson suspected, his "ceremonies of levees, birthdays, pompous meetings with Congress and other forms of the same character" in order that "a change which he believed possible" would "come on with as little shock as might be to the public mind."[29]

For this interpretation there is not one word of justification in the Washington papers. Yet the fact remained that it was the President's social behavior which opened the chink in his armor through which his opponents were able to wound him. Deeply hurt in his feelings if not in his power, he insisted that he would change his methods of entertaining if he could find out what the public wanted. The public spoke in several voices, and he did not change.

Part of the problem undoubtedly stemmed from his being the oldest man in the government.* Washington shared the general human trait of being able to move into the future more freely in matters of policy than in private tastes and behavior. His formal manners had been developed when the thirteen colonies had been quietly obedient to their "most gracious King." If Washington's preference ran to colonial living at its grandest, he came by the predilection in the most natural of ways: by being, in his youth, deprived. Again and again, Washington was to write that men judged of their situation not by actuality but by comparison. By comparison with his peers, Washington had been, as a young man, poor. He had been trapped on his mother's rundown farm because he could not afford enough feed to enable his horse to carry him to the dancing assemblies his friends enjoyed.

Washington found justification for his preferences in his sincere belief that if he behaved like an ordinary citizen he would damage the prestige needed to carry out the Presidential office. That this was altogether balderdash would be hard to demonstrate, particularly in relation to times when the entire older generation had been raised in a monarchical atmosphere. And Washington was not only self-indulgent. Although he enjoyed luxury, he hated routine formality. He pursued what he considered necessary protocol† in many ways he found un-

---

* A few years senior to John Adams and Robert Morris, Washington was eleven years older than Jefferson, thirteen than Jay, eighteen than Knox, nineteen than Madison, twenty than Gouverneur Morris, twenty-one than Randolph, twenty-five than Hamilton.

† Even today, American officials would take seriously Washington's dilemma when a merchant appeared from Holland with letters he wished to present to the President in person. Washington felt it necessary to determine whether the papers were of a public nature or their bearer was acting in a public capacity. In that case, he should go first to the Secretary of State. If he were a private person, his papers should be sent ahead "that the purport might be known before he was

pleasant. He was truthful when he told Jefferson that no one disliked more than he "the ceremonies of office."[30]

In any case, a hail-fellow-well-met manner was not for Washington an open option. The diffidence which cast such unexpected (and valuable) shadows within the blinding light of his power, made him uneasy in the presence of strangers who were examining him as a curiosity or to whom he had to be polite for official reasons. If this were the case when he was in his own world of Mount Vernon, how much more so at those levees and state dinners where his reserve came to be interpreted as monarchical frostiness!

The elderly Washington could not, in all reason, assay his position in the world as ordinary men did theirs. It is surely no usual experience to rise, as if propelled by an invisible genie, from an unexceptional starting place up and up through the welter of your fellowmen to become in the eyes of millions the greatest man in the world. When painting Washington, Gilbert Stuart, that flashy conversationalist who usually had no difficulty putting his sitters at ease, found himself utterly unable to make the stern visage before him relax. Finally, Stuart said, "Now, sir, you must let me forget that you are General Washington and that I am Stuart, the painter."

"Mr. Stuart," Washington replied politely, "need never feel the need of forgetting who he is, or who General Washington is." And he did not relax.[31]

Perhaps the most significant aspect of the vituperation against Washington's social behavior was that his opponents could find nothing more truly grave to attack. The Jeffersonian leadership were themselves so involved with slavery that they could only have found the President vulnerable as a slaveholder if he had been harsher to his dependents than was common; the opposite was the case. For the rest, although the Jeffersonians came to have their suspicions, they could find nothing anti-republican in the President's statements or his governmental acts.

---

introduced, which might be at the next levee, when he might be received and treated agreeably to the consequence he might appear to derive from the testimonials of the letters. It being conceived," so Washington continued, "that etiquette of this sort is essential with all foreigners to give a respect to the chief magistrate and the dignity of the government, which would be lessened if every person who could procure a letter of introduction should be presented otherwise than at levee hours in a formal manner." It turned out that the Dutchman was engaged in land speculation which it would have been unsuitable for the President especially to countenance.[32]

Washington attributed "the eminent advantages of our political condition" to the "valor, wisdom, and virtue" of his fellow citizens. "From the first," he explained, "they derive their freedom; the second has improved their independence into national prosperity; and the last, I trust, will longer protect their social rights and ensure their individual happiness."[33]

Paradoxically enough, Madison, after he had broken with Washington, criticized his former friend for having been too subservient to the people. Washington, he wrote, had been "cool, considerate, and cautious, . . . ever scrutinizing into the public opinion, and ready to follow where he could not lead, . . . a hero in the field, yet overweighing every danger in the Cabinet." Washington himself wrote, "I only wish, whilst I am a servant of the public, to know the will of my masters, that I may govern myself accordingly." He wished to know what the people desired so that, by granting it, he could make them happy. He had written Lafayette in 1788, "It is a wonder to me, there should be found a single monarch who does not realize that his own glory and felicity must depend on the prosperity and happiness of his people. How easy is it for a sovereign to do that which shall not only immortalize his name but attract the blessings of millions."[34]

However, to find out what the people wanted and make them happy by delivering it was not really "easy." There was the fact that "it is on *great* occasions *only* and after time has been given for cool and deliberate reflection that the *real* voice of the people can be known." The answer could not be to follow the movement of popular sentiment from day to day. "I do not mean," Washington wrote Madison in 1788, "that numbers alone is sufficient to produce conviction in the mind, but I think it is enough to produce some change in the conduct of any man who entertains a doubt of his infallibility."[35]

Washington believed as strongly as did Jefferson that popular education was the necessary foundation of a republic. He gave fifty pounds anually to the Academy at Alexandria towards the instruction of the poor. He wished that journalists "instead of stuffing their papers with scurrility" would "publish the debates in Congress on all great national questions" to afford the public "the best data for its judgment." However much "some of the gentlemen of the long robe" might object, he urged that the laws of Virginia be made so short and simple that every man could understand them.[36]

His basic effort being to get a government afloat rather than to sail one already furnished with crew and passengers, Washington regarded efforts to diminish confidence in that government as "diabolical." He could not agree with Jefferson that controversy—even if directed most extremely at the passions—was a sign of governmental health and vitality. Instead of fearing a "corrupt squadron" in the legislature, Washington was afraid of "demagogues" who, because of "prejudice and evil designs," would mislead public opinion, corrupting republican government at its very source. "There are," he warned Lafayette, "not wanting wicked and designing men whose element is confusion and who will not hesitate in destroying the public tranquillity to gain a favorite point."[37]

No city proleteriat having yet developed, Washington, when he wished to refer to the masses, spoke of "the yeomanry of the country." Land in the west offered a new life to those capable of grasping it, and the men moving across the mountains left behind them in the east a perpetual seller's market for labor. No coherent group of white citizens was trapped by American institutions in poverty.* Expecting the people to be self-reliant, Washington expected them to share the general prosperity which he was convinced the federal government was helping to foster.

Washington was not what the eighteenth century called a "leveler"; it seemed to him the natural order that some people should be richer than others; that some should command and some obey. He saw happiness as grounded on being content with your lot or else moving effectively to change it. But this did not mean that he accepted the inevitability of hardship for anyone. If he did not seek to legislate poverty away, that was because he diagnosed poverty not as an aspect of class struggle but as a result of individual misbehavior or misfortune that could be dealt with most effectively in individual terms.

---

* The extent to which American society was actually mobile has become a question of controversy among historians. It is, of course, a fact that a man with no assets could not establish himself on a western freehold without borrowing to pay for land, tools, seed, and also sustenance to carry his family until his first crop ripened. These debts sometimes proved crippling and many a pioneer was sold out. (He usually made another start even further west.) Washington seems to have regarded this as an inevitable aspect of a free economy, which could nonetheless (bad luck not intervening) be circumvented with energy and probity. As for "an enterprising man with very little money," he could by going west "lay the foundation of a noble estate."[38]

The elderly Jefferson wrote that Washington had been "liberal in contributions to whatever promised utility, but frowning and unyielding on all visionary projects and all unworthy calls on his charity."[39] Although harshly phrased, this statement contains truth. Washington was uninterested in visionary ideas that could not be, at least potentially, applied. And he did try to make a distinction between the worthy and the unworthy poor. However, his pity was easily excited. Although in the abstract he felt that scapegraces could be allowed to lie in the beds they had made for themselves, in the particular he usually relented. How often did he tell his managers to make no concessions to tenants who had cheated him, only to change his mind when he found before him the case of a particular person with particular difficulties, even if those difficulties were vices!

Towards the poor and unfortunate, Washington's philosophy was that of a neighborhood patriarch who ministered to the human problems that came naturally to his attention. Even when he had himself to borrow to pay his bills, he ordered an agent to collect no debts that would make "the widow and the fatherless" suffer. After national prominence had drawn to him many more appeals than his own pocketbook could satisfy, he felt upon occasion emotions of the kind he expressed to a woman who had been thrown into dependence by the loss of her husband during the war: "Your affecting case and others of a similar nature make me almost weary of living in a world where I can do little but pity, without having the power to relieve such unmerited misfortunes. If my means were as ample as my wishes . . ."[40]

However much the elderly Jefferson might, in retrospect, accuse Washington of callousness in relation to the people, the people responded to Washington's behavior with adulation. As a Baltimore newspaper put it, they considered him "their safest friend, as well as the most exalted of their fellow citizens, and the first of men." They looked up to him, so a letter writer pointed out, "more than they do to the Almighty, for they think he is nearer to them."* [41]

This charisma had, of course, been of tremendous value in imbuing the government with the prestige necessary to get started. It is a repeating phenomenon of history that a body of men undergoing a

---

* The reverence for Washington sometimes found peculiar outlets. After he had slept at the best tavern in Bladensburg, Maryland, which was kept by a black landlady, the other inhabitants of the town were so jealous that they invaded the tavern's backyard and wrecked the privy.[42]

major political change find a human being the most persuasive symbol about which to gather. History also reveals that at revolutionary moments dissent must be minimized or the new form that is emerging will be torn apart before it can be effectively created. Almost universally, the combination of a charismatic personality with the need to discourage dissent has resulted in a dictatorship, whether monarchical, communist, or fascist.

The worry concerning dissent rational for a man engaged in nation-building was inflamed in Washington's case by the most conspicuous weakness in his character: that oversensitivity to criticism which had plagued him throughout his career. This made all the more impressive the fact that he seems never for a moment to have considered using anti-republican methods to strike down those who opposed his policies and libeled him personally. He continued to champion the freedom of the press. He sought for Freneau's patron Jefferson not exile to some American Siberia but a continued place in his Cabinet.

Long after Jefferson had broken with Washington, he admitted that his old friend and subsequent enemy had in "scrupulously obeying the laws through the whole of his career, civil and military," behaved in a manner "of which the history of the world furnishes no other example."[43] The ballot box was still supreme. Washington had given the United States an unheard-of boon: charisma with hardly any cost.

At the end of Washington's first term, Jefferson found himself in a quandary. Since the President was not backing his beliefs, Jefferson felt that Washington's continuing charisma was dangerous; Jefferson welcomed attacks aimed at discrediting the hero with the people. Yet he still feared that the United States was not yet ready to sail without the hero at the helm. Jefferson stated that Washington was "the only man in the United States who possessed the confidence of the whole; that government was founded in opinion and confidence, and that the longer he [Washington] remained, the stronger would become the habits of the people in submitting to the government, and in thinking it a thing to be maintained. That there was no other person who would be thought anything more than the head of a party."[44]

With this verdict Hamilton completely agreed. After Washington had served some four years, the two great statesmen who symbolized the continuing divergent directions of American life were equally perturbed by the possibility that he would retire.

Washington's completing touch to the mansion house at Mount Vernon: the Dove of Peace weathervane installed in 1787. Courtesy of the Mount Vernon Ladies' Association

Washington was an aging man who had led the nation for almost twenty years. It was natural for him to look back over the path he and the United States had traveled. It was like looking down from a glorious mountaintop into a murky valley. The road that had been traversed had wound precariously among quicksands and avalanches and dizzy declivities. It seemed a miracle that he and the nation stood where they stood today. The most stupendous experiment of all, the determination whether mankind could govern itself, seemed on the verge of being proved in the affirmative.

But as he stood there in the sunlight, feeling that he should be allowed to relax now that his bones were old and his task about to be completed, there was a great bickering of younger men around him. They were talking not about the past or the present but about the future; and each faction was sure that unless the other one was suppressed, all that had been gained would be lost, that the nation would collapse either into monarchy or anarchy. The old General, the old President, who had been through so many deep, dreadful, and immediate crises, when a moment's delay would be disaster, could not fathom any good reason for all the clamor. He could not understand why these younger men were not happy to be where they were, with the ground solid under their feet; why in calm sunlight, under a smiling sky, with so much danger left behind, they had to conjure up, as it seemed to him, first out of the insubstantial air and then from across the ocean, a conflict that might indeed destroy all that had been achieved. He could hardly believe his eyes and ears. Was this a last-minute proof, after all true dangers had been overcome, that mankind was unwilling to accept the gift of peace and happiness?

Washington was too much of an optimist to accept this conclusion, and his duty was clear. He must once more, as he had so often done in the past, labor to restore peace within the cause, to draw the fangs of conflict.

Acknowledgments
Bibliography
Source References

Acknowledgments

TWO of the great libraries in New York City have given me, during my labors on this volume, not only assistance but hospitality. I have had the pleasure of working both at the New-York Historical Society and in the Frederick Lewis Allen Room in the New York Public Library.

The Mount Vernon Ladies' Association of the Union, who have so graciously preserved Washington's home, have continued their great courtesy to me. Among other institutions that have been helpful to me are the library of the Century Association, the Free Library of Cornwall, Connecticut, the Clements Library, the Frick Art Reference Library, and the Library of Congress. The editors of *American Heritage* have kindly permitted me to consult their picture files.

My wife, Beatrice Hudson Flexner, and my daughter, Helen Hudson Flexner, have helped in many ways, as have my editors at Little, Brown and Company, Arthur Thornhill, Jr., and Llewellyn Howland III. David F. Hawke kindly read my manuscript and made valuable suggestions. Joyce Ruggiero and Elsie Augenblick have expertly typed the text.

I am also grateful to Frederick B. Adams, Jr., H. H. Arnason, Julian P. Boyd, Alan Burnham, John A. Castellani, Harmon Goldstone, James Gregory, James J. Heslin, Donald Jackson, Oliver Jensen, Mary-Jo Kline, Dumas Malone, Christine Meadows, Henry Allen Moe, Richard B. Morris, Frank E. Morse, Howard H. Peckham, Charles C. Wall, and Frederick J. Woodbridge.

Bibliography

A S in this continuing biography I have tried to follow the path George Washington walked, I have traversed an ever-widening landscape. The highest lookouts reached in my first volume presented views that rarely extended beyond the confines of Virginia. During my second volume, I stood beside my protagonist in a seemingly endless succession of army camps, where concern was primarily with the needs and deeds of the Continental Army, with foreign forces on American soil or on American waters. In this volume, the action returns temporarily to Virginia; and then Washington's view opens out to include not only the entire United States but much of the known world. This enlarged outlook presented to research new and more difficult problems.

The material dealt with fell into three categories. Much the most important was documentation on the behavior and thoughts of Washington himself. Additional biographical problems were presented by the entrance, as major actors in the drama, of three more of America's greatest men: Thomas Jefferson, James Madison, and Alexander Hamilton. Thirdly, there was the need to understand the general facts, ideas, and forces with which Washington had to cope in his role as nation-builder.

The study of Washington's continually evolving personality and the examination of his behavior required no major change of approach from the earlier volumes. Washington's own writings have remained the bedrock on which this series is built. Most of the products of his pen, including almost all those in the Library of Congress, have been published in Fitzpatrick's editions of his *Writings* and *Diaries;* further documents are so scattered that it has seemed best to attempt no general list of collections but to specify each source in the appropriate citation in the references. To my first volume, I appended a discussion, which need not be repeated here, of previous biographies of Washington. The most valuable of these to my studies has remained the seven-volume work by Douglas Southhall Freeman.

If my project had required full research into the lives of Jefferson, Madison, and Hamilton, this volume could not have been completed in a single lifetime. Fortunately, I was concerned, as a biographer of Washington, only with those aspects of the personalities and careers of his colleagues that impinged importantly on him. My labor has been not to draw rounded pictures of these other men, but to show them as they showed themselves to Washington.

This approach is, of course, one-sided in relation to the great men viewed through another great man's eyes. Yet the method offers unusual and valuable insights. In particular, the mounting estrangement between Washington and Jefferson becomes more understandable if we do not visualize the protagonists as two mountains thundering at each other high above the broad American historical plain. They were, in fact, two men tugging at each other's nerves in small rooms. Thus the Jefferson that Washington saw is, if a less towering figure, more relevant to their personal relationship than the Jefferson history sees.

In my researches on Madison, Hamilton, and Jefferson (as well as the other supporting players), I have relied on a combination of manuscript and secondary sources. Those papers directly relevant to Washington I have examined. Beyond that, I have made use of historical and biographical publications. My debt is great to Dumas Malone for Jefferson, John C. Miller for Hamilton, Irving Brant for Madison.

On the third aspect of my problem, the general background, I have found insights and facts in such a wide variety of sources that an attempt to cite all the publications I have consulted would create a list both impractical to use and out of reasonable proportion to my text. Better to refer the reader to the excellent annotated bibliography appended to John C. Miller's *The Federalist Era*. A longer list, filling sixty-five pages, may be found in the sixth volume of Freeman's *Washington*.

The following Bibliography is not intended as evidence that I have studied my subject. Critics can make up their minds on that matter from the text. The Bibliography is aimed at a specific and pragmatic goal: to make it possible, by presenting an alphabetical list of titles cited, to use abbreviations in the Source References.

Adams, Abigail, *Letters*, 2nd ed., ed. Charles Francis Adams, 2 vols. (Boston, 1840).

———, *New Letters*, ed. Stewart Mitchell (Boston, 1947).

Alberts, Robert C., *The Golden Voyage: The Life and Times of William Bingham* (Boston, 1969).

Ames, Fisher, *Works*, ed. Seth Ames, 2 vols. (Boston, 1854).

Ayers, Elisha, *A Journal of Travel* (Preston, Conn., 1847).

Bacon-Foster, Cora, *Early Chapter in the Development of the Potomac Route to the West* (Washington, D.C., 1912).

Baker, William S., *Washington After the Revolution* (Philadelphia, 1898).

Bancroft, George, *History of the Formation of the Constitution*, 2 vols. (New York, 1882).

Beard, Charles A., *An Economic Interpretation of the Constitution* (New York, 1957).

Bemis, Samuel Flagg, *A Diplomatic History of the United States* (New York, 1955).

———, *Jay's Treaty* (New York, 1923).

———, *Pinckney's Treaty* (New Haven, 1960).

———, *American Secretaries of State and Their Diplomacy*, vol. I (New York, 1927).

Blanchard, Claude, *Journal* (Albany, N.Y., 1876).

Blanton, Wyndham B., "Washington's Medical Knowledge and Its Sources," *Annals of Medical History*, New Ser., vol. V (1933), 52–56.

Boudinot, Jane J., *Life, Public Services, Addresses, and Letters of Elias Boudinot* (Boston, 1896).

Bowen, Catherine Drinker, *Miracle at Philadelphia* (Boston, 1966).

Bowen, Clarence W., *The History of the Centennial Celebration of the Inauguration of George Washington* (New York, 1892).

Bowers, Claude G., *Jefferson and Hamilton* (Boston, 1925).

Boyd, George Adams, *Elias Boudinot* (Princeton, 1952).

Boyd, Julian P., *Number 7: Alexander Hamilton's Secret Attempts to Control American Foreign Policy* (Princeton, 1964).

Brant, Irving, *James Madison*, 5 vols. (Indianapolis, 1948–1956).

Brissot de Warville, J. P., *New Travels in the United States of America, 1788*, ed. David Echeverria (Cambridge, Mass., 1964).

Brooks, Noah, *Henry Knox* (New York, 1900).

Brown, Robert E., *A Critical Analysis of "An Economic Interpretation of the Constitution"* (Princeton, 1956).

Brown, Stuart Gerry, *The First Republicans* (New York, 1943).

Bryan, Wilhelmus Bogart, *A History of the National Capital*, vol. I (New York, 1914).

Burke, Aedanus, *Considerations on the Society or Order of the Cincinnati* (Philadelphia, 1783).

Burnett, Edmund C., ed., *Letters of Members of the Continental Congress*, vol. VII (Washington, D.C., 1926).

Caemmerer, H. Paul, *Life of Pierre Charles L'Enfant* (Washington, D.C., 1950).

———, *Washington, The National Capital City* (Washington, D.C., 1932).

Cauchey, John Walton, *McGillivray of the Creeks* (Norman, Okla., 1938).

Chambers, William Nisbet, *Political Parties in a New Nation* (New York, 1963).

Channing, Edward, "Washington and Parties, 1789–1797," *Massachusetts Historical Society Proceedings*, XLVII (1913–1914), 35–44.

Chastellux, Marquis de, *Travels in North America*, trans. and ed. Howard C. Rice, Jr., 2 vols. (Chapel Hill, N.C., 1963).

Chinard, Gilbert, *Honest John Adams* (Boston, 1933).

———, *Houdon in America* (Baltimore, 1930).

[433]

Continental Congress, *Journals, 1774–1789.* 8 vols. (Washington, D.C., 1921–1926).

Crumrine, Boyd, *History of Washington County, Pennsylvania* (Philadelphia, 1882).

Cunliffe, Marcus, *George Washington, Man and Monument* (Boston, 1958).

Cunningham, Noble E., Jr., *The Jeffersonian Republicans* (Chapel Hill, 1957).

Custis, George Washington Parke, *Recollections of Washington* (New York, 1860).

Decatur, Stephen, Jr., *Private Affairs of George Washington from the Records and Accounts of Tobias Lear* (Boston, 1933).

DeConde, Alexander, *Entangling Alliance, Politics and Diplomacy under George Washington* (Durham, N.C., 1958).

Donnelly, Lucy Martin, "The Celebrated Mrs. Macaulay," *William and Mary Quarterly,* Ser. 3, VI (1949), 173–207.

Dorfman, Joseph, *The Economic Mind in American Civilization,* vol. I (New York, 1946).

Drake, Francis S., *Life and Correspondence of Henry Knox* (Boston, 1873).

————, *Memorials of the Society of Cincinnati of Massachusetts* (Boston, 1873).

Dunbar, Louise B., *A Study of "Monarchical Tendencies" in the United States from 1776–1801* (Urbana, Ill., 1922).

East, Robert A., "The Massachusetts Conservatives in the Critical Period," *Era of the American Revolution,* ed. Richard B. Morris (New York, 1939).

Farrand, Max, *Records of the Federal Convention of 1787,* 4 vols. (New Haven, 1937); referred to in Source References as "F, CC."

Federalist, The, innumerable editions.

Fenno, Richard F., *The President's Cabinet* (Cambridge, Mass., 1959).

Fisher, Joshua Francis, *Recollections,* ed. Sophia Cadwalader (Boston, 1929).

Flexner, James Thomas, *George Washington: The Forge of Experience, 1732–1775* (Boston, 1965); referred to in Source References as "F, F."

————, *George Washington in the American Revolution* (Boston, 1968); referred to in Source References as "F, R."

————, *Gilbert Stuart* (New York, 1955).

————, *Steamboats Come True* (New York, 1944).

Ford, Paul Leicester, *The True George Washington* (Philadelphia, 1898).

Frary, I. T., *Thomas Jefferson, Architect and Builder* (Richmond, Va., 1931).

Fraser, Charles, *Reminiscence of Charleston* (Charleston, Va., 1854).

Freeman, Douglas Southhall, *George Washington: A Biography,* completed by J. A. Carroll and M. W. Ashworth, 7 vols. (New York, 1948–1957); referred to in Source References as "F."

Green, Thomas Marshall, *The Spanish Conspiracy* (Cincinnati, 1891).

Griswold, Rufus W., *The Republican Court; or, American Society in the Days of Washington* (New York, 1855).

Guttheim, Frederick Albert, *The Potomac* (New York, 1949).

Guttmacher, Manfred S., "Catherine Macaulay and Patience Wright," *Johns Hopkins Alumni Magazine,* XXIV (1935–1936), 309–326.

Hadfield, Joseph, *An Englishman in America, 1785,* ed. Douglas S. Robertson (Toronto, 1933).

Hamilton, Alexander, *Papers,* ed. Harold C. Syrett, vols. III–XIV (New York, 1962–1969); referred to in Source References as "HS."

————, *Works,* ed. John C. Hamilton, 7 vols. (New York, 1850–1851).

————, *Works,* ed. by Henry Cabot Lodge, 12 vols. (New York, 1904).

Hart, James, *The American Presidency in Action, 1789* (New York, 1948).

Harvard Guide to American History (Cambridge, Mass., 1954).

Hawke, David, *The Colonial Experience* (Indianapolis, 1966).

Haworth, Paul Leland, *George Washington, Country Gentleman* (Indianapolis, n.d.).

Henderson, Archibald, *Washington's Southern Tour, 1791* (Boston, :
Holdsworth, J. T., and D. R. Dewey, *The First and Second Banks*
  States (Washington, D.C., 1910).
Hopkinson, Francis, *Seven Songs for the Harpsichord* (Philadelphia [1
Hughes, Rupert, *George Washington,* 3 vols. (New York, 1926–193(
Humphreys, David, "The Life of George Washington," ms., Rosenbac
  Philadelphia; referred to in Source References as "Hump."
Humphreys, Frank Landon, *The Life and Times of David Humpl*
  (New York, 1917).
Hunt, Gaillard, *Calendar of Applications and Recommendations for*
  the Presidency of George Washington (Washington, D.C., 1893
Hunter, Robert, *Quebec to Carolina in 1785–1786,* ed. Louis B.
  Marion Tinling (San Marino, Cal., 1943).
Hurd, Charles, *The White House* (New York, 1940).
Jay, John, *Correspondence and Public Papers,* ed. by J. Franklin Jame
  ington, D.C., 1898).
Jefferson, Thomas, *Papers,* ed. Julian P. Boyd, vols. VI–XVII (Princ
  1965), referred to in Source References as "JB."
———, *Writings,* ed. by Paul Leicester Ford, 10 vols. (New York, 1
  referred to in Source References as "JF."
———, *Writings,* ed. A. A. Lipscomb and A. E. Bergh, 20 vols. (\
  D.C., 1903) referred to in Source References as "JLB."
Jensen, Merrill, *The New Nation* (New York, 1965).
———, *The Making of the Constitution* (Princeton, 1964).
Ketcham, Ralph, and Nathaniel Stein, "Two New Letters Reveal Madi
  Unmask Ghost of Washington's Unused Inaugural," *Manuscript*
  1959), 54–58.
Kimball, Fiske, *Domestic Architecture of the American Colonies and of*
  Republic (New York, 1922).
———, *Life Portraits of Jefferson and Their Replicas* (Philadelphia, 19
———, *Thomas Jefferson, Architect* (Boston, 1916).
King, Rufus, *Life and Correspondence,* ed. Charles R. King, 6 vols. (1
  1895).
Kirkland, Edward C., *A History of American Economic Life* (New Yoi
Kite, Elizabeth S., *L'Enfant and Washington, 1791–1792,* with an introd
  J. J. Jusserand (Baltimore, 1929).
Knollenberg, Bernhard, *George Washington, the Virginia Period* (Durha
  1964).
Koch, Adrienne, *Jefferson and Madison* (New York, 1950).
Langstaff, J. Brett, *Dr. Bard of Hyde Park* (New York, 1942).
Laurens, John, *Army Correspondence* (New York, 1867).
Leach, Frank Willing, "Old Philadelphia Families: Powel," *North*
  (Philadelphia), July 5, 1908.
Leary, Lewis, *That Rascal Freneau* (New Brunswick, 1941).
L'Enfant, Pierre Charles, *Plan of the City Intended as the Permanent Sea*
  Government of the United States [1791].
Lipset, Seymour Martin, *The First New Nation* (New York, 1963).
Lodge, Henry Cabot, *George Washington,* 2 vols. (Boston, 1899).
Maclay, William, *Journal* (New York, 1927).
Madison, James, "Autobiography," ed. Douglas Adair, *William and Mary*
  terly, 3rd Ser., vol. II (1945), 191–209.
———, *Papers,* ed. William T. Hutchinson and William M. Rachal, vo
  (Chicago, 1962–1967).
———, *Writings,* ed. Gaillard Hunt, 9 vols. (New York, 1900–1910), refei
  in Source References as "MH."

Malone, Dumas, *Jefferson and His Time*, 3 vols. (Boston, 1948–1962), referred to in Source References as "M."

Marshall, John, *George Washington*, 5 vols. (Fredericksburg, Va., 1926).

McMaster, John B., *A History of the People of the United States*, vol. II (New York, 1944).

Miller, John C., *The Federalist Era* (New York, 1960).

———, *Alexander Hamilton* (New York, 1959).

Mintz, Max M., "Gouverneur Morris: The Emergence of a Nationalist," doctoral dissertation, New York University (1957).

Mitchell, Broadus, *Alexander Hamilton*, 2 vols. (New York, 1957, 1962).

Monaghan, Frank, *John Jay, Defender of Liberty* (New York, 1935).

Monroe, James, *Writings*, ed. Stanislaus Murray Hamilton, vols. I–II (New York, 1898–1899).

Moon, Robert C., *The Morris Family of Philadelphia*, 3 vols. (Philadelphia, 1898), supplement, 2 vols. (Philadelphia, 1908).

Morgan, John, *The Journal of Dr. John Morgan of Philadelphia from the City of Rome to the City of London, 1764* (Philadelphia, 1907).

Morris, Gouverneur, *Diary and Letters*, ed. by Anne C. Morris, 2 vols. (New York, 1888).

Morris, Richard B., ed., *Alexander Hamilton and the Founding of the Nation*, new edition (New York, 1969).

———, "Insurrection in Massachusetts," *America in Crisis*, ed. Daniel Aaron (New York, 1952), 21–49.

———, "Washington and Hamilton: A Great Collaboration," *Proceedings of the American Philosophical Society*, CII (1958), 107–116.

Mount Vernon Ladies' Association, *Annual Report*, 1944–1968 (Mount Vernon, Va., 1945–1969).

Padover, Saul, ed., *Thomas Jefferson and the National Capital* (Washington, D.C., 1946).

Paine, Thomas, *Complete Writings*, ed. Philip S. Foner, 2 vols. (New York, 1945).

Parton, James, *Life of Thomas Jefferson* (Boston, 1874).

Rives, William C., *History of the Life and Times of James Madison*. 3 vols. (New York, 1859–1868).

Rossiter, Clinton, *The American Presidency* (New York, 1960).

———, *1787: The Grand Convention* (New York, 1966).

———, *Alexander Hamilton and the Constitution* (New York, 1964).

Rowland, Kate Mason, *Life of George Mason*, 2 vols. (New York, 1892).

Rush, Benjamin, *Letters*, ed. Lyman H. Butterfield, 2 vols. (Princeton, 1951).

St. Clair, Arthur, *Papers*, ed. William H. Smith, 2 vols. (Cincinnati, 1882).

Sargent, Winthrop, "Journal of the General Meeting of the Cincinnati in 1784," *Memoirs of the Historical Society of Pennsylvania*, VI (1858), 59–115.

Sawitzky, William, *Matthew Pratt* (New York, 1942).

Sellers, Charles Coleman, *Charles Willson Peale*, 2 vols. (Philadelphia, 1947).

Smith, John Jay, *American Historical and Literary Curiosities*, 2nd. Ser. (New York, 1860).

Smith, Page, *John Adams*, 2 vols. (New York, 1962).

Smith, Thomas E. V., *The City of New York in the Year of Washington's Inauguration* (New York, 1899).

Sparks, Jared, ed., *Correspondence of the American Revolution, Being Letters of Eminent Men to George Washington*, vol. IV (Boston, 1853); referred to in Source References as "S, C."

———, *The Life of Gouverneur Morris, with Selections from His Correspondence*, 3 vols. (Boston, 1862).

Stein, Nathaniel E., "The Discarded Inaugural Address of George Washington," *Manuscripts*, X (Spring 1958), 2–17.

Stone, William L., *Life of Joseph Brant*, 2 vols. (Cooperstown, N.Y., 1847).

Thacher, Charles C., *The Creation of the Presidency, 1775-1789* (Baltimore, 1922).

Thane, Elswyth, *Potomac Squire* (New York, 1963).

Trumbull, John, *Autobiography,* ed. Theodore Sizer (New Haven, 1953).

Van Doren, Carl, *The Great Rehearsal* (New York, 1948).

Wall, Charles C., "The Banqueting Hall at Mount Vernon," ms. of speech, Mount Vernon.

Wansey, Henry, *An Excursion to the United States of North America in the Summer of 1794* (London, 1798).

Warren-Adams Letters; Being Chiefly a Correspondence among John Adams, Samuel Adams, and James Warren, ed. W. C. Ford, 2 vols. (Massachusetts Historical Society *Collections,* 1917, 1925).

Washington, George, *Calendar of the Correspondence of George Washington . . . with the Continental Congress,* ed. John C. Fitzpatrick (Washington, D.C., 1906).

——, *Calendar of the Correspondence of George Washington . . . with the Officers,* ed. John C. Fitzpatrick, 4 vols. (Washington, D.C., 1915).

——, *Calendar of the Washington Manuscripts in the Library of Congress,* ed. Herbert Friedenwald (Washington, D.C., 1901).

——, *Diaries,* ed. John C. Fitzpatrick, 4 vols. (Boston and New York, 1925); referred to in Source References as "GW, *D.*"

——, *The George Washington Atlas,* ed. Lawrence Martin (Washington, D.C., 1932).

——, *Presidential Papers Microfilm, George Washington Papers* (Washington, D.C., 1965); referred to in Source References as "ms. LC."

——, *Writings,* ed. Jared Sparks, 12 vols. (Boston, 1834-1837).

——, *Writings,* ed. Worthington Chauncey Ford, 14 vols. (New York and London, 1889-1893).

——, *Writings,* ed. John C. Fitzpatrick, 39 vols. (Washington, D.C., 1931-1944); referred to in Source References as "GW."

Watson, Elkanah, *Men and Times of the Revolution* (New York, 1857).

Watson, John F., *Annals of Philadelphia,* 3 vols. (Philadelphia, 1907).

Webb, Samuel Blachley, *Correspondence and Journals,* ed. Worthington Chauncey Ford, 3 vols. (New York, 1892).

Weld, Isaac, *Travels through the States of North America* (London, 1799).

Wharton, Anne H., "Washington's New York Residence in 1789," *Lippincott's Magazine,* XXXIV (1889), 741-745.

Wildes, Henry T., *Anthony Wayne* (New York, 1941).

Whitaker, Arthur Preston, *The Spanish-American Frontier, 1783-1795* (Boston, 1927).

Wilson, Fraser Ellis, *Arthur St. Clair* (Richmond, Va., 1944).

White, Leonard D., *The Federalists: A Study in Administrative History* (New York, 1948).

Wirt, William, *Patrick Henry, Life, Correspondence, and Speeches,* 3 vols. (New York, 1891).

Wolcott, Oliver, *Memories of the Administrations of Washington and John Adams,* ed. George Gibbs, 2 vols. (New York, 1846).

Wood, Gordon S., *The Creation of the American Republic, 1776-1787* (Chapel Hill, 1969).

Young, Eleanor, *Forgotten Patriot: Robert Morris* (New York, 1950).

Source References

THE effort is made in these source references to be as succinct as utility allows. Had I noted all the passages in which Washington or his contemporaries mentioned matters discussed in my text, or the many excellent publications dealing in general with the historical background, I would have created an underpinning considerably more extensive than the superstructure. References are commonly to passages from which specific quotations have been taken.

Since the Bibliography gives fuller citations, the source references have been kept as brief as seems clear. When a title is repeated in the notes to one chapter, I have in the later references omitted, as superfluous, the form "*op. cit.*" Manuscript and newspaper dates are eighteenth century unless otherwise specified. The sources most often repeated are referred to by the following abbreviations:

F: Freeman, Douglas Southhall, *George Washington: A Biography,* completed by J. A. Carroll and M. W. Ashworth, 7 vols. (New York, 1948–1957).

F, CC: Farrand, Max, ed., *Records of the Federal Convention of 1787,* 4 vols. (New Haven, 1937).

F, F: Flexner, James Thomas, *George Washington: The Forge of Experience, 1732–1775* (Boston, 1965).

F, R: Flexner, James Thomas, *George Washington in the American Revolution, 1775–1783* (Boston, 1968).

GW: Washington, George, *Writings,* ed. John C. Fitzpatrick, 39 vols. (Washington, D.C., 1931–1944).

GW, D: Washington, George, *Diaries,* ed. John C. Fitzpatrick, 4 vols. (Boston and New York, 1925).

HS: Hamilton, Alexander, *Papers*, ed. Harold C. Syrett, vols. III–XIV (New York and London, 1962–1969)

Hump: Humphreys, David, The Life of General Washington, ms., Rosenbach Foundation, Philadelphia.

JB: Jefferson, Thomas, *Papers*, ed. Julian P. Boyd, vols. VI–XVII (Princeton, 1952–1965).

JF: Jefferson, Thomas, *Writings*, ed. Paul Leicester Ford, 10 vols. (N.Y., 1892–1899)

JLB: Jefferson, Thomas, *Writings*, ed. A. A. Lipscomb and A. E. Bergh, 20 vols. (Washington, D.C., 1903).

LC: Library of Congress, Washington, D.C.

M: Malone, Dumas, *Jefferson and His Time*, vols. II and III (Boston, 1951, 1962).

MH: Madison, James, *Writings*, ed. Gaillard Hunt, 9 vols. (New York, 1900–1910).

MtV: Mount Vernon Ladies' Association of the Union, Mount Vernon, Va.

S, C: Sparks, Jared, ed., *Correspondence of the American Revolution; Being Letters of Eminent Men to George Washington*, vol. IV (Boston, 1853).

1: SOLDIER'S RETURN
1. GW, XXXVII, 340–341.
2. GW, XXVII, 284–286.
3. Hump.
4. GW, XXVII, 297, 347.
5. GW, XXVII, 312
6. GW, XXVIII, 93, 436.
7. GW, XXVII, 60, XXVIII, 210, 282, 326, XXIX, 29.
8. GW, XXIX, 29.
9. GW, XXVII, 413.
10. GW, XXVIII, 6–7.
11. JF, XIX, 450.
12. GW, XXXI, 72.
13. GW, XXVII, 317–318.

2: MOUNT VERNON:
A WELL-RESORTED TAVERN
1. F, F, 195, 246ff.
2. Hump.
3. Blanchard, *Journal*, 166–167; Vaughan plan (see illustration).
4. Hump; Hunter, *Quebec*, 196.
5. GW, *D*, III, 30–31.
6. GW, XXIX, 160–161.
7. GW, XXVIII, 470, XXIX, 287.

8. GW, XXVII, 298, 305, XXVIII, 63; GW, *D*, II, 115, 357; F, F, 245–248.
9. Wall, "Banqueting."
10. Ayers, *Journal*, 8–9.
11. F, F, 80n.
12. Weld, *Travels*, 105–106.
13. F, IV, 43; GW, XXIX, 129; Hadfield, *Englishman*, 13; Hunter, 193; Hump.
14. Hump.
15. Hump; Hunter, 194.
16. Burnett, *Letters*, VII, 495n; F, VI, 34–35.
17. William North to Ben Walker, 3/9/84, ms., Historical Society of Pennsylvania.
18. F, VI, 36–37; Watson, *Men*, 278–280.
19. GW, XXVIII, 140.
20. Watson, 139.
21. Chinard, *Houdon*, xvi; GW, D, II, 419–426.
22. GW, XXVIII, 504.
23. Donnelly, *Macaulay*; Guttmacher, *Macaulay*, 315–316.

24. Catherine Macaulay Graham to GW
1/10 & 10/10/86, 11/16/87, mss.
LC. GW, XXVIII, 159, 169, 174,
203; GW, *D*, II, 381–382.
25. GW, *D*, II, 426, III, 124; Hunter,
195.
26. *GW*, *D*, II, 407, 414, 451–452.
27. Hunter, 196.
28. Custis, *Recollections,* 384–385;
GW, *D*, IV, 6.
29. Custis, 389.
30. Custis, 387; GW, XXIX, 49; GW,
D, III, 3.
31. GW, XXIX, 28, XXX, 260.
32. President of Congress to GW, 1/28/
83, LC; GW, XXVII, 302*n*.
33. GW, XXVII, 301–302.

3: FAMILY MATTERS
1. GW, XXVIII, 83.
2. F, *F,* see index.
3. GW, XXVIII, 83.
4. GW, XXVIII, 82–83.
5. Charles Armand-Tuffin to GW,
1/20/86, ms. LC; GW, XXVIII,
514, XXIX, 484.
6. GW, I, xix.
7. *Warren-Adams,* I, 228.
8. Hunter, *Quebec,* 197.
9. Custis, *Recollections,* 41; GW,
XXVIII, 312–313.
10. F, VII, 469.
11. Custis, 38–39; GW, XXVII, 492,
XXVIII, 371.
12. GW, XXVII, 465.
13. Martha to Fanny Bassett, 2/25/88,
ms. (Dr. Joseph Fields tran-
script), MtV; GW, XXVII, 465.
14. GW, XXVIII, 158, 310, XXXV, 451.
15. GW, *D*, II, 457n.
16. GW, XXVI, 41, XXVII, 485, XXIX,
25; GW, *D*, II, 410.
17. GW, XXX, 24–25.
18. GW, XXVIII, 28, 67.
19. GW, XXXII, 176.
20. GW, XXVII, 28, 210.
21. GW, XXVIII, 152; GW, *D*, II, 423.
22. GW, XXIX, 28–31.
23. GW, XXVII, 332, XXVIII, 210,
XXX, 399.
24. GW, XXI, 340–342, XXVI, 42–44;
GW, *D*, II, 372, III, 49, 51.
25. F, *F,* 116–117.
26. GW, *D*, III, 160.
27. GW, XXIX, 158–162.
28. GW, *Writings,* Ford ed., XIV, 416–
418.

4: FARMER WASHINGTON
1. Hump.
2. F, *F,* 287.
3. F, *R,* 341–342.
4. GW, XXXIV, 47.
5. Information from Charles C. Wall
and Frank E. Morse, MtV.
6. GW, XXIX, 450n, XXX, 159.
7. Hump.
8. GW, *D*, III, 15–21.
9. GW, *D*, III, 70.
10. GW, XXX, 133.
11. Custis, *Recollections,* 379ff; GW,
XXVIII, 464, XXXIII, 151; Hunter, *Quebec,* 193.
12. F, VI, 53; Hump.
13. F, VI, 6; GW, *D*, II, 357, 436–450.
14. GW, XXIX, 205, 414.
15. GW, *D*, passim., II, 334, 340.
16. Hunter, 195.
17. GW, XXVIII, 209.
18. GW, XV, 347, XXVII, 55; GW, *D*,
III, 37–38.
19. GW, XXVIII, 313, XXIX, 388,
XXX, 48.
20. GW, XXIX, 339; GW, *D*, III, 43.
21. GW, XXVIII, 185–186.
22. George William Fairfax to GW,
12/12/86, ms. LC; GW, XXVIII,
509; GW, *D*, III, 48, 118.
23. GW, XXXI, 36–37, XXXIV, 103–
104.
24. JF, IX, 449.
25. F, VI, 56; Haworth, *Country,* 56;
GW, XXVII, 271, XXXIV, 232.
26. GW, XXX, 151, XXXII, 70,
XXXIII, 439.
27. F, VI, 57–58; GW, XXX, 49–50.
28. Arthur Young to GW, 7/1/88, ms.
LC; GW, XXX, 153, XXXV, 246,
487.
29. GW, XXVIII, 244.
30. GW, XXVIII, 297–299.
31. GW, XXVIII, 331, XXX, 151–152;
GW, *D*, II, 449.
32. GW, XXVIII, 409, 423, 426.
33. GW, XXVIII, 160–161, 427.
34. GW, XXVIII, 454, 471, 479.
35. GW, XXVIII, 471, XXXI, 217–218.
36. GW, XXVIII, 423, XXIX, 74, XXX,
151–152.
37. F, VI, 58–59; GW, XXIV, 143.
38. GW, XXIX, 158–159, 212.
39. GW, XXIX, 390.
40. GW, XXIX, 65.

41. GW, XXVIII, 282.
42. GW, XXVII, 436.

5: BUSINESS WORRIES

1. GW, XXVII, 309, 320.
2. GW, XXVII, 438–439, XXVIII, 84, XXX, 2–3.
3. GW, XXVIII, 65; Hump.
4. GW, XXVIII, 423.
5. Francis Hopkinson to GW, 12/1/88, photostat, LC; GW, XXX, 196–197; Hopkinson, Seven, dedication.
6. GW, XXVIII, 379, 405; GW, D, III, 66–67.
7. Lear to Gideon Snow, 6/17/87, ms., MtV; Lear to William Prescott, 3/4/88, ms., MtV; Hump; GW, XXVIII, 474.
8. F, VI, 59–62; GW, XXVII, 344–345, XXIX, 158–159.
9. GW, XXVIII, 329–330.
10. GW, XXVII, 348–356, 362, 441.
11. GW, XXVII, 433; GW, D, II, 299.
12. GW, D, II, 288–289; Haworth, Country, 29.
13. GW, D, II, 291.
14. Haworth, 23.
15. GW, XXVIII, 293; GW, D, II, 292–293.
16. GW, D, II, 291–292.
17. GW, D, II, 294–298.
18. Crumrine, Washington County, 859.
19. Crumrine, 856–859; GW, XVIII, 111.
20. GW, XXVIII, 112, 114–115, 262, 489–490.
21. GW, XXVIII, 263, 347.
22. GW, XXIX, 85–86.
23. GW, XXVIII, 436.
24. F, VI, 32; GW, XXVIII, 269, 347, XXIX, 81.
25. Crumrine, 159–160.
26. GW, XXXI, 393.
27. Beard, Economic, 145.

6: THE CINCINNATI QUANDARY

1. GW, XXVII, 341.
2. GW, XXVII, 289.
3. GW, XXVII, 285.
4. GW, XXVII, 286.
5. Burke, Considerations.
6. GW, XXVII, 388–389.
7. JB, VII, 105–108.
8. S, C, IV, 61.
9. GW, XXVII, 393–396.
10. GW, XXVII, 400–401.
11. Drake, Cincinnati, 31–33; Foster, Cincinnati, 22ff.; Historical Society of Pennsylvania, Memoirs, VI (1848), 79ff.

7: THE ARTS OF PEACE

1. GW, D, IV, 22.
2. GW, XX, 142–143, XXVI, 422, XXVII, 219, 320, XXVIII, 514; Van Doren Rehearsal, 2.
3. F, F, 289–290; GW, XXVII, 377–378, 392.
4. GW, XXVIII, 124, XXX, 307.
5. GW, XXIV, 59n–60n, XXIV, 23, 148, XXXV, 199.
6. GW, XXVIII, 206–207, 421, XXX, 187.
7. GW, XXVII, 475, XXVIII, 4.
8. Martha to Fanny Bassett Washington, 2/25/88, ms., MtV; GW, XXIX, 520.
9. GW, XXVII, 475.
10. GW, XXVII, 475.
11. GW, XXVIII, 205, 499–501.
12. GW, XXVIII, 484.
13. F, F, see index; GW, XXVII, 373–377.
14. JB, VII, 25–27.
15. GW, XXVII, 376.
16. Thomas Blackburn to GW, 12/20/84, ms. LC; Bacon-Foster, Potomac, 45–46; GW, XXVIII, 20, 22, 24.
17. JB, VII, 59–62.
18. GW, XXVIII, 34–35, 80, 85; JB, VII, 24–25.
19. GW, XXVIII, 81n.
20. GW, XXXVIII, 214, 303–304.
21. GW, XXVIII, 53–55, 215n, 219.
22. GW, XXVII, 490, XXVIII, 89.
23. GW, XXVII, 471, XXVIII, 50; GW, D, II, 321ff.; Watson, Men, 280.
24. GW, XXVII, 490, XXVIII, 11, 337.
25. GW, XXVIII, 48, 53, 79, 144.
26. GW, D, II, 279ff.
27. GW, XXVII, 478, XXVIII, 50.
28. Flexner, Steamboats, 67–68; GW, XXVIII, 480; GW, D, II, 282–283.
29. GW, XXVIII, 265–266.
30. Watson, 281–282.
31. GW, XXVIII, 50, 73–74.
32. GW, XXVIII, 160, 188–190.
33. Hunter, Quebec, 193; Watson, 280–281.

34. GW, *D*, II, passim.
35. Flexner, passim.
36. Flexner, 84.
37. GW, XXIX, 219.
38. Guttheim, *Potomac*, 255–256.
39. GW, XXVIII, 282; JB, VII, 592.

8: THE POLITICAL SCENE DARKENS
1. F, *R*, 37.
2. F, *R*, 475–476.
3. F, *R*, chapters 52–53.
4. JF, VII, 106.
5. GW, XXVII, 49–50.
6. GW, XXVI, 482–496.
7. Rossiter, *Hamilton*, 36.
8. GW, XXVII, 58.
9. GW, XXXV, 37.
10. GW, III, 50–51.
11. GW, XXVIII, 183, XXXV, 32.
12. GW, XXVII, 294; Wood, *Creation*.
13. GW, XXVII, 415, XXVIII, 56, 421.
14. Hump.
15. Bacon-Foster, *Potomac*, 51ff.; GW, *D*, II, 354; MH, II, 198; Roland, *Mason*, II, 81–85.
16. F, VI, 66; MH, II, 198.
17. JF, VII, 592.
18. GW, XXVIII, 493.
19. GW, XXVIII, 502.
20. GW, XXVIII, 5, 234.
21. Rossiter, *1787*, 49.
22. GW, XXVIII, 487.
23. GW, XXVIII, 161.
24. GW, XXVIII, 497.
25. James McHenry to GW, 8/1/85, ms. LC; GW, XXVIII, 228–230.
26. Jensen, *New Nation*, chapters 15–16.
27. GW, XXIX, 139, 163–164.
28. GW, XXVIII, 402.
29. F, VI, 68; GW, XXVIII, 422.
30. GW, XXVIII, 422; S, *C*, IV, 131.
31. GW, XXVIII, 309; Hunter, *Quebec*, 195.
32. GW, XXVIII, 431.
33. S, *C*, IV, 136.
34. GW, XXVIII, 503.
35. Morris, *Insurrection*, 34.
36. GW, XXVIII, 503–504.
37. F, VI, 69; GW, XXIX, 4.

9: DUTY'S CLAMOROUS VOICE
1. *Pennsylvania Packet*, 8/23/86.
2. David Humphreys to GW, 10/24/86, ms. LC.

3. GW, XXIX, 27.
4. Humphreys to GW, 11/1/86, ms. LC. Burnett, *Letters*, VIII, 486; F, VI, 74; S, *C*, IV, 148.
5. Brooks, *Knox*, 194; GW, XXIX, 51–52.
6. GW, XXIX, 33–34, 153.
7. GW, XXIX, 32.
8. Morris, *Insurrection*.
9. MH, II, 278, 283.
10. M, II, 157.
11. GW, XXIX, 122.
12. GW, XXIX, 31–33, 113.
13. GW, XXIX, 52.
14. MH, II, 283–284.
15. GW, XXIX, 34.
16. GW, XXVI, 213–218, XXVII, 318.
17. GW, XXIX, 76, 120.
18. GW, XXIX, 122–126.
19. Morris, 47.
20. F, VI, 80.
21. GW, XXIX, 153, 168.
22. GW, XXIX, 153, 165.
23. GW, XXIX, 128, 176–177.
24. GW, XXIX, 190.
25. F, VI, 131n; MH, II, 315–316; GW, XXIX, 190; S, *C*, IV, 154.
26. GW, XXIX, 128.
27. Rossiter, *1787*, 24.
28. GW, XXIX, 191–192.
29. GW, XXIX, 170.
30. GW, XXIX, 153.
31. GW, XXIX, 128, 193–194, 198.
32. F, VI, 86.
33. Humphreys to GW, 3/19/87, ms. LC; MH, III, 341; S, *C*, IV, 155.
34. S, *C*, IV, 158.
35. GW, XXIX, 171, 187.
36. GW, XXIX, 158–162, 187.
37. Smith, *Curiosities*, section II, 20–21.
38. Henry Knox to GW, 4/9/87, ms. LC; GW, XXIX, 191.
39. GW, XXIX, 186–188.
40. GW, XXIX, 198.
41. GW, *D*, III, 174.
42. GW, XXIX, 208–210; GW, *D*, III, 205.
43. GW, XXIX, 210; GW, *D*, III, 205.
44. GW, *D*, III, 206–209.
45. GW, XXIX, 211; GW, *D*, III, 214.
46. GW, *D*, III, 215.
47. F, VI, 87; Monroe, *Writings*, I, 186.

10: WIDENING POLITICAL HORIZONS

1. F, *CC*, III, 20.
2. GW, XXIX, 210–211; GW, *D*, III, 216; Young, *Morris*, 168–171.
3. GW, *D*, III, 216–217.
4. F, VI, 88; GW, XXIX, 213.
5. GW, XXIX, 223–224, 457.
6. MH, II, 344ff.; Roland, *Mason*, II, 101.
7. GW, XXIX, 224.
8. F, *CC*, II, 114, 119, III, 43–44.
9. F, *CC*, III, 382.
10. F, *CC*, I, 3–4.
11. F, *CC*, III, 86–87; GW, XXIX, 153.
12. *New York Times*, 10/28/1967, editorial page.
13. GW, XXIX, 21–24, 66–69.
14. Beard, *Economic*, 144; GW, XXIX, 158.
15. Thacher, *Presidency*, 21–23.
16. GW, XXIX, 153; Rossiter, *1787*, 70, Van Doren, *Rehearsal*, 47.
17. F, *R*, 537–538.
18. F, *R*, 537.
19. GW, XXIX, 239.
20. F, *R*, 37; Van Doren, 15.
21. F, *CC*, II, 644.
22. F, *CC*, III, 469–472; Laurens, *Correspondence*, 138.
23. GW, XXIX, 236; Rossiter, 152.
24. GW, XXIX, 228, 234, GW, *D*, III, 216ff.
25. GW, XXIX, 238.
26. GW, XXIX, 239.
27. GW, XXVII, 12.
28. Brant, *Madison*.
29. F, *CC*, III, 95.
30. Rossiter, 170ff.; Van Doren, 51ff.
31. GW, XXIX, 228; Rossiter, 172.
32. GW, XXIX, 226, 233.

11: BUILDING A NEW GOVERNMENT

1. The proceedings of the convention in general: Beard, *Economic;* Bowen, *Miracle;* Brown, *Critical;* F, *CC;* Jensen, *Making;* F, VI, 88ff; Rossiter, *1787;* Thacher, *Creation;* Van Doren, *Rehearsal.*
2. GW, XXIX, 237.
3. F, VI, 88; GW, XXIX, 245–246.
4. F, *CC*, II, 363–364.
5. Van Doren, 104–105.
6. GW, *D*, III, 225; Sparks, *Morris*, I, 283–284.

7. Van Doren, 106.
8. Van Doren, 19–20, 226.
9. F, *CC*, I, 168, II, 280; GW, XXIX, 245.
10. Van Doren, 126; GW, *D*, III, 229.
11. Madison, *Papers*, I, 144–145.
12. GW, D, III, 230.
13. *Ibid.*
14. GW, *D*, III, 231.
15. GW, *D*, III, 233.
16. Rossiter, 69.
17. F, *CC*, I, 97, II, 121, 493–494, 587, IV, 57–58.
18. F, *CC*, III, 302.
19. F, *CC*, II, 462; GW, XXIX, 479.
20. Van Doren, 161.
21. F, VI, 127; GW, XXX, 396.
22. Van Doren, 165.
23. F, *CC*, II, 632; GW, XXIX, 411.
24. Van Doren, 167.
25. F, *CC*, II, 644.
26. F, *CC*, II, 648.
27. GW, *D*, III, 237.
28. GW, XXIX, 277.
29. *Ibid.*
30. GW, *D*, III, 238.

12: THE NEW CONSTELLATION OF THIS HEMISPHERE

1. Monroe, *Writings*, I, 186.
2. GW, XXIX, 278.
3. GW, XXIX, 278n–279n, XXX, 223–224.
4. GW, XXIX, 373, 403, XXX, 11, 78.
5. GW, XXIX, 324, 409.
6. GW, XXIX, 287, 380, 404.
7. GW, XXIX, 385–388, 400.
8. GW, XXIX, 285, 349.
9. F, *CC*, II, 641–643, 667.
10. GW, XXX, 299, 323.
11. GW, XXX, 299–300.
12. GW, XXIX, 466.
13. GW, XXIX, 290–291, XXX, 66.
14. GW, XXIX, 289.
15. GW, XXIX, 310, 399.
16. GW, XXIX, 376.
17. GW, XXIX, 346, 350.
18. GW, XXIX, 378, 406.
19. GW, XXIX, 401, 413.
20. GW, XXIX, 403, 426–427.
21. F, *R*, 503.
22. Benjamin Lincoln to GW, 2/24/88, ms. LC; GW, XXIX, 401, 449–453.

23. Richard Butler to GW, 4/13/88, ms. LC; GW, XXIX, 454, 459.
24. Lear to William Prescott, 3/4/88, ms., MtV.
25. GW, XXIX, 463–464, 471.
26. GW, XXIX, 488.
27. GW, XXX, 399; GW, D, III, 365.
28. GW, D, III, 366.
29. GW, XXIX, 510, XXX, 9.
30. John Porter to GW, 3/9/88, ms. LC; GW, XXIX, 471, 482–483, XXX, 120.
31. F, VI, 127; GW, XXIX, 431.
32. F, CC, III, 294.
33. GW, XXX, 77–79.
34. Rossiter, 1787, 284.
35. GW, XXIX, 516; GW, D, III, 365, 393.
36. GW, XXX, 5.
37. GW, XXIX, 525–526.

13: ON THE BRINK

1. Samuel Hanson to GW, 4/3/88, ms. LC; GW, XXIX, 443–444, 508–509.
2. GW, XXX, 178.
3. GW, XXX, 21, 34, 52.
4. GW, XXX, 96; MH, V, 249, 256.
5. GW, XXX, 16–17.
6. GW, XXX, 53, 91; MH, V, 249.
7. F, VI, 151.
8. GW, XXX, 62–63.
9. GW, XXX, 147.
10. GW, XXX, 126, 185.
11. GW, XXIX, 288, 303.
12. GW, XXX, 152–153.
13. GW, XXIX, 328–331.
14. Thomas Lewis to GW, 8/27/88, ms., MtV; Richard Graham to GW, 7/20/89, ms., MtV; GW, XXIX, 336–341, 468–469, XXX, 107, 145.
15. GW, XXX, 36.
16. Bushrod Washington to GW, 12/12/88, ms., MtV; GW, XXX, 152, 166.
17. GW, XXX, 260.
18. GW, XXIX, 479–480, XXX, 98, 119.
19. GW, XXX, 73.
20. GW, XXX, 42, 97, 110, 119, 121, 185.
21. GW, XXX, 260.
22. GW, XXX, 23–24.
23. MH, V, 270.
24. Bancroft, Constitution, II, 479.

25. Benjamin Lincoln to GW, 8/30 & 9/25/88, ms. LC; GW, XXX, 120–121, 125, 174, 190.
26. GW, XXX, 185–186.
27. Ibid.
28. GW, XXX, 296n–297n; Ketcham, Two; Stein, Discarded.
29. GW, XXX, 203–204, 310; GW, D, III, 456–457.
30. Stein, 13.
31. Stein, 10.
32. Information from Frederick B. Adams, Jr.
33. GW, XXX, 301, 303.
34. GW, XXX, 303–304.
35. GW, XXX, 213, 215.
36. GW, XXX, 239–240.
37. GW, XXX, 186.
38. GW, XXIX, 467; XXX, 189.
39. GW, XXIX, 351, XXX, 45.
40. GW, XXX, 183, 218.
41. GW, XXX, 187.
42. GW, XXX, 186–187, 199, 306.
43. Daniel Hinsdale to GW, 3/23/89, ms. LC; GW, XXX, 279, 306.
44. GW, XXX, 305.
45. GW, XXX, 76–77, 307.
46. GW, XXX, 302, 306–307.
47. GW, XXX, 302–303.
48. GW, XXX, 149, 304.
49. GW, XXX, 304, 307.
50. GW, XXX, 299–300.

14: A FRIGHTENING TRIUMPH

1. Henry Knox to GW, 3/5/89, ms. LC.
2. GW, XXX, 277–278.
3. Knox to GW, 3/30/89, ms. LC; GW, XXX, 280.
4. GW, XXX, 268–269.
5. GW, XXX, 220, XXXI, 114.
6. GW, XXX, 220–221.
7. George Clinton to GW, 3/10/89, ms. LC; GW, XXX, 251–252.
8. GW, XXX, 255.
9. GW, XXX, 222; Knollenburg, Virginia, 141.
10. Smith, Curiosities, section II, 20–21.
11. GW, XXX, 255.
12. F, VI, 164–165; GW, XXX, 285–286.
13. GW, D, IV, 7.
14. GW, XXX, 286–287.
15. F, VI, 172n.

16. Baker, *After,* 123; F, VI, 169–171; Maryland *Journal,* Baltimore, 4/21/87.
17. Baker, 24; F, VI, 170–172; *Pennsylvania Packet,* Philadelphia, 4/24/89; Sellers, *Peale,* I, 275–276.
18. *Pennsylvania Packet,* 4/24/89.
19. Baker, 125; F, VI, 175–176; GW, XXX, 290–291.
20. Bowen, *Centennial,* 50; Boyd, *Boudinot,* 162ff.; *Gazette of the United States,* New York, 4/25/89; F, VI, 180n–181n; Smith, *New York,* 220ff.
21. Lodge, *Washington,* II, 45.

15: THE PRESIDENT IS INAUGURATED
1. F, VI, 186; Smith, *Adams,* II, 753–755.
2. F, VI, 185–186; Rives, *Madison,* III, 174; M, 260.
3. F, VI, 188.
4. GW, XXX, 294–295, 427–428.
5. GW, XXX, 291–296.
6. F, VI, 212n.
7. Bowen, *Centennial,* 42ff.; F, VI, 188; GW, XXX, 293; GW, *Writings,* Sparks ed., X, 463.
8. F, VI, 190–194.
9. Ames, *Works,* I, 94; Maclay, *Journal,* 9.
10. Ames, I, 94.
11. F, VI, 197–198; Smith, *New York,* 235.
12. Maclay, 9–10.
13. Maclay, 4.
14. Maclay, 40.
15. GW, XXX, 309.

16: THE PRESIDENT AS A SOCIAL LEADER
1. M, II, 264.
2. Smith, *Adams,* II, 752ff.
3. F, VI, 182n.
4. GW, XXX, 361.
5. *Gazette of the United States,* New York, 5/2/89.
6. Maclay, *Journal,* 15.
7. GW, XXX, 319–323, 361–362.
8. GW, XXX, 320–321.
9. GW, XXXI, 53.
10. JF, I, 216; Decatur, *Private,* 43.
11. David Stuart to GW, 6/2/90, ms. LC; GW, XXXI, 54.
12. Decatur, 21, 23, 66; Smith, *Curiosities,* section II, 21.

13. Decatur, 33, 35; F, VI, 211; GW, XXX, 481, Smith, *Curiosities,* loc. cit.
14. Decatur, 28, 157; GW, XXX, 396; Smith, *Curiosities,* plate 16.
15. Adams, *New Letters,* 13–15; F, VI, 211, 213–214.
16. Wharton, *New York,* 741–745.
17. Adams, 35; F, VI, 227; Smith, *Adams,* II, 772.
18. Adams, 19; Decatur, 44.
19. Decatur, 43.
20. Bowers, *Jefferson,* 13; Decatur, 45; F, VI, 213.
21. Maclay, 29–30.
22. GW, *D,* IV, 15.
23. Maclay, 134–135.
24. F, VI, 225; Decatur, 156; GW, XXX, 296n.
25. GW, XXX, 381, 444–445, XXXI, 147–148.
26. Decatur, 40; GW, XXXI, 146.
27. GW, XXXI, 159–160.
28. Decatur, 12–13, 25, 32, 39, 42, 51; F, VI, 199ff., 226; GW, XXX, 347.
29. Decatur, 21, 51, 56, 70.
30. Tobias Lear to Clement Biddle, 5/3 & 5/30/89, mss. LC. Custis, *Recollections,* 157; GW, XXX, 348.
31. Adams, 20; Custis, 165; Decatur, 56, 65; GW, XXV, 319.
32. Baker, *After,* 298.
33. Information from Frank E. Morse; Adams, 15, 20; Decatur, 171–173; GW, XXX, 444, XXXI, 115, 154.
34. Decatur, 25; F, VI, 226.
35. GW, XXX, 498.
36. GW, XXX, 498.
37. Bowen, *Centennial,* 50; F, VI, 182.

17: FLESHING OUT THE NEW GOVERNMENT
1. GW, XXXI, 40.
2. GW, XXX, 443.
3. Langstaff, *Bard,* 168–176; GW, XXX, 348–349.
4. Adams, *New Letters,* 15; GW, XXX, 351.
5. F, *F,* 238; GW, XXX, 396, 436.
6. White, *Federalists,* 1.
7. GW, XXX, 343n, 344, 381.
8. GW, XXX, 333–335.
9. Smith, *Adams,* II, 735, 763.

10. White, 38ff.
11. Fenno, *Cabinet;* GW, XXXII, 419, 421; White, 41n.
12. White, 14–16.
13. M, II, 269.
14. GW, XXX, 431–432.
15. GW, XXX, 373ff.
16. Hart, *Presidency,* 96n; Maclay, *Journal,* 309–310; White, 61n.
17. White, 75–76.
18. Bemis, *Diplomatic,* 87ff.; Boyd, *Seven,* 14ff.; GW, *D,* IV, 15–17; Miller, *Federalists,* 13.
19. Mintz, *Morris,* 53–54.
20. GW, *D,* IV, 16–17.
21. Mintz, 178.
22. GW, XXX, 136–138.
23. Roosevelt, *Morris,* 196.
24. F, *CC,* III, 85n–86n; Parton, *Jefferson,* 369.
25. Parton, *loc. cit.*
26. GW, XXX, 496.
27. GW, XXXI, 493; GW, *D,* IV, 128.
28. Hart, *Presidency,* 317; GW, XXX, 373ff.; White, 56ff.
29. GW, XXX, 363, 441.
30. GW, XXX, 363.
31. *Federalist,* no. 73.
32. GW, XXX, 432ff.
33. F, VI, 219–221; Hunt, *Calendar,* GW, XXX, 328, XXXI, 211.
34. GW, XXX, 366, XXXV, 92.
35. GW, XXXI, 211; White, 258.
36. Decatur, 58–59; GW, XXX, 368, 370–371, 412; Maclay, *Journal,* 119.
37. F, VI, 234n; White, 118n.
38. Hart, 124n.
39. White, 132ff., 164ff.
40. GW, XXX, 414.
41. GW, XXX, 375.
42. GW, XXX, 446.
43. Mitchell, *Hamilton,* II, 21–24.
44. GW, XXX, 442, 497.
45. JF, V, 152.

18: DEATH AND DOLDRUMS

1. Robert Lewis, "Diary," 9/1/89 ms. M & V; F, *R,* 518.
2. Charles Mortimer to GW, 3/4/87, ms., LC; Dr. Robert Welford, account to estate of Mrs. Mary Washington, 7/?/89, ms., MtV; GW, XXX, 399.
3. Betty Lewis to GW, 7/24/89, ms. LC.

4. Washington, *Writings,* Ford ed., XIV, 416–418.
5. GW, XXX, 400.
6. Decatur, *Private,* 60; F, VI, 229n.
7. F, VI, 230–231.
8. GW, XXX, 436; GW, *D,* IV, 14.
9. Betty Lewis to GW, 6/16/90, ms., MtV.
10. GW, *D,* IV, 20ff., 45.
11. GW, *D,* IV, 37–38; Webb, *Correspondence,* III, 142, 144.
12. John Hancock to GW, 10/21/89, ms. LC; GW, XXX, 451–453; GW, *D,* IV, 35–36; S, *C,* IV, 289–290.
13. GW, *D,* IV, 47–49.
14. GW, *D,* IV, 50.
15. GW, *D,* IV, 52.
16. Adams, *New Letters,* 35; GW, *D,* IV, 61, 65.
17. GW, XXX, 474–476, 512; GW, *D,* IV, 74–76, 106–107.
18. JF, V, 140–141.
19. GW, *D,* IV, 65.

19: DEBTS, CREDIT, AND THE NATIONAL CAPITAL

1. Bowers, *Jefferson,* 23.
2. F, *R,* see index.
3. GW, XXI, 181.
4. F, *R,* 411–414.
5. F, *R,* 494ff.
6. GW, XXVIII, 351–352.
7. F, *CC,* III, 53–54.
8. GW, XXIX, 245–246.
9. GW, XXX, 110.
10. GW, XXX, 311n, 319–323; HS, V, 335–337.
11. Miller, *Hamilton,* 225; Mitchell, *Hamilton,* II, 21–24.
12. GW, XXX, 491–494.
13. Miller, 230ff.
14. Miller, 239.
15. Bowers, chapter III.
16. Miller, 232.
17. Miller, 241.
18. Miller, 240–241.
19. Butterfield, *Rush,* I, 345.
20. HS, XI, 428.
21. GW, XXX, 447n–448n, 509–511; JF, V, 143–144, 148–149, 151; M, II, 346.
22. GW, *D,* IV, 106.
23. JF, IX, 449; M, II, 111.
24. JB, XVI, 182–183.
25. JF, V, 168; Maclay, *Journal,* 265.

26. GW, *D*, IV, 129; *Massachusetts Historical Society Collections*, ser. VII, vol. I (1900), 36.
27. GW, XXXI, 46, 55; *Warren-Adams*, II, 319.
28. JF, V, 187–189; M, II, 299, 301.
29. JF, VI, 172–173.
30. Miller, 250.
31. Miller, 248–249.
32. JF, I, 154–168.
33. JF, VI, 172–173; M, II, 507; Miller, 251.
34. JF, V, 187–189, VI, 102.
35. M, II, 292.
36. F, *R*, 340.
37. GW, XXXI, 45; Miller, 231.
38. GW, XXXI, 30; F, *R*, 511–512.
39. GW, X, 363, XXX, 454–455.
40. GW, XXXI, 52–53.
41. GW, XXXI, 69–70; JF, V, 204–210; M, II, 302–303.
42. Miller, 255.
43. GW, XXXI, 30, 51–52, 83–84.
44. Bowers, 57; F, VI, 264n; Maclay, 319.
45. GW, XXXI, 67n, 84.

20: NOOTKA, YAZOO, AND THE SOUTHWEST FRONTIER

1. S, *C*, IV, 322.
2. GW, XXXI, 83, 86.
3. GW, XXXI, 102–103; GW, *D*, IV, 136.
4. GW, XXXI, 87–88.
5. Boyd, *Seven*, 3–8; Bemis, *Jay*, 41–48.
6. GW, *D*, IV, 137–139.
7. GW, *D*, IV, 137–139, 142–143.
8. GW, XXXI, 88; M, II, 311–312.
9. The southwest frontier in general: Bemis, *Pinckney's*; Green, *Spanish*; Whitaker, *Spanish-American*.
10. F, *F*, 151; GW, XXXIV, 99.
11. GW, XXX, 372, XXXI, 267, 320.
12. F, *F*, 88ff.; GW, XXXI, 370.
13. GW, XXXI, 369.
14. *American State Papers, Indian Affairs* (1832), I, 112; Whitaker, 375.
15. GW, XXXI, 99; GW, *D*, IV, 123–126.
16. Cauchey, *McGillivray*.
17. GW, XXX, 387.
18. Humphreys, *Humphreys*, II, 4–13; GW, *D*, IV, 53–54.

19. *New York Journal and Patriotic Register*, 7/9, 23, 30 & 8/10, 17/90; GW, *D*, IV, 90, 95.
20. Humphreys, 6, 8.
21. Cauchey, 45; GW, XXX, 76–77; Whitaker, 136ff.
22. GW, XXVII, 475.
23. GW, *D*, IV, 74–75.
24. Thomas Marshall to GW, 2/12/89, and Harry Innes to GW, 3/2/89, mss. LC; GW, XXX, 214–215, 252–253.
25. GW, XXIX, 520.
26. GW, XXX, 215.
27. Bemis, 142; GW, XXXI, 123; Whitaker, 121.
28. GW, XXXI, 87, 143.

21: VACATION TIME

1. GW, XXXI, 70–73.
2. *Gazette of the United States*, New York, 6/12/90; GW, XXXI, 93n; GW, *D*, IV, 116–121; *Massachusetts Historical Society Proceedings*, LI (1917–1918), 36–39.
3. GW, XXXI, 57, 91.
4. *Gazette*, 11/1/90; *New York Daily Advertiser*, 10/3/90.
5. Baker, *After*, 181–182, 197.
6. GW, XXXI, 160n, XXXVII, 570–571.
7. Bryan, *Capital*, 37–40, 107–119; GW, XXXI, 135, 254.
8. GW, XXXI, 131–132, 143, 155.
9. GW, XXXI, 142.

22: THE BANK OF THE UNITED STATES

1. GW, XXXI, 161.
2. GW, XXXI, 164–165; HS, VII, 173.
3. GW, XXXI, 167.
4. Bemis, *Jay*, 80.
5. M, II, 332–333.
6. GW, XXXI, 197; M, II, 328–331.
7. Boyd, *Seven*, 153–154; HS, VII, 84–85; GW, XXXI, 131–132.
8. Bemis, 81, 83; GW, XXXI, 212–215.
9. Bowers, *Jefferson*, 70; GW, *D*, IV, 159.
10. F, *R*, 397–398, 476.
11. GW, XXXIII, 488, XXXVII, 250.
12. HS, VII, 399–406; Miller, *Hamilton*, 255–277.
13. Miller, 262.
14. Brant, *Madison*, III, 328ff.
15. GW, XXXI, 216; Miller, 264.

16. *Federalist,* no. 44; M, II, 346.
17. GW, XXXI, 215–216.
18. Brant, III, 330.
19. Bowers, 77–78.
20. Brant, III, 331; HS, VII, 57–58, 97–134; M, II, 348–349.
21. GW, XXXI, 224.
22. GW, XXXI, 241–243.
23. Maclay, *Journal,* 362–364.

23. JOURNEYS AND BAD NEWS
1. *Maryland Journal and Baltimore Advertiser,* 4/5/91.
2. GW, *D,* IV, 150–151.
3. GW, XXXI, 251, 272–273, 299.
4. GW, XXXI, 261; Henderson, *Southern,* 39.
5. GW, *D,* IV, 156, 193, 195.
6. GW, *D,* IV, 161–163.
7. GW, *D,* IV, 164; Henderson, 80.
8. Fraser, *Reminiscence,* 18; GW, *D,* IV, 172–174; Henderson, 99, 184.
9. GW, XXXI, 334; GW, *D,* IV, 165, 168, 173.
10. GW, XXXI, 319, 321.
11. GW, XXXI, 319.
12. GW, *D,* IV, 195–196.
13. GW, XXXI, 294, 319–320, 328–329; Miller, *Hamilton,* 268–269.
14. GW, XXXI, 248–249.
15. GW, XXXI, 324–326; Washington, *Correspondence,* Sparks ed., IV, 361–363, 371–373.
16. GW, XXXI, 327–328.
17. JLB, I, 101, VIII, 231.

24: THE NORTHERN FRONTIER
1. GW, XXXI, 361–363.
2. GW, XXXI, 387–389, 395–396.
3. GW, XXXI, 396–397.
4. GW, XXXI, 399–400; HS, XII, 305n.
5. GW, XXXI, 402–404.
6. GW, XXXI, 320.
7. GW, XXXI, 267–268.
8. GW, XXXI, 369.
9. Bemis, *Jay,* 2ff.
10. Stone, *Brant,* II, 296–297.
11. Bemis, 109ff.
12. Bemis, 162n; GW, XXXII, 61–62.
13. GW, XXXII, 126.
14. F, VI, 329–330; St. Clair, *Papers,* II, 181–182.
15. Bemis, 74; F, VI, 329.
16. GW, XXXI, 397–398.
17. GW, XXI, 199, XXXII, 10, 20.

18. GW, XXXV, 193–196.
19. F, VI, 336–338; Wilson, *St. Clair,* 71ff.
20. JF, I, 189.
21. JF, I, 189–190.
22. GW, XXXI, 492–494; JF, I, 182.
23. GW, XXXII, 12–13, 15–16.
24. GW, XXXI, 509–515.
25. Henry Lee to GW, 6/15/92, ms. LC; GW, XXXII, 75–78.
26. GW, XXXII, 127.
27. GW, XXXII, 128.
28. Stone, II, 331–335.
29. GW, XXXII, 62–63.
30. GW, XXXII, 63; Stone, II, 328–329.
31. Bemis, 130.
32. GW, XXXI, 87, XXXII, 205–206.

25: PHILADELPHIA HIGH LIFE
1. Miller, *Hamilton,* 282.
2. HS, X, 1ff.; Miller, 282–289.
3. Miller, 301.
4. GW, XXXI, 193–194.
5. GW, XXXI, 310.
6. GW, XXXI, 389.
7. F, *R,* 318; Miller, 300.
8. Griswold, *Republican,* 272.
9. Alberts, *Bingham;* Griswold, 258.
10. Griswold, 259; Wansey, *Excursion,* 123, 136.
11. Bowers, *Jefferson,* 122–125.
12. Griswold, 260n–261n; M, II, 255.
13. Bowers, 130; M, II, 262.
14. Bowers, 130.
15. F, *R,* 335ff.
16. William Barton to GW, 8/28/88, ms. LC; GW, XXX, 87.
17. GW, XXXII, II, 32.
18. *Decatur,* 159ff.; GW, XXXI, 110–111, 136, 152, XXXV, 6.
19. Baker, *After,* 232.
20. Bowers, 131.
21. Adams, *Letters,* II, 211.
22. Fisher, *Recollections,* 208–209.
23. Morgan, *Journal.*
24. Moon, *Morris,* see index; Leach, *Powel.*
25. GW, *D,* III, 217ff.
26. GW, *D,* III, 243.
27. Alberts, 140.
28. Elizabeth Powel to Mrs. Fitzhugh, 7/?/86, and to Martha, 11/30/87, mss., MtV.
29. Elizabeth Powel to Mrs. Fitzhugh, 3/3/84, ms., MtV.

30. Elizabeth Powel to Bushrod Washington, 1/1/85, ms., MtV.
31. Leach; Moon, II, 485.
32. Elizabeth Powel to GW, 3/6–11/87, ms., MtV.
33. Elizabeth Powel to Martha, 11/30/87, ms., MtV.
34. Sawitzky, *Pratt*, 61–62.
35. GW, XXXII, 22–23; Wansey, 138.
36. Bowers, 132; GW, XXXIII, 354; JF, I, 222.
37. F, VI, 331–332, 348–351; Miller, 304ff.
38. F, VI, 349.
39. HS, XI, 433; JF, I, 178–179.
40. F, *R*, 341–342.
41. F, VI, 343–348; JF, I, 192.

26: THE GREAT COLUMBIAN
FEDERAL CITY

1. Caemmerer, *L'Enfant*, 1ff.; GW, XII, 501.
2. Caemmerer, *L'Enfant*, 127–128.
3. Caemmerer, *L'Enfant*, 82, 84; GW, XXXI, 419–420.
4. Bryan, *Capital*, I, 124; GW, XXXI, 206–208, 218–219, 226–227; Kite, *L'Enfant*, 33.
5. GW, XXXI, 200.
6. GW, *D*, IV, 152–155.
7. GW, XXXI, 256–257; Kite, 56.
8. Kite, 41–42.
9. GW, XXXI, 271, 287; M, II, 372.
10. Kite, 49–51.
11. F, *F*, 297; GW, XXXI, 295.
12. GW, XXXI, 270–271.
13. Kite, 72.
14. Bryan, 130.
15. Kite, 47–48; M, II, 375.
16. GW, XXXII, 19; Kite, 55.
17. L'Enfant, *Plan;* Kite, 52, 55–60.
18. GW, XXXI, 506; Kite, 137.
19. Caemmerer, *Capital*, 29; L'Enfant, *Plan*.
20. Kimball, *Architect*, 51.
21. Caemmerer, *Capital*, 32; Kite, 62.
22. GW, *D*, IV, 199–201.
23. Kite, 59–60.
24. Caemmerer, *L'Enfant*, 376–377; Kite, 55.
25. JLB, XXIX, 88–91; Kimball, *Architect*, 49.
26. GW, XXXI, 263–264; Kite, 51.
27. Kite, 73.
28. Kite, 67ff.
29. GW, XXXI, 394–395.

30. Bryan, 159; Kite, 76.
31. GW, XXXI, 419–422.
32. GW, XXXI, 421, 432.
33. GW, XXXI, 421.
34. GW, XXXI, 429–433; Kite, 79ff.
35. GW, XXXI, 434; M, II, 379.
36. Kite, 87.
37. Kite, 93–97.
38. GW, XXXI, 442–443, 445–446, 448.
39. Kite, 107–109, 133, 137.
40. Caemmerer, *L'Enfant*, 376; M, II, 391.
41. GW, XXXI, 372–374.
42. Bryan, 168; Kite, 122.
43. GW, XXXI, 447, 458, 461–462, 477, 479; Kite, 144.
44. GW, XXXI, 486–487; Kite, 145–146.
45. GW, XXXII, 3–4; Kite, 151, 156.
46. Kite, 151–152.
47. JLB, XXXIX, 88–91; Kite, 156.
48. Lear to Humphreys, 4/8/92, ms., Rosenbach Foundation.
49. GW, XXXI, 487–488.
50. Lear to Humphreys, 4/8/92, ms., MtV.
51. GW, XXXI, 488, XXXII, 3–4.
52. GW, XXXI, 489.
53. Kimball, *Jefferson*, 53; M, II, 384.
54. GW, XXXII, 52, 101–102; Kimball, *Domestic*, 146–164; Kimball, *Jefferson*, 53; M, II, 384.
55. GW, XXXII, 325; JLB, IX, 17; Kimball, *Jefferson*, 54–55.
56. GW, XXXII, 244–245.
57. GW, XXXII, 268–270, 371.
58. GW, XXXII, 244.

27: JEFFERSON BEGINS TO DOUBT
WASHINGTON

1. MH, VI, 106.
2. JF, I, 175–176.
3. JF, I, 174–176.
4. GW, XXXI, 261.
5. Lund Washington to GW, 4/28/90, ms., MtV.
6. JF, I, 176–177.
7. GW, XXXI, 389.
8. GW, XXXII, 86.
9. GW, XXXI, 428.
10. JF, I, 181, 185–186.
11. Bemis, *Jay*, 95ff.; Bemis, *Secretaries*, II, 44–45; GW, XXXII, 51; JF, V, 514, VI, 65; M, II, 419.
12. JF, V, 96.

13. M, II, 401–402.
14. GW, XXXI, 468–470.
15. GW, XXXVI, 219; M, II, 404.
16. JLB, VIII, 231; M, II, 401.
17. JF, I, 187–188.
18. JF, I, 191.

28: DETERMINATION TO RETIRE
1. M, II, 351, 423.
2. F, VI, 361.
3. GW, XXXII, 63.
4. MH, VI, 106n–110n.
5. GW, XXXII, 45, 74.
6. F, VI, 353–354.
7. GW, XXXII, 45–48.
8. JF, I, 198, VI, 1–6.
9. JF, I, 198–201.
10. HS, XII, 137–139.

29: PERSONAL FEUDS CUT DEEPER
1. F, VI, 362.
2. GW, XXXII, 100, 115.
3. GW, XXXII, 109–110.
4. GW, XXXII, 95–100.
5. HS, XII, 228–258.
6. GW, XXXI, 340.
7. GW, XXXII, 106, 153–154; HS, XII, 136–137, 187, 305–311, 341, 345–346, 366.
8. GW, XXXII, 152.
9. GW, XXXII, 149, 152.
10. M, II, 479–480.
11. GW, XXXII, 150–151.
12. HS, XII, 413.
13. GW, XXXII, 54, 73, 87–88, 188–189.
14. GW, XXXII, 114, 129.
15. GW, XXXII, 130, 213, 284.
16. GW, XXXII, 118, 127, 395.
17. GW, XXXII, 114, 116, 120–121; Whitaker, Spanish, 153.
18. GW, XXXII, 130–131.
19. GW, XXXII, 132–133.
20. M, II, 493.
21. JF, VI, 100–104.
22. HS, XII, 347–350.
23. JF, I, 204.
24. GW, XXXII, 136–137.
25. GW, XXXII, 135–136, 140, 156, 164, 173.
26. Edmund Randolph to GW, 8/5/92, ms. LC.
27. GW, XXXII, 136.
28. GW, XXXII, 142.
29. JF, I, 203.
30. JF, I, 203–205.

31. Elizabeth Powel to GW, 11/4/92, ms., MtV.

30: THE SHADES OF THE PRISON HOUSE
1. M, II, 476–477.
2. M, II, 468.
3. M, II, 483.
4. GW, XXXI, 189, 210.
5. GW, XXXII, 165–166.
6. Bowers, Jefferson, 179.
7. M, III, 7.
8. M, II, 482.
9. GW, XXX, 395n; JF, I, 313, VI, 105; M, III, 17, 20.
10. M, II, 23ff.
11. JF, VI, 157–158.
12. JF, I, 214–215.
13. JF, I, 214–216, VI, 157–158.
14. GW, XXXII, 354–355, 392–394.
15. M, III, 23.
16. GW, XXXII, 321–323, 355.
17. F, VII, 29; JF, I, 212–214, VI, 189; M, III, 42–43.
18. GW, XXXII, 343, 356; JF, I, 220; S, C, IV, 415–418.
19. JF, I, 206–207.
20. JF, I, 212–213.
21. F, VII, 23–24.
22. JF, VI, 153–154.
23. GW, XXXII, 54.
24. JF, VI, 153–154.
25. M, III, 52.
26. JF, I, 216–218; M, III, 52.
27. JF, VII, 24; M, III, 44–45; McMaster, People, II, 89ff.; National Gazette, Philadelphia, 12/19/92, 2/2/93.
28. JF, I, 216.
29. JF, VI, 293.

31: THE FIRST TERM SURVEYED
1. GW, XXXI, 46, 354, XXXIII, 345–346.
2. GW, XXXII, 419, 421.
3. GW, XXXIII, 249, XXXV, 103.
4. M, II; 352–354; White, Federalist, 225–226.
5. JF, VIII, 100.
6. GW, XXXI, 428, XXXIV, 253.
7. GW, XXXI, 493.
8. M, III, 343–344; Morris, Hamilton, ix.
9. HS, XI, 439–440, 442.
10. M, II, 272–273.
11. M, II, 267, 421.
12. JF, IX, 448.

13. JF, VI, 293.
14. JF, I, 230–231.
15. Chambers, *Parties*, 3–4.
16. *New York Times*, 10/23/1969, 46.
17. JF, I, 205, 215.
18. JF, I, 199, 204.
19. JF, I, 33–34.
20. HS, XI, 426ff.
21. GW, XXXII, 185–186.
22. GW, XXXII, 368.
23. Blanton, *Medical,* 58; GW, XXXII, 454; MtV Ladies' Association, *Report for 1952,* 67.
24. JF, I, 165.
25. Brant, *Madison,* III, 390; Koch, *Madison,* 34.
26. GW, XXXXII, 54.
27. GW, XXIX, 351, XXX, 186, 305, XXXII, 423.

28. GW, XXXIV, 252.
29. JF, IX, 449–450.
30. JF, I, 203.
31. Flexner, *Stuart,* 124.
32. GW, *D,* IV, 105–106.
33. GW, XXXI, 309.
34. GW, XXIX, 524. XXXIII. 23, 96; MH, VI, 310.
35. GW, XXIX, 511, XXXV, 32.
36. GW, XXIV, 24. XXVIII, 335, XXXI, 30.
37. GW, XXXI, 324–325, XXXIII, 23.
38. GW, II, 458, 476.
39. JF, IX, 448.
40. GW, XXX, 154
41. Henderson, *Southern,* 2.
42. Brant, *Madison,* III, 324–325.
43. JF, IX, 449.
44. JF, I, 204.

Index